LE CORBUSIER and BRITAIN

An Anthology

LE CORBUSIER and BRITAIN
An Anthology

Edited by
Irena Murray and Julian Osley

RIBA Trust

Routledge
Taylor & Francis Group

First published 2009
by Routledge
2 Park Square, Milton Park, Abingdon, Oxon OX14 4RN

Simultaneously published in the USA and Canada
by Routledge
270 Madison Avenue, New York, NY 10016, USA

Routledge is an imprint of the Taylor & Francis Group, an informa business

Designed and typeset in Univers by Alex Lazarou, Surbiton
Printed and bound in Spain by Grafos, Barcelona

British Library Cataloguing in Publication Data
A catalogue record for this book is available from the British Library

Library of Congress Cataloging-in-Publication Data
Le Corbusier and Britain : an anthology / [edited by] Irena Murray and
Julian Osley.
   p. cm.
Includes bibliographical references.
ISBN 978-0-415-47994-3 (hbk : alk. paper) 1. Le Corbusier, 1887–1965—
Criticism and interpretation. 2. Le Corbusier, 1887–1965—Influence. 3.
Architectural criticism—Great Britain—History—20th century. I. Žantovská
Murray, Irena, 1946– II. Osley, Julian.
   NA1053.J4L374 2009
   720.92—dc22
                                                        2008024915

ISBN: 978-0-415-47994-3 (HBK)

Contents

Contents

Contents

1.2

**Venesta Plywood exhibition stand,
Building Exhibition, London (1930)**

Photographer unknown (1930)

suggested that the post-World War II period was the appropriate time to begin the exploration of Le Corbusier's British legacy, especially since Modernism took hold in Britain at that time. And yet, British interest in Le Corbusier has had a much longer lineage, and far deeper roots, than this suggests. The sheer range of early texts from the 1920s and 1930s – here included – illustrates how British architects and critics reacted to the new phenomenon that was Le Corbusier: awe, curiosity, bewilderment, outrage and incomprehension were just some of the sentiments they expressed: clearly, he could not be ignored. The editor of the *Architectural Review* spoke for many when he wrote in 1928 that 'Le Corbusier discovered a new heaven and a new earth ... whether we agree with him or not, it is most fitting that this eager knight should enter the English lists ...'[4]

As wide-ranging as the bibliographic efforts have been in the compilation of the anthology, space-limitations have inevitably imposed severe restrictions. Since the purpose of the anthology is to provide a broad overview of both the professional and the public reception of Le Corbusier's work as author, architect, artist and social visionary, the numerous English references to Le Corbusier's individual architectural projects have, as a rule, been confined to the bibliography. For the same reason, obituaries have been omitted in favour of those critical appreciations which appeared at the time of the architect's death. The length of a number of important critical texts prevented their inclusion beyond the bibliography. The anthology includes a number of texts by Le Corbusier commissioned expressly by British editors and critics.

The editors have sought to include examples of literary and popular voices as well, sourcing texts from national newspapers such as *The Times* or *The Observer*, cultural reviews such as *The Spectator* and even from such unexpected sources as Nora Shackleton Heald's articles from *The Queen* – hardly the most obvious vehicle for Corbusian studies. Women architects and designers took an early interest in Le Corbusier's work, and the domestic interiors in his designs intrigued them: while Shackleton Heald spoke as an emancipated journalist at work, Miriam Wornum and Doris Lewis, writing as Mrs Howard Robertson, by contrast, astutely probed the residential and social implications.

Although archival documents detailing the communications between Le Corbusier and Great Britain are not included in the anthology, research in the Fondation Le Corbusier in Paris informed the broader context and selection of texts. Among the 450,000 documents housed in the Fondation – which makes it, incidentally, one of the largest and most varied monographic archives of the past century – personal correspondence with Le Corbusier's British translators, with fellow architects and collaborators, as well as with numerous architecture student groups from across Britain, add depth to the published record. Archival copies of the *Architectural Review*, *Focus*, *Plan*, *The Studio* and a number of other English titles sent by editors and correspondents to Le Corbusier's office, reveal just how well informed he actually was, and not merely about the publication of and commentary on his own work, but about the British architectural scene at large. The correspondence ranges from professional communications with Jane Drew, Maxwell Fry, Frederick Etchells, Clive Entwistle, Raymond McGrath and Bernard Feilden to a flowery greeting card from Christine Keeler, among others.

I wish to express my appreciation to the Fondation Le Corbusier in Paris, and to its Director, Michel Richard, for his interest and support. I am particularly grateful to Arnaud Dercelles, Head of Documentation and Research Centre, FLC, and his assistant Léa Demillac for responding to many queries and working patiently with the editors to provide missing illustrations for the book.

I am indebted to the Director of the RIBA Trust, Charles Knevitt, for his overall vision and his unwavering enthusiasm about all aspects of the 'Le Corbusier Season,' and for encouraging us to pursue this project.

My warmest thanks must go to colleagues who, over the past two years, contributed to research, prepared copies and provided steady support for the book. I am most grateful to Jane Oldfield and Alison Chew for their initial survey of sources and to Dawn Humm for her suggestions on Le Corbusier material in technical journals. Jonathan Ridsdale contributed immeasurably by locating material in obscure and hard-to-find periodicals. I will never discharge my debt to Robert Elwall, who with his team – Jonathan Makepeace, Cathy Dembsky, Valeria Carullo and Laura Whitton – gave most generously of his far-ranging expertise in the history of photography and who selected, collated and described the images contained in this book against the tightest of deadlines. He also influenced the decision to include a number of photographs of post-war British buildings contained in this anthology.

I want to thank Francoise McGrath who assisted by seeking the permissions from publishers and picture agencies. Patricia Pavitt carefully transcribed the texts from the originals, some of them quite difficult to decipher.

There are few epithets to do justice to the contribution of Julian Osley whose painstaking bibliographic research made this book possible. His thoroughness, determination, research skills and unwavering focus over the past two years resulted in the most extensive bibliography of British sources on Le Corbusier to date. While many texts had to be omitted from the anthology because of their length or difficulties with reproduction, Osley's bibliography forms the foundation upon which the selected texts emerge, as in relief.

Last, but not least, I would like to express my warmest appreciation to Alan Powers, a scholar of architectural Modernism in Britain, for his knowledgeable and insightful introduction to the anthology and for his ongoing support of the RIBA collections.

Irena Murray
Sir Banister Fletcher Director
British Architectural Library
Royal Institute of British Architects

NOTES

1   Stefan Buzas, E1 (2) 86, FLC.
2   Gordon H.G. Holt, 'Some French Views on Architectural Education: Interviews with Leading Parisian Architects,' *Architects' Journal*, vol. 60, 23 July 1924, pp. 117–19.
3   Adrian Forty, 'Le Corbusier's British Reputation,' in Raeburn, Michael and Wilson, Victoria (eds) *Le Corbusier: Architect of the Century*, London: Arts Council of Great Britain, 1987, pp. 35–41.
4   'Europe Discusses the House,' *Architectural Review*, vol. 64, December 1928, pp. 221–22.

LE CORBUSIER and BRITAIN

An Anthology

Introduction

Alan Powers

Le Corbusier was Britain's gateway to modern architecture, a frame through which the British tried to see something on the other side: literally the other side of the Channel, and figuratively something that they assumed to be excitingly 'other' to their preconceptions about the purpose of architecture. He was also a mirror, in which the British, hoping to see a different world, saw reflected a picture of themselves.

The proscenium frame did not hold a static picture, but a moving one, in which the hero kept returning in a different costume, with different lines. The audience changed as well, entering and departing through different doors and seeing different parts of the show. Some paid more attention to the words than others, but few left without an opinion. Adrian Forty, writing on Le Corbusier's influence in Britain in the 1987 Arts Council exhibition catalogue, *Le Corbusier, Architect of the Century*, and Charles Knevitt in the 2007/08 Vitra/RIBA catalogue both focus almost exclusively on his post-war influence, but there is a substantial earlier history, as Julian Osley's listing of printed sources and the gradual digitisation of national newspapers enable us to confirm. There was no other modern architect whose name became so well known in the non-specialist media.

Le Corbusier's appeal was initially more to a general intelligentsia and to journalists than to the temporarily conservative mood in architecture. John Summerson, in an anonymous review in 1939, recalled passing by a copy of *Vers une Architecture* (Fig. 2.1) in a Parisian shop window in 1924,

> it was obviously the work of a crank ... we knew, in those days, what architecture was. It was a matter mostly of "scholarship." But also compounded of subtle things like "artistry" and "restraint." It had much to do with Wren, whose bicentenary we had just been celebrating; it had more to do with Bush House and the Beaux Arts Albums. So we looked down our noses at *Vers une Architecture* and bought a five-franc thriller.[1]

As he discovered:

> Within a year or so it was irritating to find Le Corbusier quoted by highbrow laymen, and quoted to the disadvantage of "scholarship" and "restraint" and the rest of the

2.1
Living room in a seaside villa

From Le Corbusier, *Vers une Architecture*
2nd ed. (1924)

comfortable jargon rehearsed at No. 9 Conduit Street [then the RIBA headquarters]. Could it be that Le Corbusier was someone after all? It was consoling to know that the teachers in the schools had not heard of him. But some of the students had, and a copy of the strange new book was passed round. ... One began to look at aircraft, at silos, at the streams of London traffic, at clothes, at furniture, with a new interest. It seemed that there was an horizon beyond the Rome Scholarship, beyond successful practice, and, yes, even beyond the Gold Medal. It seemed that the real horizon of architecture was part of the horizon of modern life ...[2]

Summerson was a student at the conservative Bartlett School in London, but the *Architectural Association Journal* included a review of the French edition in 1924, by an architect member of the staff, Verner O. Rees.[3] Although Rees's few designs are in a stripped classic style, he was sympathetic to the book and its message, while two other members of the AA establishment, Howard Robertson and Frank Yerbury, introduced architects to continental Modernism through their illustrated articles in the 1920s and 1930s in the *Architect and Building News* (Fig. 2.2).

Le Corbusier's early admirers included some who became famous for different and often conflicting ideas. The architectural writer Christopher Hussey was presumably

2.2

Caricature of Howard Robertson and F.R. Yerbury

From *Architect & Building News*, 6 January 1928

HOWEVER THEY ARE EXPECTED TO SURVIVE EVEN THAT CENSURE PROVIDED THAT THEY HAVE THE CONTINUED SUPPORT OF MR. HOWARD ROBERTSON AND MR. YERBURY.

behind the approach made by Country Life Books in 1924 to publish a translation of *Vers une Architecture*, and founded a discussion circle called the *Vers* Group.[4] Hussey promoted modern buildings in *Country Life* magazine until the mid-1930s, although he became disillusioned about Modernism in later years. Evelyn Waugh, an outspoken opponent of Modernism by the late 1930s, wrote an approving review of *The City of Tomorrow* in the *Observer* in August 1929, coupling it with *The New Interior Decoration* by Dorothy Todd (editor of London *Vogue*) and the Bloomsbury critic, Raymond Mortimer.[5] Marshall Sisson, an architect who took up Modernism and then dropped it in favour of a return to classicism, was the owner of the set of *L'Esprit Nouveau* in the RIBA Library. The artist Rex Whistler, famous for his neo-Georgian murals and illustrations, found a copy of *Vers une Architecture* when he visited the British School at Rome (when Amyas Connell was a Rome Scholar in Architecture) in 1928 and temporarily impressed by its message.[6] Around the same time, another artist Edward Bawden wrote to Douglas Percy Bliss about a cookery book that their mutual friend Eric Ravilious was trying to persuade him to illustrate, showing a close knowledge and amused appreciation of the content of the book:

> He writes of giblets and entrails and the transparent architecture of jellies. Oh, very good: how Le Corbusier would have pondered over the last suggestion and no doubt would have photographed a few for his *Vers une Architecture*. Jellies, apart from scale, are not unlike Santa Sophia and the Mosquée Verte; but with more form, fuller, richer! Le Corbusier often comes very near to Rav's remarks. For instance, he says, speaking of plans, "Un édifice est comme une bulle de savon". Why? "Parceque l'extérieur est le resultat d'un intérieur."[7]

2.3
Finella, Cambridge (1929)

Architect: Raymond McGrath
Photographers: Dell & Wainwright (1929)

'Corb communicates' as Peter Smithson said in the 1950s, and goes straight into the bloodstream.[8] 'Pugin's articles excited me almost to fury, and I suddenly found myself like a person awakened from a long feverish dream, which had rendered him unconscious of what was going on about him', wrote George Gilbert Scott about reading Pugin's articles in the *Dublin Review* in 1841. Nothing, even Ruskin, had quite the same effect on British architects between this and the arrival of Le Corbusier. For a short time prior to this arrival, Eric Mendelsohn was taken as representative of modern architecture, but he did not communicate so effectively in words. The appearance of the Etchells translation of *Vers une Architecture* in 1927 stimulated many reviews, including one in the *Times Literary Supplement* by Alan Clutton-Brock, engaging in a discussion about the role of aesthetics in the face of Le Corbusier's apparently mechanistic doctrine.[9] Reading Le Corbusier, like reading Marx or Freud, could make you feel like an intellectual without much effort, and at this point, British architecture lacked much written theory.

Like Pugin, Le Corbusier introduced intellectuals to architectural texts, a process that was extended to other Modern Movement authors. In 1924, I. A. Richards began the preface of *Principles of Literary Criticism* with the phrase 'A book is a machine to think with', borrowed from Le Corbusier's most famous coinage. The Cambridge English Faculty, of which Richards was a founder, showed an uncommon involvement in modern architecture thereafter, including Mansfield Forbes' commissioning of Raymond McGrath to transform Finella, (Fig. 2.3) and, equally important, his role around 1930 as a catalyst in bringing sundered individuals outside the architectural mainstream such as Wells Coates, Serge Chermayeff and Jack Pritchard together, and thus providing a springboard for activity later in the decade. *Scrutiny*, the magazine edited by F. R. Leavis and colleagues, often reviewed books on modern architecture and planning. Less intellectually, a column on Walt Disney in *The Observer* in 1930 established Disney's importance by comparison with Beethoven and Wagner in music, and Eiffel and Le Corbusier in architecture, as the names that always came up in conversation, while a commentary on dolls' houses for the Christmas market in *The Guardian* in 1933 quipped that 'the newest home has timber gables and casement windows. It is pretty, but it is generations away from Le Corbusier. Must dolls endure all the intermediate stages?'[10] In fact, Modern Movement (or at least 'Moderne') dolls' houses were made in some quantity in the 1930s. As Reyner Banham recalled, 'Le Corbusier's was the first name of any architect, alive or dead, that I was to learn, thanks to the *Daily Mail* in about 1936.'[11]

Despite the opposite tendencies of the architectural establishment in the 1920s, there was an underlying sympathy in Britain for Le Corbusier's emphasis on Taylorism and efficiency dating from before the First World War. This aspect of his writings became the dominant received idea, led by the phrase 'a house is a machine for living in' which he himself repudiated in vain. For the more perceptive, Le Corbusier's significance came from his concern to humanise the effects of the machine, the unfinished mission of design reformers since the Crystal Palace. At the same time, from the houses at Silver End (Fig. 2.4) by Burnet and Tait in 1927 the series of modern buildings in Britain, more or less directly inspired by Le Corbusier, began to unfold. Since his was the best-known name in the field, they were inevitably ascribed solely to his influence, when the truth, if it could be established, is less simple or clear, since other sources were certainly involved.

2.4
**Le Château, Silver End,
Braintree (1925)**

Architect: Thomas Tait
Photographer unknown (1925)

Intelligent but sympathetic scepticism was a less common response than whole-sale rejection or acceptance. John Summerson, having overcome his early inhibitions, was probably the most effective commentator in this vein, from the time when he first mentioned Le Corbusier in the articles he published in 1930 in *The Scotsman*, through a series of articles and reviews. In Le Corbusier, he found a modern figure who corresponded to his own emerging project of investigating the historical relationship between classicism and romanticism in the history of British architecture since the Renaissance, which he may have linked to Jung's theory of the divided personality. Summerson's contribution on architecture to the book *The Arts To-day* (1935) made Le Corbusier its hero, and rationalised his appeal as an architect who could advance the idea of architecture as a technique of communication at the same time as it was a practical means to an end.[12] In other articles, he criticised the non-sequiturs and repetitions of Le Corbusier's writing style, and the naivety of his political vision, yet did not withdraw his admiration.

Summerson's response to the social message of architecture was measured, but for students at the end of the 1930s the effect of Le Corbusier was not simply an aspect of a cyclical process, but specific to the times. As an anonymous reviewer of Henry-Russell Hitchcock's MOMA exhibition book of 1938, *Modern Architecture in England*, commented:

> The fact that English modernists have chosen to follow Le Corbusier's lead ... must relate to national temperament and conditions. It was a particular conjunction of events which gave English architecture this chance of making what can be considered to be almost a deliberate choice. The chief element was the fact that the slump came to Britain just before any modern influence had gained secure foothold and when the schools were turning out men who in their first free years had nothing much to do but think.[13]

The Slump or Depression of the early 1930s changed the way the middle class thought, talked and acted. Modern architecture was reached through a door marked 'Desperation', heralded by W. H. Auden's famous lines of 1930:

> ... Look shining at
> New styles of architecture, a change of heart.[14]

For Auden, new architecture was a metaphor, and he soon recorded his antipathy towards Modernism as a style, but his call to the young to become more active was answered by architectural students. 'What is a highbrow?', Auden asked in 1933, 'Someone who is not passive to his experience but who tries to organise, explain and alter it', and this represented the next phase of Le Corbusier's influence.[15] For Anthony Cox, a student at the AA in the mid-1930s, 'no man, whether architect, artist, writer or philosopher, exerted so profound an influence or imparted so abundantly an energising conviction of the importance of the profession towards which we were groping.'[16] He identified the Pavillon Suisse (Fig. 2.5) (with its benefit of accessibility to any visitor to Paris) as the key site for his generation 'because of its social content and its technical mastery.'[17] In 1937, Cox was one of the authors of the AA Pantomime *Jack and Jill*, a homage to Auden and Isherwood's *The Dog Beneath the Skin* of the previous year. The final chorus ran:

> We're recovering
> What we used to lack
> Without an aphrodisiac.
> You're mistaking us
> If you're taking us
> For another flash in the pan.
> Here's the reason for
> Our recovery:
> We've made the great discovery
> That Le Corbusier
> Is the only way,
> Get a new master,

2.5
Pavillon Suisse, Cité Universitaire, Paris (1932)

Photographer: John Donat (1971)

Get a new man.
We shall build a
New community,
Men and women will
Live in unity.
We can guarantee
Perfect liberty,
Free love; Free Plan.[18]

There was poetic licence and perhaps some self-mockery in this, since Le Corbusier wasn't the only way and Walter Gropius also ranked high in the esteem of this group. Tim Bennett, the author of the music for *Jack and Jill* and an editor with Cox of *Focus* magazine, was fond of quoting 'les techniques sont l'assiette même du lyrisme' from *Précisions* to remind people that poetry did not have to be abandoned. This book, in which the poetic and technological sides of its author began to be more overtly integrated, was only translated in the 1990s, but received a warm welcome in *The Listener* in 1931 from Herbert Read, with the ending 'Le Corbusier, you see, is not inhuman; he is a poet, perhaps the greatest poet of our time.'[19] *Focus* magazine is remembered for Cox's condemnation of Highpoint II as a 'formalist' building and, in the second issue, Bennett voiced what was, one suspects, by then a general complaint that 'his own designs are fatally easy to travesty and tempting to imitate', but the emphasis was now on a deeper internalisation and assimilation of his ideas.[20] Le Corbusier's varied work of the later 1930s was reflected in random rubble walls and timber construction as much as the earlier work produced smooth white surfaces. J. M. Richards, in his widely distributed Pelican, *An Introduction to Modern Architecture* in 1940, proposed that modern architecture should become a form of regional vernacular rather than another academic style, which fitted the mood of the time. Other writers, including Summerson, were suggesting around the time of the outbreak of the war that the first phase of Modernism was now over, and that the next task was one of consolidation. These views indicate a paradox about Le Corbusier's influence, that it may be at its strongest when it is least obvious.

After the 1930s socialists had decided to put Le Corbusier's mannerisms aside in order to find the essence of Modernism, Colin Rowe emerged in the late 1940s to explain that the mannerisms were themselves the essence of Le Corbusier and, by extension, that architecture was, after all, about style. Rowe's interpretation captured the imagination of James Stirling, Robert Maxwell, Alan Colquhoun and many others who reasserted the importance of formal values in architecture and criticism, and whose influence is still felt sixty years after the first publication of Rowe's pioneering essays in the *Architectural Review*, 'The Mathematics of the Ideal Villa' (1947) and 'Mannerism and Modern Architecture' (1950). For James Gowan, looking back in 1965, 'It was not until the 1950s that we recognised fully the classical armature in Le Corbusier's work.'[21]

The confusion created by a historical master, as Le Corbusier was by the 1950s, starting in new directions, was apparent in the two articles on his work by James Stirling in the *Architectural Review*. As Banham recorded, 'the second generation of Corbusiasts were less the followers of an impassioned argument about the place of architecture in a technological culture than the admirers of a number of unique monuments standing upon specific pieces of the earth's surface.'[22]

This is not, however, what Le Corbusier is remembered for in relation to that period, but for his impact on housing design, which for many people has been his most troubling contribution to Modernism in Britain, and the most thoroughly discussed. Banham's 1965 article, 'Corbolatry at the County Hall' in *New Society* is a sample of criticism directly addressing his influence, but at this date lacking any sense of misgiving, so that Banham jocularly commends the 'businesslike and visually rewarding environment' at the Handley Street estate in Battersea, for providing 'so much cover, dead ground and general nookery for "undesirable elements" to disappear into.'[23] Seven years on, after the start of vandalism and other symptoms of urban disorder, the scales had fallen from the critics' eyes. Martin Pawley's talk at the IID Summer Session on Le Corbusier should, he felt, have been subtitled 'He's sure got a lot to answer for.' Pawley said what should have been said decades earlier:

The trouble with Le Corbusier's tremendous naïve vision was that it was a vision from above; it was in itself, in all its thinking, in all its drawing, something which was seen from a distant standpoint; seen from an aeroplane, seen from a helicopter … the failure to provide the social support system that these tower blocks need proceeds from Le Corbusier's own myopic vision.[24]

Since the 1987 centenary exhibition, the total knowledge of the history of modern architecture has increased through the work of more scholars, access to more physical buildings in former Eastern Europe, and more publications of texts and secondary works. In the process, Le Corbusier has acquired more depth of context and his impact has been modified if not diminished. Charles Jencks has had two opportunities to review the whole life story and its significance. William Curtis has provided a magisterial summary with a focus on the artistic side. Tim Benton's work has charted the shifts in focus in his work that are typical of the developing field. Helped by the increasing availability of documents, the latest generation of Le Corbusier scholars in Britain, such as Simon Richards and Flora Samuel, have looked for the man and his relationship to the inner life of the psyche and imagination.[25] Le Corbusier continues to flow in the bloodstream of British architecture (and I do mean that rather than just Britain), or, to change metaphors, to be woven into the fabric so that it is no longer possible to tell whether he is the figure or part of the ground.

NOTES

1   'Library Notes', *Architect and Building News*, vol. 159, 14 July 1939, p. 36. A copy of this piece is included in Summerson's scrapbook of journalism in the RIBA Archive.

2   Ibid.

3   *AA Journal*, September 1924, pp. 66–67.

4   See introduction by Jean-Louis Cohen to *Toward an Architecture*, London: Frances Lincoln, 2008, p. 49.

5   Evelyn Waugh, 'Cities of the Future', *Observer*, 11 August 1929, p. 6.

6   See Lawrence Whistler, *The Laughter and the Urn: The Life of Rex Whistler*, London, 1985, pp. 118–19.

7   Quoted in Douglas Percy Bliss, *Edward Bawden*, Godalming and Toronto: Pendomer Press, [1980], pp. 26–27.

8   'Mies is great but Corb communicates', Peter Smithson in 'Le Corbusier: a Symposium', *AA Journal*, May 1959, p. 254.

9   'Modern Architecture', *Times Literary Supplement*, 30 October 1927, p. 734.

10 *Observer*, 9 March 1930, p. 2; *Guardian* 16 November 1933, p. 11.

11 Reyner Banham, 'Gurus of Our Time 1: Le Corbusier', *New Society*, 14 September 1967, p. 354.

12 John Summerson, 'Architecture' in Geoffrey Grigson (ed.) *The Arts To-Day*, London: John Lane, The Bodley Head, 1935, pp. 253–88.

13 *RIBA Journal*, vol. 44, 22 May 1937, p. 746. This review could be by Summerson, who contributed to the *RIBA Journal*, often signing pieces with initials only.

14 Untitled poem, 'Sir, No Man's Enemy', W. H. Auden, *Poems*, London: Faber & Faber, 1930.

15 W. H. Auden, review of *Culture and Environment* by F. R. Leavis and Denys Thompson, and other books, *The Twentieth Century*, May 1933.

16 Anthony Cox, 'The Thirties' in 'Le Corbusier – his Impact on Four Generations', *RIBA Journal*, October 1965, p. 498.

17 Ibid.

18 Taken from a copy of the manuscript score of the music by Tim Bennett, courtesy of Doreen Benham.

19 Herbert Read, 'The House of To-morrow', *The Listener*, 25 February 1931, p. 324.

20 Tim Bennett, review of two books by Le Corbusier, *Focus,* no. 2, 1938, p. 82.

21 James Gowan, 'Post War' in 'Le Corbusier – his Impact on Four Generations', *RIBA Journal*, October 1965, p. 499.

22 Banham, loc. cit.

23 Reyner Banham, 'Corbolatry at County Hall', *New Society*, 4 November 1965, p. 27

24 Martin Pawley, 'A Philistine Attack', *Architectural Design*, April 1972, pp. 239–40.

25 See Simon Richards, *Le Corbusier and the Concept of Self*, New Haven and London: Yale University Press, 2003; Sarah Menin and Flora Samuel, *Nature and Space, Aalto and Le Corbusier*, London: Routledge, 2003; and Flora Samuel, *Le Corbusier, Architect and Feminist*, Chichester: Wiley-Academy, 2004.

Part 1

1924–1939:

The World of Tomorrow

Some Views on Architectural Education: Interviews with Leading Parisian Architects: Mons. Le Corbusier-Saugnier

By Gordon Holt

By keeping this stormy petrel of French architecture back to the end might lend credence to the view that it is good policy to write an article much as you screw up the handcuffs clapped on some bewildered bourgeois; until he sits up and takes notice. It is partly true. This young and rising architect has created and nurtured theories on architectural education so startlingly logical, but also so widely apart from those held in England, even in 'advanced' quarters, that their amazing radicalism may compel a degree of attention denied to ideas less potently charged.

The reading of Le Corbusier's book, *Towards a New Architecture*, (Fig. 3.1) made me resolve to seek this dynamic monstrosity. (I wasn't far from the conviction.) I did track him in his lair: strange to say, an office like any young architect's office, whose space, though, was punctuated by models of houses, the like of which I had never seen before. A certain dizziness overcame me, but the advent of two large horn-rimmed eyes, staring icily out of an enigmatic face, dispelled the *malaise*, and with my wits back to their proper function I was soon in battle with my man.

Here candour compels me to say that, notwithstanding a small, faithful, and increasing band of adherents, Le Corbusier is not held in pious odour by the same *monde bien pensant* (for it changes hardly at all) that exploded when, forty years before, Mons. Fr. Jourdain gave it gunpowder and caviare. He is held round the Louvre and the Rue Bonaparte to be a thinly-disguised heretic! This much, however, should be said: Le Corbusier commands attention and respect. He has delivered lectures before distinguished audiences, and under unimpeachable patronage. Further, his work and ideas are now seized upon by journalists and architects of every country, from the two Americas to Poland. What is more satisfactory, he is putting his theories into practice.

It is not easy to resume his ideas, because they burrow so deep into the soil, and go back to so many essentials that nothing less than a complete reconsideration of what makes a modern town will do.

A few staccato and bare statements may, however, serve, hence what follows are mere shorthand notes. Modern life has been revolutionized since the coming of machinery. Machinery means factories. Factories attract workers and form centres. Those centres, those factories are best near towns, on account of transport and, therefore, of efficiency and economy. As the supply creates the demand, so more factories, of all kinds, spring up.

3.1
Villa at Bordeaux constructed of mass-production elements (1925)

From Le Corbusier, *Towards a New Architecture* (1927)

Their complements are offices, also in towns. Business – that is, commerce and industry – it can be seen, is bound to expand enormously until this earth of ours is yielding its maximum. It follows that business will enlarge towns and create new ones to an extent we seldom dream of. But it *must* happen. Existing towns, taken by surprise, have not had time or the capacity to react to what, admittedly, have been sudden and portentous changes. But the lackadaisical and unscientific way modern society has chosen to cope with those cracking activities is, indeed, pathetically inadequate. Life, in our big towns, is wasteful, dangerous, and gets worse and worse. Palliatives will not and cannot do. The logic of things, the volition of progress, everything points to some striking revolution, or else to some swift evolution. Preferably the latter. But time strides on, and it is now that the great jerk should be given.

Away with slums and appalling concentrations! Away with crazy traffic! Away with timid methods of a past age. Create big; standardize, if necessary; design for future years, not for 1800. Plan as scientifically as you can; use materials that will bear huge spans, great heights, concentrated loads. Cut out almost all this silly decoration and learn to handle those gigantic and new masses of building materials with the rhythm and dignity they demand. Town houses for the workers? They will be enormous skyscrapers, veritable colonies placed, say, every 400 metres, and served, under their very foundations, by electric traffic, each block a station. The avenues those blocks will form may be like the Champs-Elysées in width, 120 metres, and although their yield for capacity per square yard will be infinitely better than what we are accustomed to, they will afford around them far more space for sun and air.

'But surely, Mons. Le Corbusier, this future town will look somewhat inhuman?'

'That is where you err. It will be nothing of the kind. Shops, restaurants, theatres, all those necessary units of a town will be there, but lower and spreading; they will link these house-towers and give scale, rhythm, incidences. They shall be fanciful or severe, plain or coloured, if you will. It is bound to come.'

'Then you hold that architects must prepare themselves for the change? The Beaux-Arts ...'

'*Cher Monsieur*' – the voice was terse and spoke with earnest resolution – 'the architects needed now must be trained to create, not abortions, but children and men, that is, beings *alive*, vigorous, and beautiful. Architecture needs eugenics.'

'You are, then, in favour of a sound technical education?'

'That is so, but it must be backed by a *real* general culture, an austere and delicate training almost self-applied. I wonder' – his eyes twinkled, his head, moved by the flux of amused memories, nodded to and fro – 'I wonder how many living architects do possess the one or the other ...'

Fascinated by large diagrams our eyes danced on the walls, and outside Paris sizzled and hummed delightfully.

Source: *Architects' Journal,* 23 July 1924

Vers une Architecture
by M. Le Corbusier-Saugnier

By Verner O. Rees

Mr. Gordon Holt has recently published a witty note on an interview with M. Le Corbusier-Saugnier in the *Architect's Journal* with special reference to his opinions on the education of architects. As the ideas of this radically minded gentleman have been so clearly and pungently set forth in his book *Vers une Architecture,* it may be of interest to attempt some sort of exposition of his ideas on architectural matters. He contends that architects have lost touch with life and are engaged only in the production of sham buildings, that they have forgotten the beauty of simple forms, and that they are afraid of the geometry of surfaces. On the other hand engineers employing geometrical forms are satisfying our eyes by their geometry, and our minds by their mathematics; they are creating clear and powerful plastic facts (witness, for instance, the great concrete hangars at Orly by M. Freyssinet (Fig. 4.1) or the grain silos in Canada). This will be seen especially in a careful examination of different modern mechanical products such as aeroplanes, motor cars, steamships, etc., in which beauty as a whole is attained by a mathematical adjustment of necessary parts.

In all the domains of industry, new problems have arisen, and also at the same time there have arisen the means of solving them. In contrast to what has happened in the past, this fact is a revolution. In building, a start has been made in mass production, for new economic necessities have come into existence, and are influencing the business of building as all other businesses. Whilst the history of architecture evolves slowly through the ages, according to set types of structure and decoration, it happens that within the last 50 years iron and cement have brought opportunities, of a great new power of construction and of a revolution in the codes of architecture at the same time. In contrast to what existed in the past we realize that the "styles" exist no longer for us, that a style for this age is being elaborated, that a revolution is taking place.

He declares that a grand and glorious new epoch is on the eve of dawning; there exist a number of works informed by the new spirit, though these will be met with mainly yet in industrial production. The different 'styles' are so many lies. Industry is invading everywhere like a river running to its destiny and is bringing us the new tools adapted to the present new era.

4.1
Airship hangar, Orly (1916)

Engineer: Eugène Freyssinet
Photographers: Chevojon (1916)

If we cast away the immobile ideas of the past with regard to the dwelling, and consider what is the object of a house from a critical and objective point of view, we will arrive at the idea of the 'house-tool', healthy and beautiful and fitted to its ends as the other tools of human existence, which are turned out by manufacturers.

'Eyes that see not' is the heading of an interesting chapter on houses.

There is one occupation' he says – 'and only one, that is, architecture, where progress is not necessary, where reigns idleness of mind, where we look backwards instead of forward. Everywhere else, the uncertainty of the morrow torments and worries humanity, and leads to a solution; if we do not advance, we go bankrupt. But in architecture we never go bankrupt. O blessed, privileged trade! Alas! ... I place myself with regard to architecture in the state of mind of the inventor of aeroplanes. The lesson of the aeroplane is not so much in the forms created, [it is necessary to see in an aeroplane not a bird or a winged insect but a machine to fly;] the lesson of the aeroplane is in the logic which has presided in the enunciation of the problem, and in the success of its realisation. When a problem is properly set, inevitably a solution is found to it.

The problem of the modern dwelling has not been set. To try and fly like a bird was not setting the problem right, consequently Ader's bat did not leave the ground. But to invent a flying-machine without memories of anything foreign to pure mechanics, that is, to seek a means of suspension and of propulsion in the air, that is to put the problem correctly; and in less than ten years all the world could fly.

Let us attempt to set the problem; let us shut our eyes on what exists.

A *dwelling* is a shelter against warmth, cold, rain, thieves, and inquisitive people – a receptacle of light and sun. A certain number of compartments destined for cooking, for work, for intimate life.

A *room* is a space in which to circulate freely, with a couch on which to lie, a chair to rest or to work in, a table to work, shelves on which to arrange quickly everything in its "right place".

How many rooms? one in which to cook, and one in which to eat; one in which to work, one in which to wash, and one in which to sleep.

These are the main requirements of a dwelling. Then why upon the pretty country houses and villas of the suburbs, these immense and useless roofs? Why these rare windows with little panes? Why then this mirrored sideboard, these bookcases adorned with acanthus leaves, these cabinets, consoles, these china and silver stand, etc? ... there is no daylight in your house. Your windows are not convenient for opening. There is no hopper-casement (vasistas) to aereate the room, such as exist in the wagons-restaurants.

Windows should serve to admit light, either a little or a great deal or not at all, or to look out of. There are windows in sleeping cars which shut hermetically or open at will; there are the great sheets of glass of the modern café which shut tightly, but which open completely, thanks to the swivel which makes them descend into the ground; there are windows in the restaurant cars, which have little louvres in glass which open to aereate a little, much or not at all. There are rolling blinds that can descend by fractions and intercept the light at will, according to the angle of their slats. But architects practice only the windows of Versailles [or Hampton Court], Louis X, Y or Z, which shut badly, which have tiny panes, and which open with difficulty.

Then M. Le Corbusier gives a list of requirements that all self-respecting tenants should exact from their landlords. These should be compiled in a booklet called the Manual of the Habitation, and the Anti-Alcoholic League or the League for the Repopulation of the Country should distribute it among all mothers and housewives. At the same time they should demand from the Government the dismissal of the professors of the École des Beaux-Arts – (!).

Here are a few of its items:

The tenant should insist on a sunny toilet room, the largest in the house, the former drawing-room for instance, one wall of which to be entirely composed of glass, opening if possible on a terrace for sun baths; china wash-basins, bath, shower, gymnastic outfit. The next room should be the dressing room. You must not undress in your bedroom. It is not very clean, and is painfully untidy. Here will be cupboards for linen and clothes not higher than 4 ft. 6 in., with drawers, racks, etc.

Insist on a large living room instead of all the many sitting rooms.

Insist on bare walls in your bed, living and dining rooms. Shelves and cupboards in the walls should take the place of furniture, which is expensive, takes up room and requires cleaning.

If you can, put your kitchen at the top of the house to avoid smells of cooking.

Buy only practical, and never buy ornamental furniture. Go to the old palaces and see the bad taste of the kings. Hang only a few pictures on the walls, and then only works of quality: failing these buy good photographs of them.

Such a house, claims M. Le Corbusier-Saugnier would be adapted to its end, i.e., to be inhabited.

The plans of the houses of to-day are conceived as furniture depositories and leave out man. To tell the truth the modern man is bored to death in his house: he goes to his club. The modern woman is bored outside her boudoir: she goes to the 'five o'clock.' But the humble people who have no clubs crowd at night under their lamp, and are afraid to move among the maze of their furniture which takes all the room and constitutes their fortune and their pride. This conception of the house is favourable to the Faubourg St. Antoine, but is nefarious to society, it kills the family spirit, because it is so uncomfortable to live in such houses.

It would hardly be fair to M. Le Corbusier to include only these extracts, where he is possibly in a somewhat playful mood. He has offered more serious meat in his book. There is his onslaught against the present conceptions of architecture, his examination of the historic periods, and the development of his ideas of practical building.

He discriminates among the masterpieces of the past. Whilst he says that the Parthenon symbolises absolute perfection in architecture, (Fig. 4.2) whilst he admires the Greeks and the Byzantines without reserve, he tilts vigorously at some of the classical idols; St. Peters, for instance, is but an attempt, a thing 'that might have been' – the result of Michael Angelo's frustrated hopes.

If, by comparison, the monuments of ancient Rome are great, it is because they are the work of master builders – 'entrepreneurs.'

From the Romans, he says, 'let us keep the brick and concrete, but sell their marble to the multi-millionaires. The Romans knew nothing about marble.'

Yet to be a constructor is not to his mind sufficient, and here he underlines with remarkable subtility the passage from the facts of building proper to architecture which is 'pure creation of the mind.'

You work in stone, wood, brick or concrete, and with these construct houses, palaces – this is building. Skill is at work. But suddenly my heart is gripped, I experience joy, I am happy, I say: this is grand – that is architecture; Art is here.

4.2
Parthenon, Athens (436 BC)

Architects: Iktinos and Kallicrates
Photographer: Edwin Smith (1962)

My house may be convenient, if so I offer thanks, as I would to the engineers of the railways or of the telephone service. Yet my heart is not touched. But the scheme of walls that is raised against the sky is such that it moves me; I feel what were the intentions in raising them – sweet, forceful, charming and dignified.

The stones tell me all that; I must cling to this place, and my eyes must contemplate something which enunciates a thought, a thought which gets clearer without words or sounds, but solely through interproportioned prismatic shapes; and these are such that light outlines them clearly; proportions which do not refer to anything necessarily practical or descriptive; they are a mathematical creation of mind; they are the voice of architecture.

With dead materials starting from a more or less utilitarian scheme proportions have been established which have moved my heart. This is architecture.

Thus also does he write about the Parthenon, which after all is nothing but the perfection of a standard (M. Le Corbusier writes 'standart' and seems to prefer the English word as more expressive of his meaning than the French word 'type'), and the standard then was the average plan of the Greek temple, which had already been in existence for a century.

When a standard is fixed, the play of competition begins, it becomes a match. In order to win one must do better than one's rival, both in the ensemble and in the details. Hence progress.

The standard is a necessary order in human work. All men have similar organs and functions. All men have the same real needs. The social order has developed through the ages and has determined classes, functions: standard needs have caused products of standard use. The house is a product necessary for man. The motor car is a product with a simple function – to run on roads – and with complex aims: – comfort, endurance, appearance, etc., and industry has been put to the necessity of standardizing it. Cars have all the same essential dispositions. Later, through the play of competition, intervenes the search for a beauty, or a harmony, beyond the brutal facts of its existence, and it becomes a manifestation of art. Here come the "style," i.e., the unanimous realization of a state of perfection.

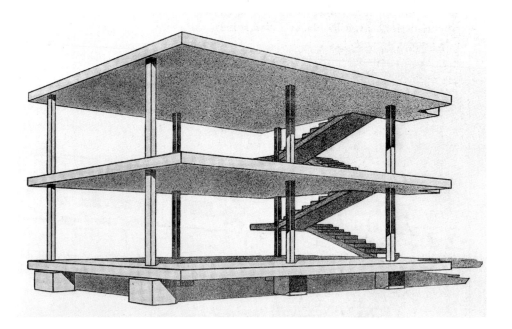

4.3
Framework for the Maison Dom-ino (1915)

From Le Corbusier, *Oeuvre Complète*, vol. 1 1910–29 (1929)

Let us show both the Parthenon and the car as two products of selection in different spheres, the former having reached its stage of perfection, the latter still seeking it. This confers a nobility on the car! Well then! Shall we compare our houses with the cars?

Here our comparison collapses, for we have no Parthenons, no standards.
In another chapter he asks,

why should not we apply this spirit of standardization to the house, which is but a tool of our life. Why should we not make houses *"en série?"* Unfortunately the necessary disposition of mind does not exist. We are still dominated by the romantic conception of the old-fashioned house. Yet the war has helped us on this road. The contractors have brought machinery, which is skilful, patient, nimble. Soon the building yards will be factories. The first effects of industrial evolution are already evident in the fact that artificial materials are gradually superseding the old natural building materials. We have heard of houses in *"béton liquide"* cast in a mould with material poured in from the top as you would fill a bottle.

M. Le Corbusier in his enthusiasm for this idea presents in his book a series of remarkable sketches of different types of houses, conceived from this point of view, *maisons en série*, the 'Domino' type, (Fig. 4.3) the 'Citrohan' type, etc., which are to answer the needs of the working man, the bourgeois, or the artist, types of different sizes and planning, but which all embody the essential requirements of the standard house – space, light, and convenience.

This string of extracts may not give an altogether true idea of M. Le Corbusier's theories and thoughts, but it is hoped that they may be sufficient to induce the reading of his book. It abounds in stimulating remarks on architectural practice and theory, all from an unusually detached point of view. He questions everything as to its efficiency and use. He measures beauty from an austere but passionate standpoint. He envies the perfection reached by the engineers, and dreams of the glories of the architecture that he hopes will arise in the New Age, perfect in its mechanical parts, magnificent and powerful in its masses and proportions, as accurately fitted to the needs and ideals of its time, as are the motor car or steamship – used in his book as starting points for discussion and comparison – to the utilitarian purposes that have brought them into existence.

Source: *Architectural Association Journal*, September 1924

Towards a New Architecture

By Harold Tomlinson

The publication of a translation into English of Le Corbusier's *Vers une Architecture* is something of an event, and the wonder is that it has not been done before. That thirteen editions should have appeared in France without an English translation having been undertaken is evidence of either a lack of initiative on the part of our publishers, or an appreciation by them of an almost incredible apathy towards architecture by the English reading public.

The dictum of M. Auguste Perret, quoted by Mr. Bartle Cox in his article on the work of the Perret Brothers, is worthy of repetition here. Speaking in 1925 at the Université des Annales, M. Perret said:

Architects speak a dead language, hence public indifference. If architects continue to speak this dead language, there is another – that of engineers – which will replace it, for the living language will be understood.

M. Perret, it was stated, 'is as strongly opposed to designs by mere engineers as he is to those by mere architects,' and Mr. Etchells, the present translator, testifies to Le Corbusier's acceptance of this creed. What was true of France in 1925 is true of England now, and those who were so fortunate as to hear M. Howard Robertson's paper on 'Modern French Architecture,' read to the [Royal] Institute [of British Architects] in the spring of the present year [1927], will realize how great are the changes that have been taking place in French architecture during the last few years.

Many valuable lessons may be learned from the translation, and one does not need to admire Le Corbusier's executed buildings to learn them. It is the divorce of *structure* from *architecture* (as if one were not an essential part of the other) that makes one fearful of attempts to introduce specialization at the present transitional stage of architectural education in this country.

Of mass production Le Corbusier has much to say, and all is to the point. The machine-made article and mass-production methods have come to stay. A small minority still bleats for a return to the adze and chisel, but the majority is only too anxious to take advantage of the inexpensive and efficient products of modern machinery. It is foolish to pretend that the worst work of a bad 'craftsman designer' is preferable to the machine-made article designed by a good artist. Incipient failures are the stepping-stones to success, and to revisualize the improvement shown, during the last five years, in the design of the machine-made door alone is to appreciate what can be done. Even the expert will admit that a dowelled door, made by well-designed machinery, is stronger than the work of any but the most exceptional craftsman. Most mass-production firms have realized that unless their wares are well designed they are severely handicapped, and architects are being forced by their clients to select, rather than to design, the smaller and less elastic units of their buildings.

On the architect, therefore, devolves the new duty of ensuring by his selection that only the fittest survive.

The history of architecture unfolds itself slowly across the centuries as a modification of structure and ornament, but in the last fifty years steel and concrete have brought new conquests, which are the index of a greater capacity for construction, and of an architecture in which the old codes have been overturned. If we challenge the past, we shall learn that "styles" no longer exist for us, that a style belonging to our own period has come about; and there has been a revolution.

It will be interesting to watch the effects of the translation on our schools of architecture. Of late, even in this country, students have begun to show their dislike for the dreary routine of the 'Orders,' and are suspicious of the threadbare statement by their teachers that 'The Orders are the only means of learning proportion.' It is not unnaturally suspected that 'The Orders are all we know' would be nearer the truth. 'Why,' says the student, 'when you have a perfectly good building, cover it up with that muck?' And, if progress lies in the teaching of the master by the pupil, this is not a bad sign.

Mr. Etchells has written a brilliant introduction to his translation, though why he has changed the title to towards a *new* architecture, is not clear. Le Corbusier, one believed, made a plea for *an* architecture, meaning that the present thoughtless copying of forms of forgotten significance is not architecture at all. In other respects the work of the translator is admirable, and his own writing well merits its inclusion in the book.

It is inevitable that the engineer, preoccupied with function and aiming at an immediate response to new demands, should produce new and strange forms, often startling at first, bizarre, and disagreeable. Some of these forms are not worth constant repetition and soon disappear into the limbo of forgotten things. Others stand the test of use and standardization, become friendly to us, and take their place as part of our general equipment.

He illustrates the entrance gate to a new lock at Liverpool, and one sees at once that it is a fine thing, and this because an element of conscious design – 'making it look right,' as well as a desire for the utmost efficiency – has entered into its conception.

In a century of development the steam locomotive has almost attained its ultimate limit of efficiency, and during this period it has also reached a high level of design. No doubt the electrical locomotive, which is ugly enough today, will be beautiful in the end, for it,

¹³⁴   TOWARDS A NEW ARCHITECTURE

PAESTUM, 600–550 B.C.

When once a standard is established, competition comes at once and violently into play. It is a fight; in order to win you must do better than your rival *in every minute point*, in

HUMBER, 1907

5.1

Eyes which do not see: Automobiles. The fixing of standards

From Le Corbusier, *Towards a New Architecture* (1927)

too, will be designed by men who will not accept past models for beauty any more than they will for efficiency. To build, as we sometimes do today, warped copies of Elizabethan houses, whose original ideal was the straight line, and to stuff the result with 'every modern convenience,' is as ridiculous as it would be to attempt to build our modern locomotives in the guise of the 'Rocket.'

Le Corbusier finds lessons for us in ships, airplanes, and motor-cars. (Fig. 5.1) Of the 'Aquitania' ... 'A seaside villa, conceived as are these liners, would be more appropriate than those we see with their heavy tiled roofs. But perhaps it might be claimed that this is not a "maritime" style ... Architects please note: the value of a "long gallery" or promenade – satisfying and interesting volume; unity in materials; a fine grouping of the constructional elements, sanely exhibited and rationally assembled.' Everybody acknowledges the truth of these statements. It is not sentiment alone which makes most 'ordinary people' love the clean lines of the steamship, and loathe its vulgar state-room and interior, even if, when architect designed, it is made 'just like home.'

In the chapter on airplanes he disproves the statement that 'the construction must be shown,' and argues that whereas the intense selection of the late war quickly produced a rapid solution of a problem (flight) clearly expressed, architecture fails today because 'We do not know how to build in a modern way – materials, systems of construction, THE CONCEPTION OF THE DWELLING, all are lacking ... Engineers have been busy ... architects have been asleep.' The force of the illustrations is not what it might have been. The airplanes are those of the first edition, and what appeared to be a clean design then looks like a museum specimen now, and one is surprised to see a statement, made by a Frenchman, that Ader's 'Avion' did not leave the ground. The 'Manual of the Dwelling,' which ends the chapter, carried out for feminine clients, might make any young architect rich, even if it did not make him famous.

Automobiles have progressed, too, and the 1921 Delage compares as unfavourably with, say, a Sunbeam of today as the 1907 Humber [...] does with the Delage. The stream-line form is generally accepted as a shape of beauty, and as it is modified by the necessities of structure, so we accept its changing form. Sometimes the best compromise which we can effect is recognized as ugly, and time is the final test; time, too, will be the test of M. Le Corbusier's teaching.

With regard to the format of the volume, for the present writer the Garamond type and the 'art' pages are an insufferable combination. One wishes that a saving had been effected by printing the line blocks and reading matter on a cheaper and more suitable paper. If the translation has a wide sale, perhaps the publisher will consider the issue of a flimsy, similar in character to the paper-backed French edition; and at a price more easily within the reach of the people for whom it could be most valuable. Is it too much to ask, also, that the illustrations be brought up to date?

Source: *Architects' Journal*, 21 September 1927

Towards a New Architecture:
When Engineer and Architect Work Together

By N.S.H (Nora Shackleton Heald)

At a recent housing conference townswomen of various classes, housewives, artists, and professional women among them, were asked to say what type of flat they would choose to have. Different though their requirements were, each had the same desire for a small space in the open air such as would be given by a balcony or a roof garden, and one vigorous statement that no dwelling should be permitted which did not provide this open air accommodation was loudly applauded. The chairman's remark that London air was so smoky that roof spaces were useless was promptly countered by the declaration that the air was rapidly becoming cleaner owing to the decreasing use of coal, and that as dwelling places are erected for long use these certain improvements of the future must be reckoned for at the outset.

This demand of the town flat dweller for an open-air space in immediate connection with his residence is not being satisfied by the greater part of the new buildings springing up in the various parts of London. The woman who owns a flat in a Mayfair block for which she may pay a rent of about two thousand pounds a year is in this respect no better served that the artisan dweller in one of the blocks of tenement flats in some less salubrious quarter, though, of course, the wealthy woman can escape from her flat and she can hire nurses who will keep her child in the Park for several hours a day. The poor woman, especially the respectable hard-working mother who keeps her house in order, is compelled to spend almost all her life indoors. She cannot, as the cottage woman can, perform an occasional domestic task at her door; she goes out only when she has an errand. Her baby, too, must stay indoors, for a woman who lives on the fourth storey cannot leave an untended child below in the common courtyard. Had she a balcony or a roof garden, she and her young children would be in better physical health and in better spirits.

Another cause for complaint in modern housing, and one which requires immediate attention, is the spoliation of the countryside by the erection of small bungalows and villas which are spreading ribbon-wise along the roads leading from every country town and village. These dwellings are the expression of a growing public desire for light and air, but they are rapidly destroying the lovely English countryside; and soon, so great is their network, even the villager will have his open country to seek.

The sad fact is that both in town and country we are allowing the erection of buildings which are out of date at the moment of their building. We do not make efficient use of new materials; we do not study how, while satisfying the urgent need for dwellings with light and air space, we can make use of the communal spirit which has arisen among us. This country, with its great tradition of pleasant domestic architecture, is being surpassed in house building by others who are using new materials in new ways.

Moreover, we are building our out-of-date dwellings so firmly that generations of households will be compelled to go on living in them, as Londoners are compelled to live to-day in the strongly built Victorian houses which are no longer suited to the lives we lead. Our houses cost more money to build and more labour to run than they should, and they do not provide the amenities we require. If we are to have efficient houses we must gain a new conception of building. We discard our old clothes; our old tools; we design new implements to take their place. Yet still we go on building, by old methods, houses which do not fit the life we want to lead.

We do not even realise the importance of this matter of building efficient houses.

The problem of the house is a problem of the epoch. The equilibrium of society to-day depends upon it. Industry on the grand scale must occupy itself with building and establish the elements of the house on a mass-production basis. We must create the mass-production spirit – the spirit of conceiving mass-production houses; the spirit of constructing mass-production houses; the spirit of living in mass-production houses.

If we eliminate from our hearts and minds all dead concepts in regard to the house, and look at the question from a critical and objective point of view, we shall arrive at the 'House Machine,' the mass-production house, healthy (and morally so too) and beautiful in the same way that the working tools and instruments which accompany our existence are beautiful – beautiful also with all the animation that the artist's sensibility can add to severe and pure functioning elements.

This quotation gives the argument of an intensely interesting book which has, after running through thirteen French editions, appeared in an English translation by Mr. Frederick Etchells – Le Corbusier's *Towards a New Architecture* [...]. The author is awake to the fact that an architecture of our own age is shaping itself. (Fig. 6.1)

Its main lines,' the Introduction to the book declares, 'become more and more evident. The use of steel and reinforced concrete construction; of large areas of plate glass; of standardized units (as, for example, in metal windows); of the flat roof; of new synthetic materials and new surface treatments of metals that machinery has made possible; of hints taken from the air-plane, the motor-car or the steamship ... all these things are helping, at any rate, to produce a twentieth century architecture whose lineaments are already traceable. A certain squareness of mass and outline, a criss-cross or 'grid-iron' treatment with an emphasis on the horizontals, an extreme bareness of wall surface, a pervading austerity and economy and a minimum of ornament; these are among its characteristics. There is evolving ... a grave and classical architecture whose fully developed expression should be of a noble beauty.

6.1
Block of freehold maisonettes

From Le Corbusier, *Vers une Architecture*
2nd ed. (1924)

It should be pointed out that the writer of the passage quoted is not using the word 'classical' in the sense which would mean that the new architecture is an imitation of the old, but rather that, like the greatest of the old buildings, the new ones owe their beauty to their suitability, their proportion and their right use of materials. Le Corbusier, indeed, takes the Parthenon and Michael Angelo's apses at St. Peter's, and, by making us see them as directly as we might see a motor car or a briar pipe, shows them to be more closely akin to a good modern concrete factory building or a Rolls Royce car than they are in 'the travesties of themselves on which architects have battened.'

These new concrete buildings (an illustration of some houses at Stuttgart by Le Corbusier (Figs 6.2 and 6.3) appeared in the *The Queen* of November 2nd), odd though they may at first appear to the English eye trained on Tudor beams and thatched gables, will not long seem strange to the average man, who, to quote again the admirable introduction,

has had an unconscious schooling through the trim efficiency of the machines and apparatus which surround and govern so much of his daily life. Already the average user of the motor car is beginning to take a keen pleasure in good bodywork, in cleanness of line and general design. It must be many years indeed since such close attention has been given to a particular aesthetic problem by so large a number of human beings.

Very wisely, Le Corbusier says that when in our epoch a problem is properly stated it inevitably finds its solution. We have not yet clearly stated the problem of the house, 'the machine for living in' as he calls it, and until we set aside our prejudices and look at the business of house building with the freshness and efficiency which we bring to the manu-

facture of ships and motor cars we are not likely to find the house which suits present day conditions.

All around us we may see that thick walls, in earlier days a necessity, are still being built, although thin partitions of glass or brick can now be used to enclose the ground floor of a twenty storey building, although the deep window embrasure made by the thick wall prevents the admittance of light. Even to-day great buildings are being put together brick by brick, and we have so little realised that concrete is an expressive material in itself, that we case in our concrete erection, with a layer of brick or stone.

Le Corbusier tells us of concrete houses built by one class of labour in three days from materials almost entirely found in the locality; thus entailing low transportation costs. These are what he terms 'mass production' houses, made from standardized units ... A significant point is the insistence that the houses shall be pleasant places with facilities for the enjoyment of leisure. The worker's house is now so uncomfortable, declares the author, that he is discontented and rushes out to spend his leisure and his money away from it; the house Le Corbusier would build would have its garden court, its large room and its roof for games and dancing.

6.2
Bruckmannweg 2 and Rathenaustrasse 1–3, Weissenhofsiedlung, Stuttgart (1927)

From *Architecture Vivante*, Spring 1928

6.3
**Double house, Rathenaustrasse 1–3,
Weissenhofsiedlung, Stuttgart (1927)**

Photographers: Bryan & Norman Westwood
(1935)

Two interesting suggestions for town planning are outlined – the City of Piles, which would have its gas and water mains, its tube trains and heavy traffic on the ground, while its houses, its roads and its quick traffic would be raised on piles twelve feet or more above them; and the City of Towers, with its sixty storey buildings surrounded by parks and wide arterial roads. To many of us, especially those who have walked the streets of New York, a City of Towers has a nightmarish sound, but a little thought will show us that our present skyscrapers are ugly because we can rarely see them, and because as they rise to replace lower buildings they convert our once pleasant streets into dark narrow gullies between dismal walls of concrete, stone, or brick. That the view of New York from a ship approaching the harbour has its surprising fantastic beauty is because the distance allows the human eye to measure the lofty buildings and realise their proportion.

So Le Corbusier would set his great towers in the midst of park-like open spaces, setting back some buildings and allowing others to be put forward, thus breaking up the long avenues and promoting the play of light and shade. He would, too, provide open terraces for each dwelling by recessing the storeys, and he would outline roofs for gardens and sports grounds.

Other schemes outlined in *Towards a New Architecture* include plans for a group of residents' lodgings, for a seaside villa, for cottages for artisans, and for terraced houses built around a courtyard. In some such plan as this last surely lies the cure for the spider-web of bungalows for each of these group settlements could provide homes for a hundred families, each of which, while sharing in the communal sports ground, lighting and power plant etc., would have its own terrace and roof garden. When planned as a unit those settlements would no more disfigure the countryside than do the great manor houses we now so much admire; beyond their areas the countryside would lie unspoiled, since the one noble building would displace a long stretch of our present inefficient make-shift villas.

It is to be hoped that this book will be widely read in England. It is, as Mr. Etchells remarks, a manifesto with illustrations, but the matter is so sound, the illustrations so well chosen, and their descriptions so informative, that the reader is instructed and has imagination stirred. Such a look might provoke a wholesome revolution in modern house building – and that merely by reminding us what we need and suggesting simply what we might have did we but insist on having it. [...]

Source: *The Queen*, 23 November 1927
The second part of the article dealing with houses designed
by Robert Mallet-Stevens (1886–1945) has been omitted. (Eds)

The Robotism of Architecture

By Edwin Lutyens
Review of *Towards a New Architecture*

This book takes you down a new channel of architectural adventure – not without the risks and perils, that all adventure pre-supposes; and Mr Etchells, in his preface, plays the part of able pilot.

M. Le Corbusier's theme is that architecture of our time should have the qualities of the machine. Efficiency and mass production are the watch-words. Houses are to be like the products of Mr Woolworth's shops – stamped out or cast in moulds and sold, I suppose, in ratios of 3d. and 6d. For such houses, Nature will provide a new humanity. Robots without eyes – for eyes that have no vision cannot be educated to see. Man may be small, but he has two eyes and can focus distance, thereby measure things. He can raise or depress his vision by the movement of his head, up, down, right or left, and with little exertion can reverse all these aspects. Mass production would destroy in man the sense of three-dimensional limitations. He would lose the pleasure of thick soft walls, dumb to noise, when compelled to live in stark noisy little boxes, where skilled plumbers take the place of house-proud maids.

Architecture, certainly, must have geometric constituents, but lines and diagrams, in two dimensions, are not enough. Architecture is a three-dimensioned art. To be a home, the house cannot be a machine. It must be passive, not active, bringing peace to the fluctuation of the human mind from generation to generation. For what charm can a house possess that can never bear a worn threshold, the charred hearth and the rubbed corner?

Humanity remains and will remain, I trust, humane. It is more likely that we shall return to the gorilla than become Robots, compelled to live in small enamelled cages. Emotion will never be controlled by sparking plugs. The logic of a French mind may make a Corbusier house, or even a Versailles, but never a Hampton Court.

M. Le Corbusier makes great play with airplanes, automobiles, and Atlantic liners, finding in them affinity to the Parthenon. They are excellent, thrilling things in themselves, and may well serve as tonics, for it is to be regretted that ugliness in a building does not kill as quickly as does a fault in their design. Physical efficiency, however, is not the sole test of a building. Phrases such as that cannot master design, or teach it; and, generally, the more discursive the literature in which they are used, the less the achievement. It is amazing to-day to see the works in brick and stone which the greater writer on beauty, John Ruskin, was able to perpetrate.

7.1
Canadian grain stores and elevators

From Le Corbusier, *Towards a New Architecture* (1927)

M. Le Corbusier tries to drive home his argument from the machine by delightful photographs of grain elevators, (Fig. 7.1) which thrill the imagination. In the spaciousness of the prairie they may stand out as magnificent objects; but take one and place it in and English valley, larded with traditional building and no formula about efficiency, and the machine would allay the horror of its aspect.

Again, 'Architecture has nothing to with styles.' Styles, however, are no lie if looked at fairly, as the recorded and oft-ill recorded experience of men's endeavours. Among the most beautiful inhabitants of the world in which we live, you might place trees, and among trees, the beech. How comes the beech to be? Created out of itself by the blind energy of its sap – no two trees are alike, yet all are akin and true to style. One may not appreciate style, but the experience of 3000 years of man's work, creative work, cannot be disregarded unless we are prepared for disaster. Again the plan regarded as a generator sounds very plausible – easily said and easily accepted, but it contains only one of these three essential dimensions. All are equally important and without any one of them the other two are moribund. In all successful architectural design you can draw no hard line. Each part is mother to the others, and the whole one a family of sweet intercourse and gentle behaviour.

In discussing the Parthenon – a pure creation of mind, of fair and fine minds in great intellectual honesty – M. Le Corbusier is profoundly emotional. Greek work is really beyond all modern conception. It is as deep in its use of light as are Einstein's problems. The ellipse to the Greeks was as the circle is to us. Every stone of the Parthenon was individual and essential to the whole. No more than four stones were identical, and no joint was horizontal. Such was their standard of reverence for a building that had to be created – a perfect unity, an entity, stable and endurable for an eternity.

The Parthenon cost three times, and the gold and ivory statue of Athene seven times, the National Revenue. How is it possible to compare such a building with an aeroplane, which one faulty stay or bolt may crash to the ground?

The appreciation of Rome comes as a relief. The assertion, however, that the Romans knew nothing of the use of marble, sweeps away one's breath. Give them credit, at least, for using it as a most precious pigment. A City of Towers (Fig. 7.2) is suggested, and it is a terrifying suggestion. How soothing later on is the view of Versailles – a work of real genius. For though you criticise it with stiff immovable neck, still, luckily, the human head can walk round and look up the avenues as well as down them. Pleasant, too, is the thought of Le Roi Soleil, on whose pillow, when in bed alone, all the axes of the avenues terminate. The men who laboured, and, I hope, enjoyed the creation could say, 'It is not we who have to bear that load.' In the City of Towers, on the other hand, with its bus-ridden elevator-tired Robots, what similar pleasure can they have?

LE CORBUSIER, 1923. A CITY OF TOWERS

The towers are placed amidst gardens and playing-fields. The main arteries, with their motor-tracks built over them, allow of easy, or rapid, or very rapid circulation of traffic.

7.2
A city of towers (1923)

From Le Corbusier, *Towards a New Architecture* (1927)

As one reads this book one is always amused, sometimes excited, sometimes angry, at the boil of M. Le Corbusier's emotions, but one never doubts his sincerity. His final prophecy is Architecture or Revolution; and we might not welcome it, if by Architecture he did not mean mass-made cages suitable for machine-made men. To avoid Revolution, great patience and long-suffering must be endured. To produce Architecture, it is the same. Sacrifice is essential and the worship of the absolute directed towards an inconceivable and ever-growing perfection.

Source: *The Observer*, 29 January 1928

Houses – Ancient and Modern:
a Home to Live In, not a Mansion for 'Occasions'

By Miriam Wornum

A house from the inside is a very different affair from the architect's elevation – especially from the point of view of the woman who has to run it. That is partly why I have been particularly interested in the houses of the most modern of all French architects, Le Corbusier. (Figs 8.1–8.3) And with his help I have tried to imagine what it would be like to live in one of them.

Corbusier's typical building is square in mass, just like a white box except for the top, which presents several strange knobs and bulges. The middle part of the house has a fashionable belt-like arrangement of a continuous row of glass windows which goes all round the sides and back. 'What a lot of window cleaning!' one thinks instinctively. The simple front door has a perfectly plain porch consisting of a piece of plaster stuck over it, like the lid of a box.

Inside are many surprises: concrete is everywhere, pavement lights are set in the stairs and corridors, radiators and pipes are made as prominent as possible by paint and position. The rooms merge into each other; some are divided only by partitions shoulder-high. Bathrooms are in the front of the house, and no pillars or mouldings offer any suggestion of decoration; but there is, in compensation, a feeling of unusual space and light. Delightful roof gardens lead off bedrooms, and at the top of the house one approaches a little turret arrangement by a twisting stairway. You can imagine the comfort of stepping on to your own roof garden in *negligée*. But one feels that such a house would be dangerous for children unless barricades were put up all over the place.

The obvious virtues of this very modern house are the flood of light and air, the roof garden, the comfort of the central heating, and the general solidity of the construction. And, above all, there is the sense that one lives in a house that is really expressive of the feeling of to-day.

I must qualify this last statement, however, as I feel that Le Corbusier and his fellow workers are too severe in their elimination of the past and all its ornament and richness. They give us a plain box and ask us to believe it is the 'last word' of the Spirit of the Age. I don't think it is. I think this age is as rich in romance, beauty, colour, and subtlety, in living and thinking, as any age that came before it. Richer in fact ...

We are not people who lead bare, stolid lives which should be reflected in bare cubes of houses. Our lives are full and busy and intense as few have been before. We have a right to

8.1
**Maisons La Roche-Jeanneret,
Paris (1925)**

From *Architecture Vivante*, Autumn 1926

richness and colour that expresses us and our ideals. The beauty of to-day is just as much our right as the beauty of yesterday was our fathers'. People who want beauty get it … always! I am sure it will come to us.

Compare the dress of the modern girl with her grandmother's. There is a lack of the richness and lavishness of the brocades and draperies of yesterday, her hair lacks the elaborateness and fantasy of her grandmother's, but … if is never out of place – one badly groomed wisp of hair puts its owner beyond the pale to-day. Her grandmother wore yards of flannel and cotton: the girl of to-day demands that her own few bits of underclothes be of the most perfect silk, chiffon and real lace. Can you say beauty is lost? This perfection in simplicity is only one phase of the difference between modern and past beauty, but it shows that we have to-day something that is distinctly ours. That 'something' should find expression in our homes as well as in our fashions and *moeurs*.

I think that one of the reasons why even the most modern of present-day architects have failed is because we are in such a transition stage that we are only just realising what a sane house should be. We have an ideal, but are groping towards the future.

Let me take you back to the house of the past and then show you what our houses express to-day. A house of the Middle Ages was a fortress, a cold, uncomfortable, dirty, disease-ridden place of safety from raids, slaughter and enslavement. Then it gradually developed into the elaborate mansion, with dark and miserable warrens for the servants, and opulent comfort for the Quality. Air and light were kept at a minimum because they spoilt carpets and upholstery. Armies of servants kept its insanitary and germ-laden

8.2
**House/studio, Allée des Pins,
Boulogne-sur-Seine (1926)**

From *Architecture Vivante*, Autumn 1926

furnishings superficially clean. Heavy, unwholesome meals were sent up and absorbed. Women and men and children died sooner because of the house and the life it made them lead. And it was responsible for much social discontent. A pleasant picture!

A modern house is lived in all the time and can barely rise to a formal 'occasion.' A place of light, air and convenience, it is healthful and reasonably clean. It has something of the freshness of out-of-doors, yet gives cosy comfort in illness or when you merely want to stay at home. The small, clean kitchen provides light meals, there are decent quarters for the maids, and, best of all, proper surroundings for the children. A little better, this.

Le Corbusier goes a step further. He brings the out-of-doors within reach of the person in the house. By heating the air of his roof-garden, he brings climate, good climate, as an adjunct to daily life. He eliminates elaborate fittings which cause extra work; but at the same time the usual comforts, as women understand them, are singularly lacking. A few built-in cupboards, a low bookcase that serves to divide two rooms, a few wooden screens here and there, seem to be the extent of his concern for the comfort of his clients. It is a house built by a man for a man, without any real thought for the woman at all. Up to now there has been such a chorus of praise and admiration from architectural writers on the amazing vitality and interest of the houses of Le Corbusier and his group that I think it is high time a woman criticised them.

The chief reason why I think one of these houses would be uncomfortable to live in is because they are built more as protests than as homes. Their designer is so 'fed-up' with the blind worship of yesterday that his creed has become 'anything that departs from this

8.3
**Villa Stein / de Monzie,
Garches (1927)**

Photographer unknown (1930s)

worship, that is new, is what we must have.' This is all right for a monument, but a home is a very different thing.

I have had it from Le Corbusier's own lips that he deliberately ignores his clients' taste, and does not care what they do to the interior of his houses. As a result I saw the builders putting into one of his houses old-fashioned plumbing discarded a decade ago. They said it was the simplest thing to do in the circumstances; but surely an architect who was really interested in his client's needs would have shown them something better.

This indifference hinges on the French habit of calling anyone well known or expect in the Arts *maître*. The amount of worship that such people get in France is absolutely unbelievable. Over here, we say So-and-so is good at his work and leave it at that. But in France one approaches the *maître* very humbly, and he condescends to do something for you. This is considered a beautiful and appropriate attitude to adopt, but I don't think it is. There are certain arts which are made to serve. A mural decorator or an architect is good when he serves his client's needs, making out of these needs a work of art. Not by ignoring them and expressing just himself. That's bad art. I should like very much to know about M. Le Corbusier's own domestic arrangements. I'd wager they are far from the last word in modern convenience.

There seem to be two branches to modern architecture. On one side are the revolution-ists who despise the public and get their modern feeling into the shell of their buildings, and, on the other, men who wish to make life easy for the public, and give them the most modern of labour-saving devices in their homes. They do make a contented, easily-run house, but they are people who are quite likely to give you a Tudor setting for your electric refrigerator. They have no aesthetic feeling for modern form and shape, and the shell of your home, so to speak, will be utterly wrong from the viewpoint of contemporary life. Why cannot there be some liaison between these schools? Why must I have either a bare, uncomfortable home designed by a man who doesn't care a jot about me and my personal-ity, but who has undoubtedly a fresh, crisp and really modern point of view, or a cosy com-fortable house that is half of this century and half of hundreds of years ago? Why should my washing machine and built-in cupboards fight against their setting?

The whole situation is within the grasp of the ultra-modern architect. He is the Artist, if he will only soften his attitude and realise something of the good side of the life of this age, and of the real people who inhabit it. If he will interest himself in them, not only as clients who give him his chance to show how modern he can be, but as people whose life is worth expressing in new architectural form, I am sure his houses will take on that quality of intimate beauty, of live-in-ableness, which up to now they have lacked. In other words, let the architect think of the women who will run his house, let him really consider her, and his house will be turned into the best thing a house can hope to be – a home.

Source: *Architect & Building News*, 20 July 1928

Le Corbusier: a Pioneer of Modern European Architecture

By Frederick Etchells

The Modern Movement in architecture which has been so pronounced a feature in the post-war life of Europe has touched this country but little; but it is evident that the attempts made to meet new conditions and in the use of modern materials and methods have aroused a great interest among us. Dr. Albert Dresdner's able article on Ferro-concrete Architecture in the April number of *The Studio* gave a careful analysis of its possibilities and its limitations, and it is here proposed to discuss the work and ideas of one of the better known exponents of the new school.

In France we may divide those architects who make a full use of reinforced concrete into the 'classicists' and the 'purists,' of whom the Perret brothers may be taken as examples of the former school, while the subject of this article, Le Corbusier, has made himself the protagonist of the latter by his propaganda and his numerous writings on the subject.

Le Corbusier is the pen-name of Jeanneret, a Swiss architect who was born at La Chaux de Fonds near Neuchâtel in 1887. He was sent to school at the early age of four and embarked on his career at the age of 13½, being apprenticed to a watch-engraver. A little later he took to architecture, building his first house at the age of 17½ and acting as his own clerk of works.

He seems for some years to have veered between architecture and work of a decorative kind, but at 20 he worked for more than a year under Auguste Perret, who with his brother was one of the first to apply modern constructional methods, particularly in the use of reinforced concrete, to the problems of modern architecture. This association with Perret opened up new horizons for the young architect, and we find him making, in conjunction with an engineer friend, technical researches into modern building methods.

A year or two later Le Corbusier made a long tour with his sketch-book through the Slav countries, the Balkans, Turkey, Asia Minor, Greece and Italy. This voyage seems to have been a turning point in his career and it was then that he came to believe that in architecture we must 'begin all over again.' The period before the war was passed in his native town mainly on decorative work, but his mind seems constantly to have returned to the subject of archi-tecture, and in the early part of 1914 he invented a unit system of building which he called the 'Domino' system; this it was only possible to apply in its entirety some years later.

Settling in Paris in 1916 he seems to have combined industrial researches with the painting of pictures of an abstract kind. Le Corbusier is a good painter of the modern school and his work is well known in Paris following on a show with Druet in 1921 and another with Léonce Rosenberg in 1923.

From the year 1922 when his book *Vers une Architecture* appeared, Le Corbusier has applied himself almost entirely to the practice of architecture and to propaganda in connection therewith. (Figs 9.1–9.5) In the same year he exhibited at the Salon d'Automne his plan for a 'Modern Town of Three Million Inhabitants,' the town of course being Paris. This took the form of a large diorama on a stand more than eighty feet long. In 1923 he entered into partnership with his cousin, Pierre Jeanneret, and since that date they have carried out a considerable number of works, mainly in the form of private houses, but including Le Corbusier's great industrial housing scheme at Pessac near Bordeaux. The dwellings consist of blocks of buildings constructed on the cellular 'honeycomb' system, by means of which each flat – or rather apartment of two storeys – has its own terrace garden, or *jardin suspendu* as Le Corbusier calls them. A complete unit of this scheme was shown in the Pavilion of the *Esprit Nouveau* at the Paris exhibition of 1925, together with a later plan for the centre of Paris – the well-known plan with its vast skyscrapers, each built in the form of a cross, and set at great distances from one another in the midst of trees and verdure. This plan Le Corbusier named the *Voisin* plan after the famous aviator and industrialist. His latest important enterprise is the design for the Palace of the League of Nations. It seemed almost certain at one moment that this interesting and provocative scheme would be adopted. It is not possible within the limits of this article to enter into the various movements and counter-movements which resulted in the dropping of Le Corbusier's plans, a result for which it is said that the English delegates were largely responsible.

Le Corbusier is an interesting architect, and he has indubitably made an important contribution to the solution of modern housing problems. He has invented a powerful slogan,

9.1
Villa Stein / de Monzie, Garches (1927)

Photographer: F.R. Yerbury (1920s)

9.3
**Villa Stein / de Monzie,
Garches (1927)**

Photographer unknown (1930s)

9.2
**Villa Stein / de Monzie,
Garches (1927)**

Photographer unknown (1930s)

From the author Frederick Etchells'
collection and used to illustrate his article

that of the house as a 'machine for living in.' A main factor of his system is the erection of an open framework of reinforced concrete piles or piers tied together by concrete floors; this arrangement undoubtedly gives to the house the possibility of a flexibility hitherto unknown, as walls, windows and internal partitions are almost independent of the structure. Another is the development of the roof garden. He describes how he has, since 1906, built three sloping roofs only, and how these were the *first* three he built. By observations made in the Swiss mountains, where the enormous falls of snow settling on to the roofs and melting, formed stalactites and tore away the gutters while the downpipes froze and burst; he found that all this damage was greatly intensified with the installation of central heating. Le Corbusier's principle is that of the slightly *concave* roof, so arranged that rain or melted snow is brought down through the *middle of the house,* i.e., through the heated part, so that a fall of snow for example is gradually melted and carried away without doing damage. Here is a principle of importance, and one easily realised by the use of reinforced concrete. But a difficulty presented itself; reinforced concrete is not a dead thing; it is constantly on the move under varying conditions of heat and cold, moisture and dryness. Instead of carrying off rain quickly it is better to try and maintain a constant degree of humidity on the concrete roof, and so a regular temperature. This can be done

9.4
**Villa Stein / de Monzie,
Garches (1927)**

Photographer unknown (1930s)

From the author Frederick Etchells's
collection and used to illustrate his article

by laying over the roof thick concrete flags on sand, with open joints in which grass is sown. The roots of the grass entwined in the sand provide a mesh through which the water filters slowly. So was born the particular type of roof garden that Le Corbusier has used constantly.

Now it is clear that such constructional innovations do not of themselves necessarily mean good architecture, and Le Corbusier's work must be judged on its merits. It will be at once apparent that he applies his principles with a rigour and a logic which are extremely annoying to many people, and stimulating to others. His work is by no means universally accepted by French critics. M. Marcel Mayer treating of Le Corbusier and his school (though not by name) as 'purists' in opposition to the 'classicists,' says:

'Se disent "puristes" ceux qui, répudiant l'expérience du passé, prétendent créer de toutes pièces, avec des moyens nouveaux, selon des idées entièrement neuves et absolues. Nous appellerons "classique" l'élite réduite qui sait adapter les moyens nouveaux aux problèmes d'aujourd'hui dans un esprit classique. A bien considérer les oeuvres que l'on nous donne de part et d'autre, nous constatons un paradoxe singulier: les "puristes" contre toute apparence, sont d'un esprit infiniment moins jeune que ces classiques. Tributaires d'un tempérament doctrinaire et dénués du véritable sens de la construction ... [etc., etc.]'

All this is a little bad tempered, and to anyone acquainted with Le Corbusier's writings would seem an entire travesty of his *intentions*, at any rate. So too M. Gaston Varenne:

9.5
House, Bruckmannweg 2,
Weissenhofsiedlung, Stuttgart (1927)

Photographer: Lossen & Co. (1927)

From the author Frederick Etchells'
collection and used to illustrate his article

Quant à ceux qui se réclament aujourd'hui plus étroitement du cubisme et prétendent être des constructeurs, ils n'usent trop souvent du béton armé que pour réaliser par ce moyen une sorte de maison géométrique, austère, nue, abstraite, qui est surtout une satisfaction donnée à leur goût de l'absolu et fort peu aux exigences de notre sensibilité et de la leur.

However, as M. Mayer admits that 'le besoin de rénovation est actuellement si vif en matière d'architecture,' there would still appear to be room for these 'geometrical, austere, bare and abstract' buildings; the adjectives are hurled as terms of abuse, but they seem to many of us to express precisely the qualities which one would like to see dominating a great deal of architectural work *at the moment*, if only as a discipline. Sensibility – the artist's sensibility – is the ultimate factor and every artist must in the end be judged by the degree of his possession of it; but in architecture at any rate it must be expressed through a number of everyday building details and methods and the need of our own time is for a rational and flexible system of construction, using *all* methods and materials that prove worthy – old and new. Out of this the good architect will emerge at the proper times, and we may remember that the greater mass of building in all periods in the nature of things cannot be called 'architecture,' but is simple utilitarian construction.

It is little use bleating about the defacement of the English countryside or the spoiling of London, unless you have something better to offer than gentlemanly *pastiches*; nor will you solve the problem of the new arterial roads and of our villages by erecting sham Elizabethan petrol-filling stations. The problem is far too serious for absurdities of this kind, and surely a rational spirit of adventure should excite us to the search for an adequate solution. Le Corbusier indicates at least one possible line of advance and we ought to be deeply grateful to him.

Source: *The Studio*, September 1928

Europe Discusses the House

By the Editor, *Architectural Review**

*Hubert de Cronin Hastings (1902–1986).
For an account of his life and contribution of
architectural journalism see Susan Lasdun,
H. de C. Reviewed, *Architectural Review*,
vol. 200, September 2006, pp. 68–72. (Eds)

Six years have passed since the publication of the last Domestic Number of the [*Architectural*] *Review*; perhaps a hundred since any Editor has been in a position to form a collection of English houses equal in quality to those shown ... [in this Issue].

Apart from flashes of wit, it is possible that the most genuine improvement apparent in the present collection lies in what the man in the street would call neatness – an effect of economy and selection which has been conspicuous by its absence from post-Regency architecture. Today we are more conscious of this desire. Thank heavens. For neatness implies a disciplined judgment; and discipline, perhaps because it is one of the qualities on which English people pride themselves, has been scoffed at by a generation of artists with flowing ties. It is clear that we have at last begun the process of tidying up.

To tidy up, however, is not an end. Neatness, though a necessary adjunct, is not Design. Before we congratulate ourselves on the sane Modernism exemplified in the English house, we may do well to ask *how* sane, *how* modern we are. To answer this question ourselves would be unprofitable – hence it has been arranged in this Issue to seek the advice of those who are in a better position to judge. The Continent has been called in to diagnose and prescribe.

First amongst Continental specialists stands one who is known in England only as a clear, thin, disembodied voice. This is Le Corbusier, a ghostly presence, who recently appeared, it is said, with a loud cry in Silver End Garden Village. What, as Mr. Hoover would say, is biting him? Why does he rend himself, crying with a loud voice, 'reinforced concrete'? And why do people in far countries spend their nights like Christian, with sighs and tears, constantly reading his book?

Le Corbusier has discovered a new heaven and a new earth ... whether we agree with him or not, it is most fitting that this eager knight errant should enter the English lists; he may be assured not only of fair, but of a keen hearing, since he speaks of the house. (Fig. 10.1)

Yet in his approach to the house even those who most ardently admire Le Corbusier's poetic sponsorship of the mechanical may feel that he is on thin ice. When he applies his principles to new problems, how excellently suggestive he is – we repeat, to *new* problems. But the problem of the modern house has been under consideration for several thousand years. Despite his roof garden and 'resources of modern technique,' Le Corbusier will surely find difficulty in rejuvenating the house.

10.1
**Maisons La Roche-Jeanneret,
Paris (1925)**

Photographer: John Donat (1971)

Le Corbusier finds no difficulty. In basing his argument on materials ('new systems of construction') he ingeniously contrives to perform this difficult thyroid operation.

There are, however, other Continental thinkers with a modern approach who do not share the views of Le Corbusier. Amongst these the very distinguished Austrian architect, Michael Rosenauer,* represents one of the most advanced groups, the Viennese: a school which is apt to look on Le Corbusier as a little bit old-fashioned ... and though neither writer has set out to haul down the other's flag, their differences are patent. Like boxers, they quarrel as they shake hands.

Briefly, Le Corbusier says:-

SCIENCE HERALDING A NEW AGE INTRODUCES NEW MATERIALS WHICH DEMAND TO BE USED, AND DEMAND TO BE USED IN A NEW SHAPE.

M. Rosenauer counters:-

NEW SHAPES ARE EVOKED BY NEW NEEDS WHICH THEMSELVES PROVOKE NEW MATERIALS.

At first sight the distinction may appear academic. The reservations implicit in each hypothesis, however, yield entirely contradictory conclusions.

Le Corbusier's hypothesis prepares the way for the following conclusion:-

NEW SHAPES HAVING BEEN DICTATED BY NEW MATERIALS WHICH DEMAND TO BE USED, THE HOUSE SHOULD DISCOVER A NEW SHAPE.

M. Rosenauer, on the other hand, would assert:-

SINCE NEW SHAPES ARE DICTATED BY NEW NEEDS, THE HOUSE, WHICH IS THE EXPRESSION OF AN ANCIENT NEED FULLY SATISFIED, DEMANDS NO NEW SHAPE.

There is here revealed by implication a fallacy and a profound truth.

If Design is to break with shibboleths many age-old prejudices and predilections must go; but if in disentangling Design from the past we substitute for traditionalism an equally conventional Modernism, we are merely exchanging one prejudice for another.

In putting the cart of *material* before the horse of *plan*, however intentionally, Le Corbusier is helping to spread a grand half-truth, the acceptance of which would give an orientation to the Modern Movement as false and as fatal as the fallacies of Ruskin in the romantic.

The profound and simple truth is that there exists in Design only one infallible touchstone – the Plan; the plan, which is the product and symbol of all the requirements, sentimental and practical; the plan projected into the third dimension.

The modern thinkers, when they are anything more than old-fashioned craze-mongers grabbing at a new brand of *art nouveau*, pin their colours to this plan, believing that the

*Michael Rosenauer (1884–1971), Austrian-born architect, who worked in London in the late 1920s and 1930s, and again in the 1950s. (Eds)

kernel in any work of architecture is the three-dimensional synthesis in which elevation and ground plan (in the smaller sense) are married. This may not be the only possible view of architecture, but it is the modern view of architecture.

The modern architect is a three-dimensional planner.

It follows, therefore that new problems and not the wilful caprices of architects are required to determine new forms of expression in this epoch; new problems which will necessitate new three-dimensional plan combinations which, in their turn, may easily demand interpretation in concrete and steel.

These can be found in the aeroplane, the steamship, the locomotive, the factory, the skyscraper, the block of flats.

But when the architect allows his enthusiasm for novelty to overcome his sense of fitness; when he makes *cast* of his plan and *matrix* of his materials, then he is acting no longer with the discipline of the artist, nor with the reason of the Modernist.

The true artist will use new materials when the requirements of his plan demand. When they are not required he will, with self-restraint, use those most fit, even to the point of being conventional.

Le Corbusier, therefore, in making out a case for new materials instead of a case for a new plan, has cut the ground from under his own feet, for he has failed to perceive that the case for new materials hangs on the question whether he can establish in the first place a case for a new plan. At the moment he has not established a case. He has merely dressed up the house in a new concrete suit with windows, two, twenty, or two hundred feet long, and put the vegetable garden on the roof so that the soot from the chimneys may manure the soil.

Some of us wear silk hats, some plus-fours, others sandals and rational dress. So far the structure of our bodies, like the house plan with its new concrete suit, has shown no inclination to justify these sensational transformations.

Thus we have in England now at this moment an opportunity to give a lead to the rest of Europe. As more or less disinterested observers of the Modernist battle we have had hitherto a better chance than most of preserving a sense of proportion. Le Corbusier and his like have done a fine service in challenging stale standards – he, above others, is calculated to appeal to our temperament since, like Kipling, to whom he may be indebted, he is a poet, the poet of the machine.

Our opportunity lies in distinguishing at this critical juncture the true from the false; in resolutely declining to be doped either by the bouncing intransigent or by the gentlemanly reactionary.

So long as we remain loyal to the three-dimensional plan, testing the metal of our materials and the virtue of our theories by their relevance to the plan which is the final court of appeal, so long shall we be acting with the traditional English common sense which Continental thinkers like M. Rosenauer find 'modern' in the genuine meaning of that hard-worked word.

Of new problems the most vital, according to M. Rosenauer, is the flat.

With cool and admirable humour he flatters our vanity, standing lost in rapture before the perfection of the English house. 'You have solved the problem,' he says; – adding unexpectedly: 'Let us turn to the next problem.' As who should say *Le roi est mort, vive le roi*.

We turn to the next problem. We find that it is the flat. M. Rosenauer believes that the day of the country house is over. The future lies in the town, and the flat is tomorrow's home. No problem which has been solved remains urgent. The artist attacks always the vital questions of his day. Thus, in the same breath as he praises the English solution of the house, M. Rosenauer proclaims its decease as a matter of vital architectural concern.

Source: *Architectural Review*, December 1929

Le Corbusier Again: *The City of To-morrow*

By P. Morton Shand and A. Trystan Edwards

P. Morton Shand

There is no writer in any field of letters who voices the modern spirit more challengingly than Le Corbusier: that 'spirit of geometry, construction and synthesis' which in its passion for simplification 'prefers the rule to the exception.' Though we may perhaps take exception to the first of these characteristics, we are bound to concede the veracity of the other two.

Le Corbusier's consuming passion for discipline and order could hardly be of Gallic origin, for 'the logical productions of the French mind' have no counterpart in the ordering of French public life. Administratively, France is *le pays de la pagei*, the land of chaos, official inertia, tax-evasion, irresponsibility, internecine parochialism, petty avarice, corruption and triumphant red tape. Le Corbusier is a Swiss from the Canton of Valais, and it is against this *pagei* that his Helvetian honesty, his sturdy and purposeful common sense revolts. France has even greater need than England of the moral electric shock such a book as this produces, for no civilised country has accomplished less in the way of social legislation, or is more backward in regard to sanitation and town-planning, than that which Le Corbusier has chosen to make his home.

With Le Corbusier the architect we are not concerned here. Daring pioneer in those new structural forms which the logical use of concrete reveals and admirable planner as he is, what he has built is of far less immediate value than what he has written. But both, though in disparate degree, have had the same effect: they have made people think. They have done even more: they have made people think for themselves who otherwise would never have realized that thinking is not merely the process of testing fresh data by the shibboleths of certain stubborn prejudices of environment, education or heredity. It is impossible for anyone whose mind is not already hopelessly petrified to avoid pondering, and pondering very hard, however involuntarily, after reading no more than a couple of pages of *Towards a New Architecture* or *The City of To-morrow*. (Fig. 11.1) His syllogisms pick us up by the roots of our hair; they shake us into elemental consciousness of our inconsistencies and hypocrisies as a dog shakes a rat; they cudgel us out of our cherished complacency and end by banging our feet down violently on a pavement of hard facts in front of our shattered illusions, or hurtling us off into space with a vigorous kick to our precious uplift of Meredithian 'fine shades and nice feelings.' All this ruthlessness is singularly wholesome for us, because we have grown too much accustomed to speculate in terms of quite

The City of To=morrow

AND ITS PLANNING

by LE CORBUSIER

translated from the 8th French Edition of URBANISME *with an introduction by* FREDERICK ETCHELLS

JOHN RODKER
PUBLISHER
LONDON * * 1929

11.1
Title-page of Le Corbusier, *The City of To-morrow and Its Planning* (1929)

unquestioned formulas. Thought, indeed, is something Le Corbusier extols above even deeds. 'In America they feel and produce,' he declares proudly, 'here, in Old Europe, they think,' as though in affirmation of the old belief that it is better to think without profit than to feel and produce without thought.

Unfortunately architectural criticism can scarcely be said to exist. How many newspapers have 'architectural critics', and how often are their services required? Yet architecture is the only art which has done more than make a tentative amateurish effort to express the spirit of the age. It does express that spirit, as all who have eyes may see. Whether we like it or not a Modernist architecture exists: an architecture radically, and above all intellectually, different from any that has preceded it. Le Corbusier is the only man who has written on architecture in this new spirit with the authority of a practising Modernist architect in such a way as to command a more than professional public. He has forced the world to think about architecture as it has not been made to do for centuries. This is a sterner and a nobler task than to charm it into a cultivated appreciation of the beauties of traditional styles with glowing purple passages, or re-editing *The Seven Lamps* and *The Stones of Venice* for the higher forms in Academies for the Daughters of Gentlemen. He has begun to make people understand that architecture must be considered as one of the vital and immediate things of life before there can be any question of regarding it as a source of aesthetic delight. We are born and die, even as we live, in some sort of architectural environment. What that environment is depends on ourselves, on the relative enlightenment or blindness of the age.

Like so many reformers before him, this practical pragmatist is accused of being a destructive genius, an iconoclast. He is; but only up to a point, and never without good cause. That the dignity of human life comes before antiquarianism may be an unpalatable truth, but it is certainly a salutary one. It is the sort of brutal and courageous axiom which helps us to brush atavistic cobwebs and the almost impalpable rust of routine from our poor muddled brains, and to reason independently when confronted by the grim reality of a problem like housing. That is why this Classicist – for that is what he really is – betrays such impatience with (unquestioning) 'respect for the past' and with 'romantic associations' which he sees as parasitic growths of the mind and impediments to rational development.

In these days the past has lost some of its fragrance, for its enforced mingling with the life of to-day has set it in a false environment.

Yet he is far more prone to admiration of the great structural achievements of other centuries than he is given credit for. Only his reverence is not squandered on those ancient monuments in which scale and purpose were subordinated to mere wealth of ornament that have hitherto inspired a rather uncritical veneration. Le Corbusier is no misanthrope, no fanatical destroyer.

Things are not revolutionized by making revolutions. The real revolution lies in the solution of existing problems.

His buoyant, practical optimism offers an eminently sane and humane justification for everything he proposes to abolish, a concrete and constructive solution to each successive imaginary difficulty raised by the torpor of procrastinators and the timidity of sentimentalists. Good must replace bad; light, darkness; Swiss cleanliness, Latin squalor; space and park-like surroundings, slum conditions and barrack tenements. And always he reverts to what he calls the 'indispensable poetry' of modern life – a different poetry from the old, it is true, but then the same fatuous charge of wanton change has invariably been brought against each age by those who have outlived the revolt of the preceding one. It is only by the 'perversity' or 'Philistinism' of these periodic reorientations that art can escape from the stultifying pedantry of academies.

The man who is accused of trying to standardize everything has written:

By its lines you can distinguish whether a machine is French, German, American and so on.

That is a sufficient answer to those who maintained that the first rather crudely geo-metrical and stereotyped forms of Modernist architecture were so inhumanly mechanical as to preclude the possibility of their containing the germs of future national styles. Le Corbusier knows that in the end man always conquers the machine, and not the machine man; just as prejudices which at first prevail over reason yield at length to the force of its persuasion.

Men's susceptibilities intervene in the midst of the most rigorous calculation. An engineer works out the section of a beam; the inquiry into the strain it will bear gives him the coefficients of tension, resistance and inertia. But the coefficient of inertia is the product of the height and breadth of the beam chosen by himself. Therefore he can choose a height for his beam whose only justification may be his own pleasure; the breadth is a necessary consequence of that height. Here you have the interven-tion of an individual personal taste, sensibility and passion: the beam may be heavy or slender.

'The streets represent an old, out-of-date state of affairs; whilst traffic represents an existing state of affairs.' This phrase resumes the whole problem. It is as though the rail-ways were to try to run express trains along the muddy ruts of tortuous country lanes instead of over the perfectly aligned and ballasted right of way of their own metals. 'The great cities have no arteries, they have only capillaries.' In other words we live in a modern mechanical world with the civic equipment we have inherited from the non-mechanical past. Thus the city is strangling itself and the very activities which are its *raison d'être*. To an ever-increasing extent it imperils the health, and even the lives, of its inhabitants. We have succeeded in domesticating speed and movement as primitive man domesticated the ox and the horse, but without finding house room for either. What must go – the canker that is at the root of all our urban troubles – is 'the corridor street':

Cities can be something better than places (and, he might have added, Palace Hotels) which are all corridors.

He has applied the basic principles of his 'Plan for a Contemporary City of 3,000,000 Inhabitants' in greater detail to the so-called *Voisin* scheme, the lay-out of which covers the central area of Paris. Admirable as are many of its aspects – especially the 'insulation' of historic monuments in tree-planted open spaces – the French are scarcely the people to be credited with the capacity for carrying out so vast an enterprise. On the other hand a *Voisin* scheme applied to Berlin sounds perfectly conceivable. Le Corbusier has given much thought to such questions as the maximum possible density of urban transport. He cites the Am Zoo station in Berlin, 'where many lines come together,' as the outstanding example of perfect synchronization of short-headway suburban traffic. In point of fact the London 'District' during rush hours holds the record in this respect. Nor is either of the two Am Zoo stations – the busy viaduct Stadtbahn or the neighbouring subterranean U-Bahn – in any sense a junction as he states.

Le Corbusier complains that it is 'almost impossible to say everything and say it in a reasonable number of words': a conviction which any one privileged to review his books is likely to reciprocate. But if he is apt to be verbose, his vehement and often difficult style is nearly always pregnant with new ideas seized impetuously in their flight. Sometimes these sudden flights from fact into fancy are a little too much even for so excellent and spirited a translator as Mr. Etchells*; as when he tries in vain to reproduce such sense as there may be lurking in the incoherent metaphor 'the centres of the great cities are like an engine which is seized.' Has the engine merely stopped, or has it been carted away bodily? The original illustrations are always to the point, but the notoriously poor quality of French blocks to some extent mars the general effect of an otherwise admirably produced and finely printed book. Mr. John Rodker has done this country a notable service in publishing it.

*In case Mr. Etchells should consider this an ungracious or carping criticism, the reviewer feels he ought to confess that having once translated an article of Le Corbusier himself, he is only too conscious of the sorry hash he made of certain rather rhetorical passages in it.

A. Trystan Edwards

Le Corbusier is an architect and town-planner and he is also a propagandist. Is it possible to be inefficient in the former capacities, yet brilliant in the latter? I believe that this is possible, and can therefore understand the amazing literary success which has attended the publication of M. Le Corbusier's books. He shouts so loudly, he bullies the reader so ruthlessly, that most people have been afraid to proclaim how few and how unfruitful are the ideas which he has set before us. Moreover, he is shrewd enough to realize that the intellectual dish he serves up, if it is to be in the least degree palatable, requires a great deal of artificial seasoning. The text of his books is interspersed with utterly irrelevant illustrations chosen from a wide variety of sources. The argument proceeds by explosions and by aphorisms which are intended to be profound, but few of which, however, will bear inspection. For instance, our author has occasion to say that

> Geometry is the means, created by ourselves, whereby we see the external world and express the world within us ... Machinery is the result of geometry. The age in which we live is therefore essentially a geometrical one; all its ideas are orientated in the direction of geometry.

This sounds really grand, almost philosophic; but not quite. He fails to use words accurately, but unfortunately this is demanded of those who claim to be so 'scientific.' His style is both slovenly and pretentious. The first sentence, if it means anything, is a platitude; the second is a misstatement, for machinery cannot be the result of geometry, its creation may entail the use of geometry but its purpose has in general nothing to do with geometry. Thus the third sentence is a *non sequitur*. The fourth sentence is an exaggeration, for geometry is but one branch of mathematics and mathematics is but one of many sciences or studies to which the human mind is addicted. And if this is a geometrical age, there is at least no evidence that the study of or passion for geometry has any place in the mind of M. Le Corbusier, for his pages do not provide the slightest indication that he has pursued the science of geometry beyond its most elementary stages. But he is writing for 'artists' and artists are always frightened by the mere mention of mathematics. To impress the reader with the fact that he is a mathematician of no mean order, he prints a page of diagrams, circles, pentagons, cubes, cones and prisms – which he has taken from the copybooks issued to the elementary schools of France.

The 'geometricality' of M. Le Corbusier's mind is mainly expressed in a love of straight lines and an unreasoning hatred for curves. The majority of roads should, of course, be straight, we do not need a 'geometrician' to tell us this, but a town-planner will occasionally find a curved road very useful and he should feel at liberty to use one without incurring the scorn of 'Modernist' architects. So many of M. Le Corbusier's contributions to the science of civic design consist of harsh prohibitions. Never a curved road, never a graceful profile of swelling dome – nothing but rectilinear forms. Surely geometry has knowledge of curves, and the human body itself is made up of them.

M. Le Corbusier has put before us what seems to him to be an ideal city. As many as 960,000 business men and clerks are housed in twenty-four gigantic skyscrapers of identical pattern. The object, he informs us, is to concentrate a great population within a small area without creating traffic congestion. M. Le Corbusier lays down the principle that the business centre of a great city must be free to expand and he allows it to expand upwards. It is not quite clear, however, whether he intends addition storeys to be placed on top of the skyscrapers as the city expands. A reference to the plan, however, shews that the number of skyscrapers cannot be increased without encroaching upon the space definitely allocated to 'Public Services.' Yet in an ideal town every part which possesses its own necessary function should be free to expend without encroaching upon the areas devoted to other functions. This is not easy to arrange but it is possible and no city can claim to be 'ideal' which does not fulfil such a condition. The problem of expansion and intercommunication of parts of the city seems to have received quite perfunctory consideration by M. Le Corbusier. The residential areas composed of housing blocks, chiefly on what he calls the cellular system, (Fig. 11.2) appear to be unrelated to any shopping centre. What is described as an industrial city is obviously an afterthought, for if this latter were an integral part of the scheme one would imagine that an attempt would have been made to provide the workers in it with a residential quarter of their own. The sports or recreational centre with a stadium is also an afterthought and placed just anywhere, and while it is conveniently situated for those inhabiting one residential quarter, there is no convenient access to it for those inhabiting the others. In fact, the scheme gives the impression of very hasty conception.

It is only in the proposals with regard to traffic in the urban centre that *The City of Tomorrow* can have any interest for modern town-planners, and even here the proposals are of doubtful value, for granted there is an open space between the skyscrapers, the congestion of traffic will occur at the bottle-neck of the skyscrapers themselves. At six o'clock every evening or thereabouts, forty thousand people must emerge from the base of each building, and even if a certain number of lifts are 'express' the majority of them must stop at each storey to pick up the passengers. Contrast this with an ordinary township of forty thousand people whose inhabitants can be discharged at innumerable points of a great many thoroughfares. Provided that a proper relationship is maintained between street widths and building heights, the old-fashioned 'corridor' street provides by far the best method of doing what every point policeman would like to do, namely, distribute the traffic as far as possible over the road areas available.

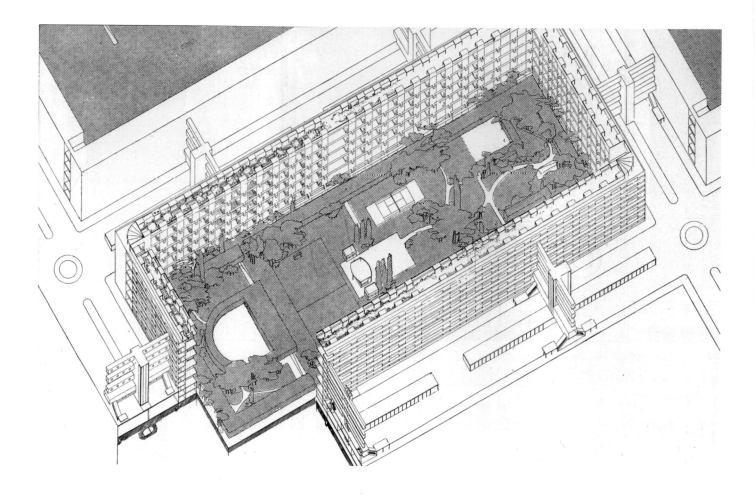

11.2
Dwellings on a cellular system

From Le Corbusier, *The City of To-morrow and Its Planning* (1929)

Moreover, the skyscraper is an inflexible type of building. When once the ground floor is determined, the floors above, with quite insignificant variation, must follow suit, whether the storeys be twenty in number or a hundred. This vertical street, unlike the horizontal one upon which M. Le Corbusier pours such scorn, cannot be altered piecemeal to suit the varying needs of a large number of different building owners, but must remain architecturally static for an indefinite period. It is surprising that M. Le Corbusier, who is so voluble about the faults of existing cities, should be unable to diagnose the mortal disease from which his City of To-morrow is suffering. The limbs are arranged in a geometrical pattern but the body is ready for the mortuary. The truth is, he has confused simplicity with order. Anyone can produce order in a city if he simplifies it so much that its human quality no longer remains. In a living organism there is both order and complexity, and both these elements must co-exist in the city also, if it is to have the breath of life. Strange as it may seem, M. Le Corbusier, whose city contains about half-a-dozen architectural forms all told, is under the illusion that for the first time he is introducing variety to the art of building which hitherto has suffered from the appalling monotony of the designs produced by its exponents. In the *City of To-morrow* the public buildings are the same plain, flat-topped 'geometrical' buildings as are the blocks of cellular dwellings. Not a spire or dome is to be seen, nor in fact any architectural feature of particular interest. What is known as architectural composition has not here made its appearance unless we are to assume that the juxtaposition of blocks of identical pattern in itself constitutes a design. Still if dullness there be, that is only in the City; the pages of the book need never be dull, for all you have to do to liven them up is to mix tables of statistics with pictures of steam engines, airships, angels and excerpts from the comic papers! And in places where the argument wears particularly thin he does not disdain the use of sentimentality or gush or the purple patch of rhetoric. We are told that in *The City of To-morrow*.

Their outlines softened by distance, the skyscrapers raise immense geometrical facades and in them is reflected the blue glory of the sky. An overwhelming sensation, immense but radiant prisms. As twilight falls the glass skyscrapers seem to glow.

This is really worse than Ruskin! But a critic, already reduced to a state of languor by the sickly-sweet aroma of M. Le Corbusier's prose, falls into a swoon when on p. 243 he reads that 'Passion, fire, ardour, faith, rapture, animation, all lead to happiness.'

Source: *Concrete Way*, vol. 2, September 1929

The City of To-morrow: the Real Revolution Lies in the Solution of Existing Problems

By N.S.H (Nora Shackleton Heald)

To mention the name of Le Corbusier to an average person is to bring forth the instant retort that the houses and cities projected by that great architect 'may be all very well for robots, but they won't do for human beings.' The objection is always the same – that the human quality in town-planning is expressed by the curved street and the wandering line.

In reality, the human line is the straight line. Man travels in a straight line because he knows where he wishes to go; it is the pack horse which wanders, picking his steps here and there to avoid an obstacle, turning aside as his attention is drawn by one object or another. Our wayward streets, as Le Corbusier points out in his latest book *Urbanisme*, which has been magnificently translated into English by Frederick Etchells, under the somewhat misleading title of *The City of To-morrow*, are based on the mule track, and to-day, with all the resources at our disposal for building, and with all our knowledge of the evils of overcrowding, of delay in transport, of lack of light and air, and of excess of noise, we still go on using the pack-donkey's way.

A visitor from Mars might suppose that human beings derived some mysterious benefit from being cooped in dark dwellings far from recreation space, and that the despairing struggle of the City worker to reach a place in tube, train or bus was his chosen evening recreation.

Yet though the idle may dismiss as revolutionary Le Corbusier's plans for a city of towers and open spaces crossed at right angles by wide streets along which graded traffic can move freely; there is little new in his ideas, though he has new means for carrying them out. The Romans of old built such cities; we see the Le Corbusier planning in Timgad, in Pekin, in Kairouan, in the fortified European towns of the twelfth century, built, as Le Corbusier says, in those

golden moments when the power of the mind dominated the rabble ... Babylon and Pekin are but examples among many; great cities and smaller ones, even quite small ones, which during certain noble periods were illuminated by talent, science and experience.

Interest in architecture is in England to-day too often confined to what is pretty or cosy or picturesque –

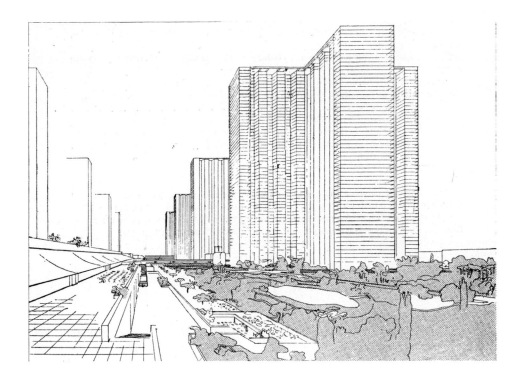

12.1
A contemporary city: the parks at the base of the skyscrapers

From Le Corbusier, *The City of To-morrow and Its Planning* (1929)

pleasant enough things in their way, but not of the essence of good building. The excursions into the study of serious architectural forms which were a part of the necessary education of the cultivated eighteenth century gentleman must have helped, one imagines, to make that amazing age what it was.

We are, in architecture and town-planning as in other matters, inclined to be too sentimental and not sufficiently critical. We seize an idea, hold it too long, and transfer it to something to which it does not truly apply. How much of our admiration for our curving streets and maze of narrow traffic ways comes, for instance, from some picture of a winding country lane or of a half-hidden village with its cottages tumbled out haphazard? Yet the village has its garden spaces and its village green, and every motorist knows how ill-adapted for modern needs is the winding lane which the pack mule first trod out, and which is pleasant enough for our own casual wanderings.

Every day the dangerous overcrowding of our cities grows more acute. Traffic congests our narrow streets; noise wears down the nervous sensibilities of the people compelled to work in them; the labour of getting from place to place as, added to the overwhelming difficulties of working in ill-lighted, airless, inconvenient buildings; the spaces for recreation are so far from dwellings that the townsfolk cannot make easy use of them. Knowing all this, we tinker away at our 'improvements' when we should re-build the hearts of our cities.

Here at last is a constructive plan, (Fig. 12.1) a scheme which exhilarates by its boldness, by its understanding of human needs for happiness, and by its completeness. The influence of *The City of To-morrow* should be immense and far-reaching.

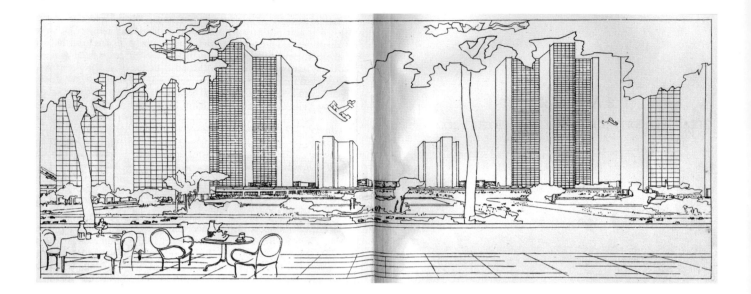

The title of the original, *Urbanisme*, might more justly have been translated as *The City of To-day* than as *The City of To-morrow*, for we have at our disposal all the means, and all the necessities, for carrying out some such plan as M. Le Corbusier proposes.

Briefly, his scheme is based on the following principles:

1. We must de-congest the centres of cities in order to provide for the demands of traffic.
2. We must increase the density of cities in order to bring about the close contact demanded by business.
3. We must increase the means whereby traffic can circulate, *i.e.*, we must completely modify the conception of the street, which has shown itself useless in regard to the new phenomenon of modern means of transport.
4. We must increase the area of green and open spaces, to ensure the necessary degree of health and peace to enable men to meet the anxieties of work occasioned by the new speed at which business is carried on.

The gates to the city, once in its wall, have changed. They are now the railway stations at its heart. (Fig. 12.2) Le Corbusier, therefore, begins to lay out his city with the station as its hub – a many-layered station, with main lines, suburban lines and tubes in superimposed storeys below ground, its booking offices above ground, and above those again its landing place for aeroplanes.

From the station come the great traffic roads going north, south, east and west across the city and crossed at right angles, at intervals of not less than 400 yard, by other roads. These roads are in two storeys, the upper one being a speed-way for light and rapidly moving traffic.

Near the centre station the city offices rise, and rise in a literal sense, for the plan admits of tower buildings sixty storeys high, each with its tube station in its basement and stretch-

12.2

A contemporary city: the centre of the city seen from one of the terraced cafés surrounding the central station square

From Le Corbusier, *The City of To-morrow and Its Planning* (1929)

ing out wings so that every room has light and air. Across open green spaces are the municipal buildings, and in a still wider circle the blocks of dwellings for the townsfolk. These would be built on the cellular principle, by which each flat has its own open terrace room, or as a 'set back' building (a 'comb building' would be an apter description, for the plan of each block of dwellings is not unlike that of a comb) which would give each dwelling light and air without the central well now considered necessary.

Parks, recreation grounds and gardens would surround these homes of the townsfolk, and the top storeys would provide further recreation space. Exercise could be taken in immediate proximity to each home.

Beyond this belt, again surrounded by gracious open spaces, would come the garden city homes of the workers who would leave the city each day when their work was done.

Such a planning would accommodate the inhabitants of a city of three millions, and yet only 95 per cent of the ground space would be built over. Business would be speeded up, communication would be easy, life would be pleasant, and noise would be greatly diminished. We have but to recall the sound of a car in the open country and it overpowering noise in a narrow street to realise how quietness would again descend to bless our distracted cars.

A further point about the Le Corbusier city is that, at its heart, it would be a city on piers. He would abolish the cost and inconveniences of our present system of burying our water, gas and electricity mains and of sinking basements. Each of his towers would be supported by piles, and the ground level of his city would contain the service pipes and accommodate the heavy and slowly moving traffic.

Goods could be unloaded at the bottom storey of the business buildings, and yet the rapid stream of traffic would be in no way impeded.

Such, very briefly, is the Scheme, which should be studied in detail in this most inspiriting book. Since the re-building of a city is a matter of the economist as of the engineer and the artist, the author has included a chapter showing how the cost of his revolution would be met.

The vital thing is to have an idea, a conception, and a programme.

And the means?

Do we not possess the means?

Haussmann cut immense gaps right through Paris. It seemed as if Paris would never endure his surgical experiments.

And yet to-day does it not exist merely as a consequence of his daring and courage?

His equipment was meagre; the shovel, the pick, the waggon, the trowel, the wheel barrow, the simple tools of every race ... before the mechanical age. His achievement was truly admirable. And in destroying chaos he built up the Emperor's finances!

In those days the French Chamber of Deputies attacked this dangerous man in stormy scenes. One day, in an excess of terror, they accused him of having created a *desert* in the very centre of Paris! That desert was the Boulevard Sebastopol, which is now so congested that every expedient is being tried to relieve it!

The book, as the previous volume *Towards a New Architecture*, is partly of the nature of a manifesto, and readers will find it full of inspiring passages, as, for example:

> The city which can achieve speed will achieve success. What is the good of regretting the Golden Age? Work to-day is more intense and is carried on at a quicker rate. Actually the whole question becomes one of daily inter-communication with a view of settling the state of the market and the condition of labour. The more rapid this inter-communication can be made, the more will business be expedited. It is likely, therefore, that the working day in the sky-scraper will be a short one, thanks to the sky-scraper.

> Then, perhaps, the working day may finish soon after mid-day. The city will empty as though by a deep breath. The garden will empty as though by a deep breath. The garden cities will play their full part. And, on the other hand, in the city itself the residential quarters will offer new living quarters to these new men of a mechanical age.

Source: *The Queen*, 24 July 1929

A Vision Realised: in a Country Villa Le Corbusier Proves his Theories

By Mrs Howard Robertson

*Villa Stein-de Monzie, Vaucresson, built for Michael, brother of Gertrude Stein, and his wife Sarah and Gabrielle de Monzie. (Eds)

Le Corbusier, the Franco-Swiss modernist architect, author of *Towards a New Architecture* and *The City of To-morrow*, is regarded by many people in this country as either a visionary or a charlatan. But in actual fact, neither description is a fair one, for his buildings as well as his writings are worthy of the most serious consideration.

The houses which he has designed show both imagination and great ingenuity in planning and detail, though the latter has in some cases suffered from the economical conditions under which his schemes have been carried out.

This was particularly apparent in the small housing scheme at Pessac, near Bordeaux, where ingenious contrivances were introduced, such as a combined cooker and central heating unit, metal windows with which were incorporated rolled steel blinds, terraced roofs presenting the aspect of a paved garden, concrete gate posts embodying the letter box, and endless other minor details which in their conception are greatly ahead of the equipment in most modest types of working-class dwelling. These ideas were all starved in execution through no fault of the architect.

One of the most recent, interesting and successful houses by Le Corbusier is a country villa at Garches* on the outskirts of Paris. (Figs 13.1–13.3) This house exemplifies most of Le Corbusier's theories with the exception of his favourite device of raising the house upon 'stilts' in order to procure increased gardens space; and it has the advantage over his other work that it has been designed to meet the requirements of a more or less 'luxury programme.' Le Corbusier's well-known ideals to a great extent have been realised in this villa: 'The house is a machine to live in'; it must be functional. Space is valuable and it must be used to the full advantage. Standardisation should be practised in the interests of economy. Light, air and sunshine are life-giving elements and should be given the freedom of the house. The flat roof replaces the traditional pitched roof, thereby giving the house an additional garden in the air.

Le Corbusier has studied his theories in a thorough manner. For example, he has been working for some years past upon the question of the flat roof. He has decided that it should drain to the centre, as the outer edges are more liable to freezing during extreme cold, and that the roof covering benefits by not being drained too quickly.

He is of the opinion that the rapid removal of moisture exposes the concrete to cracking, due to change of temperature. His concrete roofs are tarred, 'screeded', then covered

L. C. ET P. J.
VILLA, A GARCHES, 1927

with a layer of sand, and finally with a paving of concrete slabs laid with open joints. These joints are filled with earth and planted.

How different from the dull wastes of flat roofs to which we are accustomed! The open joints provide a channel for the surface water to percolate through to the sand and so gradually to drain to the internal sump; in this way the moisture is removed exceedingly slowly and an even temperature is maintained.

The house at Garches is very stimulating, though admittedly somewhat strange and even shocking to English eyes. It has, however, many unusual aspects and possibilities.

'Les Terrasses', as the house is called, stands in its own grounds, on a country road with houses near-by in the so-called *style anglais*. The landscape is typically French, grey-green in colour, spare and almost harsh. All these houses have to face the same problem – that

13.1
**Villa Stein / de Monzie,
Garches (1927)**

From *Architecture Vivante*, Spring 1929

13.2
Villa Stein / de Monzie, Garches (1927)

From *Architecture Vivante*, Spring 1929

of harmonising with this severe countryside – and notwithstanding the newness and the machine-like character of 'Les Terrasses' it looks entirely at home, and makes its pseudo-English-cum-Normandy neighbours appear somewhat stuffy and faded by comparison.

As we approach, we notice a motor car standing by the door, a happy demonstration of the relationship between the machine to live in and the other machine to travel in, both products of the twentieth century.

At the entrance gate stands another machine to live in, this time for the chauffeur-gate-keeper. It is a strange box-like edifice, severe in the extreme, with an interesting cantilever marquise which darts forward towards the gate and casts an intriguing shadow across the bright façade. The entrance door is a great panel of mottled glass which lights the living room.

The front of the house itself, like the lodge, is coloured a light cream, with black metal window frames, to which gold net curtains add a touch of soft richness without destroying their transparent lightness. In fact, the whole house has an amazing kinship with an

aeroplane. For this is a twentieth-century structure, one in which concrete does not imitate brick or masquerade as stone but reveals its true expression. The façades are supported on the floors, and these in turn are carried by internal columns, thereby leaving the whole front free from piers for a continuous band of windows, which presents a pleasing effect. A wide gravel covered drive leads to the entrance sheltered by a huge marquise which offers an almost too emphatic welcome. Flanking the doorway is a great horizontal window which lights the hall, and on its sill is a cunning slab to hold a quaint pot with its dwarf tree. This little feature expresses in miniature the whole principle of the structure.

The windows are almost continuous, of steel frames which slide one behind the other, providing in summer great bands of air and sunlight, and in winter a glimpse of countryside and trees delicately patterned against grey skies.

The hall as one enters is aglow with light; its great horizontal window descends to the floor, sending a stream of sunshine across the many coloured rugs. Why do we never light our floors? The effect is enchanting, and fine rugs take on a new and unsuspected brilliance.

13.3
Villa Stein / de Monzie, Garches (1927)

Photographer unknown (1920s)

The rugs at 'Les Terrasses' are Oriental and the rooms are furnished, not in *le style moderne*, but with old pieces rubbing shoulders in a most natural way with built-in concrete fittings and paintings by Matisse.

The hall runs up through two storeys and above our heads is light and still more light; for the bulk of this amazing house is just space. There is no drawing room, no library, no music room. Just space and light – heaps of light – and views of trees and garden. Brilliant sun falling on plain wall surfaces broken here and there by bookcases, chairs, tables, bronzes, bowls of flowers – all the things which transform a dwelling into a home.

There is actually a dining room, and it is arranged simply in an almost Italian manner with dark oak furniture and an old wrought iron ceiling lamp. And yet it has achieved a modern atmosphere.

At first floor level on the garden side is a great sheltered terrace. Above is another terrace and on the roof still another, but 'Les Terrasses' do not blanket the house. There is a thrill in all these 'open rooms.' It is stimulating to fling open a door, to step out on to a deck-like balcony, to walk smartly up and down high above the garden with the wind beating upon the face; and then, refreshed and exhilarated by sun and wind, to find sheltered comfort for lounging and reading on another terrace. The delights of the mammoth liner, without the drawbacks!

The bedrooms and baths are all in suites, served by their own staircase and private lobbies, and are fitted with every convenience demanded in this twentieth century.

Whatever may be thought of the master's portion of this unusual house there can be no two options about the kitchen, which is as charming as it is workmanlike. Round its wall runs a continuous shelf on which takes place in sequence the ritual of cooking. Nothing has been omitted, and everything is to hand.

This machine to cook in is indeed a joy to the eye and must be a joy to work in. The kitchen forms a group with its services and the servants' bedrooms, and connects with a similar garage group containing store and workrooms and plant with its water-pumping, softening, and heating, the pipes painted in gay colours to denote their circuits and functions.

In his first book *Towards a New Architecture*, Le Corbusier told us of his dreams. His house at Garches is a proof that dreams may become reality. What shall we expect of his *City of To-morrow?*

Source: *The Queen*, 7 August 1929

Cities of the Future

By Evelyn Waugh

Review of *The City of To-morrow* by Le Corbusier
and *The New Interior Decoration* by Dorothy Todd and Raymond Mortimer

The title which the publishers have chosen to fasten on to the translation of M. Le Corbusier's well-known book *Urbanisme* is justifiable but slightly misleading. Speculation about the future is always stimulating: a series of modern pamphlets has won a well-deserved success by appealing to this deeply-rooted instinct to play the amateur detective in contemporary history and to pick out from the conflicting influences of our own milieu the determining forces of the succeeding generations. But M. Le Corbusier's book has won its wide reputation on the Continent for quite different merits. He is not attempting any Utopian prophecy. The *City of To-morrow*, which he discusses, exists for the Future only in the sense that it has not yet been built To-day. He himself calls it the Contemporary City, and he presents it not as the probable result of present directions of development, but as a logical solution to a problem which already exists in an acute form all over the world.

There is practically no sense that it is not violated every time we return from the country or the sea to Paris or London or New York. Towns that have grown up haphazard along footpaths and mule tracks have become the centre of vast densely-populated areas which look inward for their life. Congested systems of transport are sapping the economic vitality of the cities just as the noise or dirt and hurry are sapping the physical vitality of the workers. M. Le Corbusier does not pre-suppose any golden age. He states the problem and with incisive Gallic logic expounds his solution, postulating only the technical equipment of modern engineering. His four aims are: to de-congest the centre of cities, to increase the density of these centres, to modify the present conception of the street to allow rapid circulation of traffic, (Fig. 14.1) and to increase the area of green, open spaces to ensure the necessary degree of repose and recreation to the workers. His book contains a cogent and almost lyrical explanation of how this can be done. Garden suburbs separated from the city by protected areas of park land still feed the offices and the works. These, with the tenement houses of the workers who live in the city, are conceived vertically, set at wide distances and constructed of steel, glass and concrete. Broad one-way arterial roads transect the city for the use of fast traffic; lower roads provide for slow-moving traffic connecting at intervals between trees. Order and health make their own aesthetic.

There is, however, a doubt that arises out of the consideration of this sane and courageous plan. How much confidence have we in the stability of an economic system that

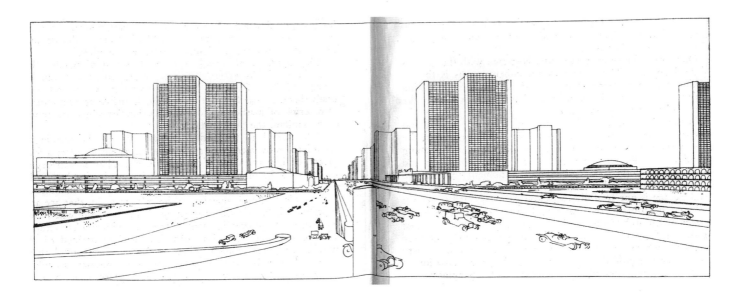

14.1

A contemporary city: the city seen from one of the main tracks for fast motor traffic

From Le Corbusier, *The City of To-morrow and Its Planning* (1929)

has so far directed itself almost unconcernedly toward chaos? and, with compensating optimism, how much fear need we have that the two determining factors of population and transport will inevitably advance in exactly their present ratio? M. Le Corbusier's city is indefensible in war, and it presupposes the continued dependence of man upon horizontal methods of transport. If his city were in existence today it would clearly be suited to our present needs. If the next generation sees, as one may confidently suppose that it will see, a period of stationary or decreasing population and of aerial transport, M. Le Corbusier's city will become as antiquated as Aigues Mortes. Perhaps the chief value of *Urbanisme* is as a social document which shows what the great cities of the world might have made of this decade if they had not chosen to have a war instead.

Miss Todd and Mr. Mortimer have a lot to say about M. Le Corbusier in their book, but they approach his work from a purely aesthetic angle. Moreover, their outlook is notably obscured by *snobbisme*; they admire his work as being *avant-garde* rather than a logical solution to a practical problem, but *The New Interior Decoration* makes a valuable companion to the *The City of To-morrow* on account its admirable illustrations. The photography and diagrams in M. Le Corbusier's book are poorly produced, often, one suspects, at second-hand. *The New Interior Decoration* contains a series of well-chosen and well-reproduced plates, which is quite the best of its kind that has appeared in England. The accompanying essay is of more doubtful quality. There are verbal repetitions that may the result of imperfect collaboration. There is also a surfeit of sociological generalization and good deal of gratuitous instruction about the history of art and taste with which anyone intelligent enough to buy the book might be assumed to be familiar. The authors, however, are to be congratulated on their championship of English decorators, whose particular genius for humour and the adaptation of traditional culture is too often overlooked by the more doctrinaire Continental architects. One or two small questions present themselves. The authors assume that fresh air, light and cleanliness are important contributions to comfort. Surely they forget that there are still large numbers of people whose work is done in the open air and who derive particular satisfaction from shutting themselves up impenetrably during their leisure? Also, all the rooms illustrated are, naturally enough, photographed when they are new and completely tidy. How will M. Le Corbusier's houses look in a hundred year's time when the patina of the concrete has weathered and the sharp angles have softened, and how do the interiors look when a family of normally disorderly habits have lived there for a few years? One cannot help feeling that iron furniture bent out of shape would be more offensive than worm-eaten wood, and discoloured concrete and rusted metal than mellowed brick and stone.

Source: *The Observer*, 11 August 1929

The City of To-morrow

By Oliver P. Bernard

Towards the end of the Paris Exposition, 1925, when the enthusiasm provoked by that international demonstration of artistic licence and luxury had become somewhat exhausted, I was invited by the Commissioner General du Section Britannique to take a stroll and record anything that seemed worthy of inclusion in those departmental reports by which departments endeavour to justify their existence. From my notes on that occasion the following extract is appropriate to this review:

> M. Le Corbusier is responsible for the only original contribution to architecture in the Paris Exposition by means of a pavilion known as *L'Esprit Nouveau*. (Fig. 15.1) As the average human being rarely makes many real discoveries in a lifetime I see no reason to qualify the expression then used to describe one of my own amongst so much that was highly decorative and generally extravagant. To come in contact with genius gives one some of that privilege that happens to such as those who once touched the hem of a great Teacher's raiment, met Isaac Newton, or listened to Abraham Lincoln; as Dumas makes an astute Cardinal say of Cromwell, 'such men, they arrive like thunderbolts!'

Give me leave to say that such a man is Le Corbusier.

The word genius as a term of human proportion may not be uncommonly applied in clubs, theatres and certain artistic circles, but is less frequently acknowledged in science and philosophy; and although it has been admitted, even in Chelsea, that there have been men of genius in architecture such application has been on aesthetic grounds of doubtful foundation scarcely noticed when such men were alive. The point which is presented in the book which I respectfully venture to review, like a naked spear-head to be touched in wonder or run against, is that Le Corbusier is very, very much alive, and his genius has already stirred the continent outside the British Isles and that of North America. Le Corbusier is an analyst of social development, but has recently been described by an English writer of architectural flattery as the only man who has ever made a very respectable practitioner of English architecture come off his perch. That perch is really another name for what is described by Le Corbusier as the line of least resistance and being long overcrowded it is to be hoped, if not anticipated, that many will be duly disturbed when

15.1
Esprit Nouveau Pavilion, Exposition Internationale des Arts Décoratifs et Industriels Modernes, Paris (1925)

Photographer unknown (1925)

they digest *The City of To-morrow* under which title Mr. Frederick Etchells has translated *Urbanisme*. Those who read this book as if it were merely a matter of architecture written for architects only will be practising a delusion which makes architecture ridiculous and disastrous. One review of Corbusier's *Towards a New Architecture*, previously translated by Mr. Etchells contained comment on the fact that thirteen editions of the original *Vers une Architecture* had appeared before the English edition. It is not extravagant to suggest that both translations, for which we should be grateful to translator and publisher, have been in preparation ever since architecture was first thought of. These works have arrived at their proper time at a transitionary stage of human locomotion which now makes the proudest cities of the world as obsolete as the 'wooden walls of old England.' To realise the suddenness of this transition, brought to a head by mechanical transport, its consequent chaos and increasing destruction of life by violence, colossal waste of energy and financial maintenance, shattering of nerves and mental equilibrium, in comparison with futile tinkering with traffic control which can do no more than direct a condition that is leaping from bad to worse; these are general aspects of citizenship which Corbusier is trying to make us understand. His analysis is not for those who think in the middle of things as they happen to be, but for everybody who can survey from the beginning that was and is without end, particularly those who are competent to attack the problems of future civic development at their source instead of turning to the paltry profits of local application and minor operation that begin anywhere and lead nowhere.

For centuries after Leonardo da Vinci thought out the principles of human flight crowds continued to jeer at those who carried on his research; quite recently New York journalists broke the heart of one Samuel Pierpont Langley who demonstrated the practicability of mechanical flight before the invention of the internal combustion engine which has now initiated a new cycle of human activity and the annihilation of all previous standards of time and energy. That millions of people will fly before this century is finished is as simple to forecast as their birth, and this is the motive that must henceforth govern all human enterprise. That the alpha and omega of aeronautical development are take-off and landings for millions sets the key plan of all cities of to-morrow. If those cities of the future are to be built on the skeletons of the present or whether new aeries of humanity will tower beside them is not a matter of architecture. That cities of to-day are already cities of the past will disturb those who concentrate their attention on preservation of monuments no more than the planetary obedience of this earth to the sun. In future archaeology will represent everything that should have been avoided in town planning and will be found lacking in that which has been its pride compared with the real romance of future efficiency. Corbusier, himself an architect, ridicules that professional incapacity to differentiate between what we see and what we know, otherwise the false romance of what is cultivated as picturesque compared with the genuine romance of reason. His reference to perambulating corpses should warm the hearts of thinkers who have long suffered and despised the trades unionism of architectural style, represented by those 'whose careers consist in recalling in their work the archaeological lessons of their youth.' A man who can pronounce this last indictment of colleagues who consider professional criticism a breach of etiquette and life-long education as sacred, will make only disciples and enemies. Yet he does not threaten all that aerial navigation must inevitably do for the world, but rather leaves that to be taken for granted by those who have vision enough to understand him. His immediate attack is directed towards present and persistent obstacles which paralyse the progress of town planning, and he classifies three cardinal barriers to that progress, namely, the law of least resistance, lack of responsibility, respect for the past. His logic and unselfish integrity is that of a republican citizen who is quite foreign to prospective candidates for social honours and professional commissions.

The thesis of Corbusier's reconstruction in *The City of To-morrow* is a process of redistribution upwards instead of outwards. His city is a gigantic machine with a centre pivot of greater skyscrapers for business, uniformly planned at great intervals instead of the chaotic and unhealthy crowding as in New York City; the first principle is preservation of close contact for business essentially required in city centres. Individuality is to be established by the city as a whole and not through a multitude of exterior expressions and architectural confusion. His advocacy of the skyscraper is clear of that prejudice and misunderstanding which makes London an ever-spreading wilderness; he merely condemns the manner in which America has adjuncted them and defeated their potential service, and there are signs that his criticism is welcomed by those who invented them. Be it said that the American nation is the only one that could have ever improved on a Swiss watch or the five

Orders of architecture, and one that builds the finest monuments but never allows a building to become a monument out of place. Having the greatest civic sense and engineers in the world to-day the United States will grasp the substance of Corbusier's analysis through experience that has never been encouraged in England, where social interference is still active enough to complicate progress with invidious distinction between who shall do a thing and how a thing shall be done.

Corbusier challenges those who are unable to associate business centres with green spaces and quotes a Turkish proverb 'Where one builds one plants trees,' adding thereafter 'We root them up,' in record of what modern traffic is doing to Paris. His insistence on the combined amenities of business and health stamps him as a super romanticist in comparison with gentlemen who ignore both those attributes in their peculiar veneration for sentimental values of Waterloo Bridge or an ephemeral example of fountain sculpture with which they would again obstruct the new Piccadilly Circus. The difference between those who never thought of Waterloo Bridge until it afforded them opportunity of writing public letters about its preservation, and men like Corbusier who regard such condition and circumstances as strangulation of a great city is a matter in which there can be no compromise, and one which is a common issue in our traffic developments. The former express a passion for what is neither an ancient monument nor an adequately serviceable structure; the latter are such who see the real romance of efficiency and recognise no other problem or solution in the crushing burden which transportation has suddenly inflicted on the ancient skeletons of our cities. It is the persistence of those skeletons which paralyse the development of even such capitals of Empire as London, and Corbusier sees the romance of their replanning where others would fondle old bones with a sentimental disregard of their menace to our future. The formula which Corbusier would apply to Paris and New York is a far more vital necessity to London. In condensed form that formula leaves nothing unconsidered: decongestion of city centres by increase of density, complete modification of our present-day conception of streets, extension of city areas of green and open spaces to ensure the necessary degree of health and peace to counteract mental and physical fatigue caused by the speed of modern business. None of these ingredients appears to be contemplated, let alone in operation, in this country to-day. Skyscrapers are prohibited, streets are being planned and constructed on old skeletons and principle of one level for all traffic, city areas are becoming more congested. It is primarily a matter of building up or spreading out; apparently our authorities are determined that we shall continue to sprawl in all directions and like house agents, and describe the process as development. Such development is like the flow of lava from a volcano, slow and devastating, seen from the air it is simply growing confusion. Who knows what educative influence flying may have on those who have been otherwise trained to consider new buildings in London as justified by their style, even before it influences plan and structure? I can almost hear Major General Sir Sefton Brancker chuckle as I write that the revolution of town planning will be brought to a head by flying; as Corbusier puts it, in this case revolution means solution. But long before flying has become a common form of human location, the increase of motor transport will have assumed proportions far beyond present statistics, and this is a perilous outlook for cities like London. Corbusier maintains that cities are the nerve centres of the country and that injury to those nerves may ruin the country. Obviously, the present schemes for road making in the country do nothing to relax the congestion of our cities, but rather aggravate it. Long before any formula of city reconstruction can be carried out other measures for traffic control will be forced upon us, however temporary and fundamentally restrictive such measures may be. They will be a direct incentive to the constructive revolution which Corbusier foresees far ahead, the population will become a disciplined body, insisting on general discipline for its self-preservation, the true communal spirit will so develop and confound the individualists. Those who once opposed trams on the Thames Embankment and taxis in Hyde Park may live to see their own private vehicles and taxis prohibited within the central area of London where either buses or trams may remain supreme, horse traffic will surely be abolished and goods delivery in the city restricted to certain hours. Such regulations seem inevitable and of no hardship. This will be a step towards that uniformity of action which ends all selfishness, and that uniformity will permeate all industry, the city of to-morrow will rise in uniformity of plan and construction throughout, it will be in order and not a multitude of styles and destructive expressions, so called individualism will give place to collectivism; as Corbusier remarks people will no longer require individual watering-cans, or other individual services as now wastefully arranged. The outer circle or residential area of the city that Corbusier describes will be as compact and as efficient as the city itself; his conception of residential uniformity is to my ordinary mind a vision of beauty which we may pardonably envy our descendants. The time, energy, health and money that is now squandered on confused thinking and living will become an inexhaustible balance to the credit of future generations who will have leisure to look back on this age as the twilight of false values, the awakening of real romance and an epoch of many problems. It is conceivable that history will record that many of those problems were analysed and their solution formulated by a great French architect known as M. Le Corbusier.

Source: *The Studio*, September 1929

The Way of To-morrow and the Traffic Problem

By Frank Pick

The Editor has asked that I write a note upon the traffic aspects of the proposal of M. Le Corbusier for *The City of To-morrow*. The essence of his proposal is to utilise the resources which modern methods of building construction – the steel frame, the tenacious cements, the adaptability and transferability of electricity, for instance – have given to us in the redesigning of our cities. First buildings, then cities. The one must follow the other. He sees his exemplar for the first stage in the skyscrapers of New York, and he sees how with fresh regulations as to buildings and city planning these skyscrapers may be turned to profitable account, piling up the population into the air to reach a high and advantageous density, but then by setting each skyscraper in an admirable and spacious setting, restoring the average density of his population to to-day's level, restoring also the amenities which the ill-controlled exploitation, the weltering discord of current building activities bid surely to destroy. His second stage he imagines on paper and provides as a grandiose plan for a new city of three million people.

M. Le Corbusier is an architect and he has some measure of the needs of people for offices, housing, and so forth. He may be a student of traffic but he is without a measure of the needs of people for movement from place to place. His orderly mind suggests that the gridiron pattern is best fitted to the development of urban areas, when already in the United States of America this pattern is proving a failure. Philadelphia is compelled to spoil its original rectilinear plan to free its streets from congestion. There must be a centre to every city. Its unity as a city depends upon the creation and sustentation of such a centre. From this centre the main arteries must run radially in all directions and the spider's web, formalised and systematised to please an architect, were a likelier road pattern and a more gracious one.

M. Le Corbusier rightly argues that roads for traffic should be straight and wide. He scorns the picturesque breaks in the street lines of M. Camille Sitte*. Yet even on the outskirts of London on our arterial roads which are not markedly straight, islands of grass – sites I fear eventually for unhappy memorials of sculptors and their clients – are being provided at important intersections, and even at little important intersections, with the express object of impeding the speed of movement. They may seem an inexcusable contradiction. First, to provide a fine new road, then to fit baffles in it. Still, on occasion, and especially within urban limits, safety makes a prior demand upon the city planner to speed. And M. Camille Sitte's theories of city planning are in full consonance, I imagine, with safety if M. Corbusier's are with speed. It is all in the point of view.

*Camillo Sitte (1843–1903), author of *Der Städtebau nach seinen künstlerischen Grundsätzen* (1899), translated into English as *City Planning According to Artistic Principles*. (Eds)

And as to width of roads, I can hardly believe that M. Le Corbusier is serious. His Roman model, his Carfax with four main arteries, north, east, south and west, they are to be 120 yards, 360 feet wide. Eighteen lines of traffic in each direction. Our Great West Road is, I believe, 60 feet wide. It is a dangerous road. With three lines of traffic in each direction at varying speeds it has become quite unsafe. What then of such an artery? The *City of To-morrow* has three million people. Greater London has nearly eight million people, yet it has no such road nor could it use such a road effectively. A network of moderate sized roads radiating in all directions and divided by centre strips with grass and trees into separate up and down roads, were more safe, more economical and more useful.

In point of fact, there has not yet been any study of the volume of traffic of a city sufficiently advanced to give a certain measure of what should be provided in city planning. As M. Le Corbusier points out himself, urban movement is a recent growth. It has multiplied itself several times in the last fifty years, but in the most highly developed cities is now showing signs of reaching a fixed and calculable level. The time is, therefore, at hand when a collation and examination of the available data some reasonable and manageable basis for a scheme of streets and railways can be worked out for cities of a given population, even for the great cities up to ten million people. It is a problem in scale and proportion, of which the units are just becoming known.

Meanwhile, M. Le Corbusier in his imaginings has brought to emphatic notice one important aspect of city planning, the need for maintaining a high density of population if railway or high-speed transport facilities are to be provided, (Fig. 16.1) if indeed a city is to live and have form and shape. A huge sprawling mass of housing is not a city. A railway is a large capacity means of transport. A railway train is a large capacity unit of transport.

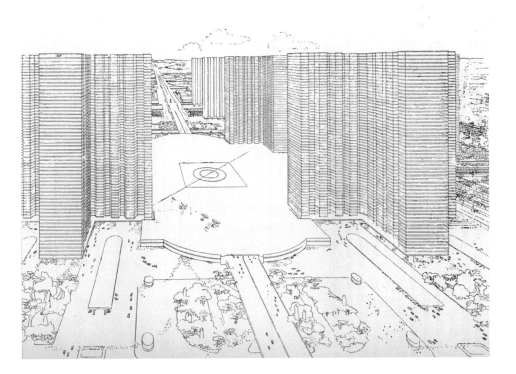

16.1
The central station flanked by four skyscrapers

From Le Corbusier, *The City of To-morrow and Its Planning* (1929)

It demands a dense passenger traffic which in turn demands a dense population. Already in New York there are skyscrapers with 120,000 people passing in and out daily, almost demanding a railway station for their sole use, and so M. Le Corbusier places beneath each one of his skyscrapers in the visionary city, a railway station. Garden cities with their twelve houses to the acre scarcely yield a sufficient volume of traffic within easy reach of a station to justify the cost of an urban railway to serve them. If, therefore, we are to enjoy in parks and open spaces the surface of the ground, the streets of houses must be set on end and even as M. Le Corbusier proposes. It is a splendid notion.

But copying M. Le Corbusier's method of exposition, I leave his book to look in the current newspaper, and what do I see?

The Times for July 12, 1929.

At a meeting of the Corporation, at which the Lord Mayor presided, yesterday, the Finance and Improvements Committee submitted a plan for widening St. Paul's Churchyard and Cannon Street to a minimum of 60 ft. between the Rotunda and Red Lion Court, and for widening Friday Street to 22 ft. between Watling Street and Cannon Street, at a total estimated cost of £61,500.

... Mr. D. George Collins proposed as an amendment that the report be referred back to the committee with instructions to bring up a scheme limited to the widening of Cannon Street from Friday Street to Red Lion Court and the widening of Friday Street from Cannon Street to Watling Street.

... In the result, both the report and the amendment were defeated by large majorities.

Then I am interested in an office building next to St. James's Park Station. (Fig. 16.2) There are nine floors above the ground floor and a central tower with excellent rooms. The ninth floor and the tower rooms may not be used. The building regulations do not forbid their erection. No one is prejudiced or harmed by their erection. Still, they may not be used. Messrs. Swan & Edgar had to build their shop to conform to the plans for the new Piccadilly Circus, but they may not use their topmost floor. Once more the building regulations intervened.

How then are we in London to begin to appreciate the grandiose schemes of M. Le Corbusier? We may not have wide streets nor may we have high buildings. No, we must observe the scale and style of a century ago. But London is four times as large. The centre of London is ten times as valuable. London has twenty times the traffic. The regulations and restrictions are the same. Just as a stray notion I have often thought it would pay London many times over to raise all its buildings, say 20 feet and convert its present street level to a basement for commercial and heavy traffic, making a new street 20 feet higher in the air for the passenger and light traffic. The traffic capacity were doubled almost for the stroke of a pen – certainly for the drafting of a regulation. But this is another subject.

And having written this, I cannot deny M. Le Corbusier the merit of having written a stimulating book.

Source: *The Studio*, September 1929

16.2
**London Transport Headquarters,
55 Broadway, London (1929)**

Architects: Adams Holden & Pearson
Photographer: Janet Hall (1999)

The City of To-morrow

By Herbert Read

Two of Le Corbusier's books – *The City of To-morrow* and *Towards a New Architecture* – have already been translated into English by Mr. Frederick Etchells [...], but I do not think they have received anything like the publicity they deserve. The French architect who has adopted the *nom de guerre* Le Corbusier is one of the most significant figures in the modern world. His ideas are expressed with great force, they contradict all the conventions of the academies, they are concerned with the most urgent problems of the day; there is, in short, no escaping them! His latest book, *Précisions* (Fig. 17.1) is perhaps no more than a restatement of the ideas already expressed in the earlier books, but the restatement is, as the title indicates, a precise one. The book consists of ten lectures which the author gave to different audiences in Buenos Aires in October, 1929, together with an introduction and various appendices. The rapid drawings which the lecturer made to illustrate his lectures are reproduced, and add greatly to the interest of the volume. Cannot Le Corbusier be persuaded to repeat his lectures in England, and not to architects only, but to all who are concerned with the great problems which demand immediate solution in our cities? But that is equivalent to a request for the lectures to be open to the public at large.

I must confess that when, a few weeks ago, I drew a distinction between the architect and the engineer, and implied that in so far as the modern architect was an engineer, he was indifferent to aesthetic values, I badly misrepresented Le Corbusier. On this very question, he draws a further distinction between the engineer and the constructor. Engineering is analysis and calculation; construction is synthesis and creation. The engineer, so to speak, leans on his measuring rod, and for the most part has no affection for the things he makes. He merely functions, and is satisfied if the result works. But a constructor like Le Corbusier has a passion for order, and order is harmony, is beauty. He describes walking along the flat sands of Brittany and coming across a solitary monolith, perhaps set up there by some primitive race. The words in which he describes his emotion would look ridiculous if translated. Here they are:

Je marchais. Subitement je me suis arrêté. Entre l'horizon et mes yeux, un événement sensationnel s'est produit: une roche verticale, une pierre de granit est là debout, comme un menhir; sa verticale fait avec l'horizon de la mer un angle droit. Cristallisation, fixation du site. Ici est un lieu où l'homme s'arrête, parce qu'il y a

17.1
'This isn't architecture – these are styles'

From Le Corbusier, *Précisions sur un Etat Présent de l'Architecture et de l'Urbanisme* (1930)

symphonie totale, magnificence de rapports, noblesse. Le vertical fixe le sens de l'horizontal. L'un vit à cause de l'autre. Voilà des puissances de synthèse.

Le Corbusier is in revolt against all the academic conventions, but would claim that nevertheless he embodies the true tradition. We have all heard of the 'orders' of architecture; but where there are so many orders, how can there be order? Le Corbusier has studied and understood the construction of the Parthenon and the Capitol; he has found the same principles embodied in a monastery in Italy, in the Eiffel Tower, and in a modern liner – economy, efficiency, and freedom. The straight line is the line of the intellect, of controlled emotions, of classicism. The rest is romanticism, confusion, the principle of muddling through! Style he regards as the expression of a prevalent state of mind: Greece, Rome, the eighteenth century – to all these ages one state of mind is common, and they have certain architectural principles in common – order, harmony, the beauty of the straight line. We have the capacity for the same state of mind; we have, moreover, all the resources which a century of scientific experiment has put in our hands: with these principles and these resources, there is literally a new world within our grasp. Le Corbusier is the lyrical prophet of this new order. Only a brain of clay will fail to respond to his enthusiasm.

His ideas fall into three main divisions, concerning the house, its internal arrangements and furniture, and what we call town-planning. Let me try to describe the situation as Le Corbusier sees it. The modern city (with a few exceptions which follow an eighteenth-century plan, like Karlsruhe or the 'New Town' in Edinburgh) is generally based on a plan determined in an age when the common means of transport was the donkey, and the donkey being an animal inclined to wander, to pluck thistles where he can see them, and generally to take the easiest rather than the shortest path, the streets of such a town are just a tangle of unmeaning tracks. The houses cluster thickly towards the middle of such a city, presumably for warmth and mutual support; all roads converge towards the centre, and though this did not matter much when even donkeys were scarce, in a day when every city must accommodate thousands of motor cars each with a potential speed of forty to sixty miles an hour, not to mention all other mechanical means of transport, the situation is such that no words are adequate to describe its absurdity. On the other hand, there are modern cities like New York and Chicago over which Le Corbusier can only weep tears: they are pathetic. Here was the opportunity and here the means to create the ideal city. What actually have we got? Vast canyons of brick and cement, down which drift the poisonous petrol-fumes of innumerable vehicles; parallel avenues bearing no relation to the density of life and traffic on each side; ragged, unmeaning silhouettes; reverberating din; no light, no sun, no gardens; just hell.

As we approach the ideal city of the future, we come, first, to long rectangular blocks of dwelling-houses, rising like a white trellis against the green parks and playing fields with which they are surrounded. If we approach closer to these blocks, we find that they consist each of a number of tenements, arranged rather like half a chessboard set vertically. The white squares are garden-balconies, one for each flat. The roof of the whole block is flat, and laid out as a roof-garden. If we look in at one of the flats, we should have a vision of flashing steel, bright lacquer, plate-glass, sunlight, flowers. Between the blocks stretch the allotment gardens, the tennis-lawns and playing fields, sufficient for all the people who live close by them. We approach nearer to the heart of the city, but as we go the veins we travel along dilate; the city opens out. We leave the heavy traffic on the ground level, and travel ourselves on elevated roadways, as swiftly as we like, for there are no level crossings. On each side of us are garden terraces, with the cafés; then the pedestrians' way, with the shops, and above the shops the soaring business blocks, not contiguous, but each rising like the monolith on the Brittany coast, a clear accent against the wide horizon, a note in this complete harmony of ordered lines, the City of Light.

This is not a poet's vision; it is a practical scheme for which Le Corbusier can give you the working drawings and the estimated cost. The cost is an immense economy. Why, then, not begin right now?

L'académisme crie: Non!

Source: *The Listener*, 18 February 1931

The House of To-morrow

By Herbert Read

I return to Le Corbusier. Three of the lectures reprinted in *Précisions* deal directly with the house, and we begin with a clear distinction between the town house and the country house. In the first case, we must remember that the constructional unit is the town; there is a complete suppression of all individuality and such houses are built, not by the foot, but by the mile. That sounds rather monotonous, but each long block represents many acres of villadom; the blocks are recessed among trees, gardens and playing fields; their long straight lines harmonize well with the towering business blocks in the distance. It cannot be denied that out of such elements an architectural beauty might be created.

As he crossed from France to South America, Le Corbusier could not help being struck by a resemblance between the liner he travelled in and the city-block of his imagination. In a cabin of only a few cubic feet a ship-constructor had designed an ideal 'machine to live in'. Space being the primary consideration, everything had been reduced to bare essentials. Not an inch of wood or metal was not serving its purpose; not a movement in man's daily life that had not been considered in the disposition of the cabin's furniture. He was looked after by an excellent steward, and in the ship's restaurant he could find a variety of food and drink such as no private house could possibly offer. If he was bored with society and the menu, he could have a special meal served in a room apart. For exercise there were long cleans decks, a gymnasium, a swimming-bath. If all this comfort, economy and convenience could be achieved in the drastically restricted space of an ocean liner, what could not be achieved on the limitless freedom of the land? The house-block in the city of to-morrow will emulate the comfort, economy and convenience of the liner; to these it will add the luxuries of space and light, of terrace, and of roof-gardens, of playing-fields and parks. The servant problem, the food problem, and many other problems that afflict the dweller in the individual house (plumbing problems, crèche problems, central-heating and supply problems of all kinds) will be solved as they are solved on the liner. The gain in freedom alone would be incalculable.

But let us now consider the country house as conceived by Le Corbusier, (Fig. 18.1) for there the aesthetic problems involved are more clearly isolated. First comes the bare structure of the house. This is radically different, for whereas the house of brick and stone must be first embedded in then earth (damp and dark) and then rise four-square on rigid walls, with a ground-floor plan that must be followed throughout its stories, the house of

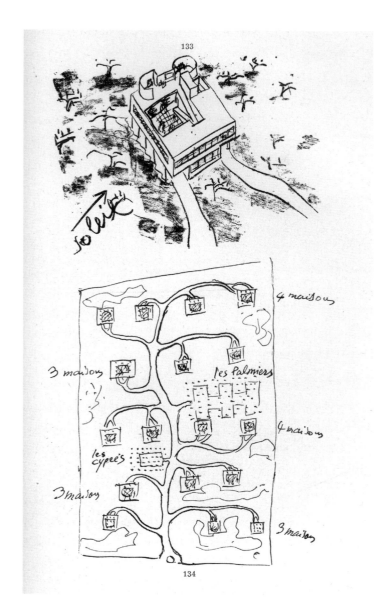

18.1

The house in the countryside: domestic life inserted into a pastoral dream

From Le Corbusier, *Précisions sur un Etat Présent de l'Architecture et de l'Urbanisme* (1930)

to-morrow will rise clear of the ground on steel piles. The whole house will be lifted like a box in the air, the ground being left free for traffic, for shelter, for gardens. The floors will be built on to the upright piles, and the walls of the house will hang from the ceilings, thus reversing the usual order, and making each floor independent of the other. Windows, no longer being restricted by the structural importance of the walls, can be as large and as long as desired. '*Je compose avec la lumière*', claims Le Corbusier. The roof of this house is flat, and on the roof is a garden, a sun-trap; and why not a small gymnasium?

Perhaps that is enough to give the reader an adequate idea of the outer appearance of the house of to-morrow. Before going inside, let us consider what objections can be taken to its appearance. All that I ever heard reduce to the same complaint: it is just like a box!

18.2
Villa Church, Ville d'Avray (1929)

From *Architecture Vivante*, Spring 1930

But, as Mr. Bernard Shaw once said, what is wrong with a box? Nothing, of course, so long as it is a well-designed box. If the proportions are right, such a box on a hill-side will look as well as a yacht at sea. It is only necessary to get rid of our prejudices. When we come to the private house we have to contend, not so much, with academic tradition, but rather with age-long usage – not with style, but with habit. A house with a sloping roof seems a part of nature; but actually it was a machine with a functional purpose, designed to throw off rain and snow at a time when man could not design any other means of keeping the wet out. But functionally a sloping roof is so much waste space; and aesthetically it has no exclusive rights.

Inside the box we revert to the example of the cabin in the liner, with all the transforming difference made by the possibility of unlimited light. (Fig. 18.2) There being no restriction in the placing of the walls on the floor, the individual rooms can be just as big or small as we like. But the great difference is in the furniture, or rather in the absence of furniture. If a house is designed as a machine to live in, all our needs and all our movements can be foreseen. Cupboards and presses, bookcases and wardrobes, can be designed in the right proportions and built in where they are required. What else do we need? Tables and chairs of various sorts and sizes, but little else – the rest is decoration. For tables and chairs we should again consider function in terms of material. We should again consider light and space and cleanliness. Such considerations would lead us to steel and plate-glass; and furniture in these materials is already available. But here again new ideas must contend with age-long prejudice. The beauty of steel furniture will be denied, but only by those who have not used it. The colour, the surface, the natural forms of chromium-plated steel are very different from similar qualities in walnut or oak, but their claims to aesthetic consideration are real. We have given up contending that the old horse-coach was a more beautiful object than the modern motor-car. We must with equal justice begin to consider whether the steel chair is not at least as beautiful as its Chippendale ancestor.

It will, of course, be said that this is all very well; the house of to-morrow will be very beautiful and very hygienic, but it will be very inhuman. But Le Corbusier protests that everywhere he has sought for houses that were built by men, and not by architects, houses that just happened. In such houses he finds true harmony, true disposition of spaces, utensils, light. The ideas are there; apply the resources of modern technology and you will get the same *natural* plan achieved with efficiency and fervour. Le Corbusier, you see, is not inhuman; he is a poet, perhaps the greatest poet of our time.

Source: *The Listener*, 25 February 1931

The Vertical Garden City

By Le Corbusier

*Highpoint 1, North Hill, London N6, 1933–35 (architects: Lubetkin & Tecton). (Eds)

I believe that in periods of a new beginning, in epochs of the birth of new civilizations, ideas must be human before being national. This because nations are only artificial products of circumstance. I have visited the large block of flats just completed at Highgate*. (Figs 19.1–19.3) This beautiful building sets a question of principle: to follow tradition or to break with it? I reply unhesitatingly by stating my personal point of view; a new tradition must be created.

In England, undoubtedly, there exists a very strong domestic tradition. England, seen from the air, is a green country, subdivided by high hedges into a crazy paving, based on some system which is incomprehensible, but whose effect is very clearly defined. From above, it seems impossible to alter the subdivision which was devised in the remotest past. I leave it to whoever it may concern to study this question; it would be very interesting to explore it.

But the aeroplane goes on, and passes over London. A colossal spectacle, amazing phenomenon. From Croydon, the suburbs stretch out of sight, multiply, and follow one upon another. The earth, in all its vast extent, is covered with them. Suddenly, a town – the Town; but we have already passed over it. It was the City. After it, the puzzle of suburbs goes on again.

Let us stand on the solid earth again; let us undergo the daily lot of 10,000,000 inhabitants, walking on the ground and going about their business. 10,000,000 inhabitants, in the course of their ordinary occupations, make the London street intense, magnificent, and seething with life. The traffic, resolving the paradox of terrific distances, bus, tube, tram, taxi, car, roll us on an irresistible torrent. The buses are splendid – red, covered with beautiful lettering; tall, strategic towers. The lay-out of the London tube impresses me by its size, its pleasantness, and the comfort put at the passengers' disposal, and by the care the public takes of the accommodation it has been given.

The breakwaters of the torrent are the London shops – full of goods, polished glass, clean marble, and brilliant brass. One feels the abundance of merchandise, the weight of production, the quality. Then, involved in this violent adventure, the martyred pedestrian. What adaptability; what perseverance; what resignation, and what optimism! He does not revolt (not yet); he accepts a new rôle that was unknown to his ancestors.

This intensity of life in the street is an entertaining distraction, enthralling in its dynamic quality. But it is crazy, so stupid it makes one cry. More than that, it is an economic disaster.

19.1–19.3
Highpoint One, London (1935)

Architects: Lubetkin & Tecton
Photographers: Dell & Wainwright (1935)

What statistician would consent to calculate the capital which could be mobilized from the gigantic expenditure represented by the consumption of petrol and tyres of all these vehicles; and, above all, by the hours wasted by the innumerable workers who toil at production and distribution. We, with this capital emerging triumphantly, could achieve a new vindication of realistic town-planning, and the page would be turned. Then only, after life would begin – the new epoch with its new towns ...

What I have just said will let me return to Highgate. Where does this pedestrian go after his day's work in London? He goes home to his little two-storey house. London has millions of these houses, each with its little bit of garden.

The house is probably, even certainly, very intimate; but what kind of intimacy is it? The windows open on to those of the next house; it is a few yards from one front door to the next. The landscape? – invisible from the garden, the street, or the window.

Let us examine the question from another point of view: those 10,000,000 individuals are spread out to the horizon thick as sand. Naturally a tradition grows up and creates a way of thinking and acting, which becomes specifically that of the Londoner, and, by imitation, probably that of the Englishman. It is rightly said that there is an English tradition, but founded upon what? On these exact phenomena of circulation and housing – phenomena which are deficient.

When the village was a village, when London was a normal town, when the motor car, the bus, and the Underground were still in the dim future, the proportion was different; it was radically different, possible, human. Proportion existed; it is no more.

I think I felt around me, in my London journey, a certain tiredness and desire for change. This terrific extension has led to a dislocation of everyday life, and to the weariness of the people: slow and penetrating symptoms of disintegration. This, at any rate, is apparent – certain of the vital elements of modern life have been strangled: the civic qualities which activate the spirit of the citizen outside the simple obligations of work, especially the feeling of participation in a common enterprise, in a work which is visible, whose function one can understand, through which one walks, which exists materially, optically, and plastically. I speak of a town; of a town which represents the spirit of an epoch, a spiritual event.

Have modern times the right to create their own towns, to manifest their spiritual significance? I believe that this tradition, which we recognize as existing, is broken and smashed today by the paradox of a town immeasurably extended, and I believe that a new tradition is being born which will safeguard all that was the prime motive power of the preceding tradition. It will be the new tradition of vertical garden-cities, made possible by modern technique. It will replace the horizontal garden-cities by giving what those have ceased to give, bringing what they have ceased to bring; everyday joys, much more real than the illusions of today. Our immense progress will bring immense benefits.

The vertical garden-city:

(a) brings the solution of modern speed: the separation of automobile and pedestrian routes. The whole site is at the disposal of the pedestrian, out of danger from cars.

(b) gives facilities for the organization of communal services: liberation from domestic slavery, of great importance for women.

(c)   safeguards the site: creates a real landscape and provides the opportunity of admiring it, by means of eloquent avenues superimposed one upon another.

(d)   restores the land for useful purposes, one of which, at least, is to provide sport facilities at the very feet of the houses; another, if necessary, to provide vegetable gardens for intensive cultivation; much more interesting than the traditional small garden system.

So we find in Highgate the seed of something, the seed of a vertical garden-city as opposed to the horizontal extension. The building is large enough to be an example, a demonstration, a proof. The response of the public, also, is eloquent; it is enthusiasm. Almost all the flats are let, before the block is finished. Thanks to the construction on stanchions, the ground floor is no longer that part of the building usually sacrificed, where strangled rooms crowd around access corridors to the staircase, between heavy carrying walls. The ground floor here extends like the superb surface of a lake, absorbing easily the lines of traffic of different speed and direction; the cars into their own door, pedestrians elsewhere, services elsewhere again. Perambulators and bicycles have easy access, the cars are garaged in the right place. But more than circulation, this surface contains real parking spaces: a huge hall, full of light and air, extremely attractive architecturally, and leading with enormous virtuosity towards the two vertical services of stairs and lifts. And here again, full light from top to bottom of these essential services.

The top is no longer composed of an academic pitched roof folk-lore: it is a product of reinforced concrete. A great area of repose, broken only by wind-screens and shelters from the sun and rain which stand out against the sky. From the roof the view on all sides is incomparable: framed in concrete bays the whole sky appears, and the forests, and the garden suburbs, and the church spires, and the distant roads. A spectacle. When it is finished, plantations of bushes and flowers will give this roof garden of a new era the necessary intimacy and pleasantness … Here then are two new events brought about by modern technique; the stanchions with a distribution of circulation on the ground floor, and the roof garden accessible by lifts – now the current means of vertical transport. Between these two new elements are inserted, with all the standardization capable of uniting efficiency with economy, the sixty flats. These are of two types; they could, if necessary, be of ten or more; standardization of structural elements leaves perfect liberty for architectural initiative.

These flats possess the most important factor of all domestic architecture: sun and space and intimacy. What do interior subtleties matter? They take second place behind this predominant reality; immense bays, opening on the country. Before fixing the standard of these flats, the architects have studied the question of interior arrangement very skilfully and profoundly. It is worth while, when one multiplies one's experience by sixty, to do it well. The result of standardization is here an excellent quality in the smallest details; well studied, once and for all, they extend their benefits to the whole building. For a long time I have dreamed of executing dwellings in such conditions for the good of humanity. The building at Highgate is an achievement of the first rank, and a milestone which will be useful to everybody. It is amusing to point out here the obstinacy with which the conservative and reactionary spirit tries to maintain its position. Highpoint could only be constructed because until today the local regulations did not consider at all the problem of building in height. These rules were created chiefly for the building of normal houses of the garden-city type. The architects of Highpoint were able to sweep away, as a torrent sweeps a dam, the feeble resistance which these regulations were able to oppose to them. The building grew but, as soon as it was up, the authorities gave the alarm; they immediately added a clause forbidding the repetition of such an adventure. This is characteristic; it is also heartbreaking. It might have been imagined that the legislation was really created to give freedom to intelligent initiative. No. The regulations are blind tyrants, red-taped and bureaucratic. When a new building legislation, a free legislation, induces the builders not to perpetrate anachronisms, but to open, on the contrary, the door to modern times, for the total transformation of architecture and town planning, this transformation will be the gift of modern technique.

Source: *Architectural Review*, January 1936

The Voice of the Prophet

By J.N.S (John Summerson)
Review of *La Ville Radieuse* and *Aircraft*

Le Corbusier repeats himself. He is not content to say a thing once, or twice, or a dozen times. Mere statement is not enough; he writes not to inform, but to persuade; not to persuade, but to convince. So he volleys his matter in violent paragraphs, shot off at machine-gun tempo, always at the same targets. Wherever you open his books they seize your attention, assault your peace of mind, inflame your curiosity. But if you are sufficiently old-fashioned to read books attentively from beginning to end you may find his method infuriating.

La Ville Radieuse is a development of the scrap-book technique used by the author in his previous works. It is a large oblong book, of the size and proportion associated with bound volumes of Bach's organ works, and is extremely awkward to hold. The illustrations comprise photographs, drawings, newspaper cuttings, fragments from catalogues, engravings and the author's own hasty scribbles, reproduced direct, and often almost impossible to decipher. The book has a certain order and coherence of its own, however, and is divided into eight sections, each with numerous subsections. A great deal of the matter is reprinted from other sources, and this naturally results in repetition and overlapping. Moreover, the author does not hesitate to reproduce the same picture twice if it serves to reinforce his argument at different points. And all through we are bombarded with aphorisms and slogans, capital letters and italics. Maximum emphasis is the great objective. As the author himself says, the book 'expresses the hammering rhythm of present-day life, the accelerated, violent growth of a new phenomenon – urbanism.'

The first section of the book is headed 'Preliminaries.' It is really no more preliminary than any other section, but comes as near as any to telling us what any reader of Le Corbusier naturally wants to know: what are the author's political beliefs? Le Corbusier avoids this delicate issue, but declares himself a revolutionary, 'along strictly professional lines.' His plans are his revolutionary programme. 'It is LIFE which has impelled us to these plans. We must obey LIFE. The plan defines objectives, and demands action ... Revolutionary action? – and by revolutionary is meant destructive. Not at all; constructive predominantly and absolutely.'

Thus, the architect sticks to his plans; the yawning gulf between their creation and their realisation does not seem to trouble him. We have the plans; we have the means. Put the plans into execution, and there will be no need to bother about the class struggle or the overthrow of capitalism. Follow a logical programme of living, and everything will come

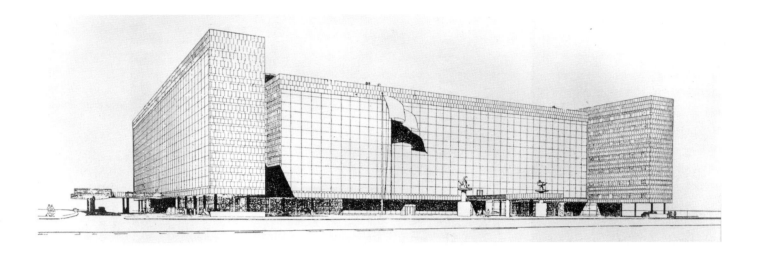

20.1

Design for Centrosoyus

From Le Corbusier, *La Ville Radieuse* (1935)

right. This, in short, is Le Corbusier's attitude; the attitude of an individualist and a romantic. It is not surprising to find him defending individual liberty in the face of Moscow's disapproval. 'I regard the sanctity of personal freedom as the corner-stone of all modern urban development,' he wrote in his *Réponse à Moscou* (1930). 'Collective discipline,' he says, elsewhere, 'is only valuable in so far as it makes for the liberty of the individual.'

The second section of the book is headed 'Modern Technics.' Here Le Corbusier outlines many concepts which are by now familiar to those who know his works and his writings. Such, for instance, is the concept of the structural skeleton which leaves both the plan and elevations absolutely free; again, we are familiar with the concept of the lofty living-room rising through two low stories devoted to cooking, bathing, sleeping, etc. A more revolutionary notion than these is that of the hermetically closed window separating the conditioned air within the building from the unwholesome bacteria-laden atmosphere without. The author wished to put this theory into practice in his Centro-soyus building in Moscow, (Fig. 20.1) but apparently even the ultra-modern-minded Soviets (as they then were) would not stand for that, and accused their architect of an intellectual affinity with the morbid bourgeois mind of H.G. Wells. 'One can only regret,' comments Le Corbusier, 'that the Russians involve problems of respiration with those of political doctrine.'

Le Corbusier conceives history as a vast, helpless organism, which may spread into channels of horror and destruction, just as a river may flow into dark unwholesome chasms, unless its course is checked and guided. With the third section of the book we come to a consideration of what modern living conditions might be and ought to be, and this, in turn, is preparatory to showing us the 'radiant city,' with a description of which the next section is concerned, and which, 'inspired by the laws of the universe and of the human body, contrives to bring to man of the machine age the *essential joys* of life.' These 'essential joys' consist of healthy and beautiful surroundings, and opportunities for exercise just round the corner. 'The materials of urbanism,' says Le Corbusier, 'are sun, sky, trees, steel and concrete.'

It is important to note that in his *Ville Radieuse* Le Corbusier sets his face against two types of layout which have achieved considerable repute on the score of logic and practicability. One is the 'terrace' type of housing, pyramidal on section, each layer of flats set back behind the one below. The other, more important, is what the Germans call *Zeilenbau*, that is to say, blocks set in rows, all looking the same way. His criticism of this arrangement is that it creates the 'corridor-street,' which he looks on with especial disfavour, not merely because of its monotony, but because of its disastrous results in case of gas attack from the air, the gas lurking in the channels formed by the buildings.

Section 4 brings us to *La Ville Radieuse* itself, described in the series of extremely fine drawings exhibited at the Brussels congress of the *Congrès International d'Architecture Moderne* in 1930. The design is Le Corbusier's most impressive exploit into the world of unrealised possibilities, and is a crystallisation of much that is best in contemporary thought. A great deal of nonsense has been talked about this 'city of the future' (which, as Le Corbusier bitterly points out, is no Wellsian fantasy, but merely the unbuilt city of the present), and innumerable misconceptions have been spread abroad by people who have not taken the trouble to look twice at the design before passing judgment on it.

This hypothetical town is divided into three main sections: the residential quarter, the manufacturing quarter, and the business quarter. The famous and much-illustrated cruciform skyscrapers belong, not to the residential quarter (as is so often stated), but to the business quarter. The residential buildings are laid out in spacious arabesque formation whose action pattern is (surprisingly enough) a matter of aesthetic choice. The orientation of the arabesques and the positions of the flats in each section is worked out in detail after the general pattern has been settled. Infant schools, crèches, and parking spaces are distributed within the arabesques with the most satisfying ingenuity, but rather less inviting is the way in which football grounds, bathing-pools and tennis-courts are packed in among the rest; surely a better place for these would be in the country which so closely borders the *Ville Radieuse*.

One of the later sections of the book, labelled 'Plans,' is of special interest. It comprises illustrations (accompanied by the inevitable explosive comments) of some of Le Corbusier's most remarkable projects, and leads off with the great *Plan Voisin*, which proposed to clear a vast area of Paris, north of the Ile de la Cité, and cover it with eighteen of the cruciform skyscrapers and a number of lower buildings laid out in arabesque formation. Then there is the gigantic scheme for Algiers, described in great detail, there is the beautiful League of Nations design, and rejected schemes for Antwerp, Moscow, Stockholm, and elsewhere. All these reveal the genius of Le Corbusier much more clearly than any of his writings can do. Here are no mannerisms, no naïve enthusiasms, but only a tremendous lucidity, a power of synthesis such as one recognises only in the greatest minds of the past.

Finally, there is a design for *La Ferme Radieuse*, made in response to some peasants who wrote to Le Corbusier after the first publication of *La Ville Radieuse*; (Fig. 20.2) and the book closes with a short section, stating laconically the alternatives before humanity: mobilisation for war, or mobilisation for peaceful reconstruction. The same resources are available for both; the same discipline, the same large-scale organisation. 'Can it be as simple as that?' the reader is made to ask on the last page; 'a mere tilt of the scales in favour of GOOD instead of EVIL.' Alas, one has but to glance at the headlines of the papers or the skyline of London to know that it is not quite so simple as that.

20.2
Farmhouse of industrialised and standardised construction

From Le Corbusier, *La Ville Radieuse* (1935)

20.3
Cover of *Aircraft: the New Vision* (1935)

In the smaller of the two books before us, Le Corbusier pays homage to man's achievements in the air. (Fig. 20.3) As he knows nothing of the technique of aircraft there is nothing to tie him down to matters of fact, and he romances excitedly about the new viewpoint, the new scale, the new tempo of an air-minded world. For sub-title he calls his book *L'Avion Accuse* – the aeroplane indicts. He shows us air pictures of confused planning in London and Paris. 'The eye of the airplane is pitiless.' Again, 'the eye now sees in substance what the mind formerly could only subjectively conceive,' and we are shown geometrically planned Dutch fortifications of the Middle Ages, spread out below like a carpet. Then there is a bird's-eye view of Le Corbusier's scheme for Antwerp, showing charming arabesques of the *Ville Radieuse* type, threaded with paths and gardens.

It is an irritating book, with its flashy introduction, advertising the NEW AGE of the machine in the same terms as up-to-date advertising agencies use for new toothpastes and aperients. Nevertheless, as part of Le Corbusier's campaign against contemporary smugness it is effective and characteristic. The make-up and production are clever; the photographs are beautiful and coherently arranged (though why the captions should be banished to the end of the text and rendered nearly useless it is difficult to explain). In short, the book is a mixture of naïveté and artistry, which will be accepted or rejected according to the reader's mood or taste.

Le Corbusier is a great man, and for that very reason it is forgivable, indeed necessary, to indict that part of his literary output which is theatrical and sensational; for what remains, both in his thought, and still more in his architecture, is of the greatest moment. Le Corbusier has one of those rare minds in which intellect and vision are perfectly co-ordinated. Individualist as he is, he is a great leader, and the least homage we can aware him is our constant and attentive admiration.

Source: *Architect & Building News*, 10 January 1936

Radiant City and Garden Suburb: Corbusier's *Ville Radieuse*

By Godfrey Samuel

The architectural fantasies of Wells and Korda at the Leicester Square Theatre are perhaps little more than inflations of the modern luxury interior. What is bad is their conception as the shapes of things to come. They belong to that school of thought which talks of Futurism and Ultramodernism. When Wells broadcast an appeal for prophetic opinions, in 1932, *The Listener* invited Le Corbusier, among others, to reply. He did so, and pointed out very clearly that the things were here, it was only the shapes that were to come. Men of to-day were simply living in cities of yesterday. (The Mayor of Algiers had just told him that his now famous new plan for the town would be very welcome in a hundred years' time.) Procrastination is the easiest escape of all.

On the broader principle, however, Wells, Le Corbusier, even the Mayor of Algiers perhaps, are agreed. Our business is to bring about the highest degree of order combined with the widest extent of human liberty, a contradiction in terms to some, but no more of a contradiction than the wild freehand shape drawn on the sheet of graph paper.

That has always been the aim, it is the means of achieving it that changes, and the machine age of the last hundred years has brought the biggest changes of all. Unfortunately for city-making, Machinery coincided with Democracy. Mediaeval Catholicism had given direction to urban life through churches. The Aristocracy of the Renaissance had done much the same through palaces. Democracy had no such unifying factor to offer. The whole problem was mishandled, and in the general social confusion it is small wonder that sensitive spirits were driven to attempt escape, either back into the good old days (any good old days would do) or out into the primitive present of the countryside. So much for liberty; though even in the countryside the ignorant application of the Town Planning Acts is now paralysing it. These painful discords continue with us in the town aggravated by a thoroughly ill-considered attempt to get some sort of order. Hence our neo-Roman grandeur, starting literally above the heads of the populace, crushing by its superhuman scale any small civic joy the humble citizen may feel. (Thank God, and Pick, for the Underground!)

Not Hausmannisation, as in Kingsway, for instance, but humanisation is what we need. That is the first and most fundamental of Le Corbusier's pleas, a return to human scale and natural human desires, if indeed we know what these are, for under the stress of acquiring means to satisfy them, they themselves have become contorted almost out of recognition.

'Vivre, rire, être maître chez soi, et ouvrir ses yeux dans la lumière, dans le soleil, les ouvrir sur les vertes frondaisons et sur le ciel bleu.'

Apparently this emphasis on individual liberty is responsible for Le Corbusier's running wrangle with the Soviet Union, an argument at cross purposes (with some genuine differences of opinion on building technique in the background), which is a major tragedy. For the Soviet Union could provide the two essential conditions for serious urban planning, a land publicly owned, and an organisation with a will, while Le Corbusier could give the Soviet doctrine a clearer and nobler expression than the neo-classical absurdities to which they seem to be returning.

The individual man, and Le Corbusier's individual is a very real man, provides the 'programme' for the smallest unit of the urban pattern. This is based on the principle of neat functional planning for those purposes that call for it, and owes much to the design of ships' cabins and wagons-lits. (It would be interesting to know whether this rationalised living makes any part of the appeal of Holiday Cruises, or whether it is simply a matter of leisure, fresh air and new company.)

The next unit in the pattern is set by the individual car. Le Corbusier has been one of the first to recognise this, though he leaves the permanence of this system of transport unquestioned. He points out that the twenty-fold increase in horse-power means a complete change of scale in what might be called the second urban unit. After a series of thorough and well-presented studies of the problem, he concludes that the grid of streets now requires to be enlarged about three times, roughly up to a quarter-mile mesh. (Bus-stops in London are about half-a-mile apart.)

The second problem of circulation is safety, as between car and car on the one hand, and car and pedestrian on the other. Le Corbusier's solution is convincing. Visualising more clearly than most the real three-dimensional character of a city, he would have us give up the ground level *entirely* to the free circulation of pedestrians and to the establishment of such pleasures as tennis, boating and sitting in the shade. The cars lead their own lives some fifteen feet higher up with a properly worked-out system of ramps and bridges to avoid all crossing. The advantages of such a solution over the much published 'City-of-the-Future' type, with first floor pavements for pedestrians, is obvious on close analysis.

With these two general groups of data in mind, Le Corbusier insists on the prime importance of the buildings dominating the circulation. The 'corridor street' and the common practice of fitting blocks of buildings into any old shape left by the network of roads is more responsible than any other feature of contemporary town-planning for the inhumanisation of the city. It states, in effect, that cars are more important than men. Let those who profess to see in Le Corbusier's school of thought the domination of the machine, bear that point in mind.

On this question of machinery he has been grossly misrepresented. 'The house as a machine to live in' is a phrase that has been contorted by those who fear machines to mean some kind of devitalising of the inhabitant. It is symptomatic of a whole group of reactions towards the idea of the Machine. So many people in this country still take what might be called the Ruskinian attitude. Ruskin's passionate eloquence was designed to turn the men of his day from the broad and level arterial road to Mechanisation, back to the strait and narrow path that leads to Hand Craftsmanship. Le Corbusier with a no less passionate and often surprisingly similar eloquence reminds us that the machine is our servant and that if we grasp it firmly and work it with a will, knowing what we want, far from inducing the spiritual impoverishment which was Ruskin's obsession, it will present us with opportunities of enrichment undreamed of (even by H. G. Wells). If anyone still imagines Le Corbusier to be a soulless utilitarian he will be quickly disillusioned by a glance at this book, or its predecessors. Pre-Hitlerian German housing blocks, for example, supposed to be part of 'the Movement' are condemned with vigour on grounds of spiritual poverty.

The several town-planning schemes prepared by Le Corbusier and Jeanneret during the past thirteen years (his interest in town-planning dates only from 1922) form the most important part of this collection of papers. Together with the introductory material and an appendix on rural planning – which must, however, be condemned as superficial inasmuch as it takes for granted the contemporary and probably outworn unit of production, the individual farm – they present a fair summary of the Le Corbusier doctrine of Town-planning.

Build up on the principles we have discussed, it is worked out with that incredible vitality and almost vegetable sense of form which have given Le Corbusier a place in international architecture unoccupied since the time of Palladio.

The schemes fall into two main types. The more important is the *Ville Radieuse*, the *Plan Voisin* for Paris (1922) and the Antwerp Scheme (1933). Forty-storey cruciform blocks widely spaced are surrounded and contrasted with continuous fifteen-floor meanders, with free ground circulation everywhere and a quarter-mile mesh of roads at a higher level. The publication of so many plans is bound to involve a certain amount of repetition, which, though valuable in a propagandist work, is liable, when added to the author's natural tendency in the same direction, to irritate. Each scheme, however, is well worth studying in relation to its own particular problems, especially those which have had a financial plan worked out, for while the financial advantage of large-scale planning in general is obvious, this kind of solution involves rather different considerations from that of the satellite town, which is the standard English answer of the day.

The second type of scheme is that prepared in sketch form for Rio de Janeiro (1929) (Fig. 21.1) and worked out in great detail for Algiers (1929–1932). (Fig. 21.2) Here the special problem is the lie of the land, a mountainous coast with all level parts already occupied. Le Corbusier's solution in principle is the construction of great viaducts for traffic running from hill to hill with tiers of dwellings, varying, of course, in number, below them, and in some cases also above. The idea is not quite so convincing on account of the less clear domination of building over circulation, but the architectural grandeur of such schemes would be more than Roman, while human scale and common human delights need not, as Le Corbusier shows, be lost.

A scheme of the *Plan Voisin* type would be an adequate solution for any large city, even London. Since it is no Utopian affair and should be seriously examined, we may well ask how far its principle could be applied here. There are, of course, many special points to be borne in mind.

In the first place, the attitude of the Englishman to London is rather different from that of, say, the Frenchman towards Paris. Paris is first and foremost the centre jewel of France; the country outside exists for the sake of Paris, and every man's ambition is to live there.

21.1
Sketch made in an airplane – birth of an idea for Rio de Janeiro (1929)

From Le Corbusier, *La Ville Radieuse* (1935)

In England, on the contrary, cities are really no more than necessary evils, required by the machinery of economic exchange. Every man's ambition is to live in the country, and the equivalent of the Paris salon is the country house-party. The interest of the wealthy or educated in the affairs of London are usually for that reason based more on a sense of duty than on affection, and the results are all too apparent. On the other hand, this sense of duty is at the moment more highly stimulated than for many years past, and County Hall, or rather one man in it, shows that he can think broadly on the subject.

In the second place, the success of such schemes depends partly on a feeling of solidarity among the inhabitants of each unit. The units of, say, 1,500 families in this case would be something like a ward, but it is doubtful whether Londoners are capable of a real sense of ward-solidarity. That sense is important, for it is the soundest guarantee against spiritual monotony in such a comparatively uniform town. It may be mentioned that the overall density of population in the *Plan Voisin* works out at 1,000 persons per hectare, say 100 families per acre, with far better open spaces than are given by anything we do now.

A third difficulty would be the intense conservatism of most Londoners, a quality shared in this case with citizens abroad, which in recent years has taken the form of an indiscriminate preservation mania. Those who criticise this habit, often consider that it is nevertheless

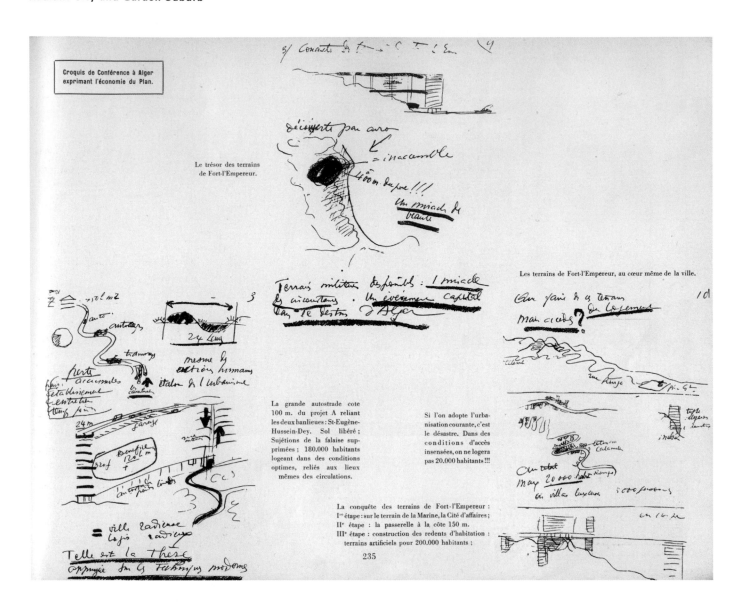

21.2
Sketches explaining the economy of his plan for Algiers

From Le Corbusier, *La Ville Radieuse* (1935)

an error on the right side as a safeguard against vandalism, but it is surely more of a crime to prevent the seeds of our own age ever fructifying than to allow the fine flower of a past age (not perhaps the very finest) to wither. Actually it may be that many of our preservation maniacs take this view, and that if something as grand as Carlton House Terrace could be produced for the new order, Carlton House Terrace might be allowed to go.

Fourthly, there is this horror of the machine and its 'artificial' products, and the widest possible use of the machine is, of course, essential for the making of a city of this kind. Le Corbusier confesses that in his younger days he had a great distaste for such 'artificial' materials and that he only came to prefer them when he realised that they were merely improved by man for the better service of his 'natural' needs. Human nature, real human nature, must come before sub-human nature.

Fifthly and finally, the question of social reorganisation. Here the most pressing need is the public ownership at least of urban land. Most of us concerned with building in London know this quite well, though some of us are afraid of being dubbed communists and losing our practice. We must decide now, however, whether we are going to try and hammer out an equitable plan to-day or wait for a revolution to-morrow.

The opposing school of thought, associated with the name of Sir Raymond Unwin, favours the satellite town, but there are overwhelming arguments against it. The confusion of urban and rural life results in devitalising suburban conditions instead of a clear distinction between town and country. The lack of organic life in the satellite, apart from a few forced and self-conscious activities, is as depressing as the lack of a true citizenship for the individual. Transport becomes uneconomic, and the city proper degenerates into a chaos of drudgeries. There are many undeniable merits in the garden city area, and it is certainly an improvement on the model artisans' dwellings of Queen's Park, but fundamentally it is an escape from the problem.

It would seem, however, that even if development on the general lines of Le Corbusier's schemes were sponsored by the Beaverbrook, the Rothermere and every other press, it would be effectively hindered; but do not let us be too certain. It is in essence the right answer, and in time it may even percolate behind the Ionic capitals of County Hall. Some of the detailed proposals may be more readily considered, such as the plea for legalising the balcony dwelling, a double height living room of, say, 15 ft. with the lesser rooms 7 ft. and full cross ventilation (Programme of La Sarraz, 1928*). (There are helpful suggestions for the building industry as well, such, for example, as the advantages of a standard height of door with varying widths in place of our present peculiarly arbitrary classification.) But the value of the book lies in its general doctrine and in the superbly sane approach behind that doctrine. It may have in it a touch of what Frank Lloyd Wright calls the Café Philosopher, but it is at least a clear objective statement, and to that extent more valuable than an Autobiography.

In its presentation it is a delight to the eye (and no less to the fingers and the nostrils) an achievement considering the difficulties under which these things are done in a depression; and it is not a luxury book; its type was not specially designed, nor was the paper hand-made in Japan, but it might well supersede many such volumes on the hall table. The selection of photographs and drawings – some of them illustrative, some purely symbolic – and the skill with which they are laid out, are noteworthy. The value of the frontispiece, a black and white reproduction of one of the author's paintings, is more doubtful.

An English translation should be considered, less for the sake of architectural students, who will devour it anyway, than for those members of our local town-planning authorities who are deterred by the French, for Le Corbusier has been too long considered merely a stimulant for the schools, or at best a private inspiration to some of our moderns.

Source: *Journal of the Royal Institute of British Architects*, 4 April 1936

*Inaugural meeting of the Congres Internationaux d'Architecture Moderne (CIAM). (Eds)

The Crystal Palace: a Tribute

By Le Corbusier

The Crystal Palace (Figs 22.1 and 22.2) no longer exists. What has disappeared with it was not a curiosity, but one of the great monuments of nineteenth-century architecture.

That century had a strange destiny. It engendered the architecture of the modern world, exemplifying it in immense and splendid structures. This architecture was the fruit of discovery, of the joy of creation, and of enthusiasm. The mind of man suddenly began to compass unguessed and amazing perspectives. The iron and glass which were furnished by the rising new industries allowed unprecedented forms to be evoked, dimensions such as one may say architecture had never known. I mean the dimensions of those vaulted buildings and huge covered markets that were as light within as fields seen under the open sky. They were built of iron and glass. The international exhibitions of that age of discoveries offered fruitful opportunities for realizing structures of this kind. In London as in Paris stupendous palaces were raised ... but these were fated to gather about them all the worst excrescences of the successive stages of a rising tide of bourgeois revulsion. While the new world was being born the forces of reaction rose *en masse*. Academism invaded government departments, the schools and institutions. Never had architecture sunk to such a low ebb. The most baneful temper prevailed. It gained the day, and as a result those magnificent vaults of iron and glass which had been the heralds of a new age were demolished right and left.

By some miracle the Crystal Palace still remained as a last witness of that era of faith and daring. One could go and see it, and feel there how far we have still to go before we can hope to recover that sense of scale which animated our predecessors in all they wrought.

In every country and under all forms of government the last onslaughts of the spirit of reaction are now striving to crush our endeavours. We are accused of being demented or irresponsible. And the real tragedy is just that these witnesses in our defence are no longer extant. When, two years ago, I saw the Crystal Palace for the last time, I could not tear my eyes from the spectacle of its triumphant harmony. The lesson was so tremendous that it made me feel how puny our own attempts still are. But I felt, too, how eminently justifiable and practicable our proposals are, *if only they get a chance*. In them we are simply following the same line of development as the great constructors of the nineteenth century had traced.

22.1
**Crystal Palace, Sydenham, London
(1854)**

Architect: Sir Joseph Paxton
Photographers: Dell & Wainwright (ca. 1936)

Architecture is not a manifestation of the styles of the schools. It is a way of thinking, of achieving order, and of expressing contemporary problems in terms of materials. Today, when the whole world has got to be refashioned, our towns as the countryside, and great communal undertakings appear both urgent and inevitable, we have more need than ever of the assurance that we can forge ahead – more need than ever of not being afraid to see too clearly or too big.

That 'uniformity,' of which so much has been heard among the various arguments used to assail the New Architecture, offered a convincing example of its plastic possibilities in the Crystal Palace, where all was grandeur and simplicity.

Source: *Architectural Review*, February 1937

22.2
Crystal Palace, Sydenham, London (1854)

Architect: Sir Joseph Paxton
Photographers: Dell & Wainwright (ca. 1936)

The MARS Group Exhibition:
the Elements of Modern Architecture

By Le Corbusier

*The MARS (Modern Architectural Research Group) exhibition was held at the New Burlington Galleries, London, between 11 and 29 January 1938. (Eds)

On January 19th [1938] I dropped out of an airplane into the midst of a charming demonstration of youth, which revealed the architecture of tomorrow to be as smiling as it is self-reliant. Much has certainly been accomplished. It is no longer a case of fighting a battle all over the world, but of a victory already won in every part of it.

The characteristic quality of the New Architecture – and therefore of this MARS Exhibition* – is that it anticipates the needs of mankind. Consequently, it substitutes dwellings which vouchsafe their inmates all the essential joys of life for the gloomy dens built during the last century. The New Architecture springs from the depths of the human heart. That is why it has launched a deliberate crusade against brutality, indifference, selfishness, and stupidity. This generous sentiment has prevailed because it knew how to dispose of the marvellous resources which the Mechanical Age has put into our hands. Those constructive weapons were the fruit of a *Technical Revolution*. Thanks to it, the sensibility of our generation has been able to discover or create those new forms which the modern dwelling embodies.

These have been perceived more or less clearly, though often intuitively. That MARS, the British national group of the international federal organization known as *Les Congrès Internationaux d'Architecture Moderne*, has been able to plan and produce this magnificent exhibition in London is sufficient proof of this. (Figs 23.1 and 23.2) C.I.A.M., as the parent body is usually called, was founded in 1928 at the Château de La Sarraz, in Switzerland – not to solve the general economic problems of modern architecture, but to affirm its moral principles which had been outraged by the jury's verdict on the competition for the Palace of the League of Nations at Geneva. Though that conference awoke vital echoes in a score of different countries, it was as much the quality of heart as that of mind of the enlightened men who took part in it which brought into being these various national groups.

In this London exhibition you are confronted by men of good faith and goodwill, men with the enthusiasm and sensitiveness of artists, who found their architectural faith on the heart of man, imbued with the tender aspiration to shape a home for it that shall be truly such on every day in the year. But to do so they have to face the gravest problems of planning, sociology, and economics – problems which raise the question of *action* as the only answer to *inertia* and *routine*.

But there is another reason why MARS has been able to score such a brilliant success. Important industrial enterprises and wealthy commercial organizations appreciated the

23.1
**MARS Group Exhibition, New
Burlington Gardens, London (1938)**

Photographer: Alfred Cracknell (1938)

23.2
**Architecture and garden landscape
area, MARS Group Exhibition, New
Burlington Gardens, London (1938)**

Photographer: Alfred Cracknell (1938)

generosity of mind which animates the Group, and have contributed so liberally to its funds that it was possible to stage this exhibition under conditions I have never seen approached elsewhere. Is it Old England's greatest secret that, in her chosen hour, she always knows how to blend the noblest ideals with the measured realities of hard economic facts?

What strikes one particularly in this exhibition is the elegance, the intimate eloquence, of its sequence of presentations, none of which could possibly alarm anybody. The visitor is led by the hand, and almost imperceptibly finds himself convinced by one after another. The sunshine of innumerable electric globes suffuses every room in the gallery with the soft atmosphere of springtime. The pictorial argument adopted – a selection of photographs chosen from the whole world – is so arranged that from every angle the pure prisms of the New Architecture can be seen rising out of sunlit trees and lawns, or from the water's edge. There are great glass bays bathed with light; interiors lovingly proportioned to the human scale. Some rooms have been actually reproduced with their furniture so as to offer the visitor a concrete fulfilment of the expectancy born of all these photographs.

The party I attended in this setting was a crowd so delighted with all it saw as to let itself be gently carried away by the promise of town-planning, construction, and technology – things which by all the rules ought to have been invincibly tedious and forbidding. But the only memories of these the guests took away with them were of the lyrical appeal of those poems in steel, glass, and concrete. The New Architecture can no longer be reproached with being mere insensitive and soulless technics. The MARS Exhibition will prevent the repetition of such calumnies as these.

The greater task still lies before us. The benefits of the New Architecture must not be confined to the homes of the few who enjoy the privilege of taste or money. They must be widely diffused to as to brighten the homes, and thus the lives, of millions upon millions of workers. That is the present position in all its earnestness, and that is why our generosity impels us to pursue this aim and assure its triumph. It necessarily postulates the most crucial issue of our age: a great campaign for the rational re-equipment and proper utilization of whole countries regarded as indivisible units. Granted a due aesthetic sensibility to form, that campaign will enable us to carry out vast undertakings, like the rebuilding of our towns, in a spirit of grandeur, nobility, and dignity. When the hour for it strikes, planning – urban, regional, national, international – will become humanity's omnipotent orderly officer, the universal disposer, the Supreme Architect.

In very truth our epoch holds out the promise of a fresh cycle of architecture that shall express the new Mechanistic Civilization we are now entering on – a civilization that has no reason to prove inferior to any which have preceded it, and ought to be worthier, purer, more resplendent than all of them.

One must be allowed a little indulgence to weave such luminous dreams as these after seeing the MARS Exhibition, for that exhibition was one where youth and enthusiasm have expressed themselves in purity and precision.

Source: *Architectural Review,* March 1938

Le Corbusier: Review of *Le Corbusier & Pierre Jeanneret: Oeuvre Complète 1934–1938*

By John Summerson

In a bookshop on the Boulevard St. Germain, during the summer of 1924, we noticed Le Corbusier's name for the first time. It was a copy of *Vers une Architecture*. We did not buy it. It was the work of a crank (anybody could see that), probably of some ignoble layman trying to put it across the profession. We knew, in those days, what architecture was. It was a matter mostly of 'scholarship', but also compounded of subtle things like 'artistry' and 'restraint.' It had much to do with Wren, whose bi-centenary we had just been celebrating; it had more to do with Bush House and the Beaux Arts Albums. So we looked down our noses at *Vers une Architecture* and bought a five-frame thriller.

But there was no escape. Within a year or so it was irritating to find Le Corbusier quoted by highbrow laymen, and quoted to the disadvantage of 'artistry' and 'restraint' and the rest of the comfortable jargon rehearsed at 9 Conduit Street*. Could be it be that Le Corbusier *was* somebody after all? It was consoling to know that the teachers in the schools had not heard of him. But some of the students had, and a copy of the strange new book was passed round. Of course, one could not take it *seriously*, this sort of thing. It was as bad as this man Mendelsohn and his crazy tower at Potsdam. Still, it was clever, suggestive. Perhaps even more than that. Somehow this foreigner, this outsider, this man who had never heard (one supposed) of Wren, managed to connect things up in a way that was surprising, but – one had to admit it – right. One began to look at aircraft, at silos, at the streams of London traffic, at clothes, at furniture, with a new interest. It seemed that there was a horizon beyond the Rome Scholarship, and, yes, even beyond the Royal Gold Medal. It seemed that the real horizon of architecture was part of the horizon of modern life ...

And so a generation grew up. To-day Le Corbusier is the name which, next to Wren and Lutyens, the English layman knows best. With Picasso and Einstein and Freud he stands for the new, the queer, and in nine cases out ten, the suspect. To the student he is everything – the epitome of a movement, the harbinger of a new order. It no longer takes three years to discover him; the first-year student's first excursion into design is more likely to be the Pavillon Suisse than with, say, Hampton Court or the Piccadilly Midland Bank. There can be no architectural school in Europe, perhaps none in the world, where Le Corbusier's influence, his aphorisms, his idioms, have not penetrated.

All this being so, and what need we say of the book before us except that it records very admirably the last five years of the great man's works, including the town plans for

*Royal Institute of British Architects. (Eds)

24.1
Project for the Bata Pavilion in the Exposition Internationale des Arts et des Techniques dans la Vie Moderne, Paris (1937) as illustrated in *Oeuvre Complète, vol. 3 1934–38* **(1939)**

From *Architect & Building News,*
14 July 1939

Nemours and Zlin, the Education Building now in progress at Rio, the competition scheme for the Paris art galleries of 1937, the model village, several small houses, the Pavillon de l'Esprit Nouveau (with the rejected scheme for the Bastion Kellermann), and a number of other designs unknown in this country. (Fig. 24.1) A few essays by Le Corbusier and others do not substantially increase the value of the book, whose main purpose, like that of its three predecessors, is to record and illustrate work in progress. To the Le Corbusier fan the book, is of course, essential.

Source: *Architect & Building News,* 14 July 1939

Part 2

1940–1949:

Building upon the Canon

Contributors

Lionel Brett
Gordon Holt
Colin Rowe
John Summerson
and
Le Corbusier

The 'Poetry' of Le Corbusier

By John Summerson

Part of a Lecture Delivered at the Warburg Institute

It is common to hear Le Corbusier described as 'the poet of the Modern Movement.' It was different in the nineteen-twenties; then we were struck by the dissonance of his formal arrangements and the harshness of his industrial-looking silhouettes. It took most of us a long time to swallow the Ozenfant House (1922). (Fig. 25.1) But now he is 'the poet.' His later work has shown in what direction the earlier work was moving, and his whole achievement seems, in a profound, revolutionary sense, romantic.

It may be useful to inquire what this means. How and why is Le Corbusier a 'poet' and a 'romantic'? Let us take a look at what he has done during the last fifteen or twenty years.

The Ozenfant House was, certainly, a turning point. Behind it was the period of experiment, mostly on paper – the 'Dom-ino' and 'Citrohan' standard types, the writing of *Vers une Architecture*, the period of education under Perret and Behrens; the first revolts from the Art Nouveau of L'Eplattenier and the decorative manner of Hoffmann. After the Ozenfant House came a few years of intensive development, till maturity was definitely reached with the Garches Villa of 1927.

In the thirteen years since this house was built Le Corbusier has changed little. He has tackled bigger problems with no loss of vitality and incredible mastery of his own innovations. He still shows no signs of becoming the mannerist of his own school. But by 1927 one can recognise the *fait accompli*. The Le Corbusier revolution is a fact.

In what exactly does this revolution consist? A good approach here, I think, is the Euclidean one of saying: Suppose the answer to be so-and-so and see where it leads us. Suppose, then, that the Le Corbusier 'revolution' is a projection of the point of view of nineteenth-century materialism as propounded, say, by Viollet-le-Duc. This would mean that what he has done has been to set up the engineer's criterion of 'performance,' and, within the humanistic framework of geometrical rules represented by his *tracés regulateurs*, to bring together every available resource of engineering and industrial production in order to effect efficient solutions of building problems. In other words, that he has taken Perret's rationalisation one step beyond Perret and detached it from its tenuous Beaux Arts anchorage, leaving aesthetic considerations practically at the mercy of empirical standards of efficiency.

That is the interpretation which was placed upon Le Corbusier's work when his first great innovations – the Ozenfant House, for instance – came before the public. That vulgar

25.1
Ozenfant house, 53 avenue Reille, Paris (1924)

Photographer: Lance Knobel (ca. 1984)

word 'functionalism' was coined to express this point of view. 'Functionalism' stood for a theory of design for performance; it stood for the introduction of engineering standards into architecture to replace aesthetic standards. Le Corbusier's deliberately hyperbolic description of a house as a *machine à habiter* was adduced to support the view that just as a propeller, mathematically designed for efficiency, produced a beautiful shape, so a house designed with equal precision would turn out equally, and as inevitably, graceful.

I need hardly say that the 'functionalist' theory will not bear a moment's examination, and that the parallel of the propeller is meaningless. The design of a propeller is a circumscribed problem in the circumscribed science of aerodynamics. It is a calculable problem. The design of a house is not circumscribed at all. It is incalculable. If you try to formulate the problem presented by a house you will find so many alternatives – so much scope for what laboratory workers call 'aesthetic choice' – that by the time you have made a watertight formulation of the problem you have already designed the house.

'Functionalism' was a journalistic derivative of Le Corbusier. Its chief importance has been as a weapon in the hands of fools who have triumphantly succeeded in showing how wrong it is of modern architecture to be what it is not, never has been, and never could be. I cite the 'functionalist' nonsense here because, when its utter fallibility is exposed, we are brought right back to the original issue in a categorical form, and we have to ask ourselves: What is the nature of the aesthetic sanction in Le Corbusier's work? For aesthetic sanction there must be. In the design of any object not strictly controllable by calculation intuition leaps ahead of logic, adumbrating a pattern to which logic, somehow or other, conforms. Look at any building you like, as remote as you like from consciousness of aesthetic purpose, and you will notice how as soon as a choice of alternatives comes before the builder he inevitably conforms to some dimly perceived tradition of formal arrangement. There is no escape. The aesthetically negative building is a virtual impossibility – as much an impossibility as that abstract, uncivilised, unspoiled savage dear to seventeenth-century philosophers.

I believe that, in the case of Le Corbusier's architecture, the aesthetic sanction derives from the modern school of painting – the school which comprises Braque, Léger, Juan Gris, and the monumental, all-embracing Picasso. I suppose it is really pretty obvious that this is so, even if Le Corbusier, who is usually the best guide to his own psychological indebtednesses, has not, so far as I know, said so himself. But then painting has always been so much part of his life that he might very well not be conscious of the process of deriving and converting of which he has been the agent. Le Corbusier has been at the centre of French artistic life ever since he was discovering the ethnological treasures of the Trocadéro, when Picasso and Modigliani were discovering them. He is a painter himself (under the name of Jeanneret) whose canvasses clearly owe very much to Léger and hardly less to Picasso. He is not a great painter, but he has been a worker in the same laboratory as the great painters, knows how to use their tools, and is completely identified with their artistic outlook. How could he help but bring the painters' revolutionary aesthetic to architecture?

I suppose that anybody who is familiar with non-representational painting and has a feeling for it must sometimes have the experience of seeing commonplace objects in chance relationships which, as it were, 'speak the language' of the painters – which suggest, for a second or two, the poetry of a Picasso *collage* or a Braque still-life. It is something of this kind which, developed to an extraordinary intensity, enables Le Corbusier to collect ideas, methods and forms from every quarter – from industrial technique, from cheap building practice, from local vernaculars, from machine design – and bring them together into a single whole which has an architectural quality rarely, if ever, surpassed.

Perhaps, on the face of it, you will think there can be very little in common between, say, one of Léger's complex organisations of remembered fragments and Le Corbusier's simple rectangular houses. Superficially true. The link with painting cannot be read easily in the elevations; it goes much deeper than that. Le Corbusier knows, what the Ecole des Beaux Arts has known and taught for two centuries, that the genesis of a building is its plan – 'le plan générateur,' he calls it. If you would see the connection between a Le Corbusier building and the French tradition of painting, put one of his later plans side by side with a painting or drawing by Picasso (or Léger if you like; though, in spite of Le Corbusier's obvious devotion to this painter, it is Picasso who is more plainly reflected in his work).

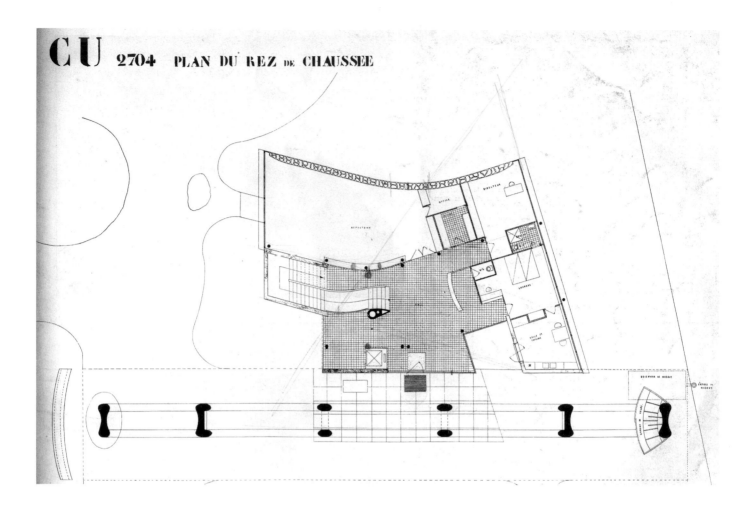

Put the plan of the Garches Villa or the Swiss Students' Hostel (Fig. 25.2) beside the Picasso Harlequin … I think you will agree with me that there is complete harmony between these two productions. The lines make a rather similar sort of counterpoint; there are the same tensions in the curves. One is even tempted to be quite literal: to find Harlequin's sharp nose (or noses) in the plan and tiled flooring in Harlequin's clothes! To convince you of this close and intimate relationship between an architect's and a painter's work it might be necessary to show you many more plans and many more paintings than is possible here. My point is that it is the formal discoveries of the modern painters which have rendered Le Corbusier's revolution in architecture possible. It is a most remarkable instance of the way in which graphic artists, working in considerable isolation, in a remote 'laboratory' atmosphere may influence, ultimately, the whole architectural language of Europe, and, indeed, of the world.

Having said this much about the connection between Le Corbusier's architecture and modern painting, I feel I ought to say it again in quite different terms. It is so easy, by narrowing down an argument, to distort it into speciousness. I can see some horrid textbook of the future saying: 'Le Corbusier's planning was much influenced by the drawings of

25.2
Pavillon Suisse, Cité Universitaire, Paris (1932)

From Le Corbusier, *Oeuvre Complète, vol. 2 1929–34* (1935)

Pablo Picasso' – which is sheer nonsense. That comparison I gave was merely a pointer-reading. Behind it is the new outlook of the modern painters – the new emotional pattern made by their observations of the world. These Le Corbusier shares; it is these which make his buildings what they are. Further than that I will not presume to go.

Now, if Le Corbusier has something of the painter in his make-up, he also has very much of the poet. He has the poet's penetrating imagination, which sees the reverse logic of every situation, sees that what appears absurd is perhaps only more profoundly true than what appears to make sense. His architecture is full of those contraries which have an extraordinary, exciting logic of their own. Writing this, I am reminded of two lines of Wyndham Lewis's*:

*One-Way Song (1933). (Eds)

> Ring all bells backwards, enter by sally-ports,
> Make towers of wells, night clubs of lunch resorts.

That matches, rather well, the poetry of Le Corbusier. Tell him that 'The house stands in the garden.' He will say: 'No, the garden stands in the house,' and prove it in one of his buildings. Tell him that 'A house is four windows, with walls for privacy and shade.' Put it to him as axiomatic that a park is a space for recreation in a town. He will say: 'Nothing of the kind; in the future the park will not be in the town, but the town in the park; work is an incident in life, life is not an incident in work.' In the details of planning this passion for opposites is ubiquitous. To take one example: We habitually think of a chimney breast as an excrescence from the wall of a room; so Le Corbusier gives us a room which is loosely arranged round a free-standing chimney breast. And – one last example – Le Corbusier is the great apostle of fresh air, so what does he do but advocate that all windows shall be hermetically sealed – so that scientifically cleansed air can be pumped in!

All this is so like poetry that – well, it is poetry. Le Corbusier 'makes towers of wells' and 'enters by sally-ports.' It is far on the way to Surrealism, which it seems to me is most of the time a literary, poetic activity, whether manifested in poetry, paintings, sculpture, *objets trouvés*, or what you will. Recently, Le Corbusier designed a week-end cottage with an open fire burning in a grate in the courtyard. Isn't that very nearly a painting by Magritte?

These relationships with poetry and painting seem to me to show pretty clearly what the 'romanticism' of Le Corbusier means. It means that he has a power of synthesis exactly comparable to that of the major poets and painters of our time. This has enabled him to bring together the tradition of 'abstract' or 'constructivist' painting and the very diffuse traditions of experimental architecture, and present them to the world, for the first time, not merely in combination, but as a new unity – as the resultant of many converging forces, which, until his arrival, no man was big enough to grasp all at once. It is a prodigious imaginative achievement, which one can only compare with, say, Michaelangelo's inauguration of the Baroque; and that comparison is interesting because in both cases you have a man with a strongly poetic imagination, who is also a painter, entering the field of architecture and setting a new direction.

Source: *Architect & Building News*, 5 April 1940

Corbusier

By Gordon Holt

So much harm is told me of this man, and I see so little of it, that I begin to suspect obtrusive merits in him that snuff out the merit in others.

La Bruyère

Commissioned two months ago by *Building* to enquire, in France itself, upon the stage reached by French Reconstruction (the results of which enquiry will appear later in this review), I was led to interview M. Raoul Dautry, State Minister of Reconstruction and Urbanism, and also some of his professional advisers, namely: Messrs. Auguste Perret, membre de l'Institut, Le Corbusier, and André Lurçat. All three names are well known to architectural circles outside France and all three were at one time or another symbols of a radical break from custom. Bluntly, they were rebels, and, to a varying extent, still are. Thus, they form the 'left' wing of that body of professional men called together by M. Dautry to advise him upon the architectural, the town-planning feasibility and merit of whatever plans – previously approved by Departmental authorities – shall be submitted to rebuild France's ravaged towns.

Such initiative gives us a measure not only of M. Dautry's broad-mindedness but also of the whole country's determination that this time (as compared with 1918 and after) France shall not leave unused the best talents of her sons.

To date, the Minister has entrusted Le Corbusier with the replanning of Palisse-La Rochelle, a maritime region besieged and wrecked by the British a dozen times through the centuries, and now partly, though seriously, wrecked by the Germans at the end of their occupation. M. Dautry has also teamed with him Marcel Lods to develop St. Gaudens, small industrial town up in the Pyrénées where petrol has been discovered and which, for obvious reasons, the French Government are anxious to enlarge on efficient lines. Lods is a most capable architect; he was mentioned in a recent article on French prefabrication.

A third assignment has, since the war, come in L.C.'s way, but not through the Ministry. In its hasty retreat one of the German armies totally flattened St. Dié, in the N.E. of France. Faced with a complex task, M. André, the town architect, asked L.C.'s help, the more readily as the inhabitants brought pressure to bear not, let it be said, to discredit the local man, but because they remembered the shocking mess made of northern towns and villages after the last war by authorities of little repute, and hungry jobbers. (Fig. 26.1)

26.1
Model for the civic centre of St. Dié (1945)

Photographer: Walter Dräyer (1957)

The other appointments – like all others throughout Metropolitan France, whether decided by boroughs or the Ministry of Reconstruction – are of quite recent date. The truth is, France has not yet got off the mark; or, to be exact, the organism is set up and over a hundred towns boasting more than 50,000 souls have had a qualified architect or town-planner put in charge of their reconstruction plans, but these last are only now being studied. It would therefore seem unreasonable to expect for many months French equivalents to the fine designs already turned out over here, as at Bristol, Liverpool or Coventry. Still, they will come; we may confidently await admirable solutions.

André Lurçat's sketch plans, part of Perret's for Le Havre, and L.C.'s for Palisse-La Rochelle, I have been privileged to scan in their respective offices. None of the three goes farther than a rudimentary stage. Strangely enough, the Ministry keeps cagey about them; it fears, as other Ministries in the past often have suffered, indiscretions ventilated in the Home Press, premature disclosures. Be this as it may, anyone who has peered behind the veil is urged to reticence, if not complete secrecy.

An unfortunate embargo. I am afraid it may rob this article of much current interest. Nevertheless, enough remains to focus afresh the thoughts of British architects upon a personality that has not only made L.C. what he is – bull to some, red rag to others – but promises added surprises. I base the prophecy, hedged with sobering ifs, upon the one undeniable and indeed constant characteristic separating his work from the work of other famous architects. It can be spelt 'departure,' the steady shaking of premises hitherto accepted. Since renewed activities may be expected from him, it should not be amiss to consider its progress and influence.

Proper approach must be effected through its general development, only thus can one weigh the causes behind the squibs and grenades that he hurled from 1920 onwards.

To give him his due, the squibs are few; they concern minor things, furniture gadgets, no more; the rest proceeds from two sources esteemed so far as the intellect goes but far less relished whenever they gush forth into our life. Indeed, when stiffened with puritanism, logic can be a nuisance, it takes so little account of details, positively spurns customs. L.C. has more than a normal quorum of either; he also has been endowed with a quality not unseldom found, so to speak, stuck on to logic and puritanism: pugnacity.

My acquaintanceship with L.C. goes back over twenty years. I think I am correct in stating I was the first to introduce him to Anglo-Saxon architects. Of course it was less my text than the scandalous photographs illustrating it that, like so many stones, disturbed our placid pool. What far cry from the gabled domesticities of Dawber, the finialled town architecture of Blomfield and Lutyens, their regard for precedence, texture, and other gracious relevancies (at least, we thought them so) to the naked, rude, hatless cubes offered to our gaze without one word of apology – on the contrary, with exceedingly blunt manifestos.

True, on this side of the Channel not everyone damned such monstrosities; a few minds had been stuck, some years before, by the plea of Wyndham Lewis denouncing, in his Caliph pamphlet, the whole tribe in favour of engineers and painters: let these alone build our bridges, museums, and houses. So there were already doubts and fulminations; but how far between such outbursts and how little did they penetrate! The profession they influenced not a whit; insular continuity, prejudices, proved strong enough to ward off skirmishing blows.

Heavier ones more often applied still came from the Continent, from whence, pretend our diehards, issue most of our misfortunes; France, Germany, little Holland were suspected areas – and particularly France; in France, Paris, where lived and worked Swiss-born L.C.

I saw him again in 1924, again a year later, during the Paris exhibition of Decorative Arts; a fourth, fifth and sixth time through the 1928–30 period, marked by the furore caused when the dubious awards that ended the international concours for the League of Nations palace was in some respects at its highest. Placed first, then, in deference to academic susceptibilities, pulled back to rank *ex aequo* with other premiated designs (over 800 were sent in) L.C.'s design gave rise to a mighty row; it also spurred on its way the old tag about blessings in disguise, for, albeit he lost the commission to an Italo-French team, L.C. by his most able and pertinent scheme gained, at one stroke, a deserved celebrity. He has been on the map ever since.

The reason? Logic, undodgeable in the end. We distrust it. By dubbing a man a doctrinaire, we mean to damn that rigid process of thought that bores its way up, regardless of consequences, to the fulfilment of an idea; whereas, on the Continent, a doctrine will always be a most respectable thing, valuable to boot, since it requires both canon and discipline.

L.C. calmly, repeatedly, calls himself a doctrinaire.

In their earlier days L.C. and the painter l'Ozenfant (now in the U.S.A. after some years in England) edited the periodical *L'Esprit Nouveau*, wherein aesthetic doctrines and, to a lesser extent, social theories, were applied to painting and architecture. Their drift led toward much severity, known as purism, still practised.

Five years before L.C. began practice, together they had written a book, *After Cubism*, in which the germ of valid theories can be found. Soon afterwards l'Ozenfant asked his friend to build him a house and studio; followed by coupled residences at Auteuil for Messrs. Jeanneret and La Roche, this last a wealthy patron of Picasso, Braque, Léger and others. Besides ramps instead of stairs, these two houses for the first time saw the emergence of the framed *pilotis* or piers upon with L.C. later was to place, freed from ground ties, most of his buildings and all his staggering projects for 'cartesian' skyscrapers, the huge cross-like or double-Y buildings, kernels of his 'Radiant Town.'

Between 1923–26 should be placed the garden-city at Pessac, near Bordeaux. (Fig. 26.2) Fifty houses were erected from standardised ferro-concrete elements; prefabrication

26.2
Housing at Pessac (1927)

From *Architecture Vivante*, Autumn 1927

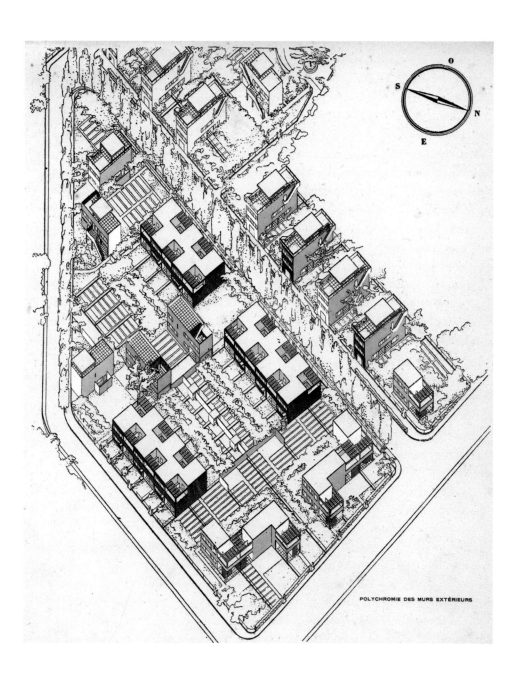

POLYCHROMIE DES MURS EXTÉRIEURS

(though the word was then unknown) was born. Polychromy reigned among their façades. It is impossible to say whether, after further trials, it might have succeeded or not; the odds are that it would, because L.C. has a subtle eye for colours, lines, and volumes. The fifty-first house was barely up when the time-bomb placed months earlier in the municipal services bringing water, gas, electricity on the site exploded, no longer were those service available; sabotage had been carried out after a virulent campaign. To be known, to pioneer, may be sweet; it also brings, and creates, bitterness.

It seems far too little known outside France that L.C. is no less a painter than an architect; throughout life he has sketched, painted forms, above all their relationship. This accounts for his place in that narrow stream of artists who, like Michael Angelo, da Vinci, Picasso, were possessed by more than one form of art if their appetite for universalism was to be satisfied. Nowadays, we have become accustomed to so much specialisation that we fail to gauge the harm it can do. It is a hearty sign when a painter turns to clay – an architect towards brushes and oil colours.

Corbu (as some affectionately call him) has done so from the time he met l'Ozenfant; and never given it up. Over 200 oil pictures, hundreds of drawings irreproachable in fracture as fastidious in conception, must be put to his credit. Five exhibitions in Paris, one at Zurich, each a one-man show, provide some test of his quality; London, New York or Stockholm may have theirs too. It should be added, to complete this aspect of L.C.'s creative work, he has carried out mural paintings, [among them] ... two murals done at Cap Martin on the Riviera, designed for himself 25 years ago by Badovici, the architect; the house, if small, is very pleasant, a low white rectangle lapped by the Mediterranean. L.C. adorned it six years ago*.

In 1924 L.C. erected two more houses, for the sculptor Lipschitz and his painter-friend Mietschaninoff, at Boulogne-sur-Seine; another on the lake of Geneva. In all three he struggled with a problem since become insistent, how to achieve compactness without sacrificing the cultured needs of our epoch, how to reconcile both within the calls for an open-air life. He found a solution that has been copied the world over.

This world became still more in his debt after three further experiments which went a long way to confirm the astonishing nature of his originality, though but two were of any size. The first in time – and the smallest – was his Pavilion for *L'Esprit Nouveau*, built within the Decorative Exhibition grounds. I say the date, 1925, heralds the beginning of a period that future historians of architecture should not forget, because certain crucial principles and methods were then evolved by L.C. 'about' configuration or shell-form, relationship of levels within that shell, elasticity of internal arrangements, use of ground freed by *pilotis*; not least though not yet quite apparent, the consequences implicit in a bolder handling of horizontal fenestration.

The *Esprit Nouveau* pavilion embodied the principle – come by fortuitously – that, whenever feasible or reasonable, nature should participate out *and in* the house. A tree stood in the middle of the site; L.C. incorporated it, built round it. Everyone gasped; well, the thing is now familiar in Europe and the two Americas.

At Garches, in the large villa commissioned by Mr. de Monzie, relative (if I mistake not) of the celebrated American writer, Gertrude Stein, the fabric is big, spacious and of course

*E-1027, Roquebrune-Cap-Martin (1926–29) (architect: Eileen Gray). (Eds)

26.3
Villa Savoye, Poissy (1931)

Photographer: John Donat (1971)

26.4
Villa Savoye, Poissy (1931)

From *Architecture Vivante*, Summer 1931

experimental throughout all its parts: it displays chronic tantrums among floor levels internal gardens, gardens above the top floor. We are in 1927. In 1928 came Villa Savoye at Poissy, (Figs 26.3 and 26.4) whose reduced ground floor, less than a third of the house area, adumbrates a *parti* perfected in the Swiss Pavilion built at the *Cité Universitaire* of Paris two years later, and also at the Centrosoyus for Moscow.

The Centrosoyus Palace, followed in 1931 by the immense and truly amazing 'Palace of the Soviets,' (Fig. 26.5) also at Moscow, are two colossal jobs that all too soon became super-worries. The first, the Co-operative Headquarters, was the object of a limited competition in 1928, and was won by L.C., who visited Moscow where he twice revised his

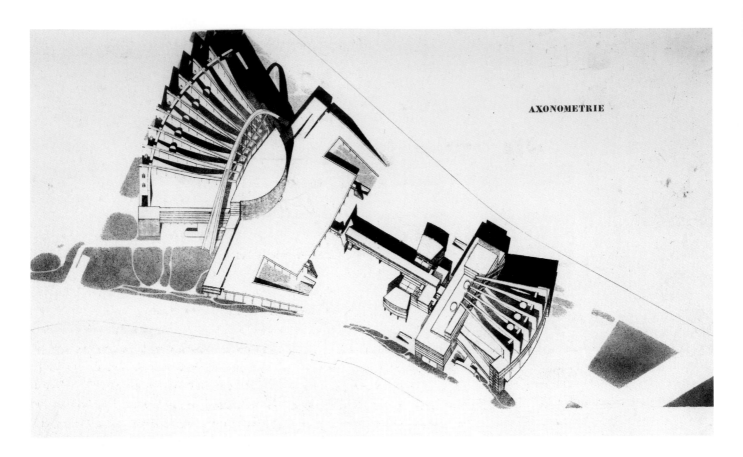

AXONOMETRIE

scheme before building operations began. He saw its seventh floor completed in 1930. Various reasons have held it up since.

In 1931 the U.S.S.R. government chose him for another limited competition, the Palace of the Soviets. His plans were greatly favoured. Bolt from the blue: academic circles who, for political motives, had started intense propaganda lauding classical Russian culture, asked that 'the people' decide who shall be the winner; the people dutifully chose peristyles.

We must look upon the completed work of L.C. as if each job had been an experiment. He himself holds this view; every *chantier* proved a laboratory where technical novelties were tested. Since he made no bones about it, and, in fact, warned his clients that what he was about to build, though their house, was his trial, an experiment, we should praise the stout-heartedness of both architect and patrons, and remember that the last were Continentals, people to whom risks made an appeal. The trait marks a degree of love-in-ideas that an Anglo-Saxon finds hard to reach: how can such things take precedence over the cash-nexus? It also explains why, on the whole, significant impacts upon the tiny world of art come from abroad, Picasso, L.C. might exist in England; they could not live there.

Faith acting amid great perils, such appears the lesson to be drawn from Le Corbusier; a finer one is difficult to conceive.

Source: *Building*, October 1945

26.5
Competition design for the Palace of the Soviets (1931)

The Future of the Architectural Profession

By Le Corbusier

STANDARDISATION

'Do you believe that the future of architecture lies in the direction of standardisation of design and production?'

The terminology used no longer holds good to-day. The word 'architecture' to-day is to be understood rather as an idea than as a material fact. 'Architecture': to put in order, to organise ... in the best possible way ... both spiritually and materially, etc. ... This idea is relevant to innumerable activities, and involves a multiplicity of products: the hull of a liner, an aeroplane, a motor-car, a wireless set, all the varied machines of a centralised electricity system – are these devoid of architecture, or are they nourished by it? I will not reply here, but I will take the liberty of posing the question in other terms.

(a) Do you believe that the future of the building of houses and towns lies in the standardisation of design and production?

I will complete the question by a further interrogation:

(b) Can architecture, with its recognition of higher spiritual values, lend itself to the creation of standardised designs?

(a) 'Do you believe that the future of the building of houses and towns lies in the standardisation of design and production?'

This is certainly my profound conviction; in fact, it is the cause and effect of all my investigations into architecture and town planning since 1922. (*Une Ville Contemporaine de 3 Millions d'Habitants* – Paris, Salon d'Automne.) (Fig. 27.1) To justify this, one must first accept a fundamental postulate:

The Machine Age was born one hundred years ago. During its first epoch, 1830–1930, the machine has shaken the structure of society to its very foundations.

Little by little it has destroyed the artisan tradition; it has raised up new gangs of workers; the calculators (engineers), the chemists, the innumerable physicists devoted to objective research of practical value, the mechanics, most of whom form a technical elite hitherto unknown. The age has created new methods of production: machines making other

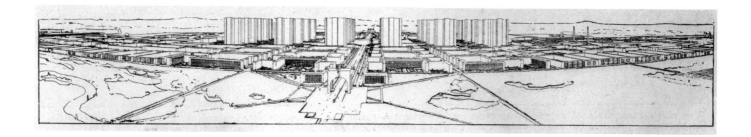

machines. The new machines can supply our daily needs – food, clothing, and amusement, all of a high standard, with amazing rapidity. Another group of these machines gives us speed; a third, energy replacing bodily effort.

This rapid replenishment of food, clothing, or pleasures, has overthrown age-old habits of economy and frugality, and has awakened new desires and created new needs which henceforth must be regarded as essentials.

Speed has permitted the rapid transference of all these products, as well as of human beings, to all parts of the world. Age-old notions of time and distance have been swept away and replaced by a completely new use of the solar day, and this has resulted in an unforeseen division of labour. The family has been torn asunder, society has undergone a violent and incessant upheaval; the concentrations of productive power have dragged together untold masses of workers.

Energy (steam or electricity) has made possible gigantic undertakings under a régime of democratic appearance, whereas formerly such enterprises were only possible, if possible at all, by slavery.

In forty years, through the advent of electricity, the eternal solar rhythm has been upset and altered: night is no longer the signal for sleep. Far from it. Innumerable activities are born of the night which henceforth is vanquished.

This stupendous epoch, the first hundred years of machinery, has forged amazing tools for a society whose every dream seems capable of immediate realisation. The tools are created. The forces, the powers are here.

But during this age of technical achievement, all that was previously the very foundation of society was smashed and laid waste. Man was molested. He was merely looked upon as 'a hand', as a unit of production. Human equilibrium foundered. A page of human history had been turned. We were thrust forth upon another venture – a new venture.

Equilibrium is upset. All is crumbling. Everything must be readjusted – harmony, *the* harmony must be established. This can only be done on the basis of a fundamental factor – the only factor worthy of consideration: the dignity and happiness of man.

Man standing over his machines, commanding his machines, exacting from them the lightening of his labours, man demanding from the vast effort which has just been made, material benefits, happiness and harmony – that is my vision of the future.

The second era of the Machine Age has begun, the era of harmony, the machine in the service of man.

27.1
A contemporary city for three million inhabitants (1922)

From Le Corbusier, *Oeuvre Complète, vol. 1 1910–29* (1929)

This means the undertaking of great works for the equipment of modern society, equipment in towns, dwellings, means of transport, territorial planning, etc. ...

I reply, therefore, to question *(a)*: The task developing upon the second era of the Machine Age – towns and dwellings – is so immense that it constitutes purely and simply the new and gigantic programme of industrial production. Towns, dwellings, farms and agricultural villages: these are to be the products of this new industrialism.

Unsatisfactory processes and results are the concomitant of the old methods of construction (wood, brick, or stone). Neither the machine nor modern methods of work organisation can be applied to them. The advantages of nineteenth to twentieth century equipment cannot be exploited. To-day the problem of towns and dwellings can only be sensibly contemplated if key industry lends itself wholeheartedly to the enterprise.

Houses must no longer be constructed on the site itself with an uncontrolled method of working, and subject to the vagaries of the weather. The house, in all its elements, from the ground upwards, must be fashioned in the metal construction sheds of the manufacturing centres, using metal, wood, or artificial products in the same way as the motor-car is manufactured on a mass-production basis.

But what sort of houses and what sort of towns are we to have from now on? That is the question.

At the moment the town and house specialists – the architects – are absorbed in contradictory controversies, often academic or sophistical, in this time of urgency, when industry is ready to supply our every demand.

These controversies lead nowhere. Styles, ancient or modern. That is not the question. The question is this: modern towns in which man can live serenely, joyously, bring up his family, care for and develop his body, care for and develop his soul, and avail himself, if he so desires, of the greatest possible individual liberty and, with equal freedom, reap the benefits of organised collectivisation.

The problem of the dwelling implies that of the town. Architecture and town planning are only one subject. Let us reply to question *(a)* by saying: It is only by searching for standards which are useful, true, and human, both biologically and psychologically, that big industry will be able to take over building operations, hitherto subjected to ruinous methods which recognise in no way the benefits of our technical conquests. Further, in reply to question *(b)*: *Can architecture, with its recognition of higher spiritual values, lend itself to the creation of standardised designs?* My answer is a decisive 'Yes'. Dwellings and towns, microcosm and macrocosm, shelter for individual, family, and collective life, the very *'emanation'* of the life of a society, of a civilisation, requires organisation of the highest quality for the biological and psychological benefit of man, and *consequently demands the architect*.

But where is the architect who is the architect in this matter? I am convinced that here it is a question of a new spirit in architecture, with new men or men of adaptability, courage and the desire to align themselves with very new conditions. These conditions are of two sorts: first, the answer to be given to fundamental human needs, alike in all classes of society, and that implies a drastic revision of our conceptions of space, and organic arrangements, and an extensive knowledge of technical conquests ... the architect

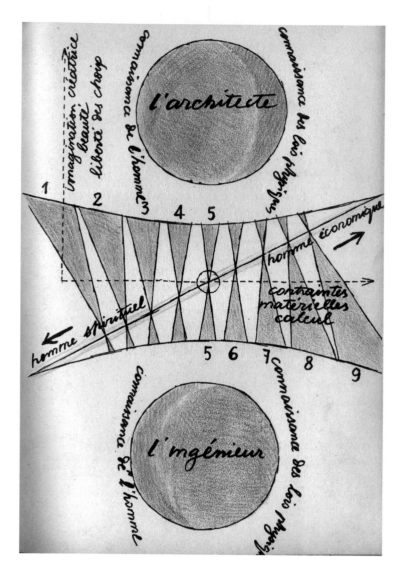

27.2
**The tasks of construction divided
between the architect and the engineer**

From François de Pierrefeu and Le Corbusier,
La Maison des Hommes (1942)

devoting his time to dwellings is akin to the naturalist – he becomes a sort of savant studying 'the animal-man'. Secondly, the reply to be given to all the imperative requirements,
although infinitely elastic, of industrial undertakings; and that implies a very close contact
with the world of industry, working methods, materials, and organisation, etc., and the
architect in this case is akin to the engineer; it is an exacting form of thought which is
expected of him. (Fig. 27.2)

In short, he is more 'architect' than ever. He is an architect in the sense that those were,
who constructed the 'houses' of the past, which possessed every virtue, the best available
technical processes, the most efficient sizes and arrangements. Pleasant, efficient, and economic, where sanity reigned and expressed itself *poetically*. In those times the very word
'architect' was not used. The house was in fact 'folk-lore' (this applies to houses of all countries and civilisations until the advent of the schools and with them – academicism).

SURVIVAL OF THE ARCHITECT

If so, does it mean a technical upheaval for the architect, or will the immense field revealed by the 'science of shelter' supply work for all?

The reply depends solely upon the quality of the professional men concerned – the architects. There are some 'for whom it is too late'; but they can console themselves in executing traditional works well enough during the period of evolution of the towns and dwellings.

I believe, from personal experience, that the new tasks require of us illimitable vigilance, devotion, curiosity, constancy and imagination. Nothing is easier than to construct an accidental type. Once a standard is established it acts like a trap or barrier at each step; the difficulty is immense and all but exceeds the energy of a single man. The question is to discover what standard to adopt, and what requires standardisation. It is in this search for standardisation that towns and dwellings may be brought to their perdition by the application of inhuman standards imposing upon us a crushing boredom, or may, on the contrary, bring forth grace, variety, flexibility, and the infinite manifestations of personality.

I think, therefore, that the 'science of shelter'; as you call it, makes its appeal to a new spirit, and, consequently, to those who are imbued with it. And it is not only the young who should be animated by this spirit.

The future of architecture is certainly not at stake: All the countries of the world have to equip themselves completely in a multitude of things infinitely more numerous than before.

In passing let us pay tribute once again to the crazy book of M. Camille Mauclair, *L'Architecture: Va-t-elle Mourir?* This work defines the issue. Of what does this prophet of woe speak? Of 'Architecture' considered as an activity which to-day has declined, not as this noble and necessary duty: to construct the New Age, whose realisation will bring to mankind 'the essential joys' by proper planning of town and countryside. This 'Architecture', which is in its death throes, was merely one of the forms of the dusk which falls upon the end of a civilisation. There were good intentions in this 'Architecture', but at the same time it harboured all the forces which bolstered up the malevolent reign of Vanity, Imbecility, Plunder, Indolence, and Money. This architecture is dead, yes. Decked out pretentiously in a motley of feathers, embroideries, and decorations, it has prevailed throughout the nineteenth and twentieth centuries and killed the *architectural sense*. It was merely an alien pageant, having nothing in common with our conception of true architecture, *this idea of organising in the best possible way, both materially and spiritually.* With such a gigantic task before us there is no need to wonder whether there will be work for all.

ARCHITECTURE AND THE ECONOMIC SYSTEM

Do you think that in any consideration of the future of architecture the fundamental question is: What economic system will prevail? And, if so, under which economic system will architecture best thrive?

This question touches upon ideas to which my continual work in architecture and town planning has forced me to reply by adopting a clearly defined principle and position amidst the chaotic and tumultuous life of to-day.

The plan is the dictator. Let everyone in his own particular sphere draw up plans in keeping with the new times by getting to the bottom of the question himself, so that he realises what can be done both materially and technically from to-morrow. This mighty task of preparation, these plans, will supply the answer to all questions, they will reveal what measures to take, what laws to make, and the men to be placed in key positions. To-day, in all countries, the same sterile answer is made to the accumulated evils: 'We haven't the necessary laws – it is against the regulations – vested interests are opposed to it – it is useless to contemplate anything whatever which is new, efficient or truthful – circumstances are against it.'

We must, therefore, denounce the circumstances, but denounce them with exactitude. And for this purpose it is necessary to commit oneself to an act of optimism which consists in drawing out on paper definite plans, technically possible, of all that can transform existing evil into immediate good.

Once these plans are made the discussion is closed, and doubt is swept away and replaced by the assurance that: *here is what can be done at once*. Here are New York, Chicago, Paris, and Moscow, such as they should be. No preconceived régime must stand in the way of *the plans*. What are the forces which oppress us to-day? They are merely preconceived régimes: despite the diversity or opposition of doctrines, confusion, and error reign on all sides through lack of plans. The technicians have not done their duty. The régimes, whatever they be, *are not informed, they know not in which direction they are travelling* (in the sphere which occupies our attention). Seen from the planet Mars they would look like machines running empty, without supplies of raw material; *the plans for the equipment of the Machine Civilisation have not been drawn up.*

My line of conduct is to take up my position on the basis of *the plan*: with my feet firmly planted upon it, I can affirm with conviction that such and such initiatives must be taken. The plans will show that in order to safeguard the indispensable benefits of individual liberty, profit by collective effort, and put a stop to the frenzied wastefulness of our present-day towns, it is necessary to prepare for the realisation of communal enterprises. To-day, we must rescue from misery millions of human beings, victims of neglect and egoism. Build dwellings, reform the cellular unit of our towns, equip the countries of the world – that is the task that lies before us all.

Source: *Plan: Arch. S.A. Quarterly*, no. 2, 1947

The Mathematics of the Ideal Villa: Palladio and Le Corbusier Compared

By Colin Rowe

There are two causes of beauty – natural and customary. Natural is from geometry consisting in uniformity, that is equality, and proportion. Customary beauty is begotten by the use, as familiarity breeds a love to things not in themselves lovely. Here lies the great occasion of errors, but always the true test is natural or geometrical beauty. Geometrical figures are naturally more beautiful than irregular ones: the square, the circle are the most beautiful, next the parallelogram and the oval. There are only two beautiful positions of straight lines, perpendicular and horizontal; this is from Nature and consequently necessity, no other than upright being firm.

Sir Christopher Wren

Palladio's Villa Capra, called the Rotunda, has, perhaps more than any other house, imposed itself on the imagination of subsequent generations, and as the ideal type of central building. It has become part of the general European experience. Mathematical, abstract, four square, without apparent function, its dry aristocratic derivatives have enjoyed universal diffusion; when he writes of it Palladio is lyrical.

The site is as pleasant and delightful as can be found, because it is upon a small hill of very easy access, and is watered on one side by the Bacchiglione, a navigable river: and on the other it is encompassed about with most pleasant risings, which look like a very great theatre and are all cultivated about with most excellent fruits and most exquisite vines; and, therefore, as it enjoys from every part most beautiful views, some of which are limited, some more extended, and others which terminate with the horizon; there are loggias made in all four fronts.

When the mind is prepared for the one by the other, a passage from Le Corbusier's *Précisions* is unavoidably reminiscent of this. No less lyrical, but rather more explosive, he is describing the site of his Maison Savoye at Poissy.

Le site, une vaste pelouse bombée en dome aplâti ... La maison est une boîte en l'aire au milieu des prairies dominant le Verger. Il est à sa juste place dans l'agreste paysage de Poissy. Les habitants venus ici parce que cette campagne agreste était belle avec sa vie de campagne, ils la contempleront maintenue intacte du haut de leur jardin suspendu ou des quatre faces de leurs fenêtres en longueur. Leur vie domestique sera inserée dans un rêve virgilien.

The Savoye House as been given a fair number of interpretations: it may be a machine for living in, an arrangement of interpenetrating volume and external space, another emanation of space, time and architecture. It is probably all these things; but the suggestive reference to the dreams of Virgil, and a certain similarity of site, solution and feeling put one in mind of the passage in which Palladio describes the Rotunda. The landscape there is more agrarian and bucolic, there is less of the untamed pastoral, the scale is larger, but the effect is somehow the same.

Palladio, writing elsewhere, amplifies the ideal life of the villa. Its owner, from within the fragment of created order, will watch the maturity of his possessions, and savour the piquancy of contrast between his fields and his gardens; reflecting on mutability, he will contemplate through the years the antique virtues of a simpler race, the harmonious ordering of his life and estate will be an analogy of paradise.

The ancient sages commonly used to retire to such places, where being oftentimes visited by their virtuous friends and relations, having homes, gardens, fountains and such like pleasant places and above all their virtue, they could easily attain to as much happiness as can be attained here below.

Perhaps these were the dreams of Virgil. Freely interpreted, they have gathered round themselves, in the course of time, all those ideals of Roman virtue, excellence, Imperial splendour and decay, which made up the imaginative reconstruction of the ancient world. It would have been, perhaps, the landscape of Poussin that Palladio would have longed to penetrate, to roam among the portentous apparitions of the antique: it is possibly the fundamentals of this landscape, the poignancy of contrast between the disengaged cube and its setting in the *paysage agreste*, between geometrical volume and landscape which has the look of unimpaired nature, which lie behind Corbusier's Roman allusion. If architecture at the Rotunda forms the setting for the good life, at Poissy it is certainly the background for the lyrically efficient one; and if the contemporary pastoral is not yet sanctified by conventional usage, apparently the Virgilian nostalgia is still present. From the hygienically equipped boudoirs, pausing while ascending the ramps, the memory of the Georgics no doubt interposes itself, and, perhaps, the historical reference adds relish as the car pulls out for Paris.

A more specific comparison that presents itself is that between Palladio's Villa Foscari, the Malcontenta, and the house which in 1927 Corbusier built for M. de Monzie at Garches. (Figs 28.1 and 28.2) A diagrammatic comparison will reveal the fundamental relationships.

In general idea, as can be seen, the system of the two houses is closely similar. They are both conceived as single blocks, with one projecting element and parallel principle and subsidiary façades. Allowing for variations in roof treatment they are blocks of corresponding volume, eight units in length, by five and a half in breadth, by five in height. In both

28.1
Villa Foscari, Malcontenta (1560)

Architect: Andrea Palladio
Photographer: Edwin Smith (1963)

cases six 'transverse' lines of support, rhythmically alternating double and single bays, are established; but the rhythm of the parallel lines of support, as a result of Corbusier's use of the cantilever, differs slightly. At the villa at Garches it is ½: 1½: 1½: 1½: ½, and at the Malcontenta 1½: 2: 2: 1½. In plan, Corbusier thus obtains a sort of compression for his central bay, and interest seems transferred to his outer bays, which are augmented by the extra half unit of the cantilever; while Palladio secures a dominance for his central division, and a progression towards his portico, which focuses interest there. In both cases the projecting element, terrace or portico, occupies 1½ units in depth.

It is to be observed, that those (rooms) on the right correspond with those on the left, that so the fabric may be the same in one place as in the other, and that the walls may equally bear the burden of the roof; because if the walls are made large in one part and small in the other, the latter will be the more fit to resist the weight, by reason of the nearness of the walls, and the former more weak, which will produce in time very great inconveniences and ruin the whole work.

Palladio is concerned with the logical disposition of motifs dogmatically accepted; but he attempts to discover a structural reason for his planning symmetries. Corbusier, who is proving a case for structure as a basis of the formal elements of design, contrasts the new system with the old. He is a little more inclusive.

Je vous rappelle ce 'plan paralysé' du maison de pierre et ceci à quoi nous sommes arrivés avec la maison de fer ou de ciment armé.

plan libre

façade libre

ossature independante

fenêtres en longueur ou pan de verre

pilotis

toit jardin

et l'intérieur muni de casiers et débarras de l'encombrement des meubles.

Palladio's structural system makes it almost necessary to repeat the same plan on every level of the building; and point support allows Corbusier a fairly flexible arrangement; but both architects make a claim, which is somewhat in excess of the reasons they advance. Solid wall structures, Palladio declares, demand absolute symmetry; a frame building, Corbusier announces, requires a A:B=B: (A+B). Thus he indicates the ideal with which he would wish his façade to correspond, although in actual fact the figures 3:5–5:8 thus represented are only approximate.

Palladio also provides his plan with cryptically explanatory dimensions, and thus the rooms comprising the suites of three can be read as a progression from a 3:4 to 2:3 relationship. They are numbered 12:16, 16:16, and 16:24.

The façade is divided vertically into four main units, the two central ones being really a single division by their common expression as portico. The horizontal divisions are complicated by the introduction of the order, which presupposes alongside the 'natural' proportions, a series of purely 'customary' relationships. In fact these horizontal divisions are uneven although, as the figures show, they roughly approximate to a division into fifths – a fifth part to the attic and approximately three-fifths of the remaining wall surface to order and entablature.

Corbusier also divides his façade into four units; but in his case horizontally. The two central units are partly unified by their placing alongside the garden terrace, and could be considered as corresponding to Palladio's *piano nobile*. The vertical divisions are in the relationship indicated by the equation (3:5), which Palladio uses horizontally. In both cases there are elaborations in detail of dominant, complicated by imposition upon subsidiary system. It is by vertical extension into arch and vault, diagonal of roof line and parapet, that Palladio modifies the geometrical asperities of his cube; and the use of the circular and pyramidal elements with the square, seems both to conceal and amplify the real nature

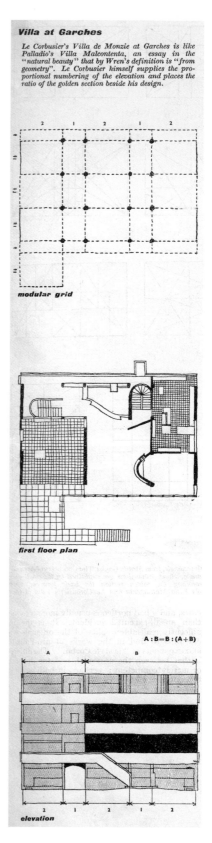

Villa at Garches

Le Corbusier's Villa de Monzie at Garches is like Palladio's Villa Malcontenta, an essay in the "natural beauty" that by Wren's definition is "from geometry". Le Corbusier himself supplies the proportional numbering of the elevation and places the ratio of the golden section beside his design.

modular grid

first floor plan

A : B = B : (A+B)

elevation

28.2

Villa Stein / de Monzie, Garches (1927)

From *Architectural Review*, March 1947

of the volumes. Some of these resources are the prerogatives of solid wall construction, freedoms of the *plan paralysé*, and the introduction of arched forms and pitched roofs is a liberty which Corbusier at Garches is unable to allow himself. In the frame building it is not, as in the solid wall structure, the enclosing walls that are a dominant, but the horizontal planes of floor and roof. The quality of partial paralysis, which Corbusier has noticed in the plan of the solid wall structure, in the frame building is transferred to the section. Perforation of floors giving a certain vertical movement of space is possible; but the sculptural quality of the building as carving has disappeared, and there can be none of Palladio's firm sectional transmutation and modelling of volume. Extension must be horizontal, following the established horizontal planes; free section is replaced by free plan, paralysed plan by paralysed section; and the limitations in both cases are equally severe; as though the solid wall structure had been turned on its side, the former complexities of section and subtleties of elevation are now transferred to plan.

The shapefulness and spatial audacities of the Garches plan continue to thrill; but it is an interior which seems to be regulated by the intellect only, operating, as it were, inside a stage vacuum. There is a permanent tension between the organised and the apparently fortuitous. To the intellect it is clear, to the senses deeply perplexing; and it seems not to be possible to stand anywhere in it, at any one point and receive the palpable impression of the whole. Both buildings can be absorbed from without; but from within, in the cruciform hall of the Malcontenta, there is a clue to the whole building, which is crystallized and focused there. At Garches, the theoretical equidistance between floor and ceiling conveys an equal importance to all parts of the volume in between. Allowed a sufficient height, it might be treated as a single volume, but otherwise the development of focus becomes a somewhat arbitrary proceeding. Corbusier accepts this limitation, and accepts the principal of horizontal extension; at Garches the central focus has been consistently broken up, concentration at one point is disintegrated, and replaced by a peripheral disperson of incident. The dismembered fragments of the central focus become, in fact, a sort of serial installation of interest round the extremities of the plan.

The system of horizontal extension comes up against the rigid bounding lines of the rectangular block, which is fundamental to the programme. Elaborate external development is, therefore, impossible, and Corbusier logically employs the opposite resource, inversion in the place of extension, gouging out large volumes of the block as the terrace and the roof garden, and exposing them to the outer space. Thus the peripheral incident, which replaces the focus, sometimes becomes one and the same with the inversions, which represent an essentially similar feature to Palladio's vertical extension.

This system of regular diffusion of interest and irregular development of points of concentration, throws into intense relief the geometrical substructure of the building. A comparable process to that in the plan takes place in the elevations, where the horizontal window treatment conveys equal interest to the centre and verge of the façades, and produces similar disintegration of vertical emphasis and displacement of the central feature. Elimination of focus immediately transfers interest to extremities of the block, which acquire a clarity and tautness, as though they were trying to restrain the peripheral incident from flying out of the block altogether.

A specific comparison is less easy to make between the Villa Rotunda and the Savoye House of 1930, the houses which seemed to provoke it. The problem, although at first it appears to be more severe, in actual fact offers a wider range. The emotional impression, concentrated in two fronts at Garches and the Malcontenta, is diffused here through all four, resulting in a more complex internal disposition and a greater geniality of external effect. The structural system of the Poissy house is less clear, and its central character is somewhat discounted by the cantilevered prolongations of what are presumably the east and west façades; and by the 'directed' expression of the ground floor, with its *porte cochère* and utility entrances. There is a noticeable easiness and lack of tension in these façades; but there are analogous developments from the earlier houses in both cases. Such are Palladio's development of central emphasis in both plan and elevations; and Corbusier's extended interest throughout his façades and dispersing of focus. The complicated volumes of the roof gardens replace the Palladio's four projecting loggias are replaced within the block as the first floor roof garden, which could also be considered, as the dominant element of this floor, to correspond to the domed saloon of the Rotunda.

Symbolically, and in what might be called the sphere of 'customary' beauty, these two groups of buildings are in different worlds. Palladio sought complete clarity of plan, the most lucid organisation of conventional elements based on symmetry, as the most memorable form of order, and mathematics as the supreme sanction in the world of external forms. In his own mind his work was essentially that of adaptation, the adaptation of the ancient house; and at the back of his mind were always the great halls of the Imperial thermae, and such buildings as Hadrian's villa at Tivoli. He has several schemes of archaeological reconstruction of Greek and Roman domestic buildings, based on Vitruvius and Pliny, and incorporating elements, which in Greek and Roman practice would have been found only in public buildings, but which he regarded as general. Rome for him was still alive, and if the ancients had adapted the temple from the house, their large scale planning was no doubt similarly reflective. Development was, therefore, less a matter of innovation, than an extension of ideas already implicit.

Corbusier has an equal reverence for mathematics, and would appear to be sometimes tinged with a comparable historicism. He seems to find a source in those ideals of *convenance* and *commodité* displayed in the ingenious planning of the rococo hotel, the background of a social life at once more amplified and intimate. The French have an unbroken tradition of this sort of planning; and one discovers, in a Beaux arts utilisation of an irregular site, elements which, if they had not preceded Corbusier, would have been curiously reminiscent of those suave boudoirs and vestibules. Corbusier admires the Byzantine architecture of the Mediterranean world, and there is also present a purely French delight in the more comprehensible aspects of mechanics ... the little pavilion on the roof at Garches is at the same time a temple of love and the bridge of a ship, the detail is precise, the most complex architectural volumes are fitted with running water.

Geometrically, both architects may be said to have approached something of a Platonic archetype of the villa, which the Virgilian dream could be held to represent. The idealisation of the cube house must lend itself very readily to the purposes of Virgilian dreaming. Here is set up the conflict between the contingent and the absolute, the natural and the abstract; the gap between the ideal world and the too human exigencies of realisation receives its most pathetic presentation. The bridging must be as competent and compelling as a well-executed fugue, charged as in these cases with almost religious seriousness, or sophisticated, witty allusion; it is an intellectual feat which reconciles the mind to the fundamental discrepancy of the programme.

Palladio is the convinced classicist with the sixteenth century repertoire of well-humanised forms. He translates this 'customary' material with a passion and a high seriousness fitting to the continued validity that he finds it to possess; the reference to the Pantheon in the superimposed porticoes; to the *thermae* in the cruciform saloon; the ambiguity, profound, in both idea and form, in the equivocal conjunction of temple front and domestic block. These are charged with meaning, both for what they are and for what they signify; and their impression is poignant. The ancient house is not re-created, but there is in its place a concrete apparition of antique virtue, excellence. Imperial splendour and stoicism: Rome is there by allusion, the ideal world by geometry.

By contrast, Corbusier is in some ways the most ingenious of eclectics. The orders, the Roman allusion, are the apparatus of authority, customary, and in a sense universal forms. It is hard for the modern architect to be quite as emphatic about any particular civilisation; and with Corbusier there is always present an element of wit, suggesting that the historical reference has remained a quotation between inverted commas, possessing always the double value of the quotation, the associations of both old and new context. The world of classical Mediterranean culture, on which Palladio drew so expressively, is closed for Corbusier. The emblematic representations of the moral virtues, the loves of the Gods and the lives of the Saints, the ornamental adjuncts of humanism, have lost their former historical monopoly. Allusion is dissipated at Garches, concentrated at the Malcontenta; within the one cube the performance is mixed, within the other, Roman. Corbusier selects the irrelevant and the particular, the fortuitously picturesque and the incidentally significant forms of mechanics, as the objects of his virtuosity. They retain their original implications of classical landscape, mechanical precision, rococo intimacy; one is able to cease hold of them as known objects, and sometimes as basic shapes; but they become only transiently provocative. Unlike Palladio's forms there is nothing final about their relationship; their *rapprochement* would seem to be affected by the artificial emptying of the cube, when the senses are confounded by the apparent arbitrariness, and the intellect more than convinced by the intuitive knowledge, that here in spite of all to the contrary, there is order and there are rules.

Corbusier has become the source of fervent pastiches, and witty exhibition techniques; the neo-Palladian villa became the picturesque object in the English park. Content is different in both cases, and a bad portico is usually more convincing than an ill-executed incident. It is the magnificently realisable quality of the originals which one fails to find in the works of neo-Palladians and exponents of *le style Corbu*. The difference is that between the universal, and the decorative or merely competent; perhaps in both cases it is the adherence to rules which has lapsed.

Source: *Architectural Review*, March 1947

Intervention during the Discussion on Architectural Expression by CIAM, Bridgwater, on September 13, 1947

By Le Corbusier

I experienced a profound happiness when I heard [Sigfried] Giedion demanding that we should place art at the summit of our preoccupations. I was deeply moved yesterday when I heard our president [Cornelis] van Eesteren unveiling what hides in his innermost heart and thought: his subtle discrimination in art and in philosophy. After our hard week of work, see now how the blossoms unfurl.

For twenty years, since I was first submitted to the discipline of my own effort, I have known with certitude that the one fact, in the world, in the present immense shifting of forces, the real question, the essential thing that has to come, is the *re-formation of the modern consciousness*.

Cogito, ergo sum. For each one of us, in the consciousness of each, this is to learn to recognize the nature of the new light that must shine on our enterprises and, in consequence, determine the programme of our work.

It is through personal experiment, through private work. It is through the participation of each in the construction of the whole. The whole will be made new by the innumerable multiplication of molecular efforts. The responsibility is upon the individual.

The first era of machinery disseminated chaos; the disaster of a prodigious century, magnificent in its scientific, moral and spiritual conquests. Everywhere lies disgrace, an unspeakable ugliness, a default of grace, of smiles, the evasion of goodwill ...

But there is no reason to despair; all the elements of construction exist, at hand – an immense crowd of *means*. Harmony alone is absent, since no one has had the time, nor the taste, nor even the idea of giving thought to it ... *Harmony* is the great word of the present time: *the setting of all things in harmony! Attaining the reign of harmony over all things!* And, so doing, to provoke the burgeoning,

the bursting,

of the poetic phenomenon!

Poetry! The word should be pronounced. Poetry, that cannot exist but by the presence of relationships. Relationships create an interplay between precise objects, precise ideas – but never among the mists of ambiguous intentions. These exact objects and objectives are so placed that from their relations surges the prodigious, the unexpected, the unsuspected, the astounding, the miraculous.

29.1
Group photograph of the participants, including Le Corbusier, at the Congrès Internationaux de l'Architecture Moderne (CIAM) conference, Bridgwater (1947)

The MIRACLE of precise relations occurs beneath our eyes, by the operation of the most mathematical exactitude.

But our efforts are capable of producing this miracle! For whom is this miracle? For a public.

For what public? It has been said – for the people.

I shall say: for men. It is a matter between one man and another man.

It is an individual addressing himself to his brothers. And the common work is, in the hour of its birth, held in the hands of *whoever has the responsibility.*

This man addresses his work to strangers. But to strangers who exist,

> who are there,

> who wait,

and for whom *EMOTIONS, ART*

are as deeply needed as water and bread.

These unknown men exist in modern society, perhaps at decisive posts. There are men at the command of essential trains of wheels in the life of a country which may be guided by their decisions and attitudes toward ugly or beautiful destinies. *Certain among these men need the nourishment of poetry.*

In an hour of industrialization, of collective enterprises which can bring security, abundance, a joy in living, and can save the world from imbecilic catastrophe – in the hour of all the indescribable possibilities capable of transforming into harmony the stupid disgrace which now degrades us, the person acquires a startling value; and the person exists, receiver and transmitter of human emotion.

I say this to you: behind our collective problems, which have held us together for twenty years in a productive and overridingly friendly union, the responsibility rests deep within each one of us.

Harmony will result from the true expression of the modern consciousness.

Source: *Architects' Journal*, 25 September 1947

The Space Machine: an Evaluation of the Recent Work of Le Corbusier

By Lionel Brett

Nous voulons nous donner de vastes et d'étranges domaines
Où le mystère en fleurs s'offre à qui veut le ceuillir
Il y a là des jeux nouveaux des couleurs jamais vues
Mille phantasmes impondérables
Auxquels il faut donner de la réalité

Guillaume Apollinaire

Le Corbusier is a painter, a poet, only accidentally an architect. An intimate sympathy with the nature of materials, an easy felicity of structure and a sense of scale, these three vital attributes of the born constructor are not specially prominent in him. It doesn't matter much, because these things do not travel. They can only be apprehended from the building itself, whereas it is well known that the phenomenon of Le Corbusier is not what he has built but the ideas he has exported. It remains a puzzle (which the latest volume does nothing to solve) how these carelessly assembled picture-books, with their impudent doodlings, their pretentious but half-baked *esquisses*, and their tantalising omissions, have leapt the barriers of language (including the English translation) and become the student's bible from Helsinki to Rio.

But first perhaps one ought to substantiate these criticisms. Let us take this fourth volume of the complete works, covering the period 1938–46 and recently published [*Oeuvre Complète 1938–46*]. It is exciting to open the wide canvas cover. Has the leader kept his place at the head of the revolutionary party, or is he merely repeating the successful slogans and finding himself among the conservatives? It must be reported that the successful slogans are repeated word for word, but Le Corbusier remains in power, because no Robespierre, no smiler with the knife, has yet appeared on the horizon. This is fortunate. The principles of modern architecture which Le Corbusier states and restates are not yet understood outside a tiny band of brothers. Until they are in the curriculum of every school and as much a part of Everyman's mental apparatus as the multiplication table and the internal combustion engine, they must be repeated *ad nauseam*. The danger is that some clever Judas among the disciples, tired of being good, may sell out to frivolity and nostalgia before the new lesson has been learnt.

Le Corbusier in this volume gives no hint of concession to a change of taste. In fact, he starts with a sketch for a monument which comes nearer the Teutonic expressionism of the early Mendelsohn than one would believe possible. The most interesting of the other pre-war projects is an ingenious model of the infinitely extensible Museum, inspired by the spiral growth of the snail's shell, with which Le Corbusier had been experimenting for some time. This flat swastika-shaped building seems destined to act as foil to the soaring slabs of the *Cité d'Affaires*, and sure enough we find it in this role in the scheme for St. Dié. Some house projects of this period (with one exception oddly labelled, 'Clarke Arundell'*) are of a lower level of inspiration than the masterpieces of the twenties. They are also more than usually difficult to read. Le Corbusier plays with a double lean-to roof, falling towards the centre. This produces a curious and uncomfortable centrifugal feeling on the end elevations (the opposite of the ridge roof) and creates problems in the section which do not seem to be realised. Has anyone thought out the aesthetics of sloping ceilings? One rule must surely be that where a space has a dominating axis imposed by bed, window or fireplace, the slope must be in the direction of that axis and not at right angles to it.

In 1940 the fall of Paris separated Le Corbusier from his silent but invaluable cousin Jeanneret, and from that date Le Corbusier signs his work alone. Like others, he fills the war years with skyscraping reconstruction projects, the first years of peace with schemes for mudhuts for D.P.'s. Of the former, the new *Cité d'Affaires* for Algiers, latest of a long series of studies for the port, is worked out in some detail and illustrated by really impressive models and drawings. (Fig. 30.1) The general conception has some affinity with the Rockefeller Centre, but with two important differences; first, the fully developed use at Algiers of different levels for traffic segregation; secondly, the far richer texture of Le Corbusier's latest elevations. With an arrogance reminiscent of Leonardo the architect thus describes his building:

*Project for an Ideal Home (1939) in association with Clive Entwistle (1916–76). (Eds)

30.1
Design for an administration building in the Quartier de la Marine, Algiers (1942)

From Le Corbusier, *Oeuvre Complète, vol. 4 1938–46* (1946)

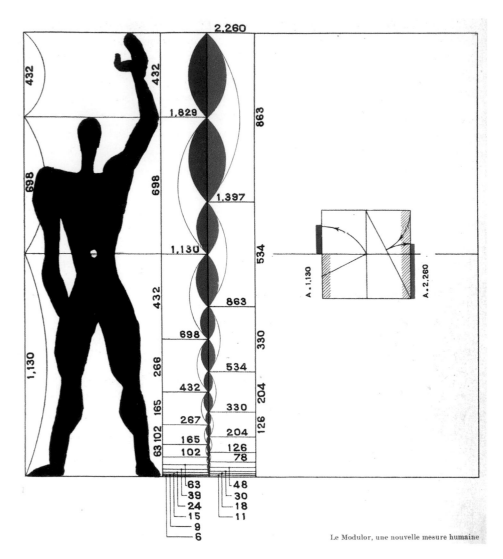

Le Modulor, une nouvelle mesure humaine

30.2
The Modulor, a new measure of man (1945)

From Le Corbusier, *Oeuvre Complète, vol. 4 1938–46* (1946)

Unité étincelante d'une oeuvre architecturale. Ici règne la section d'or, ayant donné l'enveloppe harmonieuse, fourni le prisme impératif et pur; marqué la cadence, proportionné à l'échelle humaine, permis les variations, autorisé la fantaisie, réglé de bas en haut l'attitude générale. Cet édifice de 150 mètres de haut, est assuré contre tous risques: l'harmonie est en chacune de ses parties. Et nul désaccord avec notre sensibilité n'est possible.

Le Corbusier's use of the Golden Section is well known. (Fig. 30.2) He has the same superstitious belief in it as had Lutyens. Although it is arguable that with 'regulating lines,' as with statistics, you can prove anything, one must concede that Le Corbusier's system (which he has now patented) has preserved him from the solecisms which other modern architects (Frank Lloyd Wright, for instance) commit at intervals. Yet with all respect to the master's definite statement to the contrary, there is a disturbing ambiguity of scale about this great façade. Covering one-third of it is a key pattern of loggia-like sun-breaks, the scale of which is exactly double that of the rest of the elevation. And this arbitrary doubling of the scale corresponds to absolutely nothing on plan. If there are eternal rules (and Le Corbusier evidently believes there are) this design breaks them. The result is not a success.

It was during the war period that Le Corbusier first realised the full potentialities of the *brise-soleil*. Roasting in their giant glass-houses, it is surprising that the tenants of modern buildings had not demanded this solution long ago. Rescued by the egg-crate, the wall of glass survives, and we gain the possibility of a rich repetitive pattern, exactly the kind that appeals to modern sensibility, and capable of considerable variation. The best-known illustration of the new effect is, of course, the superb Ministry of Education building at Rio de Janeiro, built under Le Corbusier's direct inspiration. I cannot resist quoting here Mr. Clive Entwistle's delightful tribute, which sums up so neatly Le Corbusier's benefactions to modern architecture.

> Je saisis cette opportunité pour vous remercier de la part de tous les jeunes d'ici, de votre dernier don à l'architecture: le brise-soleil, élément splendide, clef des combinaisons infinies. Maintenant, l'architecture est prête à prendre sa place dans la vie. Vous lui avez donné une squelette (ossature indépendant), ses organes vitaux (les services communs du logis); une peau fraîche luisante (le pan de verre); vous l'avez mis debout sur ses jambes (les pilotis); posé un joli chapeau sur sa tête (les arabesques du toit-jardin). Et maintenant vous lui donnez des vêtements magnifiques s'adaptant aux divers climats! Evidemment, vous devez être un père fier! ...

So excited is Le Corbusier by his discovery that he does not hesitate to use it on sunless elevations.

Most convincing and fully realised of the wartime schemes is the armament factory known as the *Usine-Verte*. Though the idea of the 'factory in a garden' is far from novel in England, Le Corbusier links it rationally enough with his well-known schemes for a Linear City. This gets industry into the genuine country, enables great windows to open on to *des perspectives paysagistes*, and is something quite different from the modern English trading estate with its slap-up elevations, its patches of precarious lawn and its squalid backs along the railway.

During these years and the first months of peace the atelier devoted a good deal of time to the problem of temporary housing, (Fig. 30.3) working along lines exactly opposite to our own: unskilled labour and manual techniques, standard layouts but flexible interior arrangements. What we are shown of this research is not impressive. If one were to be reduced to *pisé* walls and log roofs, it is unlikely that one could command the site organisation to erect these long terraces with their subtle modular variations, exact dimensioning and expensive standard elements – or if one could one might just as well build permanent houses of a decent size and be done with it.

There follows, however, a relief from all this fooling in the form of a reconstruction scheme for the destroyed Vosges town of St. Dié. This exhilarating project is in the direct

30.3
Design for a Unité d'Habitation as transitional housing (1944)

From Le Corbusier, *Oeuvre Complète, vol. 4 1938–46* (1946)

line of descent from the great *urbanisations* of Paris, Antwerp, Buenos Aires, Boulogne, Algiers, Nemours, etc. Going back over its antecedents, one notices at once the steady movement away from the frigid geometry of the *Plan Voisin* for Paris (Fig. 30.4) towards variety of grouping and (almost) informality – but not quite, for Le Corbusier gets his strongly emotional effects by methods as coolly deliberate as Le Nôtre – and as mysterious to the Englishman. In the use of different levels to separate pedestrians from traffic there is also an enormous improvement here. The over-elaborate viaducts and clover-leaves which dominated the earlier projects are dispensed with and separate circulation contrived with delightful ease and simplicity. For all its right angles, there is an Attic grandeur about this plan for St. Dié. Unlike so many of the earlier projects, dominated by mechanism and cruel to the ant-like individual, this twentieth-century aeropolis would, if it could be built, exalt our civilisation. In fact, one wonders whether human beings as one knows them – fond of slums, fish and chips, overcrowded cafés, romantic ill-lit alleys – could quite live up to these splendid but austere spaces, or get much fun out of them in the hot sun or the rain.

The book ends with working drawings and models for a *Unité d'Habitation de Grandeur Conforme* to house 1,600 people, which is to be erected at Marseilles. Le Corbusier leaves us in no doubt of the significance of this great building as the culmination of his life's work.

Après vingt années de préparation inlassable, années pendant lesquelles ces problèmes furent constamment étudiés, l'occasion est donc fournie de mettre dans la pratique, ce qui fut mis au point théoriquement.

30.4
Centre of Paris showing Plan Voisin skyscrapers (1925)

From Le Corbusier, *La Ville Radieuse* (1935)

Il s'agit donc ici, d'une prototype, à vrai dire d'une proposition formelle de conditions de vie pour la civilisation machiniste présente.

Once again, the critic is more or less bludgeoned into silence. And indeed the size of the job is formidable, the ingenuity with which the various flat types are fitted in is so remarkable that one has no doubt that this is the highest residential density yet achieved on earth. Criticism becomes mainly a job for the sociologist. Yet if these are really working drawings it may also be legitimate to suggest that the Mediterranean has the wrong climate for corridor access, that whatever the structural system the noise of living-rooms will be audible in bedrooms immediately below them, that nine-tenths of the flats will be almost sunless in mid-winter, and that descending 20 floors to collect the pram from a garage for 200 would make any mother dream of Hampstead Garden Suburb. There may be answers to these minor-criticisms, but there can be no justification for the excessive fatness of the whole block, which gives a horrid cell-like section to each dwelling and many dark and ill-ventilated corners. This is, of course, another example of Le Corbusier's weakness in the section, which Mr. Colin Rowe was, as far as I know, the first to demonstrate as a weakness inherent in frame construction. One need only flip the pages of any of the *Oeuvres Complètes* to notice at once the contrast between the fluid grace and lucidity of the plans and the rigid slabs that slice across the sections. Just as we escape from the weight-bearing wall we look like being crushed in true Hegelian style by the floor slab.

The English translations in the book as first printed are so fantastically bad that they make quite good comic reading. The publishers decided that their best course was to issue an apology and some re-translations in a separate leaflet tucked into the endpapers. Unfortunately, the apology and the re-translations are not right either. This detail is only worth mentioning as an example of the happy-go-lucky atmosphere which makes one wonder for a moment whether the author is serious either.

Yet when all is said Le Corbusier's greatness remains absolutely unimpaired by the kind of holes I have picked in his latest book.

Do I contradict myself?
Very well then, I contradict myself
(I am large, I contain multitudes).

The answer comes back in poetic terms, because it is only in terms of poetry that Le Corbusier's enormous influence can be defined. If there is a clue to the puzzle stated at the beginning of this article, it is to be found in the last caption in the book: 'C'est la splendeur de l'espace!'.

O to realise space!
The plenteousness of all, that there are no bounds,
To emerge and be of the sky, of the sun and moon and flying clouds, as one with them.

Le Corbusier's achievement lies not in any buildings but in his intuition of the power of the machine to enlarge the boundaries of human experience, and in his brilliant gift of communicating this intuition.

We have other sources of power ... more pure, nor less serene, than that of the hermit spirit which once lighted with white lines of cloisters the glades of the Alpine pine, and raised into ordered spires the wild rocks of the Norman sea; which gave to the temple gate the depth and darkness of Elijah's Horeb cave, and lifted, out of the populous city, grey cliffs of lonely stone, into the midst of sailing birds and silent air.

Source: *Architectural Review*, November 1947

Address to the Students of the Architectural Association School

By Le Corbusier

I am going to begin by talking to you about harmony, which goes all the way from architecture to music, and I shall end by giving you a few ideas about the new palace of the United Nations. Moreover, as you have asked me to give you my ideas for the next hundred years, I propose to say what I think may happen next year.

What I am going to say now may sound stupid, but it constitutes the basis of architecture. The fundamental measure for the appreciation of architecture is provided by man, and the current idea that a man can stand in the centre of a circle and have simultaneous perception all round is one which we cannot accept. Man has his eyes in front and not behind or at the sides, and it is in this way that he gains his impression of architecture. The idea that he can see in all directions at once is pure illusion; he sees things in a consecutive order, in sequence.

This process of perception is mathematical, and the miracle of numbers can open the door to an extraordinary richness and harmony. We must extend to architecture the principles of measurement and proportion which can be given to us by numbers. After thirty years of research we have created what I call the *Modulor*, which will soon be put at the disposal of all architects. It is a measure which obeys the laws of the requirements of the golden mean and of the human figure. We have thus been able to create a tool of measurement going almost from zero to the infinite, from a "microbic" measurement of 1/15,000 mm to the circumference of the earth, 40,000 km, containing 272 increasing intervals.

There is another reason for creating this measure. The modern world finds itself in constant movement, so that contacts are made everywhere at the same time. We find an analogy in music, which is made up of sounds which are physical events and absolutely continuous. In solving the problem of representing a phenomenon which was continuous and unlimited in a form of writing made up of a few signs, what was done was to take the possibilities of hearing of the human ear and to recognise laws which are of a biological, physiological kind, and on the other hand to take mathematics, finding in numbers the possibilities of extraordinary combinations and thus creating the musical notation known as the Doric scale. In this way it was found possible for the consciousness and imagination of man to be written down and transmitted across space and across time, thanks to the miracle of the door opened by numbers.

31.1
**Le Corbusier shown on a return
visit to the Architectural Association
(1953)**

31.2
Le Corbusier seen talking to J.M. Richards on a return visit to the Architectural Association (1953)

In architecture, which is a visual matter, man took the measurement which was nearest to himself – the foot, the span of the hand, the forearm, the finger, the thumb. In the early days this was sufficient, but today contacts between one part of the world and another are much closer, and people and ideas and manufactures travel all over the world, so that the difficulty has arisen of the existence of two methods of measurement, very different from each other and in fact irreconcilable; on the one hand the scale of the foot and the inch, the scale of the Anglo-Saxon world, and on the other hand the metric scale. The metre was introduced at the time of the French Revolution by scientists who forgot that the circumference of the earth is not important for us, and that we do not measure houses with the circumference of the earth. The advantage of the metre, however, is that it is part of the decimal system.

The system which we have created now can be used in a similar way to the notation employed for music. It is in the form of a series based on the golden cut, and can be expressed in millimetres or in feet and inches, thus bringing the two systems of measurement into agreement. It is a system, however, which cannot give intelligence to imbeciles, but by its proper use the proportions and harmony of music may be realised in architecture. After all, the mode of music is the nearest to architecture, and music, like architecture, is concerned with time and space. Architecture began to lose its human reality when it forgot that man has eyes only in the front of his head. That is the *grand mal de l'academisme* and the danger even of classicism.

Let us consider how music can be expressed in architecture. In a good town plan we find nuances and finesse, and finesse is one of the joys of architecture and of civilisation. The buildings should make a rhythm of architectural music.

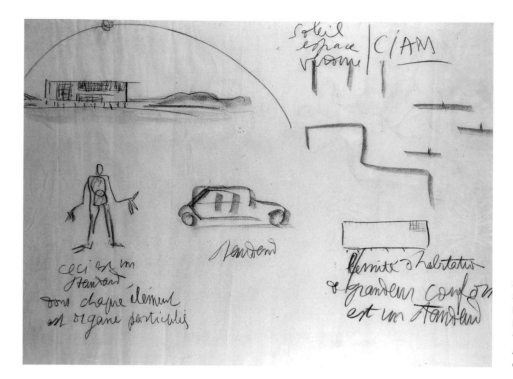

31.3
Sketch of the Unité d'Habitation, Marseille, and the Modulor made by Le Corbusier to illustrate his lecture, 'The Golden Section', given at the Architectural Association, London, during its centenary year (1947)

In dealing even with such a humble building as a small factory, by the right method of proportioning the building we can introduce music in counterpoint and fugue. There is no symmetry; a building is a single thing, but in it we can use four kinds of measure. The first is the distance between the piles which carry the building; the second is the measure used for the glass façades. It is altogether different from the first; it has nothing to do with it; it plays its own music. The third measure is used in the framework, and the fourth is given by the dimensions of the glass which covers it. These measures play their own music, but they have the secret of harmony, of the golden cut, and they allow us to make something which smiles by reason of its proportions, by the calm that reigns there. Even in so modest a building as a factory it is possible to introduce, therefore, a quite delicious harmony.

We have adopted these principles in a great building which we constructed at Marseilles, which contains 1,600 people. This immense building obeys entirely the proportions of the *Modulor*. (Figs 31.3 and 31.4)

The unit of habitation of adequate size, *l'Unité d'Habitation de Grandeur Conforme*, is the key to a synthesis which is both individual and collective, the harmonious solution of the individual and collective equation which architects will bring to modern society, which will bring happiness to its homes and social force to its developments, permitting the phenomenon of participation, the true condition of joy, which will drive away the egoism which destroys both individuals and peoples.

We still have our old customs and our old habits and our old cities, but a modern consciousness has come into being everywhere and will be manifested by architecture. The nature of our buildings will be transformed in the years to come. In the Middle Ages there

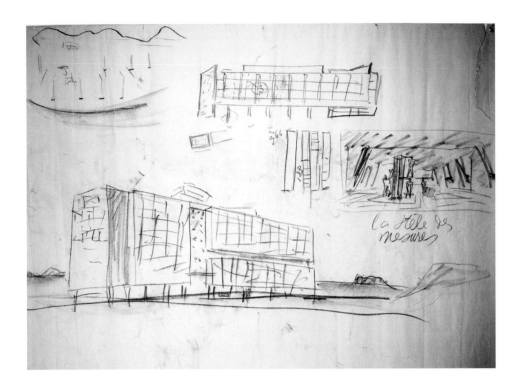

31.4
Sketch of the Unité d'Habitation, Marseille, made by Le Corbusier to illustrate his lecture, 'The Golden Section', given at the Architectural Association, London, during its centenary year (1947)

was a monk who prophesied that all the earth would be covered by a mantle of churches, but instead of churches we shall see the tools of what is a machine civilisation. Architecture will cease to concern itself with decoration and will be interested in the welfare of man in his home, in his work, in his institutions and so on, and with the housing of things, of institutions and of gods.

Let us see how standards become established, and let us appreciate just what we mean by the word "standard." To set up standards is not to construct pieces of standards. A man is a standard with organs which breathe, a digestive organ, an organ of movement, an organ of prehension and an organ which controls them all. He is a standard of which the elements are organs. You find the same thing in a motor car, which is also a standard in which each element is a particular organ. There is no repetition either in the man or in the motor car. The standard which I suggest should be adopted by us is the *L'Unité d'Habitation de Grandeur Conforme*. In a discussion at the Ministry on Tuesday last, the Director of Works said to me: "But then your house is against your theory; it is not a standard." We pointed out that the thrust of the wind necessitates different calculations from one end of the building to the other, and differences of stress and torsion necessitate different calculations from the bottom to the top. Nature, if it were to make the house, would make all the elements different – of the same family, but different. In a tree all the elements are of the same family, but there are different nuances. The standard is not in the single element; it is in the whole. That is very important, because we have got to make the politicians and the economists realise that the major expense is in the design of the prototype, and if the Ministry will pay the architects, the country will save money.

We have to have new conceptions of town planning, and to re-establish natural conditions. In considering the geography and topography of any part of a country, we find that at an early stage earth roads appear which follow the *Thalweg*, and other roads meet them and form a crossing-place at which a town grows up. Later, after the roadway, comes the railway, and perhaps the waterway. There are two forms which the dwellings there may take: the collective unit, and the family house for those who do not like collective living. The great transformation which modern town planning has brought about is what may be called the 'linear' industrial city, as opposed to the old radioconcentric city which generally exists at road junctions.

In looking to the future I must apologise for not concerning myself with politics, but I am interested not in politics but in human conditions. Everybody seems to be against this method of approach, but if you adopt it you will discover how the human study of architectural phenomena can lead you by way of harmony to a fresh consideration of essential problems which should enable us as architects to teach those who are concerned with administration.

You may complain that although I am an architect I have not been talking about architecture. As a matter of fact, I never stop talking about architecture. Let me consider now the application of these principles which I have outlined to a building. Let us take the case of a simple building with two floors and a glass façade, which, thanks to modern progress, may have conditioned air at a temperature of 20–30 degrees C. The people who work in this building will be uncomfortable; there will be warmth everywhere, but the people themselves will be cold, because they will lose heat by radiation to the colder area of the window. This I would describe as the catastrophe of the modern glass façade. To find a solution for this problem we shall have to have a double glass front and the circulation of warm air in the space between the two sheets of glass. I call this a 'neutralising wall' (*mur neutralisant*), and it stops the radiation from the warm body to the colder window.

That is all very well in the winter, but in the summer we have different conditions; although the infrared and ultra-violet rays are broken by the glass the visible rays pass through and transform themselves on absorbent surfaces into heat energy, so that in summer it will be very hot inside the building, and we must find a solution for this also. The solution will be to put in the rays of the apparatus necessary to ward off the rays of the sun and prevent the entry of direct sunlight. This will be done by a type of *brise soleil*, and you will find this area even in the old, traditional architecture; you find it in Spain and in Africa, and you find it even in temperate zones. It has the effect of admitting sunlight in winter but excluding it in summer.

The architectural evolution which I have been describing has, as you will see, nothing to do with style. It is the work of those who are prepared to abandon historic tradition and undertake a modern adventure.

Consider New York for a moment. We have a Fifth Avenue, for example, a very congested street, and in the implacable climate of New York the sun fills what is almost a sort of cavern between the buildings with warm vapour. In spite of this, the architecture is of a traditional type; the buildings have a steel framework, but the façade consists only of small windows occupying 20–30 per cent of the area. There is a great temptation to go in for the all-glass façade, which would provide what I would call the Cartesian skyscraper, based on reasoning, where all the essential human problems are solved in terms of modern techniques, and which might make the poet exclaim "Ou sont les styles d'antan?"

Coming to the headquarters of the United Nations, we shall need a large assembly hall and at least eighteen other large rooms for meetings, adapted for their special purpose by the provision of sound insulation and facilities for photography, television, radio and so on, where people from all over the world can make speeches and provide a spectacle for the crowd. The real work, however, will be done by these people in private conversations, and conditions will have to be provided which will keep them in good humour. For this purpose they must be in touch with nature, with the countryside around, the gardens and the sun. People cannot be good humoured where the sun is excluded. In such a building, therefore, place must be found both for artificial and for natural conditions.

The delegates will be there only from time to time, but we have also to consider the officials, who will be there every day, and we must provide internal means of circulation which will enable some 5,000 members of the secretariat to go about their business conveniently. To provide comfort in cold weather we must have our *murs neutralisants*, and to provide against the fierce summer of New York we must have our *brises soleil*.

We shall have on the borders of the East River, therefore, a building larger than Versailles. We shall have an underground parking-place for vehicles, and with the earth taken from the foundations we can make little artificial hills to hide the Coca-Cola sign which dominates the site, and on these we will plant trees and create a sort of artificial countryside. I call this the Valley of the Nations, the green valley, in the desert of New York. We shall have a second building for the secretariat and a third for the delegations and special agencies, while on the water-front there will be a little landing-stage for the boats which will bring tourists to see the whole place.

It is thus an exceptional opportunity which is offered to our American friends, with the collaboration of the other nations. This town of New York is formidable, catastro-faeric, fantastic. It is impossible altogether to like it; half an hour of love is succeeded by half an hour of hate. Skyscrapers and little houses are intermingled in complete disorder, and what I call the Valley of the Nations will make a fantastic contrast with New York. I hope that New York itself will gradually be transformed and will find the way to human and natural conditions. Twelve years ago, when I visited New York for the first time, I was interviewed by about twenty journalists who asked me what I thought of New York. I told them that I thought the skyscrapers were too small, which seemed to stupefy them. I should like to see the problem of the skyscraper faced by what I have called a Cartesian approach, by the way of reason.

I should like to say three things in conclusion. First, I thank the President for inviting me here; it is a great honour. Secondly, I hope that another time you will provide me with something to wipe my hands on after using chalks. Finally, all that I have to say to you, as the fruit of a life spent in struggle, is that you must have faith, you must have courage, and you must be *hommes vivants* and not bother too much about diplomas and artificial papers.

(*The lecture was given in French and illustrated with sketches on the blackboard*)

Source: *Architect & Building News*, 2 January 1948

Part 3

1950–1959:

Architecture and Recognition

Le Corbusier's Unité d'Habitation

London County Council Architect's Department Housing Division

Le Corbusier's Unité d'Habitation *in Marseilles* (Fig. 32.1) *has been more disagreed about than any other building going up anywhere since the war– besides being the subject of wilder rumours. As a fair sample of the diverse opinions which informed observers maintain about it, here is a discussion held recently by members of the Housing Division of the London County Council Architect's Department and their guests; it serves as introduction to a full account of the building ... and ... it will be seen that, however much speakers differed about the social and structural aspects of the* Unité d'Habitation, *about its aesthetic qualities – and in particular, curiously enough, the 'humanity' of its scale – there was no disagreement at all.*

Kenneth Easton

At the end of the war the Marseilles Municipality commissioned Le Corbusier to help them solve their housing problem and in doing this presented him with a full-scale opportunity of realizing the ideas of a lifetime – the design and erection of a vertical garden city. After 25 years of paper planning and production of evolutionary projects, Unité d'Habitation No. 1 has taken shape and is now nearing completion. This building and the ideas behind it have probably engendered more heat 'for and against' than any other building since the war and it is our purpose here to invite first-hand reports from six architects who have recently made the pilgrimage to Marseilles. My contribution therefore must be broad and brief.

Before going to Marseilles I had collected some general information about the four sites, the seven governments and the three contractors who had gone down during the progress of building and I had pored over and speculated upon the published information and the progress photographs that were available. It seemed to me that this elegant rectangle raised up on *pilotis*, housing 1,600 people in two-storeyed flats and providing most of the amenities of a neighbourhood unit, was clearly the fusion of idea of two men – Corbusier the social philosopher and Corbusier the modern romantic architect.

It seemed clear too that the complete integration of structure and form and the high degree of standardization should fulfil Corbusier's claims that the building would be speedily and economically built; the vague reports that work was rather slow and that costs were mounting alarmingly seemed difficult to credit. The internal planning itself, the thin slices of double-storeyed living accommodation 12 feet wide and 60 feet long, lit only at the ends,

32.1
Unité d'Habitation, Marseille (1952)

Photographer: Emmanuel Thirard (1996)

and served only by internal roads, artificially lit and ventilated, seemed more doubtful, and this sort of doubt struck at the whole economic conception of planning vertical houses.

However, as a background to the building I decided to first take stock of Marseilles and the Marseillais.

The second city of France, and surely her first for noise and perpetual bustle, is Mediterranean rather than French in its way of life. Its vigorous and multitudinous inhabitants, a fifth of whom I believe are Italian, live, eat, shop, and carry out their business in the open air along the wide boulevards of their busy *Canebière* and around the picturesque harbour and horseshoe of sunny quays of the *Vieux-Port.*

How, I wondered, could 1,600 of this essentially 'agora-minded' and volatile community ever be happily contained in this great rectangle on the outskirts of the town?

Mixed feelings, however, do leave one with an open mind and it was in this state that I boarded the tram which left the boulevards and the high buildings of the town behind, passed the stadium and the villas dotted among the eucalyptus and olive trees of the outskirts and fetched up level with a contractor's board announcing that this was 'Unité d'Habitation No. 1' and that Le Corbusier was the architect. (Two facts which, by the way, are known to everyone in Marseilles.)

At first sight the building looks deceptively small, the seventeen storeys sitting on the truly heroic *pilotis* seems a masterpiece of deliberate understatement. Scale, the treatment of planes, patterns and surfaces are as magnificent as the bad finish of the precast concrete work is deplorable. Both inside and out – and this includes the *jeu d'esprit* on the roof – I found a building which was always interesting and often exciting. The demonstration flat which is completed and furnished makes magnificent use of its 1,000 square feet (costing about £1,100 before devaluation) and has excellent services and equipment.

Of course if you are not wildly enthusiastic during or immediately after a visit to any Corbusier building it is unlikely that you ever will be, and later, after I had left the site and had recovered myself physically and mentally, I found some doubts, which are summarized in the following questions, still persisting.

1.   Does the whole approach and conception of Unité give us the sort of building which can properly fulfil our current sociological functions?
2.   Have the full benefits of such a scheme been curtailed by limiting it to one block instead of to a group of blocks?
3.   Will the final capital cost make it a failure in quite another way by demanding rentals which are too high for the people for whom it has been designed?
4.   Is this the beginning of vertical housing in concentrated densities and if so is it a solution which we can accept and agree to develop in this country?

I shall not attempt to answer these questions now but simply throw them out for discussion.

Moholi and King

Although Unité is on monumental scale it should not be regarded only for its architectural features. It is the culmination of twenty-six years' study of urban development, and its sociological significance is perhaps more important to planners than its architectural conception. Indeed its architecture is the physical expression of certain sociological precepts.

For the first time Le Corbusier is now executing the ideas which he has for so long propounded in his writings. And like all great artists he has in many respects relied on intuition rather than scientific method and analysis in order to create a building which will fulfil its anticipated social functions.

The Unité must not be considered as the ultimate realization since it is proposed to be the first of a number, which will then comprise his long cherished dream of *une cité-jardin verticale*. Its name is a guide to its accommodation, since it is designed for the social life of a small community. In addition to 330 flats for 1,600 people (at a density of 139 to the acre) it will contain a post office, a shopping centre on the 7th and 8th floors, a library and restaurant, an hotel for guests, club-rooms, a clinic on the top floor and a running-track and gymnasium on the roof; while a swimming-bath and a school are sited in the 11½ acre grounds surrounding the building. These, by contrast in size, will provide a foil to the architectural mass of the building.

Perhaps a comparison between Unité and one of London's largest blocks of flats will help to clarify some of the more tangible town-planning factors involved. Dolphin Square,

Westminster, (Fig. 32.2) is one of the most 'luxurious' blocks of flats erected during the inter-war period; designed as a quadrangle, its multi-storeys enclose an area laid out with gardens, terraces and tennis courts, and cater for different sized families. It has its own restaurants, dance hall, laundry, gymnasia and squash courts. The whole conception aims to provide a social refuge from the immensity of London. Occupying a site of 7¼ acres, its population density of 415 persons an acre, a figure that far exceeds the maximum density of 200 persons an acre for London advocated in the County of London Plan. Although this figure is considerably greater than the density of the Unité d'Habitation (139 per acre) can we truthfully say that Dolphin Square has a closer resemblance to a beehive than Unité? A balanced judgment can only be made when other Unités have been erected and occupied for some years, and I therefore leave the issue as a matter for your conjecture. (Further interesting density comparisons are the proposed LCC development at Princes Way, Wimbledon, where 1,600 people are to be housed in an 'open' park site of 27 acres and the residential area of Lansbury (Poplar and Stepney)*12 acres, 1,500 persons, 125 per acre.)

32.2
Dolphin Square flats, London (1937)

Architect: Stanley Gordon Jeeves
Photographer: Sydney W. Newbery (1937)

*The first phase of the Lansbury Estate formed the Live Architecture Exhibition, part of the 1951 Festival of Britain. (Eds)

Max Gooch

In explaining the structure ... the clearest way is to start from the individual flat and work outwards.

With 1,600 persons closely packed into one block, sound insulation obviously becomes a major problem, and this has probably been the greatest single factor influencing Le Corbusier's structural design. Each flat is a box, complete in itself, made up of light prefabricated panels of dry construction whose dimensions are based on the *Modulor*. (Figs 32.3 and 32.4) These boxes are assembled inside the structural frame, but do not touch it directly. They rest on joists of pressed steel spanning between the main frames, but insulated from them by pads of lead.

The main structure of the block is of in situ reinforced concrete, and the shuttering for this is quite crude, being knocked together from rough timber. There is no use of standard metal moulds as one might have expected. However, the concrete comes out remarkably clean. Only at every third floor is there a solid concrete slab, to provide a fire-break. The intermediate floors are of the same type of dry construction. Outside the main frame the floor slabs cantilever to form balconies, and on these stands the exterior cladding of precast elements has surprised some people familiar with the precision of the Pavillon Suisse, but I think this is quite deliberate, and that Corbusier realized that an assemblage of smooth precise slabs on this scale would be intolerable, a point borne out, in my opinion, by some recent American office-blocks. On the in situ work of the ground floor too the board-marks are clearly shown (*béton brut*), and all this seems to me a great contribution to the architectural handling of concrete.

32.3
Play area in the children's room, housing unit prototype, Unité d'Habitation, Marseille (1952)

Photographers: Photographie Industrielle du Sud-Ouest – Bordeaux (1949)

32.4
Bas-relief of the Modulor, Unité d'Habitation, Marseille (1952)

Photographers: Kenneth Easton and Peter Carter of the London County Council Architects Department (ca. 1951)

32.5
Unité d'Habitation, Marseille (1952)

Photographers: Kenneth Easton and Peter Carter of the London County Council Architects Department (ca. 1951)

The main structural frame, seventeen storeys high, stands on the *sel artificial* – the classical Corbusier device as used in the Pavillon Suisse – some 30 feet above the natural ground. This massive slab collects the point loads from the closely spaced columns above and transmits them to the huge portal-framed *pilotis*. (Fig. 32.5) As an example of the careful study which Corbusier gives to form it is said that he spent several months arriving at the exact form for these *pilotis*, and in his Paris office is a precise model of one of them in plaster, about five feet high.

Thurston Williams

What I have to say is entirely impromptu – an attempt to recall certain immediate personal sensations on visiting the site. In the first place I was impressed by the fact that Unité seemed less vast than I had expected; this is probably due to the excellent proportioning of the building (though how far this in turn is due to the *Modulor* I would not like to say). The use of strong colour in the reveals of the balconies is perhaps a bit violent but when the whole building is completed in this manner we will be able to judge better whether this use of colour has achieved its object which is presumably to lighten the dead character of so much exposed concrete.

Generally speaking one would say that the aesthetic quality of the conception is beyond dispute … but in execution the performance falls rather short, the constructional methods being almost mediaeval in their crudity. This is particularly unfortunate where the reinforced concrete so handled is left exposed. My own criticisms, however, are of a more sociological character. Firstly, the attempt at completeness made by the inclusion of shops, post office, library, clinic, etc., within one single building must be a limitation to the social life of the inhabitants; one can well imagine that the housewife will have little need and less inclination ever to leave the building at all for days on end. And this seems particularly unfitting to the temperament of such people as the Marseillais. The conception seems to dominate rather than to liberate.

Finally, there are those rumours about rising cost of the project; and unless the final rentals are within the reach of the workers for whom it was originally planned, it will have failed in its principal objective.

W. G. Howell

I don't think it is possible to understand the Unité as a contribution to urban architecture if it is considered merely in its present isolated setting.

When Corbusier was called in to build apartments for the Marseilles Municipality, no plan of development for the city existed, and the lack of any such plan is reflected in the chaotic rebuilding in the old port. It is unlikely that anything built in an unplanned milieu can produce out of the blue a patch of balanced urbanism. Therefore I suggest that, in discussing this aspect of the project, we examine it as it is used in the plan for St. Dié.

This post-war project by Corbusier for rebuilding a small town in the Vosges represents the most recent development of his ideas on urbanism. In the plan, Corbusier shows eight Unités, closely related to broad pedestrian ways leading into and through a series of 'piazzas,' from which runs another broad pedestrian route across the river to a *place d'industrie*, the centre of gravity of a group of factories which stretch along the river-bank. All vehicular traffic is isolated on different levels.

The eight Unités form a series of vertical streets within a few minutes' walk of the town centre, and are set in a landscaped park with schools disposed around them. Then, from this highly concentrated centre (something like 250 people to the acre), long ribbons of low houses run out into the countryside along parkways, which are separated from the main approach roads to the town. These two, the vertical street related to the piazza and the horizontal street radiating into the countryside, are clearly differentiated in the plan, each an imaginative interpretation of a particular way of living.

The only reservation I would make here is that I would like to see a higher proportion of houses – in St. Dié the proportion is three persons in flats to every one in the houses, though there seem to be provisional sites for more houses.

Bearing in mind this setting one may discount Thurston Williams's fear that there would be no incentive for the housewife ever to leave the building. What in fact Corbusier has suggested is that the people living in flats should be given the choice of communal facilities and services both in their own buildings and in the town centre five minutes' distant. We give them no such choice, but force them always to go out. Corbusier also makes it possible for those who live on the ground to shop or have a drink eight storeys up, whereas the flats we build are inaccessible to non-residents.

Two further points we should study in this exciting and beautiful building – first, the idea of a whole structure, a whole set of components, a whole series of spaces, designed on a system of dimensions all harmonically related, and all related to the human figure. Everyone who has seen the building testifies to the human and domestic quality of the building, contrasting with what Easton has called the heroic scale of the *pilotis*. To what extent the quality of the building derives from the use of such a geometrical system, or to what extent it is a result of the handling of such a system by a very great artist, we might discuss.

The other idea which seems most relevant to us is the development of the principle of the deep, narrow-frontage flat. The saving in external walling, maintenance cost and heating must be enormous, and if you want to know just how exciting and generous an interior of these proportions can be, I can only advise you to go to Marseilles.

Philip Powell

My immediate reaction is that this is a very lovely building – even the trial colours on the balconies. Some speakers have objected to these, and I would agree that anybody with pretensions to 'good taste' would not like them. I found their strength stimulating. (Especially, I remember a very wicked green.)

The poor craftsmanship in the handling of the concrete was very evident – as it happens, most effective in the case of the in-situ work and probably giving an intentionally rough effect. But I am not so sure I agree with Mr. Gooch that the roughness of the precast concrete work is intentionally contrived to avoid monotony.

Incidentally, I tried running round the semi-circular end of the running-track. There is no banking at the moment, and the bend is so sharp that unless it is very steep indeed I visualize runners reaching parapet level at full speed and flying off the edge of the building.

But I have been asked to consider how far the Unité has an immediate application to our own housing problem. The principle of the deep slice plan is, in point of fact, traditional to the Victorian terrace-house and can be arranged, as in the Unité, to give good light in any flat. It would be particularly suitable over here for studios. However, I have some doubt about the advisability, in this country, of a bedroom overlooking a living-room except in studios. I would like to see double height flats with double height gardens as opposed to the minimum size box balconies, even if this meant (for financial reasons) the reduction in area of some of the rooms inside the flat. That, of course, means 'away with the Housing Manual.'

Most people with families of any size prefer houses with gardens. But the possibility of twenty- or thirty-storey blocks, suggested by the Unité (yet reserved for smaller families) mixed with two- or three-storey compact house-with-garden development, seems to be the only rational approach to high-density planning.

Instead of alternating two- and three-storey houses or flats with five-, six- or even eleven-storey blocks of flats on, for instance, a thirty-acre site, we might divide the site in half, giving one half over to two- and three-storey garden terraces and the other half to, say, two twenty- or thirty-storey blocks of single, two and three room flats, giving, I feel, a happy contrast between the domestic, small-scale effect of the houses with their small enclosed open spaces and the blocks of flats standing in wide public gardens. Of course the present system of subsidies might artificially make this development, with its increased number of houses, more expensive – in which case, scrap the present subsidies system. And the present by-laws would make a thirty-floor block of flats impossible – therefore scrap the by-laws too. [...]

Source: *Architectural Review*, May 1951

The Vertical City

By Colin St. John Wilson

The recent decision by a Town Planning Appeal Tribunal to reduce the height of a proposed block of flats at Wimbledon has drawn attention to one of the crucial issues in the re-planning of our cities. Further attacks in the press upon the use of 'skyscrapers,' together with the appearance of the L.C.C. Development Plan, prompt us to consider once more what we really want London to be.

There is a general agreement upon the diagnosis in the 1942 County of London Report of the basic evils of London: depressed housing, traffic congestion, inadequacy of open spaces, jumbled zoning and continued 'sprawl' into the countryside. But the nature and appearance of the solutions vary considerably since they will depend upon one of two basic attitudes of mind towards city-life in general.

Fear and disgust at these evils have obliterated from the minds of some people any idea of the city as a desirable place. Such an attitude will demand reduction of scale, dispersal of population, dilution of conflicts. At the opposite pole there are those who maintain a positive acceptance of the grand scale of city-life together with a conviction in our capacity to create on this scale in an orderly and bold way.

To clarify these two reactions we may reduce the discussion to the particular issue of housing. The extreme 'negative' case is illustrated by the man whose sole dream is to possess a 'cottage, an acre and a cow.' Multiply that dream by 2,000,000 and its impracticability becomes obvious; but, as an extreme example of one type of development, the 'horizontal garden-city,' it is very revealing. Low densities spread thinly are bound to cover more virgin countryside just at a time when demands upon domestic agriculture make this particularly undesirable. Technically, the construction of the free-standing house, together with the necessary increase in lengths of service and roads, is unnecessarily costly. And aesthetically, a desert of front doors staring at each other across an access road precisely defeats the desire for 'freedom from monotony' which brought it into being.

This particular form of the 'horizontal garden-city' is not seriously proposed by anyone to-day as the answer to London's housing shortage: but its basic assumptions and attitude of mind are often present behind many proposals which claim powerful sponsorship. There are those who maintain that the scale of London has always been 'intimate' in comparison with Rome, Paris, or New York. This extraordinary effeminacy promises to convert London into the most overblown and 'tasteful' village in the world: three- and six-storey blocks of flats with the pitched roofs, peep-hole windows and 'folky' details of the current Swedish revival, picturesquely sited around market-places, have been offered to us in the name of 'live architecture.'

This, on the contrary, can lead to an architecture of 'cold feet': fear of city-scale, fear of the machine, fear of everything that the architectural innovators of the past twenty-five years have promised us. It is symptomatic of that post-war loss of nerve which, from a sense of guilt towards the scientific methods and machines that have been used for destruction, reacts with a split-minded desire to retreat into a world of cosiness.

The 'positive' attitude of mind which regards the large-scale city as desirable can best be demonstrated by another extreme example. For the 1937 Paris Exhibition, Le Corbusier proposed a 'live architecture' reconstruction for a condensed quarter of Paris – the 'vertical garden-city.'

Structurally, the basis of this solution is the tall slab block raised off the ground on 'stilts', roads for vehicles are also raised above ground level, which is thus freed throughout the site as open space for park-land, where children and pedestrians are at last safe from traffic. Each block of flats is sited among trees in a park, twenty to thirty floors high, with wide and splendid views (like that, for instance, from the top of Primrose Hill). The concentration permitted by vertical planning may free sufficient space for houses with gardens for the larger families. The scaffolding around the Victoria Tower, Westminster, which last summer gave it the appearance of a block of flats, provided a fine example of what the true scale of London could be.

This is a conception which uses in a positive way all the original technical capacities of our day rather than abusing or rejecting them: mastery of the machine rather than fear of it is accepted as the only way to rediscover the 'human' city. Its plastic expression is as far removed from artiness as the design of aircraft. Its whole spirit is one of clarity and imagination; and the last hundred years have proved that these are not just pretty embellishments but desperate necessities.

The idea is simple enough and has an organic inevitability about it: all over Europe it is gaining ground – in Rotterdam, Hamburg, Marseilles, (Fig. 33.1) Nantes, Milan, Frankfurt ... Complexity enters only when we consider the instruments by which to achieve it. In London the archaic building regulations that prevailed at Wimbledon are not the only opponent to buildings over 80 ft. high, as Lansbury has shown. Cuts in capital expenditure have already made nonsense of the most modest proposals for road improvements. Our building industry, in comparison with the car, ship or aircraft industries, is farcically antiquated. But we have got the best town-planning legislation in the world, and recent housing schemes proposed by the L.C.C. and rumours of the use of twenty-storey blocks in the provinces give evidence of an exhilarating attempt to open up new ground.

These are small beginnings, but they must be carried out without compromise in order to achieve both the greatest possible advantage from them now and their easy assimilation into more advanced schemes in the future. Some 'risks' must be taken, for instance, central heating and the freeing of space around the 'stilts' of large blocks must be maintained against short-termed accusations of 'wastage' of space.

33.1
Unité d'Habitation, Marseille (1952)
Photographer unknown (1950s)

It is by such means that those who are not obsessed by fear still hope to achieve a city that is both disciplined and imaginative and self-confident, that city whose function Aristotle described as being 'to make men happy.'

Source: *The Observer*, 17 February 1952

Concerning Le Corbusier

By Frederic J. Osborn

The fountain pen is mightier than the drawing pencil; so one is tempted to think when reading architectural books of today. Perhaps it is another symptom of social progress. When Macaulay said that as civilization advances, poetry declines, he may well have been wrong; but there is a better case for the expectation that as literacy advances, architecture must decline. So much more is to be found in books and journals as you sit in an armchair than in accessible streets as you walk about.

Ruskin, who did not realize this, certainly profited by it, and created an architectural revolution in a new arena – the dreams of the great circulating-library and magazine-buying public – as well as, to a less extent, the external world of building. It is almost a hundred years since, in his Edinburgh *Lectures on Architecture and Art* (1853), he propounded, with terrific assurance and no small effect, his beautifully confused aesthetic principles. Vivid and immensely important moral truths and aesthetic half-truths were strung on a frail thread of unphilosophic argument. Thereby Ruskin won his permanent place in this history of architecture and art. There he is for all time. The fact that it is now obvious that on this subject he wrote a lot of gorgeous nonsense cannot deprive him of his niche in the temple. He was a force. He moved opinion.

Le Corbusier has also won his place in the record. Whether a commendable fact or not, he is a fact. He has influenced many minds in many countries. Whatever critics may think of his ideas or his expressions he has proved he can interest and stimulate readers. The illustrations he puts in his books have the attraction of doodles that look as if the doodler could draw if he liked. And his written texts, like brief staccato syllabuses for chapters, leave room for the belief that he could fill them out into real chapters if he liked – that a complete philosophy of aesthetics could be produced if there were world enough and time. Ruskin's thoroughly wrought periods and paragraphs, noble tone, and beautifully executed drawings, by making the very most of his argument, disclose its limitations to any critical reader. It is very much more difficult to fasten on the fallacies in Le Corbusier's philosophy because he does not even attempt to connect up the components that might go into it. But you don't have to have an absolutely water-tight philosophy to find a following and to leave a mark.

Perhaps Le Corbusier's most influential book is *Towards a New Architecture*, first published in France in 1923, and in England in 1927. At the time I was as much irritated by the author's neglect to digest and systematize his ideas as I was interested in some of the ideas themselves. It is clear now that his dominating and effective inspiration was a replacement of the 'architectural' by the 'engineering' concept of building; but he fogged this quite intelligible thesis by an unsuccessful attempt to distinguish architecture as the custodian of 'beauty' from good engineering as the custodian of 'harmony'. Neither his theory nor his practice has ever convinced me that he has any grip on the meaning of 'beauty' or the conditions of its creation or evocation. But I do see that he has a genuine passion for mechanical progress and scientific novelty (the enthusiasm of Macaulay, H. G. Wells, Northcliffe, and nine out of ten healthy British or French boys). Consistently with this, he welcomes mass-production; deprecates tradition; finds older things stuffy, and new things exciting; is sympathetic to change of any kind that has the mechanistic glitter or severity; and does not mind whether an invention is useful, so long as it expresses adventure or power. The space-rocket seems to be a sort of symbol of the aesthetics this outlook produces.

The 'engineering' enthusiasm is so vital a factor in modern feeling and is so widely shared that clearly it could have some relation to aesthetics; but I cannot see that in any of his books Le Corbusier gives us any principles for 'architecture' in his own sense of construction made beautiful as well as harmonious. I am sure he is right that there is a beauty that is more than harmony, but I suspect you would have to bring in elements of memory, association, or tradition, as well as of fundamental preferences in shapes and colours, to establish canons of beauty sufficiently widely shared to be applicable to architecture. I suspect that the complete shutting-off of tradition was the death of 'architecture' in any sense distinguishable from 'decent building'; but it may have had to die – there is no ground for assuming any art is immortal. And there is much to be said for decent building.

Leaving these difficult issues, I come to the theories on which the Marseilles experiment is based. Foreshadowed in several previous books, the idea of l'Unité d'Habitation is very fully elaborated in *Concerning Town Planning* (1945) and *The Home of Man* (1946). In the latter book F. de Pierrefeu shares the authorship; he states the same ideas in a more *legato* and continuous style.

Since the Industrial Revolution, Man, we are told, has mocked Nature. The natural pattern of settlement, discouraged by the steam railway and the automobile, is again changed by the aeroplane, which (it is not explained why or how) restores natural harmony. Profit is no longer the aim. There is (I summarize too brusquely) a unity of man and the cosmos. Architecture and Planning are the spirit and heart of the epoch. The sun is a primary phenomenon (with this I cordially agree). It dictates the size of the agricultural unit (this is not demonstrated). Architecture develops from within outwards (so does everything). Grass and flowers are the natural police force of town planning (the Green Belt idea – admirable). Streets and internal courts are contrary to human well-being. And Venice (all streets) is the ideal town. The chaotic city, with its narrow traffic streets, viewless windows, nasty smells, and suburbs spreading like 'great leprous stains' is a prison. It hands out to its customers 'miles instead of sunrays, stinking car exhausts instead of pure air, and in place of silence, a tumult murderous for nerves'. And so 'man reaches the end of his life without once having had the chance to catch upon the mirror of his conscience, framed by the landscape of creation, one glimpse of his real appearance'. And 'an enormous mass of working hours' is 'destined to useless transport'.

Thus more wittily, though less judiciously and persuasively, than Ebenezer Howard, Le Corbusier and his colleague expose the pretentions of the modern city – carrying their criticism as far as a moral denunciation of the speculators and usurers who have so built it, and the 'blind public authorities' who have allowed it to be so built. These 'worldly but cunning' persons have transformed the 'bare and sombre prison' at first produced by the machine era, by means of 'a whole glittering arsenal of disguises, neon lights, shouts, and songs', into 'a regular palace of mirages'. They are accused of enslaving all ranks of society, of rupturing the economic balance of human groups, of depraving standards of living, of promoting war, even of the corrosion of the very soul of citified man.

A more raging, tearing indictment of the great city has never been made. Compared with it the curses of the Hebrew prophets, the satires of Juvenal, the descriptions of Dickens or Zola or Maxim Gorky or Eliot Paul, or the analyses of Lewis Mumford, all look like a considerate white-washing. We of the garden city school of thought have sometimes been charged with over-stating the case against the congested, corpulent metropolis; but beside Le Corbusier we are tender, simpering, mealy-mouthed, timidly complaining babes.

Yet if you put on smoked glasses to reduce the atomic-fission glare and hectic coloration of Le Corbusier's picture, you can detect that his essential criticism of the metropolis is the same as Howard's. What they both dislike, and what humanity dislikes, is the squalor of the canyon street, the shortage of sun and space in the home, the grasslessness and gracelessness of the ensemble, the waste of time in daily travel, the damage to the quality of the person and of society through the destruction of local community.

Anyone who can enter imaginatively into the working of the youthful mind in times of revolutionary change and war and much insecurity, and in places where city depersonalization has already taken effect and balanced criticism is absent, can understand the appeal of Le Corbusier's violent and exaggerated dramatization of facts open to everyday observation. If Eliot's *Waste Land* could strike deep into the soul of some types of deracinated persons whose interests have turned inward, this devastating picture could equally capture some whose interests have turned outward and tend to be constructive. Le Corbusier quite rightly asks us to regard him as 'a sort of poet'.

Le Corbusier, however, has not stopped at a poetic extravaganza on the theme of the existing city as he sees it. Nor did he begin with that vision. All the indications are that his criticism of the city has been developed to support by antithesis another vision that goes further back into his life and is far more fundamental to his make-up. I think his dominating prepossessions are, like those of many architects, essentially visual, and inventively visual – those of the painter or sculptor, whose urge is to make new forms in shape or tone. He started as an engraver, and was a painter before he was an architect, and an architect before he was a student of cities. His passion for mechanical progress and discovery is as strong as his visual passion, and both preceded his interest in ways of living, social affairs, and economics – of which subjects he hardly shows a moderate amateur grasp. This would not handicap him as an artist, architect, or engineer if he confined himself to such specializations. But it is disabling when it comes to prescribing the sort of city suitable for family life, industry, trade, culture, and the other purposes of society.

34.1
Sketch showing how land is released for pedestrians by raising buildings on pilotis

From Le Corbusier and François de Pierrefeu,
The Home of Man (1948)

The Home of Man is a rough but fairly complete specification of l'Unité d'Habitation – the vertical village of which the exemplar is now nearing completion in Marseilles. (Fig. 34.1) The presentation in this book is most vivid and entertaining: little batches of short sentences are interspersed with many of those expressive doodles. (Students need to be warned that some of the doodles are seriously misleading through their distorted scales.) Paris is the guinea-pig city chosen for dissection: it is shown as having a centre of 'urban desert' – dark, congested, cut off from nature – and all around it the 'garden cities of exile and disillusionment'.

That Le Corbusier uses the term 'garden cities' for the suburbs that the garden city movement was the first to oppose, illustrates the astonishing limitations of his reading. A poet need not read or listen; a philosopher should; a social planner must.

Study of this specification for the dwelling of the future shows that it is inspired by two enthusiasms. The first is for the open countryside as a daily spectacle; this most people probably share; those in temperate climates who revel in the 'urban' or enclosed sensation are few. The other is for the technical possibilities of lofty buildings as an expression both of scientific power over materials and of creative imagination; this is not so widely felt, but most people understand it. In Xanadu did Kubla Khan ... On Manhattan did the Chrysler Company ... and if it comes to that, in pyramids and obelisks and church spires and skylons so did generations of men. There should be outlets for this endemic aspiration without immolating living beings in the vertical features.

Placing buildings on stilts, so that the landscape is in theory uninterrupted by them, caters for both Le Corbusier's enthusiasms. And so does the idea of the wall of glass. These are new things made possible by modern construction: therefore they should be done. The stilts seem to 'free' the earth below. The glass wall seems to bring the largest possible slice of landscape into the room.

To show these possibilities of modern technique is proper: there will be occasions when they should be used. But Le Corbusier preaches the high flat building on stilts as the future normal standard. He would rebuild the million cities in this way at 366 persons an acre overall, with cars carried on overhead roads and all the ground between and under the buildings open to pedestrians. And certainly this would look a lot more interesting and spacious than the cities look today. For business districts already overcrowded a reconstruction on these lines would be an improvement.

But if there were not already a congestion problem in cities, it is very doubtful if it would prove economic or convenient to build to great heights; the elevator is not inherently a quicker means of transport than the surface vehicle. For planners the transport problem is that of disentangling wasteful from useful periodic movement. Movement, vertically and horizontally, could be as expensive in a million city on Le Corbusier's pattern as on the present pattern.

To reconstruct a city on these lines would clearly be enormously costly. Le Corbusier shrugs off problems of finance, though he talks much of economy: 'For the inventors, the realists, the strong, who tilt at life with courage, money dies, and with this love of money.'

For the Home of Man, however, apart from the colossal extra cost (which the Marseilles realization illustrates), I am sure Man himself, and still more Mrs Man, will think the proposed solution flouts too many vital functional considerations. Even the aesthetic argument for it, in these books, has to be supported by fallacious diagrams. The doodles rightly reiterate that the human eye normally sees horizontally from five and a half feet off the ground, and dramatic scenic effects, with slab buildings among trees and mountains, are sketched from that viewpoint. But the detestability of suburbs is proved by dotting masses of little houses as if they were studs on a rubber doormat seen from above – quite out of scale and with no hint of vegetation.

In fact a well-laid-out housing estate can look delightful from the air. But if it looked monotonous from that angle, that is not the way the occupiers see it. From five and a half feet up every garden of reasonable size has its own prospect; the views are of buildings, trees, earth, and sky in multitudinous forms varying with the skill of the planners and the taste of the residents. They may well produce a far greater sum of aesthetic satisfaction than a single landscape with dwellings packed into spaced-out towers.

However, Le Corbusier's romantic mechanistic fantasy does have a spectacular appeal, and his lively propaganda for it is stimulating and enjoyable. I would not wish to induce anyone to live in a city on his pattern; but just as I went to see the film of Wells's *Shape of Things to Come*, hoping they would not come, so on reading these books I felt that if ever anyone built something on these lines I would have to go and see it. [...] It is a very conspicuous object in the eastern suburbs of Marseilles, near a range of the barren hills that enclose the city. Standing up on its massive *pilotis* or stilts, 185 feet high, 420 feet long, and 75 feet wide, the building gives an impression of overpowering strength and weight rather than of domesticity or elegance. (Fig. 34.2) Noah's Ark, 450 feet long and 75 feet wide, must have looked homely by comparison, since it was only 45 feet high.

The stilts struck me as needlessly swollen, rather brutal, more anxious to demonstrate the colossal quantity of material they are carrying than to 'free the ground' or to offer views of the landscape on the other side of the building. The ground seemed indeed about as much 'liberated' as under the London Bridge railway arches. As an amenity the scenery discernible through the chinks seemed insufficient to compensate residents for the extra sixty-foot return journey between earth and home. But the actual façades, with their horizontal accent, and their many loggias or balcony recesses, painted on the flanks with hard bright colours like the Hertfordshire schools, were interesting and lively.

The building contains 337 dwellings, housing at average occupation 1,463 persons. (Fig. 34.3) Of these 220 are for families of four to eight, and have an area of 1,046 square feet plus two balconies of 63 square feet. There are seventy-nine smaller flats, for no-child or

34.2
Unité d'Habitation, Marseille (1952)

Photographer: J.M. Richards (ca. 1953)

one-child families, the latter of about 640 square feet, and twenty-two larger, the biggest, for ten persons, having 2,455 square feet, and four balconies.

The internal planning is complex and has much technical fascination. There are seventeen floors, one of which (the eighth) is to be a shopping centre. Most of the 'flats' have two floors, thus resembling what are now called maisonettes. Public access is by means of corridors in the core of the building, which in general are on each third floor only, so that the lifts are on the 'skip-stop' principle. But whereas in most skip-stop buildings you walk up or down one storey to the front doors on intermediate floors, in l'Unité all the front doors are on the lift-corridor level, and you go down or up stairs inside each 'flat' to either the living-room or bedroom floor.

Living-rooms are two floors or 14½ feet high; bedrooms and kitchens 7¼ feet. Thus the part of the living-room nearest the window and loggia is very well lighted and attractive. But the kitchen, reached by an open staircase in the living-room, is far back from the window, dark, and very cramped, and the great depth of the building means that much of the space towards its core is without natural light. Bathrooms, showers, lavatories, and a plenitude of cupboards are tucked away in this central core; but the transverse passage

34.3
Children's room, housing unit prototype, Unité d'Habitation, Marseille (1952)

Photographers: Photographie Industrielle du Sud-Ouest – Bordeaux (1949)

space is so extensive as largely to cancel the economy in public corridors. Also it can be argued that the internal stairs cancel the one advantage of flats over houses. Many bedrooms are 6 feet wide, 7¼ feet high, and 25 feet long, with an end window only. Though specially designed dwarf cupboards are placed at the head of beds, light is very weak at the end of such a room, and there is no place for other furniture.

Thus, though the floor space provided seems generous, much of it is reduced in value by darkness or is virtually passage space.

No definite figures of cost have been issued, but I was informed by an official that the total cost to March 1952 was 1,800 million francs: £1,850,000, or £5,400 a flat. The type of construction – a mighty concrete framework into which are inserted separate flat units resting on lead pads and insulated with glass wool – cannot conceivably be cheap. Experienced French architects told me they thought the quoted cost an under-estimate; but the building had been in progress six years, and prices were lower in the early years. The cost today might they thought be 60,000 francs a square metre; or £5,880 for the flat of 1,046 square feet.

This sized flat was offered for sale at £3,575 including ice-box, cooker, cupboards, and other fittings at £175. The purchaser had to find £1,075 and the £2,500 balance could be paid off in thirty-five years at £90 a year. For space-heating, window-cleaning, lifts, garden upkeep and insurance he pays £60 a year. He also pays for electricity used for water heating, cooking, and lighting.

Half the flats were for sale, to owners of war-damaged dwellings and others; and half for letting, to civil servants and others. The loss on the building is borne by the Government, which has undertaken the scheme. The loss would appear to be around £2,000 a dwelling, which rivals our own housing subsidy for the blue riband for extravagance.

I think it unlikely that any profit rental will arise from the avenue of shops and offices on the eighth floor or the restaurant, club rooms, or play-ground facilities on the roof. A group of 1,400–1,500 people is too small to support a shopping centre, and occupiers are more likely to shop outside than outsiders to shop inside.

The conception of a self-sufficient community on this scale is not in my opinion sound, and while it is good to provide clubrooms and playground facilities in any residential area, high up inside a building is not the most convenient site for them.

Thus I am bound to conclude that, even if it is held that housing densities of 150 or more persons per acre are so firmly established in towns that they must be perpetuated (which seems to me planning defeatism), the arrangement posed by Le Corbusier in the Marseilles building is entirely unsatisfactory. It does not provide the best accommodation possible even in multi-storey flats. The depth of the building involves waste of space and bad lighting, and its height and complexity involve excessive building and upkeep costs.

On the whole the most interesting feature of the scheme is the two-floor apartment having one room double the height of the others. This may be usable in future luxury dwellings – though not for families with children. And I am sure there must be constructional expedients of value in so ingenious a scheme. But L'Unité d'Habitation has nothing to do with a solution of the social housing problem or with the planned redevelopment of great cities.

Source: *Town & Country Planning*, July & August 1952

Selection of Speeches made at the Presentation of the Royal Institute of British Architects' Royal Gold Medal to Le Corbusier on 31 March 1953

35.1
Le Corbusier

Photographer: Sam Lambert (1950s)

Howard Robertson (RIBA President)

On the recommendation of the Council of the Royal Institute of British Architects, Her Majesty the Queen has approved the award of the Royal Gold Medal for 1953 to Monsieur Le Corbusier, of France. I need hardly say what an enormous pleasure it is to have Monsieur Le Corbusier with us this evening. He has come from France today; he has been photographed a few times and he has made three broadcasts; but he is a man who takes punishment lightly, and he is standing up very well to his trials.

A number of people are going to speak about our guest tonight, and I am not going to say very much; I shall leave it to others. There are, however, two things which I should like to say about M. Le Corbusier. One is that his name is known and respected as an architect all over the world. To an extraordinary degree it is a household word. The other thing is that as an architect he has never been interested in what architects have to do to earn their living; he has earned his living, but he does not care about it. He would leave any job which did not interest him and refuse any work, however fat the fee, in order to do something which appealed to his artistic integrity. It is a tremendous thing for an architect to do that, and I think that it is about the highest compliment which I could pay him as a man.

Sir Herbert Read

I shall beg leave to speak very briefly about Le Corbusier the poet. Yes, M. Le Corbusier is a poet, a great poet. I am told that he actually writes verses, though I regret that he does not publish them, or at least I have not seen them. We all know that he paints pictures, and that if he had not been so busy as an architect he might have taken his place among the leading painters of our epoch. There is a close stylistic relationship between the paintings and the architecture; they are alternative expressions of the same spiritual harmony.

M. Le Corbusier also writes books (Fig. 35.2) – vigorous, vital books in a prose that sparkles with metaphors and images, with aphorisms and with crystal-clear logic. All this constitutes a complex activity which can only be called poetic, an imaginative process which is unique in our time and which exerts an influence far beyond the spheres of architecture and town planning. Le Corbusier is a man with a poetic vision of life, not a poetic vision of buildings and cities only but rather a vision of a poetic way of life, a new manner of living. Life in that vision is above all radiant, not only *La Ville Radieuse* but also *la vie*

35.2
Cover of *Des Canons, des Munitions? Merci! Des Logis ... S.V.P.* (1938)

radieuse. He has said in one of his books, and it is the key to all his activities, that the concept of life itself must be changed, and indeed that we should begin by investigating the nature of happiness. That is the first necessity; the rest, including a new architecture, will inevitably follow.

'What should we build with?' he asks, and he dares to answer 'Not with steel and cement, but with love.' Steel and cement, all the modern techniques, are given to us for this purpose, to express our love of life and of man. They are the raw materials of a visual love poetry. The techniques are the foundations of lyricism, of poetry. Revolutionary? He admits it, he glories in the fact, but at the same time he explains that he is a revolutionary who has never had but one master, the past. He has ranged through the world in his studies of the past. He is probably the most travelled, the most international architect since the Middle Ages. He has learned from that experience that it has always been the poet who has shown the new way and revealed the new truth.

In *When the Cathedrals were White* – and only a poet could have thought of such an evocative phrase – M. Le Corbusier has pointed out that the whole universe was raised up by an immense faith in the energy, the future, the harmonious creation of a civilisation. Le Corbusier has that immense faith. He is not just any kind of poet; he is an immensely optimistic poet. He believes that the present is creative, creating with an unheard-of intensity. He believes that a great epoch has begun, a new epoch. To that great epoch he himself has contributed the paradigms, the prototypes. That is why we honour him today as the poet who has given us a new vision of the future, and not only a vision but the beginnings – white, limpid, clean, clear and without hesitations, a new world opening up like a flower among the ruins – his own poetic words, again apt to describe his own poetic creations ... we honour a great poet.

Mr Robert Matthew

I have been asked to say something tonight in particular about M. Le Corbusier and town planning. Let me say at once that this is, of course, to say something almost about his whole life and work. I do not imagine that in his mind there are two compartments, one for architecture and the other for town planning. If one could characterise his approach it would certainly be one of wholeness, an indivisibility, the subtle but enormously important relationship of the part – in the case of town planning, of the innumerable parts – to the whole.

It is no accident, I imagine, that Corbusier the *urbaniste* and Corbusier the inventor of the *Modulor* are one and the same. The relentless search for order, the search for proportion and the discovery of its roots in the classical golden ratios is the inevitable expression, to my mind, not only of his disgust at the pathetic disorder of our 19th and 20th century towns, but also of his persistent belief – and this must be tremendously to his credit, in view of his own experience – in the possibility, if not the certainty, of the emergence of harmony in human affairs.

For far too long Corbusier's town planning schemes, fertile, audacious – I would say revolutionary, but with great respect to Sir Herbert Read and the *Evening Standard*, I do not know whether Corbusier would entirely accept that phrase today – for far too long these remained on paper, in the realm of theory. A window on new worlds, in the organisation of urban space, had been opened, and in the years between the wars the whole world – in so far as it was young, progressive and architectural – was drawn to his atelier in Paris.

What they saw there – and they could see this nowhere else in the world– was nothing less than a new affirmation of the rights of man, the rights of man in terms of sun, light, space, quiet, trees and grass. The translation of this book of rights into architectural terms has, I imagine, been his constant work and recreation. The wonder is that, with so little opportunity before the war to put into practice his theory, a consistent development was possible at all. That this was so, however, is now a matter of history, as anyone comparing his early studies for *La Ville Radieuse* with, for instance, his post-war reconstruction schemes can immediately appreciate.

Today the situation is different, quite different. M. Le Corbusier is here, there and everywhere, advising, designing, creating, from India to New York and from South America to Marseilles. His life-long studies in the functions of the city are now put to the test of practical achievement, and everyone here will wish him well in his great work for the present and for the future. These studies, knitting together the technological possibilities of building with radical solutions to, among other things, the seemingly intractable problems of traffic circulation, have for long now been recognised as a fundamental contribution to 20th-century town planning technique. Even some of the world's largest bureaucracies have not been entirely impervious to these ideas.

Bureaucracies and academics! These have been the substantial windmills at which this Don Quixote, this wandering knight – and here, with great respect. I have used his own words – has unremittingly tilted. Academies, for their fine words and fair gestures, masking a basic lack of understanding of 'cities in evolution'. Bureaucracies, for their power-driven politics, obscuring and confusing where there should be directness and simplicity. This, indeed, is his characteristic; his approach is nothing if not direct, alike to his problems and to his critics.

His notebooks are a miracle of direct statement. I know of no one who has depicted the urban scene with equal economy of line and certainty of effort. In these thousands of sketches lies the development of his thought from the rigid geometry of the university-quarter-caravanserai of the early 1920s and the *Plan Voisin* for Paris to the highly imaginative plan for St. Dié in 1945, with its disciplined informality and differentiated traffic levels, and still more in the new capital of the Punjab, which has already, before it is built, become one of the most celebrated cities in the world.

The description by M. Le Corbusier of the plans for this city of Chandigarh given at the C.I.A.M. meeting in England in 1951 is, I think, an excellent example of his brevity of statement and his clarity of aim. Describing the various functions of the city plan, he comes after a number of other headings to the heading 'industry', and he makes but one terse comment: 'This is not an industrial city!' Let bureaucracies take a lesson from this brief but adequate statement!

I must confess, however, that all his statements are not equally illuminating. In English, at any rate, I find some of his books difficult to follow. His prose is explosive, telegraphic, sometimes highly enigmatic. This may well account for the criticism, which has long been current here in the past, that Le Corbusier is a town planner who is out of touch with everyday life as we in this country know it. Those who feel this, however, need only turn again to his drawings and illustrations. These are the real expression of his comprehension of the human problem in all its variety and contradiction. His earliest book in English, *Towards a New Architecture*, starts with a picture of the great Bell telephone building in New York, but it finishes with a picture of briar pipe. The constant theme of his urban sketches is the re-establishment of nature. The distance covered by an hour's walking, he has said, is a surer measure than abstract numerical scales – and I believe that he practises, in this respect at any rate, what he preaches.

To M. Le Corbusier, town planning must be the spontaneous expression of human needs. Legalistic complications are only there to be surmounted or swept aside. The law of the land, he says, is that it shall support houses, and not that it shall support the unmerited ascension of private fortunes. Nor does he readily acknowledge limitations. 'Compensation' – the great bogey of all town planners everywhere – 'can be seen,' he says, 'in a new light if it is taken to mean the creation of fresh and splendid conditions of life for the townsman. That would indeed be compensation.' How true this is! It is, in fact, no more than the other side of the planning ledger, but how often it is ignored, though not by M. Le Corbusier! To him, first things are first, and these are human values.

The conclusion to his 1951 C.I.A.M. contribution is in these words: 'I have tried to show that *life* forges the tools.' In these days of great tyrannies, it is our privilege in our own sphere of architecture and town planning to recognise this life force through the incorrigible individuality of M. Le Corbusier, and in doing honour to him, as we do tonight, we do some small thing to cherish the vital flame.

Mr. W. W. Wells-Coates

It is a very great privilege to be here today to speak in honour of M. Le Corbusier, the master whose disciple I have been for many years. Corbusier, with Gropius and others, founded the International Congresses for Modern Architecture, the C.I.A.M., which have developed and represented to architects and allied technicians, and indeed to the world, new concepts in architecture and town planning for the past 25 years.

As a representative of C.I.A.M. in this country, through the MARS Group, which is celebrating its 21st birthday this year, I have received from leading C.I.A.M. members in other countries a number of messages of congratulation on this occasion, and I should like to quote a few of these. From Delgo, Ernesto Rogers and Peresutti, our friends in Milan, we have this message: 'Very pleased R.I.B.A. giving great reward to Corbusier. We take part most heartily in the honour of sending our congratulations and best wishes.' From Richard Neutra, of California, comes the message: 'Corbusier has added a stupendous impetus to modern design and to modern thought.' From Dr. Giedion, the Secretary-General of C.I.A.M., in Zürich, we have a message which ends with the words: 'Corbusier is more brilliant than ever today.' Walter Gropius says: 'His abundance and the fertility of his genius determines Corbusier's place in history as that of the Leonardo of our time.' Lastly, from Sert, who is Gropius's successor at Harvard and President of C.I.A.M., we have a message saying: 'In the name of C.I.A.M. and also my own, please convey to the R.I.B.A. heartiest congratulations for setting example to all other architectural societies by granting Gold Medal to the most outstanding architect of our time.'

Le Corbusier is known to us as a poet, a painter, a philosopher, a master architect and an outstanding leader of men. He is also a gay and inspiring companion and friend. But above all I would name him an inventor, an innovator, a discoverer, the initiator of a new world of forms. Corbusier is the architect's architect. He is the prophet of new developments, the sure master of form, the prolific delineator of new terms and new themes in this transitional age for architecture. He has done more to consolidate our thoughts and inspire our actions than any other living man.

In spite of singularly fierce opposition from persons and personalities, including often many amongst his own profession, and from committees and authorities, both national and international, Corbusier has throughout his life been the most resolute fighter for form and reform in life. He has pointed sure ways to the future of architecture. He has influenced through his teachings and his example to architects throughout the world ten thousand times the number of clients they might otherwise have had.

This is no ordinary occasion. The Royal Gold Medal of the R.I.B.A. is not being presented to an ordinary man; it is a great man who honours the honour bestowed upon him today.

Le Corbusier (speaking in French)

I have listened with interest to the speeches which have been made, and I am conscious of the kindness shown to me in doing me this great honour. I wish to admit, what I think that you have recognised, that it is always the human being, man, that I have sought to study, not as a professional architect but as a discoverer, and also as a traditionalist. I have always had my feet in the past, and my head in the past too. My roots are in the past, though not in the Dark Ages of the academies. At the same time, I have tried to take a step towards the future. It has been my object always to be simple and direct, to be both an engineer and a poet.

After all these flowers which have been showered on me, I should like to try to show you another aspect of Le Corbusier, Le Corbusier as a cab-horse. If tonight I am wearing this magnificent medal, it is because I was a cab-horse for more than forty years. During all that time I worked for all the days that God made, and often in the evenings as well, with one aim in view, to follow the truth and let my conscience be the judge of whether my work was good.

Before you presented me with all these bouquets I received, like a true cab-horse, many blows with a whip, but this did not alter my outlook or change my aims. I should like to tell you something about what happened to me, because it will perhaps show you at what a price one can perhaps succeed in making something of one's life. In all my life of more than sixty years I have never had commissions from the State and only had one official client, and that was for the Unité d'Habitation at Marseilles. I was asked 'Will you make a great building for these people?' and I replied 'Yes, on one condition, that I am not to be bound by any rules.' They agreed, and so I started work on this building, which embodies a great many of my proposals for the modern town, the town of today. I was governed by the cosmic laws of space, by my respect and admiration for nature, by the needs of the family and the recognition of the home as the fundamental unit of society and the hearth as the centre of the home. My work there has its roots in the past, in the Grande Chartreuse, which for fifty years has appealed to me by its harmony and its perfect association of the individual and the collective.

This is the positive part of what I have done. I have created something at Marseilles, as I realised when on 14 October last, at 9 o'clock in the morning, I saw it completed and inhabited. There was general agreement that it was magnificent, and I was the first to say so. I always had confidence that it would prove to be so, in spite of all the attacks that were made upon it, and on 14 October of last year I realised that here was a new achievement not of an architect but of the constructive spirit of our time.

Now let me tell you something which will show you that I am, after all, modest. I began in 1923, when I built a village at Pessac. For eight years this village remained uninhabited, because for eight years it was refused a water supply, until in the end the Government had to intervene. In 1925 I built the pavilion *L'Esprit Nouveau* at the Exhibition of Decorative Arts in Paris. It was the most hidden-away building in the whole exhibition, and came upon you, as you went round the exhibition, as a sudden apparition, as something wholly unexpected. The international jury wanted to give me a diploma of honour, but one of the best architects in France, himself a medallist, protested; he said 'Whatever it may be, it is not architecture.' The battle, you see, was already joined.

Then there was the competition for the new League of Nations building in Geneva. Twelve kilometres of plans were submitted, and I sent in about a hundred metres. That was not accepted, for reasons which I thought were little short of abominable. That was followed by plans for the Centrosoyus building in Moscow, which were first of all accepted, but then they wanted a balcony on the façade, and in the end my proposals were dropped. I was asked to prepare plans for the Palace of the Soviets, and these were first of all accepted and then declined.

In 1935 I decided to go to America for a change of atmosphere, and there I found – you may not believe it, but it is true – Americans who were suffering at that time from an inferiority complex. A model of my design for the Palace of the Soviets was exhibited – of all places! – at the Rockefeller Foundation in New York, where it aroused the admiration of young Americans. That model, two metres long, is in the museum of the Rockefeller Foundation. Another project on which I worked at that time was refused on the dual plea that it was revolutionary and out of date.

With some Brazilian architect friends I worked on plans for a Ministry building in Rio de Janeiro. (Fig. 35.3) That building was actually put up during the war. I found out that it had been through seeing an illustration of it in an English magazine.

35.3
First project for the Ministry of National Education and Public Health, Rio de Janeiro (1936)

From Le Corbusier, *Le Corbusier et P. Jeanneret (septième série)* (1936 or 7)

Then came the reconstruction of France after the occupation. Everybody seemed to be working on this, and the Minister who was responsible said to me, 'What are you reconstructing?' I replied 'Nothing, Mr. Minister.' He said 'Well, you built a town once. Why not reconstruct that?' He made inquiries from his staff, and they told him that all the work had been allotted to somebody or other, so he said 'Well, there is always La Rochelle. It is not destroyed at present, because the Germans are still there, but the Allied Armies are closing in, and in a fortnight it will be destroyed, and then you can rebuild it.' Happily, however, it was not destroyed, and so I did not have to rebuild it.

I ought also to mention the town plan for Algiers. Over a period of years I made a number of plans without any fee for a new town, and people said 'If it could come true it would be marvellous', but it did not come true. Algiers was the last of such plans. I made a plan for Barcelona which was accepted by everybody, but then the revolution came. I made a plan for Stockholm, but they said that they recognised the hand of the author, and it was put on one side. There was a plan for the left bank of Antwerp in 1933. In 1938 I did a plan for Buenos Aires, but seven years later one of the Ministers said 'If we bring in Corbusier, it will seem to show that we can't do it ourselves.' A plan for Bogota was accepted, but then there was a political revolution.

All that represents the work of a cab-horse. It meant a vast amount of work by head and hand and collaboration with large numbers of people. My plan for La Rochelle, which was a good plan, was silently put aside. At St. Dié, which I was asked to rebuild, people said 'Are you going to make us live in huge barracks?' and everybody, from the bourgeoisie to the workers, rejected the idea. The other two great disappointments I have had are over that big building for the United Nations in New York (which cost about the same as my whole town of Chandigarh) and the Unesco building in Paris. That shows you a little of the nature of the work which I have accomplished during my career.

I should like to say once again how much I appreciate this Medal which I have received from Her Majesty the Queen, and I thank you once more.

Source: *Journal of the Royal Institute of British Architects*, April 1953

A New City for India

By Le Corbusier

In February 1951 we started the town-planning project of the city of Chandigarh. It involves the most modern principles, the objective expression of the clearest theories. For example, the applications of the 'Green City' idea, with all its consequences: the freedom of the pedestrian and his separation from motor-cars. In Chandigarh the motor-car will be replaced almost entirely by a network of different kinds of buses, each taking different kinds of passengers, and travelling at full speed without ever meeting a pedestrian or any other obstacle or untimely crossing. The bus stops are 400 metres apart.

This really extraordinary development has its roots in the Bogotá town-planning scheme which we worked out in Colombia, but there its principles were applied to an old city. Its second application was to the town-planning of Marseille-Sud. At that time, Unesco had commissioned me to write the first article on town-planning to appear in its world-wide review. This article was an explanation of the *Loi des Sept Voies* (law of the seven systems of access), necessary for providing a site with its provincial, regional and urban connections, right down to the last road which ends at the very doors of the houses.

This theory brings a very necessary clarity to complex and confusing problems. Chandigarh, for example, has a forty-kilometre network of streets which take only fast mechanical traffic: not a single doorway opens on to them. Here is an administrative and municipal achievement which deserves notice.

Another significant feature introduced into Chandigarh is the *Modulor*. The *Modulor*, a scale of mathematical dimensions taken from the human body and invented in 1942, has been applied in the construction of the Boulevard Michelet building at Marseilles, and is spreading more and more widely over the world. Here, at just the right moment for town-planning, is a harmonic scale based on the relevance of human beings to every architectural size. By the miracle of numbers, the reduction of dimensions to a common measure, or to a measure of the same harmonic type becomes the indispensable intermediary step for prefabrication and mass production. The words 'mass production' will no longer be a byword for monotony and boredom. Thanks to the *Modulor*, limitless diversity and mathematical harmony are being reintroduced into the surroundings of men's lives.

Adaptation to climate, a difficult problem, has been overcome in Chandigarh. The Indian climate is extreme: ten months of burning sunshine and overwhelming heat and two months of torrential rain, the monsoon. In the modern buildings of Bombay or New

Delhi, confusion is rife; the symphonic problem of climate has not been understood. Modern architecture, foraging through manuals and magazines from all over the world, blindly absorbs French, American, Indian, German, English or Scandinavian discoveries and shapes. Confronted with this inconsistency, we felt the need for a 'climatic screen,' and we have created it. This at last makes it possible for the problems of breathing and of human behaviour in extreme climates to be set straight. It automatically gives the architectural answer. In Chandigarh, accordingly, the large buildings are provided with large parasols or umbrellas. The shade will protect them, and natural air currents will partially limit the disadvantages (and sometimes the advantages) of air conditioning – advantages or disadvantages which, in any case, are very expensive.

The problems of shade had already attracted me in Barcelona in 1931. The sun-screen was born. Its first application was to the Palace of the Ministry of Education and Public Health in Rio. Now, in India, the sun-screen, restricted up till now to façades, is taking possession of the roof and, what is more, is showing us how air-currents can be used. This is a science which from now on is going to develop into a real physics of the architecture of things.

Whatever the sun demands, rain demands just the opposite. The parasol then becomes an umbrella. The umbrella sheds such a volume of water that it becomes necessary to solve hydraulic problems. This led me, in my plans for the Capitol at Chandigarh, to new combinations, stamped perhaps with beauty and grandeur, in any case with originality. I believe them to be endowed with permanent value.

The Capitol group, comprising the Government buildings, crowns the layout of the city; it is the city's head. Certainly, not for a long time has the occasion arisen (or at least been taken) for building a group which has such importance from the aspects alike of architecture, technique and town-planning. Consider, for example, the protection of pedestrians from motor-cars, thanks to the rational application of the theories of the *Ville Radieuse*, and the designing of houses in relation to sun and winds. The plan which we have developed during this year of work is capable of beauty.

But there is one very relevant consideration: India is poor, very poor. I have been asked to keep to budgets which are really very low; to cut to the limit. On this condition, I have been given a free hand. I have been able to bring to the solution the experience of a whole life. By an eloquent classification of working functions and materials; by the use of contrasts and analogies, of harshness and softness, of sharp and soft lines. I have been able to create an architecture full of variety, made of rough concrete blocks (I propose the phrase: 'the splendour of rough concrete'), and of thin layers of concrete, five to six centimetres thick, which are either simple or twisted in form. The whole is whitewashed inside and out, relieved by the violent polychromy of the fabrics which will serve as curtains. They alone will supply the thunder of colour so necessary to set off the whitewash and the concrete.

The work has gone forward rapidly. The High Court Palace first: in less than a year the plans were finished and the construction begun. (Fig. 36.1) Next came the *Palais des Ministères*, or Secretariat. This, too, is in the nature of a prototype for office buildings in a fierce climate. The plans are completed. Next comes the Assembly, a rectangular building 100 metres long and 110 metres wide. (Fig. 36.2) Finally, the Governor's Palace raises its expressive silhouette.

36.1
High Court, Chandigarh (1955)

Photographer: Jo Newsom (1997)

36.2
The Assembly, Chandigarh (1960)

Photographers: Bryan & Norman Westwood
(1960s)

Not far from here stands the monument which I was asked to design for this capital city – the 'Open Hand,' an idea which has been preoccupying me for a long time. The Open Hand stands sixteen metres high, emerging from what I have named the 'Well of Thought.' In short, a group which may prove moving in its lines, its symbolism and its ideas, and will bring a strangely new note to the illustration of an architecture springing from contemporary sensibility, ethics, and aesthetics.

Between the Assembly and the High Court runs a promenade about 400 metres long, paved with stones. It will be enlivened (at the request of my colleagues in Chandigarh) by the presence of what they have called 'the Signs' tokens of urbanity or of a certain philosophy of life.

Source: *The Observer*, 10 May 1953

Painting and Sculpture of Le Corbusier

By Reyner Banham
Review of the Exhibition at the Institute of Contemporary Arts, London, 1953

Had Le Corbusier never written a book, nor ever built a house, he might not have become a Commander of the *Légion d'Honneur*, and certainly would never have been awarded the Royal Gold Medal for Architecture this year, but he would have been remembered as one of the Masters of the *Ecole de Paris*, one of the heroes of post-Cubist painting.

The achievements of his career as architect have overshadowed his work as painter and sculptor, (Fig. 37.1) and those few who are acquainted with the whole of his output in these fields do not often prize them highly. Yet they have a particular significance now that we begin to see that the Modern Movement in architecture has its foundations not only in material and functional revolutions, but in a visual revolution as well, and the recent exhibition of his paintings and sculpture at the Institute of Contemporary Arts was revealing as well as timely.

These oils, watercolours, lithographs, drawings and sculptures are too little known, too little studied, for us to appreciate them fully, as yet, as works of art, but their importance as laboratories of form is manifest. (Figs 37.2–37.4) They throw a penetrating light on the aesthetic mechanisms of his architectural creation, and, in those barren periods when he had no chance to build, they lead us on to the next achievement in construction, anticipating its innovations. Long before his first 'Modern' buildings were erected, the early still-lives of 1918–19 give evidence of a mania for precision and for geometrical forms so pure as to be almost devoid of substance, elaborated from drawings of meticulous linear construction, based on a system of *tracés regulataires*, anticipating the insubstantial and subtly-proportioned façades of the Ozenfant and La Roche-Jeanneret houses.

Yet, by the time these were built his painting had passed on to those large compositions, called *Puriste*, in which objects of daily domestic familiarity combine together in grave and formal dances of candy-coloured transparency, sharing and exchanging contours. Though these bottles and jugs, plates and pipes, were the customary bric-à-brac of the cubist still-life table, he and his fellow purists gave them a new significance – they are not merely pretty forms on which the painter may improvise, they are also, as he and Ozenfant expressed it in a chapter of their forgotten book *La Peinture Moderne*, to be praised for having 'the peculiar virtue of being standardized, for being closely associated with man and in scale with him ... they serve man most directly, are to him like extra hands and fingers, of an intimacy and banality so great as hardly to interest him.' Thus he promoted the products of mass-production to the status of a kind of serially-produced folk-lore, came to

37.1
**Le Corbusier in his studio on rue
Nungesser-et-Coli with his sculpture
Totem (1951)**

Photographer unknown (1951)

37.2
Violin and its Case (n.d.)

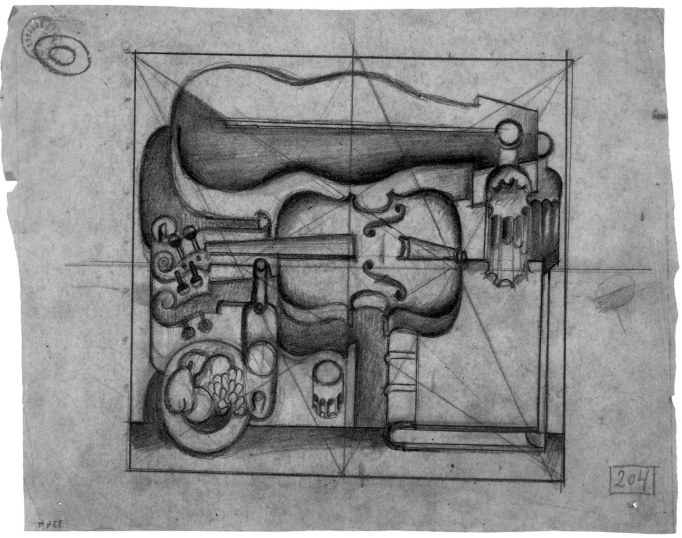

37.3
Still Life of the Esprit Nouveau Pavilion
(1924)

37.4

Woman at Pedestal Table with a Horseshoe (1928)

terms with the machine on a note of lyricism, and at the same time laid the foundations of many later important architectural researches, such as the *Modulor*, and the standardization of domestic equipment.

This period of the purest Purism ended with a show of stronger earthy colours and freely manipulated forms, which received their architectural realization in the Villa Savoye, a habitable still life table of concrete. But again, having made his peace with the machine, he was already moving on to other considerations in his painting, and the human form appears, together with a note of fiercer and more full-bodied plasticity, in works which often distil a dark disquiet, as if the rising tide of Surrealist anxiety was engulfing him as well. But, a year after this menacing picture, the frustrating thirties ended on a note of cheerful and rumbustious gaiety, the great murals at Cap St. Martin.

When the further frustrations and sterility of the war were over the new buildings were so different from those of the thirties as to appear the work of a different man, yet the paintings of the intervening years were full of clues of this new development. And there was in addition a new plastic adventure, a new laboratory of formal experiment – sculpture. The fat and confident detailing of Marscilles, its swaggering and pachydermatous legs, the rough romantic finishes, had all been worked out in the polychromed sculptures [an example of] which was shown completed in the exhibition and is signed by Le Corbusier and Joseph Savina* [...].

These large wood-carvings were undertaken by him as experiments towards a sculpture intended for an architectural setting, but under their influence his buildings have begun to create bold plastic effects, and in the Capitol of Chandigarh, the new administrative centre for the Punjab, the crowning achievement of his career, the emphasis is everywhere sculptural – the same plastic sensibility has carved and modelled the landscape [...], moulded and manipulated the concrete masses of the buildings, and shaped the purely sculptural features, which animate and punctuate the plan.

Government House is the most astonishing creation of this sculptural force, but the forms and perforations of the Courts of Justice, and the roof structures of the Secretariat, also bear witness to its power. Yet he continues to paint, and one of his recent pictures, shows that even the most abstract and intellectual of his conceptions, the *Modulor*, is for him a matter of visual, as well as technical, consequence and full of decorative possibilities of its own. His creative power as artist continues unabated, and he is emerging now as one of the truly original creators of the age. Just as the growth of the human embryo summarizes the more general process which, in *La Peinture Moderne*, he termed *La Formation de l'Optique Moderne*. All the elements are there: – the absorption of the past, the submission to the laws of geometry, the confrontation with Cubism, the comprehension of the machine, the study, continued at Chandigarh, of natural and human form (and of natural and human behaviour), the three-dimensional experience of sculpture – through all these stages he has passed to emerge the confident master of materials, both massive and light, natural and synthetic, self-coloured or painted, the assembler of magnificent and cunning plays of volume in the sun.

*Joseph Savina (1901–83), wood-carver, cabinet maker and sculptor. (Eds)

Source: *Architectural Review*, June 1953

Garches to Jaoul: Le Corbusier as Domestic Architect in 1927 and 1953

By James Stirling

Villa Garches, recently occupied, and the two houses for Mr. Jaoul and his son, now near-ing completion, are possibly the most significant buildings by Le Corbusier to be seen in Paris to-day, for they represent the extremes of his vocabulary: the former, rational, urbane, programmatic, the latter, personal and anti-mechanistic. (Figs 38.1–38.3) If style is the crystallization of an attitude, then these buildings, so different even at the most superfi-cial level of comparison, may, on examination, reveal something of a philosophical change of attitude on the part of their author.

Garches, built at the culmination of Cubism and canonizing the theories in *Towards a New Architecture*, has since its inception been a standard by which Le Corbusier's genius is measured against that of great architects of this century. Inhabited, again by Ameri-cans, after 15 years' splendid isolation, it has been painted in a manner more *de Stijl* than the original: walls white inside and out, all structural members black and single planes of primary colour on areas of lesser consequence. It is never possible to see more than one coloured plane from any single viewpoint. On the principal façade, the underside of the entrance canopy is painted sky-blue as the underside of the slab over the terrace. Inside, one wall of the living area is painted yellow, etc.

As with the deserted Poissy, the deterioration at Garches was only skin-deep; paint decay, broken glass and slight cracks in the rendering; there has been no deterioration to the structure nor any waterproofing failures. Though the landscape has thickened consid-erably to the rear of the house, trees have not yet grown close against the main façades; where this has happened, at La Roche, Cook and Pleinex, the balanced asymmetry of the elevations, as total compositions, has been grossly disfigured. The one instance among the Paris buildings where the trees are sympathetic is the Pavillon Suisse where they have grown the full height of the south elevation, significantly one of the most repetitive façades that Le Corbusier has produced. In more extreme examples of additive elevations, as in many American buildings, the presence of trees, naturalistic incidents, might almost be considered essential. The disemboweled machine parts of the Armée du Salut outbuild-ings have a similar juxtaposition to the neutral backdrop of the slab.

If Garches appears urban, sophisticated and essentially in keeping with *l'esprit parisien*, then the Jaoul houses seem primitive in character, recalling the Provençal community; they seem out of tune with their Parisian environment. Their pyramidal massing is reminiscent

38.1
Maisons Jaoul, Neuilly-sur-Seine (1954)

Photographer: Emmanuel Thirard (1996)

of traditional Indian architecture and they were in fact designed after Le Corbusier's first visits to that country. Frequently accused of being 'internationalist' Le Corbusier is actually the most regional of architects. The difference between the cities of Paris and Marseilles is precisely the difference between the Pavillon Suisse and the Unité, and at Chandigarh the centre buildings are indebted to the history and traditions of a native Indian culture; even a project for the Palace of the Soviets makes considerable reference to Russian constructivism. Therefore it is perhaps disturbing to counter the Jaoul houses within half a mile of the Champs-Elysées.

Assuming that the observer has become familiar with the architecture of Le Corbusier through the medium of glossy books, then the first impression registered on arriving at the Jaoul houses is unique for they are of the scale and size expected, possibly because of the expressed floor beams. Usually, the scale is either greater or smaller than anticipated, that of Garches being unexpectedly heroic.

Differing from the point structure and therefore free plan of Garches, the structure of Jaoul is of load-bearing, brick cross-walls, cellular in planning by implication. It would, however, be a mistake to think of these buildings as models for cross-wall architecture as this aspect is visually subordinated to the massive, concrete, Catalan vaults occurring at each

floor level. These vaults are to be covered with soil and grass to resist thermal expansion and the timber shutter-boards have been set to leave a carefully-contrived pattern. Internally one-inch solid steel tiles are positioned at approximately fifteen-foot centres to resist diagonal thrust into the brick walls. At the external centre point of these vaults, bird-nesting boxes are formed, and occasionally concrete rainwater heads are projected from the side-beams, though the pipes drop internally. Rising from the underground garage through to the top of each house are dog-leg stairs, cast in situ; they are a development from the Marseilles fire-escape stair, with the treads cantilevered either side of the vertical concrete slab. By English standards, the brickwork is poor, but then the wall is considered as a surface and not a pattern. Masonry, rubble, or, perhaps more rationally in view of the vault construction, mass concrete walls could be substituted without difference to the principle of design.

Perhaps the only factor that Garches and Jaoul have in common is the considerable influence of the site on both. All Le Corbusier's buildings tend to fall into one or two categories: those in which the peculiarities of the site are a paramount factor in conception

38.2
Housing, Ham Common, London (1958)

Architects: Stirling & Gowan
Photographer: Colin Westwood (1958)

Influenced by Maisons Jaoul, Neuilly-sur-Seine (1954)

38.3
Falmer House, Sussex University, Brighton (1964)

Architects: Sir Basil Spence Bonnington & Collins
Photographer: Henk Snoek (1962)

Influenced by Maisons Jaoul, Neuilly-sur-Seine (1954)

– most notably the Armée Salut – and those where the site is of little consequence, being subordinated to a preconception or archetype, e.g. the Unité. To some extent this may account for the lack of inevitability, sometimes felt with buildings of this latter category, most particularly the Pavillon Suisse where, except as an archetype *per se*, there seems little justification for raising the building above ground, there being no circulation or view through. If the entrance hall, approachable from any direction, had been under and not to the rear of the slab, the raising of the block would not appear so arbitrary. None the less, the town-planning ideas which generated this form retain their urgent validity.

The exact relationship and planning of the two Jaoul houses have been motivated by the nature of the site. The circulation is on two levels and of two kinds. Cars drive straight off the road into the garage, a large underground cavern from which separate stairs rise through to each house. Walking circulation is above this garage on what appears to be natural ground level but which is a made-up terrace on which the houses stand. This level is linked to the road by a ramp. The differentiation of circulation on super-imposed levels and free movement around the houses are reminiscent in another medium of the suspended routes into the Armée du Salut.

At Maison Jaoul the only entire elevation that can be seen from a single viewpoint is to the rear and has to be observed over the garden wall of the adjoining private property. Owing to the narrowness of the plot, all other façades have to be viewed either episodically through the trees or close up at an oblique angle. The solid-void relationship of the exterior does not appear to follow any easily apparent scheme. This is a development from Le Corbusier's earlier work where at La Roche the drawing board elevation also cannot be seen at right angles and the studied balance of window to wall is destroyed. This is due not only to the trees which have grown since but especially to the necessity of viewing the elevation at a sharp angle.

The hierarchic presentation of external elements occurs also in the work of Frank Lloyd Wright, where the most important feature is the corner, and this may account for much of the undergrowth against the façades proper. It may be argued that the only exterior which can maintain interest, as the eye moves at an equal distance around the corner, is the cage or box. The most notable example of this is the Lake Shore Apartments where it would be inappropriate to suggest a 'principal façade'. Poissy almost comes into the category of the box, but only on three sides; the fourth, receiving no undercut, becomes a vertical plane differing from the dynamic horizontality of the others. At Garches there is no point in moving around the corner for there is a very definite axis and the side elevations are of little consequence, their window openings positioned functionally make no attempt to arrive at a formal composition. The site boundary lines, defined by tall, closely planted trees, are about six feet from each of these side elevations, making it almost impossible to see them. The long façades, on the contrary, may be seen head on from a considerable distance by the approaching visitor and their balanced asymmetry is masterfully exploited.

Internally, space departs radically from the structure; an explosion in terms of Cubist space is contained within the four peripheral walls which externally give little evidence of this phenomenon, contained except where it escapes and rushes out along the direction of the terrace, to be finally dissipated in the heavy landscape. However, space is not contrived for the sake of effect only, it invariably has a psychological as well as a functional context. For instance, on passing through the front door, the immediate double height and the presence of a stair indicate that the main floor is above. Similarly, the diagonal spatial stress across the first floor suggests the route through the house.

The main living areas are flooded with an even intensity of light, but, where accommodation and circulation are of lesser consequence, natural lighting becomes more restricted and as one moves through the house a continuous contrast in definition is attained. 'The elements of architecture are light and shade, walls and space.' The natural light which penetrates to the interior of the Jaoul houses is consistently subdued and not dissimilar to that found in many Frank Lloyd Wright buildings.

Eventually somebody will have to consider the numerous similarities between Le Corbusier and Wright, and their common differences from the work of Mies van der Rohe. For instance, the pattern of circulation, repetitive on all floors as in the Pavillon Suisse and many of Le Corbusier's larger buildings, becomes in some of his and Wright's domestic works a route so complex and involved, as at Pleinex, that it is with the greatest difficulty that the stranger finds his way out. To a lesser extent, that applies at Jaoul and again, similar to Wright, the spatial effects, though exciting, are unexpected, encountered suddenly on turning a corner or glimpsed on passing a slit in the wall. Where double height does occur in one of the living rooms it appears as a dead area, having no secondary use such a the vertical height of the Unité flats which lights and ventilates the bedroom. If the space inside Garches can be considered dynamic, then here it is static; there is certainly no question of being able to stand inside and comprehend at a glance the limits of the house, as at Garches.

Implicit in the structural system, rooms tend to small boxes with the living areas more generous. The internal finishes have a greater variety and richness of surface than at Garches, where, with the exception of the floor, the materials, though not the form, of the walls and ceilings are neutralized. Inside Jaoul, concrete is left shutter-marked, walls are plastered or brick fair-faced, floors are tiled and there is considerable variety and quantity of timber and, most significantly the ceiling or underside of the vaults is frequently finished in a dark clay tile which cannot be expected to amplify 'the magnificent play of light on form'. The 'fourth wall' – the incorporation of shelving and opaque materials into the window opening – is symptomatic of Le Corbusier's recent attitude to surface depth. Windows are no longer to be looked through but looked at. The eye finding interest in every part of the surface *impasto*, does not, as at Garches, seek relief from the hard textureless finish by examining the contours and form of the plane.

Maison Jaoul is no doubt dimensioned according to the *Modulor*, a development from the application of the golden section by regulating lines as at Garches, where it is possible to read off the inter-relations of squares and sections as the eye traverses the façade and where, internally, every element is positioned according to an exact geometrical hierarchy. In fact, Garches must be considered the masterpiece of Neo-Palladianism in modern architecture, conceived in plan, section, elevation from two proportions, which, owing to their particular inter-relationship, achieve an organic or harmonic whole as distinct from an additive total. The variety of dimensions available from the *Modulor* are considerable and as Bodiansky* has said; 'there is always a figure near at hand to adjust to'. This considerable flexibility may create a visually non-apparent geometry, as at Jaoul, but here the restrictions of the site already mentioned must be remembered when considering whether this is a valid criticism.

Garches is an excellent example of Le Corbusier's particular interpretation of the machine aesthetic. The body of the house, built by quite conventional means for its time, has skin-walls of concrete block rendered to a monolithic, poured or sprayed effect; an aesthetic for a structural system not yet in being. Yet while Garches is not the product of any high-powered mechanization, the whole spirit of the building expresses the essence of machine power. To be on the first floor is to witness the Mumfordian end product of

*The structural engineer of the Marseilles Unité.

203

twentieth century technology, 'the silent staffless power-house'. The incorporation of rail-road and steamship fabrication is decidedly technocrat and the integration of architecture to specialist requirements extremely considered as the boiler-house disposed like an industrial engine-room or the timber-strip flooring obviously laid by ship's carpenters. The type of detailing in synthetic materials here and at the Armée du Salut is almost the last of the steam-age period; crude maybe, it is nevertheless powerful. After this date, the number of synthetic materials per building increases, and, as at the Pavillon Suisse, the detailing becomes more refined but somehow less memorable. There is no reference to any aspect of the machine at Jaoul either in construction or aesthetic. These houses, total cost £30,000, are being built by Algerian labourers equipped with ladders, hammers and nails, and with the exception of glass no synthetic materials are being used; technologically, they make no advance on medieval building. The timber window-wall units may be prefabricated but as with technology one suspects that prefabrication must begin with the structure.

To imply that these houses will be anything less than magnificent art would be incorrect. Their sheer plastic virtuosity is beyond emulation. Nevertheless, on analysis, it is disturbing to find little reference to the rational principles which are the basis of the Modern Movement, and it is difficult to avoid assessing these buildings except in terms of 'art for art's sake'. More so than any architect of this century, Le Corbusier's buildings represent a continuous architectural development which, however, has not recently been supplemented by programmatic theory.

As homes the Jaoul houses are almost cosy and could be inhabited by any civilized family, urban or rural. They are built by and intended for the status quo. Conversely it is difficult to imagine Garches being lived in spontaneously except by such as the Sitwells, with never less than a half a dozen brilliant, and permanent guests. Utopian, it anticipates, and participates in, the progress of twentieth-century emancipation. A monument, not to an age which is dead, but to a way of life which has not generally arrived, and a continuous reminder of the quality to which all architects must aspire if modern architecture is to retain its vitality.

Source: *Architectural Review*, September 1955

Le Corbusier

By Peter Smithson

Contribution to the 1959 Symposium on Le Corbusier organized by
the Architectural Association

Le Corbusier is a great visionary and this is more than being an idealist or revolutionary, for a visionary can make other people's minds take alight almost as a by-product of his personal struggle. And I hold that with Le Corbusier there would be no *modern architecture as an ideal*, although there would be modern buildings.

Le Corbusier's vision was of a humane, poetic, disciplined, machine environment for a machine society. Now it will be held that the definition of a machine environment was the work of the Futurists, but for me their environment was *dominated* by machines. Le Corbusier's dream of a *Ville Radieuse* has the machine firmly under control, and even though some of his aesthetic techniques may have been carry-over ones he was never confused that an appropriate environment for machine-age man was his all-over objective. His dream was of a city of shining towers in a sea of trees, with the automobile used at the scale at which it is a moving poetic thing and not a stinking object – an essentially controlled, *quiet* environment with the energies of transit and communication channelled and not randomly and wastefully *displayed*.

He saw at once that the skyscrapers were too small – that the reason for the decay of the metropolis was undermechanisation not overmechanisation. The essence of Futurism was the *display* of mechanisms and this is an early nineteenth century attitude towards machines. In the twentieth century the machine has become more and more suppressed and the aim is for it to be taken for granted as a service – for example using lifts has become absolutely mindless, it is as simple as walking in the country.

The idea that the metropolis is still worthwhile is central to Le Corbusier's thoughts, although his vision is communicated by different means to different people; speaking as only for my own generation by the Armée du Salut (Fig. 39.2) to some or the Pavillon Suisse to others; or by his writing. But their minds are equally illuminated and become *capable of independent action*.

As to the buildings themselves as objects, I hold that, although Berlin in the twenties generated quantities of heat, only with Le Corbusier did *other people* catch fire. The German movement was rational and severe more than anything else. In spirit it was a continuation of previous tradition – nineteenth century rationalism. It certainly not one which would make a man leave home and start a new life, which I hold Le Corbusier's work could.

39.1
TUC Congress House, London (1957)

Architect: David du Rieu Aberdeen
Photographer: Colin Westwood (1957)

The symposium was held in this building influenced by Le Corbusier's Centrosoyus

39.2
Cité de Refuge, Paris (1933)

Photographer: John Donat (1971)

39.3
German Pavilion, Barcelona (1929, recreated 1986)

Architect: Ludwig Mies van der Rohe
Photographer: Roland Halbe (1999)

39.4
Villa Savoye, Poissy (1931)

Photographer: John Donat (1971)

By definition there could be no Modern Movement before there was a machine aesthetic and this did not come in being in 1851 or even in 1909, but arrived between 1923 and 1927. *De Stijl*, essentially a continuation of *Art Nouveau* even if it did hint at machine fabrication, has to be fully absorbed before a real dead-pan anti-art machine aesthetic can be said to have arrived. Compare, for example, the 1917 Rietveld chair with that of Mies in 1936.

The Germans certainly found a way of making buildings that responded to the new feeling for the machine – the houses at the Bauhaus, the Gropius exhibitions or the Barcelona Pavilion (Fig. 39.3) are wonderful – but, some how, at least in England, it was, and is, the Villa Savoye (Fig. 39.4) that makes the old architecture look really ridiculous.

One only has to compare the buildings by Mies with those by Le Corbusier at the Weissenhof Siedlung (1927) to see what I mean. *MIES IS GREAT BUT CORB COMMUNICATES.*

Both masters really struggle with same essential problems over the decades. Le Corbusier's struggle with the reinvention of the house culminated in the Unité, and caption on the panel in the exhibition [Walker Art Gallery, Liverpool] (Fig. 39.5) 'First appearance of a modern form of dwelling' is really true, and he has been struggling since Pessac to achieve it. And in my opinion he had already achieved it in a certain way at Pessac which

39.5
Le Corbusier exhibition, Liverpool (1958)

Photographer: Stewart Bale (1958)

if you compare with, for example, the housing at Frankfurt by Ernst May you can really see how Le Corbusier's first concern has always been with an exciting, moving, image of a new environment. In this his first housing project, as at Nantes one of his latest, mechanism and mechanised techniques (such as repetition) are there, but they are not given absolute importance. It is the way of life that is important.

These arguments do not diminish the work of German architects, especially Mies van der Rohe, but give a special place to Le Corbusier for somehow breathing life into most of us here as architects.

Source: *Architectural Association Journal*, May 1959

Part 4

1960–1969:

Goodbye to the Giant

Contributors

Reyner Banham
Jane Drew
Philip Powell
Walter Segal
Basil Spence
Peter Yates

Our Debt to Le Corbusier

By Basil Spence

There are two kinds of architects, just as there are two kinds of farmers, Le Corbusier was a seed farmer producing a great number of ideas which he did not fully develop but scattered around and left to be taken up by others.

It was a strong strain, which I think will last for a long time. We see it in many places in Britain, particularly in housing, and its influence will probably outlast anyone else's in modern times – Frank Lloyd Wright's, for example.

Le Corbusier really thought about getting architecture down to earth, making it relate to people and the changing world. He made a break from the academic and eclectic philosophy which had been prevalent before.

I first came across him when I was working in Edwin Lutyens's office on designs for the Viceroy's house in Delhi. I read his *Towards a New Architecture* (a banned book in that office).

Some of the things he said then have been disproved. He himself didn't later really believe in 'if a thing functions, it is bound to be beautiful' and 'a house is a machine for living in.' But they made his point that a machine is not a thing without aesthetic significance.

Have I myself been influenced by him? It is awfully difficult to know whether one is influenced or not in particular cases. But one believes in his philosophy.

His forms changed, as mine have changed. He broke away from glass boxes to more plastic forms. When I was doing Coventry I was already tired of glass boxes, and at the same time Le Corbusier, unknown to me, was doing his Ronchamp Chapel (Fig. 40.1) – he had moved away from the transparent to the enclosed plastic form.

The main influence we see in Britain is in flats – Roehampton shows it most clearly. (Fig. 40.2) Le Corbusier's idea was exploited and improved slightly. The L.C.C. architects did extremely well. I was President of the R.I.B.A. when we gave the London Architectural Medal to them. Housing in Sheffield (Fig. 40.3) and the town centre at Cumbernauld (Fig. 40.4) also reflect his ideas.

My own scheme for the Gorbals, in Glasgow, (Fig. 40.5) just now completed, was influenced by him a long way back. In 1928 he did a theoretical scheme for houses with gardens which was never carried out; that is reflected in the Gorbals.

His conception of tall buildings goes back further still. In 1922 he foresaw that tall blocks could liberate the ground around them.

40.1
**Chapel of Notre-Dame-du-Haut,
Ronchamp (1955)**

Photographer: Emmanuel Thirard (1996)

40.2
Alton West Estate, Roehampton, London (1958)

Architects: London County Council Architects Department
Photographers: London County Council Architects Department.
Photographic Unit (1959)

40.3
Park Hill Estate, Sheffield (1961)

Architects: J.L. Womersley, Sheffield
Architects Department
Photographer: Bill Toomey (1961)

40.4
Town centre, Cumbernauld New Town (1967)

Architects: Geoffrey Copcutt and Hugh
Wilson
Photographer unknown (1960s)

40.5
Flats, Hutchesontown C, Gorbals, Glasgow (1965)

Architects: Sir Basil Spence Glover & Ferguson
Photographer: Henk Snoek (1965)

Has he done any harm? I think if you became a slave to any idea in architecture it would do harm – even if you followed Palladio, for example. You have to accept the challenge of quality, and then apply it to what already exists, trying to make it part of the environment.

Le Corbusier condemned other architects like Frank Lloyd Wright, but Wright condemned him, so it was mutual. He was a very jealous person.

I do not care for his Chandigarh building and town-planning in the Punjab; it is too European and theoretical. His arrogance was typically Gallic, and he sometimes ignored the requirements of ordinary people – this was the paradox of his philosophy.

I have just been to India, and I have heard it said that when Nehru was alive he and Le Corbusier never discussed architecture – they always talked about his fees. I remember asking Nehru, 'How on earth do you reconcile the gentleness of India with Le Corbusier's force?' He replied, 'I simply don't know.'

What do I value most highly of Le Corbusier's work? I think his religious buildings; he was a religious man. I would say Ronchamp is a perfect small construction.

Source: *Sunday Telegraph,* 29 August 1965

The Unknown Giant

By Walter Segal

Never following mercenary motives, never seeking compromise, but, on the contrary, finding our reward in creative search which alone is the joy of life we have covered the entire chessboard of architecture from the humblest detail to the important planning of towns. We have seen in our studio in the rue de Sèvres young, enthusiastic and devoted men from many countries ... The generous help of the young allowed us to undertake tasks ... with which, perhaps, we could contribute to the solution of the great problems of contemporary architecture.

Thus wrote the forty-two-year-old Le Corbusier in the introduction of the first volume of *Oeuvre Complète* in 1930. A western Swiss like J. J. Rousseau, Charles Edouard Jeanneret possessed, like him, that unique mind so supremely intuitive and passionate and equally so logical and rational which, with singular talents, lifts such men's contributions far above the level of their contemporaries and turns them into forces that give direction to history.

In the ever-changing vocabulary of modern architecture no name is so overwhelmingly evident as Le Corbusier's; no man's vitality, not even that of Picasso, has been put so incessantly, obsessedly and remorselessly to such a wide variety of tasks or achieved as much both in volume and content; few possessed his courage, mental elasticity and the *élan* needed to triumph over a series of set-backs.

What emerged from these efforts was, by all standards, astonishing and held right to his end – and beyond – the attention, interest and admiration of his own generation and the passionate devotion of two younger generations: Le Corbusier never seemed to age. He spoke of the autumn of his life but it was an autumn which never made one think winter a possibility. What his *vieillesse verte* might have brought is not to be measured.

Above all there was that atmosphere about the man, about his buildings, his drawings, his writings. He wrote staccato, far too passionate to endure the struggle with carefully measured expression, far too impulsive to exhaust himself in patient argument. His drawings and his innumerable sketches are statements of great charm and integrity: they mean to explain, to convince, never more. At one time his manner of drawing broke into the field of conventional architectural draughtsmanship and presentation and established a new idiom of expression which spread all over the world. Every period in architecture makes its own medium of drawing: the masters of the Baroque used charcoal, the Classicists defined

41.1
Le Corbusier with Mulk Raj Anand in Le Corbusier's studio

Photographer: Marilyn Stafford (1960s)

contours with thin, carefully drawn, lines. Le Corbusier stands out among those who developed the drawing language of our time.

It is difficult to write of the experience which exhibitions of his work conveyed in the twenties but many will remember the indelible impression made by those plans and gently tinted isometrics which opened a new and wonderfully possible world to the young eye. And how is one to describe the spell of his buildings? Like Rousseau he thought of simplicity, of happiness, of joy. But his amenity was not the amenity of upholstered and cosy comfort, nor, indeed, was it austerity in the common sense. He dreamt of light, of the warmth of the sun, of an unforgettable view like in his first sketches for the Ministry of Education in Rio. Thus it came that his buildings transcended purpose and function, that they drew people to them irresistibly and not so much seeking whether purpose and performance were properly served (though nobody could ever accuse Le Corbusier of extravagance). Purpose and performance can always be attended to by those who come after with great assiduity because this is their *raison d'être*; the task of those that come first is to transmit insight and show that it is feasible and Le Corbusier was such a man.

41.2
32 Newton Road, Bayswater, London (1938)

Architect: Denys Lasdun
Photographer: John Havinden (1939)

Influenced by Villa Cook, Boulogne-Billancourt (1927)

41.3
St Michael's Theological College Chapel, Llandaff (1959)

Architect: George Pace
Photographer: Stanley Travers

Influenced by Chapel of Notre-Dame-du-Haut, Ronchamp (1955)

41.4
Row house, 82 South Hill Park, London (1956)

Architects: Stanley Amis and William & Gillian Howell
Photographer: John Pantlin (1956)

The dimensions of the row houses were worked out according to the precepts of the Modulor

41.5
Couvent Sainte Marie de la Tourette, Eveux-sur-l'Arbresle (1957)

Photographer: Monica Lehmann (1960)

41.6
St Peter's College, Cardross (1967)

Architects: Gillespie Kidd & Coia
Photographers: Thomson of Uddingston

Influenced by the Couvent Sainte Marie de la
Tourette, Eveux-sur-l'Arbresle (1957)

The step still quickens, the mind still becomes alert as one approaches one of his buildings just as they did when one went to see his early houses in Vaucresson (1922), in Auteuil (1923) where the *toit-jardin* made its first appearance, the maison Cook in Boulogne (1926) prototype, if ever there was one, of a modern town house, the villa in Garches (1927) with its wonderful garden façade, the houses in Stuttgart (1927), one of them the first flesh-and-blood maison Citrohan, and the near-square house Savoye in Poissy (1929) with its body lifted on *pilotis* and its enclosed terrace garden. Who can forget the Ministry of Education in Rio (1936–45) with its façade of *brise-soleil*, the 1930–32 Pavilion Suisse in the Cité Universitaire in Paris or the plan for a *ville contemporaine* (1922) which showed that the skyscraper had a place in the modern town and was the first attempt of a modern architect to deal with the problems of urbanism in the first quarter of the twentieth century, followed by the even more radical *cité radieuse*?

Or the Pavillon de l'Esprit Nouveau (1925) the first L-shaped patio house with hanging terrace garden as elements of a multi-storeyed block of maisonettes developed from its 1922 predecessor? Or the 1930 deck-housing of Algiers? And the Unités d'Habitation, the chapel of Notre-Dame-du-Haut in Ronchamp, the Palace of Justice in Chandigarh, the monastery La Tourette near Lyon?

This architect who indeed covered the entire chessboard of architecture and carried his own contemporaries and the young architects of two generations with him to the last, who himself was held in his development by no narrow confines even of his own making but continued to extract from his endeavour all he could give, leaves a wonderful heritage: a flexible every-ready openness to architectural exploration and a host of architects in all countries whom he encouraged and inspired with his work (Figs 41.2 to 41.6) and the single-minded devotion of his life. No man can do more.

Source: *Architects' Journal*, 8 September 1965

Le Corbusier: Appreciations

By Philip Powell and Jane Drew

Philip Powell

Le Corbusier's influence has been enormous – that by now is a platitude. To me, personally, he is the one architect who, time and time again, has made something so beautiful, so romantic even, that criticism is suspended. Sheer pleasure takes its place – in the interior of the chapel at Ronchamp, for example; the foyers (not the debating chamber itself) of the Parliament Building in Chandigarh; the roof terrace of the Villa Savoye, Poissy (Fig. 42.1) and the south face of the Swiss Pavilion in Paris. Le Corbusier, although nearly eighty when he died, was still in his creative prime. It is this which makes his death a tragedy.

Jane Drew

There have by now been many obituaries of Le Corbusier, but so far as I know none of them gives a real picture of the man himself, the way he lived, what he stood for and the kind of person he really was.

As I have had the luck to know Corb fairly well; a close and intimate association at Chandigarh, and a continued friendship since; I would rather attempt this kind of appreciation than one of the very carefully documented ones which include a list of his achievements and the part he played in the Modern Movement in architecture.

For these I refer the reader to the *Sunday Times* (5.9.65) and the long obituary notice in *The Times* (28.8.65) which sets out in full his life's work in architecture but, significantly, without mentioning his painting, sculpture, tapestries, enamels and so on.

Corb was a poet with a sense of humour. His life was governed by principles – his own. He got up early in the morning and would usually paint or draw or do a collage. At the age of seventy he was still quite able to rise at 6 o'clock in the morning and start work. He spoke scathingly about people who said they never had time and then complained of lack of achievement.

This early morning work was something for which he gave his imagination free rein and he would often return to a subject again and again. Some of the drawings and paintings he has given me have two different dates on them; the first the date and usually the place where he first worked on the idea, and then another date years later when the final drawing or painting was done in another place.

The reason that Corb was able to do a master plan for Chandigarh almost in a single week was that he had been thinking about the problem for so many years. All he had to do was to apply the solution to the terrain in question.

After breakfast he used to go to the office and very often shut himself in to work, not allowing himself to be interrupted by telephone calls or visits; no matter who the caller or visitor might be, ambassador or any other important person. He worked with extreme concentration, searching for principles and applying them; he had the French power for grand analysis, his principles he translated in what to him were interesting artistic forms, never allowing himself to be ruled by scientific logic although he thought of logic and science as most useful tools. In the afternoon he was more available but he liked working with only one person at a time.

His expressions were pretty vivid and not easily translated into English! The ones he used to characteristically categorise his day, for example morning concentration – 'il faut serrer les fesses' – in the afternoon – 'il faut approfondir le problème'. This philosophy led him to work only with those who understood. He disliked meeting new people unless he had a very good reason to believe that they had some special quality which would prove sympathetic with his own. In the evening he would go for a walk with a friend – Max, Pierre or myself. After dinner we sometimes listened to music, but usually we joked, talked or told stories; and occasionally he would work on a translation he was making of Shakespeare's sonnets into French.

42.1
Villa Savoye, Poissy (1931)

Photographer: Emmanuel Thirard (1994)

He was not a good reader though sometimes if he had a good book on a subject like climatology he would study it with interest. He thought the general architectural press appalling, full of irrelevant material (especially the American and the English papers). He said everything depended on one's point of view of what mattered in life. To him the sun, the trees, the green, the quiet, the magic of night mattered and were necessarily a part of life. There had to be a balance of other things.

He was a man of great method and integrity (both to his own standard). He dated every sketch. He worked like a carthorse – his own expression – to do his work well. He cared little for normal codes of conduct and agreements. I once acted as translator between him and Nehru. He said to Nehru, apropos the High Court fees – 'I have spent twice as long thinking on this as I thought I would have to and naturally I am charging twice what I said I would'. Nehru took this and understood. Corb was not, however, really interested in money. He cared for his principles, his art and his ideas. He saw no dividing line between his architecture, sculpture and painting, or his prose or way of life.

42.2
Cover of *Modulor 2* (1955)

His treatment of concrete now fashionably known as brute for him was *brut*, meaning raw. He shuttered it with wood to try and give it texture and life. He disliked the smooth, glossy skin which had become so fashionable as an aim for architects and interior design-ers. He was very unpretentious and believed absolutely in the importance of art and artis-tic creation. He liked strong colours and bold forms and hated what he called sweet pea colours on buildings but his proportions were at the same time delicate.

His letters were always illuminating and revealed the man. In a card to me from Egypt where he was drawn himself sitting on a on a pyramid he says, 'and this time Jane, it is not a square peg in a round hole!'. Another letter praising something I had done says that the difference between a great and little architect is a matter of millimetres – there is no detail in architecture – everything is important. In reply to another letter when I was trying to persuade him to come to the Architectural Association and had ended my letter with the words *'en espérance'* he wrote back saying that *en espérance* in French meant pregnant I must immediately tell him by whom! In another, he says architecture is weight.

He was a very warm and generous friend. He often said he felt happiest working with a woman, recalling also the long association with Charlotte Perriand. He adored his mother. He loved humanity, as was shown intrinsically in his *Modulor*, (Fig. 42.2) an attempt to humanise proportion, yet in many ways he lived like a monk. In later life he regretted his decision not to have children – a decision he made believing that an artist should be dedi-cated to his work (his change of view came when he stayed with Nivola and his children, his refuge in New York).

He hated the American way of life, the waste in New York, the silly cocktail parties, the unpoetic life. I remember driving with him to Idlewild Airport when he left America where he had been given the most magnificent adulation. He turned to me and said, 'These people are mad; Paris could live for a month on the waste this city makes in a day'.

His loss is something I feel it will take generations to appreciate. We need someone like Corb living now to put technology in its place – someone with his extraordinary breadth of spirit. I mourn him.

Source: *Architects' Journal*, 15 September 1965

Le Corbusier: a Personal Appreciation

By Peter Yates

At the death of an old man who was a good friend suddenly age is gone, what you remember is the man in his prime.

Rue Nungesser et Coli, Porte Molitor, 1944.

Le Corbusier apologised, 'See how we are under the Germans.' His dark brown leather jacket looked completely worn out. His shoes had thick wooden soles like sabots with uppers of straw basket work, and lined with cat fur.

We sat at the white marble table in the dining room which links like the web of an H Le Corbusier's small living room to his large studio. The American was going on and on about Frank Lloyd Wright. I looked at Le Corbusier. His thoughts were elsewhere. He was a stone god: inhuman, expressionless, strange.

'Can we see your paintings?' I said.

He came out of his chair like an eagle, and his eyes shone. 'You like painting? You are a painter yourself?'

And round that marvellous room he went, full of excitement, pouring armfuls of drawings on to the low tables, drawings of stones and women and flowers and fish and fircones. There were thick portfolios labelled 'drawings L. C.' down through the years, and neat brown paper parcels protecting mounted drawings, and labelled 'Bulls,' 'Women,' 'UBU's.'

Suddenly he said 'There was a little music hall at Blackfriars where we used to go and see Charlie Chaplin.'

And I thought of the fancy dress ball in America where he had gone in green trousers and a red shirt with blue sleeves and a black disc on one cheek. But no one noticed him, they were all mandarins and cardinals and *rois-soleil* and laden with silk and jewellery, and how dull it was, he said, with none of those little nude women that make a party go.

He was back with a vast roll of canvasses that he unrolled, hurling each across the floor, one after another, wrestlers and lovers; stones, bones; giant women with purple fruits and rainbow scarves, great shells perforated by the sea, chestnut leaves unfurling out of sticky buds. Fishes and clouds and rocks and ropes. A highly controlled fury of shapes and colours, brought masterfully to extremes, a pabulum of work as important as Picasso. And more, bearing the experience of form that was to become Ronchamp and Chandigarh.

'Who has seen all this?' I asked.

43.1
Gas Council Engineering Research Station, Killingworth (1968)

Architects: Ryder & Yates & Partners
Photographer: Bill Toomey (1968)

Designed by the author of the article and
heavily influenced by Le Corbusier's work

'Very few,' he said. 'I have not exhibited since 1925.'

He showed how he worked, on writing paper thin enough to trace one drawing from another; retaining some parts, altering others. Using coloured chalk then brushed over with water to unify the colour and bring it to the edges of its form.

In all these drawings there was a wildness and accidental life not evident in the monumental and more finely coloured hard-edge oils.

'Would you like one, choose which you like,' he said, shovelling 50 or so on to the table.

I found three nude giantesses, one bright pink, one grey and one white with bright blue hair, all holding hands and sitting on a rock. I fell in love with them.

'You like them?' he asked, wrote my name in the corner the word 'amicalement' and signed it Le Corbusier.

The French troops were later to tell me that the German women looked like that. The American liked them, too, but said they'd bust his family's bridge parties back in Boston.

'Jean Cocteau was here last night, and he bought ten.' I told him they were going to rebuild the Crystal Palace. He beamed.

He hadn't liked St. Paul's; it wasn't even big, and the mouldings were sloppy – a man should draw with all the strength of a man – but the Crystal Palace – nothing so fine had been built since!

'We must go in for this competition,' he said.

Later, working in Soho on the Pyramid scheme for the Crystal Palace we had a telegram from New York to announce his immediate arrival in London. In Chelsea for three exhausting days and nights he talked of towns and dwellings and good brother man, and ran like a happy boy when his wife 'phoned from Paris.

He was always full of wise advice. Never compromise on a design, give it all you have and it will shine like a jewel – and whoever judges it will recognise its quality.

The League of Nations scheme was chosen by a committee of academic judges because it shone out from the others like a diamond.

'You have many different methods of doing drawings. You know all the tricks, but volumetric and linear representation should never be mixed. When I was your age I didn't know what to do either. So I drew bottles. You know the two different kinds of shadows?'

'Yes,' I said.

'In that case,' said Corbu, 'you know everything.' 'It is no good drawing anything once. Draw it 20 times; alter, improve, and you will begin to see its possibilities. That is the secret of architecture.'

Another time he said, 'Where are the coloured pencils?' and taking a fistful he drew out all the different circulation systems in separate colours. 'That is the secret of architecture.' Always a continuous torrent of wise advice. He hated meaningless scribble, and building up of textures.

'People who draw like that have their heads full of spiders.' Talk full of slogans and parables. You were always learning his chance remarks were more deeply significant than you had thought at the time. He found a drawing I had done of a chain of cumulus clouds in a curve mirroring the coast. 'I have a drawing like that,' taking a paper out of his pocket, and for the first time in England was seen the *Modulor*.

This is a good dimension, and this and this.

Tick these off 2.260; 1.130; 698. These are based on the proportions of my own body. With these you may design anything. But shortly after, at the Architectural Association, he began, 'This is a 6 ft. Englishman.'

It was early November, and as we stepped out into the fog there were two small boys with black discs on their cheeks and a monster in a red mask propped up in a pram. It looked like Père Ubu.

'What is this?' asked Le Corbusier, and his face lit up.

I said 'They're remembering Guy Fawkes, who tried to blow up Parliament.'

Corbu looked absolutely delighted, and he poured all his change into the little boy's hat.

Source: *Northern Architect: Journal of the Northern Architectural Association*, September 1965

The Last Formgiver

By Reyner Banham

All genius is embarrassing, and never more so than in the immediate aftermath of death. Supporters of the deceased giant busy themselves with the public record to ensure that the good (in defiance of the normal entropy of reputation) shall live after him. Detractors, convinced that their hour has finally struck emerge from the woodwork – only to find that everyone is applying the law of *de mortuis* to the last letter of *nil nisi bonum*. When the dead genius has attained a measure of acceptance as widespread, total and unquestioning as that enjoyed by Le Corbusier, when his supporters are in such total command of the media of communications as were Corb's, the chances are that the festering resentments of the detractors, when they finally burst through the crust of conventionalized approval, will provoke a reaction so destructive of his reputation that it may take generation or more to set the record straight.

Apart from the deliciously truthful memoir of his domineering and satyrish attitude to women which appeared, amid gasps of scandalized horror, in *The Guardian*, the writers of Le Corbusier's necrologies have seemed determined, by their vacuity, sentimentality, name-dropping and ignorance, to make the reaction – when it comes – so explosive and disastrous that the reputation will be destroyed finally and forever. The gullibility, for instance, of those who praised his ability to `extract lyricism from technology' (etc., *ad nauseam*) would be comparable to that of the courtiers who failed to observe the non-existence of the Emperor's new clothes, but for the fact that the non-observation of the demonstrably non-existent had gone on so long that the clothes had become old, the topic so boring that – apart from a few brave voices like that of Denys Hinton in his letter to the *Architects' Journal* – small boys had given up trying to point out the obvious to their CIAM-besotted elders.

The observable facts of his built designs are that most of his most celebrated 'machine age' effects were achieved with very primitive building technologies, descending, in later designs, to plain fakery (those spray-on walls at Ronchamp, those sky-hooked vaults of the Law Courts at Chandigarh), what time the writings if his declining years revealed an ever-deeper ignorance of the intellectual disciplines that kept the technologies of his life-time moving, and he delighted himself (with the childishness of an old man) in such `technological' discoveries as the interference patterns produced by superimposing two transparent grids. This discovery has little that is interesting, or even significant, to do with the

44.1
**Le Corbusier with Walter Gropius,
Marcel Breuer and Sven Markelius
discussing the design of the UNESCO
building, Paris (1952)**

Photographer unknown (1958)

progress of technology, but that fact that these patterns caught his eye five years or more before Op Art hit the galleries, points to something that is significant about Le Corbusier and interesting about the times in which he lived: he was the fashion-master of his age. He was ever first in the hearts of his fellow professionals because he was always first on the beach-heads of aesthetic (never technological) adventure. Just as the US marines never stormed an atoll or captured an island without finding *Kilroy was here* chalked on some handy surface, so no sudden rush of aesthetic adventure in architecture between 1925 and 1965 ever reached its objective without finding slogans in the old master's familiar hand already scrawled across the scene. As Alison Smithson once said, with the kind of resigned exasperation usually reserved for discussing elderly relatives, 'When you open a new volume of the *Oeuvre Complète* you find that he has had all your best ideas already, has done what you were about to do next.'

This is by no means a gift to be despised. To enjoy this kind of command over the quasi-conscious and semi-rational preferences and prejudices of men, has been the source of vast political power to some, immense wealth to others, has founded religions that brought empires to their knees. History has not been shaped solely by deep social ground-swells, inexorable economic forces, new sources of power or improved means of communication. It has also been decisively shaped by unforeseeable individuals (Lenin, Gandhi, Martin Luther King – but also Christian Dior, Elvis Presley, Jackson Pollock) whose power to utter the right word, turn the necessary gesture, has made great trends conscious and comprehensible, defined the forms in which history, and their contemporaries, could recognize the drift of events.

The *quality* of the utterance or gesture made by these historical formgivers has no bearing, it seems, on its charismatic effect. Gandhi could speak foolishly, King irresponsibly, Lenin stupidly, without their ceasing to be great and compelling leaders. Corb could be as flashy as Presley, as ridiculous as Dior or as mulish as Pollock on a bad Monday, and yet his slightest doodle would be as persuasive as his longest-pondered design to architects of most generations in most parts of the world. The bitterness of British architects seasoned in the service of the Raj, who complained that Le Corbusier was offering to solve the architectural problems of India on the basis of a merely tourist acquaintance with the sub-continent, was made the more sour by their helpless recognition that these solutions would impose themselves on practically everybody – including themselves, as like as not. Within the confines of architecture as currently practised, and the compass of architectural history as currently studied, his achievement is overwhelmingly clear – he was the outstanding formgiver of what may prove to be the last form-dominated epoch of architecture. He was, perhaps, less fundamental a formgiver than Auguste Perret, whose trabeated conception of concrete structure underlies even Le Corbusier. He was less radically inventive than Frank Lloyd Wright, but far more imitable. The evidence of the eyes is that for thirty years he discovered, codified, exploited, demonstrated – even invented – and gave authority to more forms than any other architect around. To walk across the grass at Alton West is to inhabit a total environment created largely and consciously in his image, (Fig. 44.2) but to drive down Sunset Boulevard is to be constantly reminded that men who never heard his name have been able to go to work on clichés borrowed at

44.2
Alton West Estate, Roehampton, London (1958)

Architects: London County Council Architects Department
Photographer: Bill Toomey (1958)

second or third hand from his notebooks. From him the Modern Movement in architecture learned most of its international language of architectural expression, and the fact that this language expresses practically nothing of interest for the second half of the twentieth century is the movement's fault, not his, and detracts nothing from his personal achievement in imposing it.

Source: *Architectural Review*, August 1966

Part 5

1970–1987:

Rejection and Reappraisal

Contributors

Peter Allison
Brian Appleyard
Christopher Booker
Alan Colquhoun
Peter Cook
Maxwell Fry
Louis Hellman
James Palmes
Martin Pawley
Gavin Stamp
Phil Windsor

Le Corbusier: 'Architect or Revolutionary?'

By Peter Allison

Considering the amount he published, it is surprisingly difficult to formulate from his writings a 'straight' interpretation of Le Corbusier's purposes. The first difficult is to create a sufficiently wide 'mental gap' to be at all critical. This is particularly so with *Vers une Architecture*[1] whose contents have so far influenced our notions about architecture that to actually read the book can very easily seem like wading through a sea of platitudes.

The second difficulty is to do with the form of the writings themselves. It is well known that both *Vers une Architecture* and *Urbanisme* consist basically of articles which had been published independently in *L'Esprit Nouveau*, and that *Précisions*, Le Corbusier's second book on planning, is largely a reprint of lectures he delivered on his South American trip in 1929. But in *La Ville Radieuse*, (Fig. 45.2) probably his most carefully considered book, written between 1931 and 1933, he continues to utilise the same form i.e. to assemble the whole book from relatively short pieces written at different times – of which only a small number had been previously published in *Prélude*, the monthly organ of the Central Committee for Regionalist and Syndicalist Action. So that what we are effectively being offered is not self-conscious and highly structured argument, but rather intriguing glimpses into a private journal.

This is certainly not the way in which Le Corbusier intended his writings to be received, but it does start to account for their general form and some of their content, and the highly personal nature of some of his comments.

Within the context of his book Pevsner had no need to consider Le Corbusier as one of his pioneers of modern design, but is somewhat unfair in his comment that Le Corbusier 'tried in his writings to make himself appear one of the first-comers'.[2] Le Corbusier was perfectly well aware of the work of his immediate predecessors and seldom failed to credit their achievement,[3] but clearly he did not find it altogether satisfactory – 'the vacuum-cleaning period' as Ozenfant called it. As early as 1908 he was writing: 'My concept is now clear ... I have 40 years in front of me to reach what I picture to be great on my horizon, which is still flat at the moment.'[4] By 1923 the exact breadth of his concept is more clear: 'Architecture is the first manifestation of man creating his own universe, creating it in the image of nature, submitting to the laws of nature, the laws which govern our own nature, our universe.'[5] It requires not just new buildings but a 'new spirit', which he claims already exists, and 'the attainment, universally recognised, of a state of perfection universally felt'.[6]

45.1
Le Corbusier with, amongst others, William Tatton-Brown, Cornelius van Eesteren and Serge Chermayeff, at the construction site of his Pavillon des Temps Nouveaux at the Exposition Internationale des Arts et des Techniques dans la Vie Moderne, Paris (1937)

Photographer: Monte Bryer (1937)

45.2
Pedestrians in the air, vehicles on the ground

From Le Corbusier, *La Ville Radieuse* (1935)

This seemingly nebulous ideal was the spur to all Le Corbusier's early writings, beginning with the essays in collaboration with Ozenfant on Purism: 'The means of executing a work of art is a transmit-table and universal language.'[7] And always the arguments with which he attempts to substantiate his vision are rhetorical rather than rational: a collage of observations, memories, ideas and impressions, which he is continuously revising but never condenses into a final form – that would have contradicted his only basic principle, 'No beginning and no end'.[8] This accounts for his apparent repetitiveness, and the fact that he seldom ever repeated himself exactly.

Another important, and related aspect of Le Corbusier's early writings which is known about but not generally appreciated, is the extent to which they were affected by the experiences of his early life, that is during the period before he finally settled in Paris in 1917, aged 30. The basic facts are simple enough. He was born in 1887 in La Chaux-de-Fonds, a small watch-making town in the Swiss Jura, and at the age of 14 enrolled at the local art school to train as a watch case engraver, the occupation of both is parents. Here he was taken up by the 'emancipated pedagogue' L'Eplattenier who eventually persuaded him to turn to architecture, and gave him his first commission. From then (1906) until the outbreak of war, when he returned to La Chaux-de-Fonds, he travelled extensively throughout Europe and the Near East: first to Italy, then Budapest and Vienna, where he worked briefly for Joseph Hoffmann, then on to Paris and 15 months with Auguste Perret; in 1910 to Munich, Berlin and Peter Behrens' office; then on again to Prague, Vienna, Budapest, Belgrade, Serbia, Rumania, Bulgaria, Turkey and Greece.

Obviously these years mark Le Corbusier's[9] progress from the status of a talented provincial art student to that of a trained architect known and respected by some of the most eminent members of the profession in Europe. But from the only published document of this period, a letter written from Paris in 1908 to L'Eplattenier, it is equally clear that the going was not always easy: 'I began to suspect that architecture is not simply an eurhythmy of forms but something else, but what? I didn't really know. So I studied mechanics, then statics, then the strength of materials. They're difficult, but they're beautiful, these mathematics, so logical, so perfect! ... Those eight months shouted to me 'logic, truth, honesty, burn what you loved, and adore what you burned.' The architect should be a man with a logical mind; an enemy of love of the plastic effect; a man of science but also with a heart, an artist and a scholar. I know this now but none of my masters could tell me, luckily the elders know how to communicate with those who consult them. Egyptian and Gothic architecture were conditioned by religion and available materials. The art of tomorrow will come, because humanity has changed its way of living and thinking.'[10]

It is possible to identify, in latent form, many of the themes of his later writings in this letter – a substantiation of my suggestion that they are at least partly autobiographical in nature. But what I find much more suggestive is his repeated assertion that architecture is not simply a matter of form. Could it be that he had discovered within himself an immense potential for understanding and manipulating form – certainly this is the evidence of his contemporary drawings – but had decided that for an architecture of the future something more, or something different, was necessary – logic, mathematics, science? 'Burn what you loved, and adore what you burned.' For the next 30 years form and all plausible alternatives he could find to it as a basis for postulating the renovation of architecture, became the complementary poles around which his thinking crystalised. But undoubtedly their most clear – and most confusing – expression is to be found in his first book, *Vers une Architecture*, published in Paris in 1923.[11]

Vers une Architecture

The only extended critique of *Vers une Architecture* of which I am aware is the relevant chapter in Reyner Banham's *Theory and Design in the First Machine Age*. He starts by explaining that he is dealing with 'one of the most influential, widely read and least understood of all the architectural writings of the twentieth century',[12] but then immediately dispels any hope of enlightenment with this gross generalisation: 'Two main themes can be distinguished at once, and can be roughly labelled Academic and Mechanistic. All the essays can be put under one or other of these headings in terms of their main subject-matter, and they are grouped in the book in a manner which emphasises this distinction.'[13] On this basis he briefly describes the contents and organisation of the book and then concludes: 'As will be seen, although the book opens on a Mechanistic note, the chapters which actually deal with the virtues of machinery are firmly sandwiched between two sections whose main function is to rehearse the more Abstract and Classical – *large et sévère* – ideas of the Academic tradition, so that the reader who goes straight through the book gets the impression that he is being conducted through an orderly argument in which machine-design stands as a necessary intermediate stage between certain Abstract fundamentals of design and the glories of the Parthenon.'[14]

Banham's summary classification into Academic and Mechanistic material undoubtedly provides a convenient means of outlining the form of *Vers une Architecture* but neither word if applied to the text of a particular essay would adequately indicate its contents. His choice of such loaded words is also misleading: Academic, especially, amounts to a deliberate denial of one of Le Corbusier's most explicit attacks – 'The Grand Prix de Rome and the Villa Medici are the cancer of French Architecture'. And the suggestion that the whole book was carefully contrived to deceive the unwitting reader into believing in a non-existent argument is hardly fair when the first eight pages are devoted to a detailed summary of its total contents.

The mistake Banham has made here is the very obvious one of assuming a direct correlation between the illustrations, which are usually of engineering achievements or good architecture, and the text. As the titles of the different sections usually follow directly from the subject-matter of the illustrations, such a correlation is clearly suggested. But although Le Corbusier was undoubtedly stimulated by the formal properties of Ozenfant's[15] photographs, or his own drawings, his purposes were much wider than merely to justify his own 'aesthetic prejudices'[16] and are made explicit in the text, sometimes in parallel with the illustrations but often only by elliptical reference to them.

'THE ENGINEER'S AESTHETIC AND ARCHITECTURE – two things that march together and follow one from the other – the one at its full height, the other in an unhappy state of retrogression.'[17] Thus Le Corbusier begins his first book and almost too abruptly informs us what it is going to be about: the decline of architecture, with evidence and reasons, and the importance of architecture – otherwise its decline would not matter. The argument of this chapter, crudely put, is to denigrate architects, to praise engineers, then to recall with nostalgia 'this thing called ARCHITECTURE, an admirable thing, the loveliest of all'.[18] The state of architecture is blamed on the 'national schools' which 'mystify young minds and teach them dissimulation and the obsequiousness of the toady'. Instead architects should follow the example of engineers who 'employ mathematical calculation which derives from natural law, and their works give us the feeling of HARMONY'. He finishes the chapter by outlining his intentions in the next three sections of the book: THREE REMINDERS TO ARCHITECTS, an attempt to re-establish the neglected fundamentals of architecture; EYES WHICH DO NOT SEE, professedly addressed to 'big business men, bankers and merchants', who as clients are also to be held responsible for 'the present evil state of architecture'; and 'finally, it will be a delight to talk of ARCHITECTURE after so many grain stores, workshops, machines and skyscrapers'.

MASS, the first reminder, begins with that incredible aphorism 'Architecture is the masterly, correct and magnificent play of masses brought together in light', followed by some straight Purist theorizing on the use of primary forms and an appeal to 'our forefathers': 'Egyptian, Greek or Roman architecture is an architecture of prisms, cubes and cylinders, pyramids or spheres: the Pyramids, the Temple of Luxor, the Parthenon, the Coliseum, Hadrian's Villa.' Only in conclusion does Le Corbusier turn to 'the American grain elevators and factories, the magnificent FIRST-FRUITS of the new age'.

SURFACE, the second reminder, deals with the problem of how 'to leave a mass intact in the splendour of its form in light' and at the same time 'to appropriate its surface for needs which are often utilitarian'. Thus 'the surface of the temple or factory is in most cases a wall with holes for doors and windows; these holes are often the destruction of form; they must be made an accentuation of form'. Le Corbusier's solution is to take over the engineering technique of using 'generating and accusing lines' to divide up surfaces according to their geometrical properties – which obviously depends on the surfaces, and their respective masses, having distinct geometrical properties to begin with. The illustrations are all of industrial buildings, including Gropius and Meyer's Fagus factory, except the first which is of the Belvedere Courtyard – 'The engineers of today find themselves in accord with the principles that Bramante and Raphael had applied a long time ago.'

Having established mass and surface as 'those elements which are capable of affecting our senses, and of rewarding the desire of our eyes',[19] it only remains 'to dispose of them in such a way that the sight of them affects us immediately'.[20] Hence THE PLAN which 'determines everything; is the decisive moment'. Its purpose is to establish 'a primary and pre-determined rhythm: the work is developed in extent and height following the prescriptions of the plan, with results which can range from the simplest to the most complex, all coming within the same law. Unity of law is the law of a good plan: a simple law capable of infinite modulation … so we get the astonishing diversity found in great epochs, a diversity which is the result of architectural principle and not of the play of decoration. The plan carries in itself the very essence of sensation.' All this with axonometrics from Choisy's *Histoire de L'Architecture*.

Between the THREE REMINDERS and EYES WHICH DO NOT SEE Le Corbusier inserts a separate chapter, still intended for architects, entitled REGULATING LINES – essentially an expansion and substantiation of his suggestions on 'generating and accusing lines'. Their purpose is to create order in any dimension – 'a basis of construction and a satisfaction'. As a constructional means they provide the geometrical basis necessary to lay out a plan, section or elevation with the desired 'unity of law', together with a system of measurement – 'on the human scale' – to ensure accuracy. The satisfaction comes from imposing on nature a system of order, which is itself a paraphrase of the laws of nature'.[21] To clarify these ideas Le Corbusier refers to the example of 'a primitive temple', and then discusses a series of elevations, mostly historical but finishing with three of his own designs.

So far we have been treated to little more than a series of stimulating history lessons, based on personal experience and reflection, and the assumption that as architecture worthy of consideration existed previously – 'A product of happy peoples and a thing which in itself produces happy peoples' – it might exist again, given 'a new spirit'. To this end, both the text and illustrations have served the same purpose – to draw a parallel between past achievements and the most advanced of contemporary building techniques – and the correlation between them has, on the whole, been close. In EYES WHICH DO NOT SEE this correlation begins to break down as the argument of the text, though still dependent on the illustrations, becomes at once more general and more urgent. Again there are three sections.

LINERS starts with an attack on the 'decorative arts' and their irrelevance at a time when machinery has become 'a new factor in human affairs', when engineers 'have conceived and constructed these formidable affairs that steamships are.' Architects too are responsible for the same kind of irrelevance; they are 'stifled by custom' – and ancient by-laws – and ignorant of the latest building techniques. They are also party to the common confusion between decoration and art; art depends upon an understanding of its epoch, decoration does not. 'The steamship is the first stage in the realization of a world organised according to the new spirit.'

AIRPLANES are not only an example of the kind and scale of achievement which architects should attain to, they also provide an exemplar of machine invention and production. 'When a problem is properly stated, in our epoch, it inevitably finds its solution.' Le Corbusier then refers to the 'commonplace' arguments of younger architects, that 'the construction should be shown' and 'when a thing responds to a need, it is beautiful', and dismisses both as inadequate. But because of a failure to fulfil any basic needs, 'it is not possible that the higher factors of harmony and beauty should enter in ... the problem has not been stated as regards architecture'.

Once the problem has been well stated 'it is necessary to press on towards the establishment of standards in order to face the problems of perfection'. This is the theme of AUTOMOBILES, but the argument becomes somewhat diffuse due to the introduction of the Parthenon as an example of perfection achieved – the motor-car being in a state of evolution only. According to Le Corbusier's logic, the setting-up of standards ought to be a direct consequence of stating the problem: 'A standard is established on sure bases, not capriciously but with the surety of something intentional and a logic controlled by analysis and experiment.' The next stage, once a 'type-solution' has been established is to check the details and so improve the over-all performance. This is the lesson of the motor-car.

Later, in case he has not been totally convincing or possibly to reveal his final intentions, he reassures us that 'Phidias would have loved to have lived in this standardised age ... Before long he would have repeated the experience of the Parthenon.' Thus, 'after so many grain stores, workshops, machines and skyscrapers', we come to ARCHITECTURE.

Taken together, the contents of the Engineers Aesthetic and Architecture, Three Reminders to Architects, Regulating Lines and Eyes which Do Not See amount to a fairly complete description of the means by which 'this thing called architecture' might be resurrected. But clearly the exact nature and use of these means has been dominated by a total preconception concerning the highest qualities of which architecture was, or might be, capable. Its ingredients were the distilled experiences of his early life – as I briefly described them – of which by far the most dominant was his appreciation of the architectural achievements of the past. In this respect, ARCHITECTURE is both an admission and an explanation. There are three chapters: The Lesson of Rome, the Illusion of Plans, and Pure Creation of the Mind; and the Lesson of Rome has four parts: Ancient Rome, Byzantine Rome, Michaelangelo and Rome and Ourselves.

ANCIENT ROME begins with some general history: 'Rome's business was to conquer the world and govern it. Strategy, recruiting, legislation: the spirit of order. In order to manage a large business house it is essential to adopt some fundamental, simple and unexceptionable principles. The Roman order was simple and direct.' For Le Corbusier, these characteristics also distinguish Roman architecture: 'The Parthenon, the Colosseum ... Absence of verbosity, good arrangement, a single idea, daring and unity in construction, the use of elementary shapes. A sane morality.'

BYZANTINE ROME dwells on the simple but satisfying qualities of the Church of S. Maria in Cosmedin: 'The design is merely that of the ordinary basilica, that is to say the form of architecture in which barns and hangars are built. The walls are of rough lime plaster. There is only one colour, white; always powerful since it is positive.' But despite its modest appearance, S. Maria in Cosmedin had been built on a geometrical basis i.e. with 'the sense of relationships and the mathematical precision thanks to which perfection becomes approachable.' But what is this perfection and how will we perceive it? 'There exists one thing that can ravish us, and this is measure or scale.'

Having started with a great civilisation, Le Corbusier finishes with a great man, MICHAELANGELO, 'the man of the last thousand years as Phidias was the man of the thousand years before'. Intelligence and passion are what makes these men: 'There is no art without emotion, no emotion without passion. Stones are dead things sleeping in quarries but the apses of St. Peter's are a drama ... As the man, so the drama, so the architecture.' Then almost as a premonition of his own future, Le Corbusier reflects how easily such talent is wasted; 'But foolish and thoughtless Popes dismissed Michaelangelo; miserable men have murdered St. Peter's within and without!'

ROME AND OURSELVES is an attack on the Academies for their indiscriminate appreciation of Renaissance Rome, much of which Le Corbusier considered to be in bad taste.

Just as the lesson of Rome provides historical justification for the arguments of Mass and Surface, so does THE ILLUSION OF PLANS for the Third Reminder to Architects. The end purpose of the kind of architecture Le Corbusier has been postulating is to have a clear intellectual and emotional impact, hence his demands for pure forms, pure colours – like white – and the geometrically pure division of surfaces. But more important is his insistence on the importance of the plan, and its potential to organise diverse elements within a unity of rhythm. Such a unity cannot be contrived although it must be intentional; it is the result of emotions clarified into thought. 'The plan is the generator ... it is a plan of battle. The battle is composed of the impact of masses in space and the morale of the army is the cluster of predetermined ideas and the driving purpose.' The rest of the chapter is devoted to describing some basic 'predetermined ideas' illustrated by examples from his travels in the Mediterranean.

The first is a PLAN PROCEEDS FROM WITHIN TO WITHOUT and consists, as Banham naturally delights in pointing out, of descriptions of the Green Mosque at Broussa and the Casa Del Noce at Pompeii, as seen by a visitor 'proceeding from the outside inwards'. But the intention is clear enough; the interior of a building provides an opportunity both of great freedom and great control: 'You are captured, you have lost the sense of the common scale. You are enthralled by a sensorial rhythm (light and volume) and by an able use scale and measure, into a world of its own which tells you what it set out to tell you.' In this respect the exterior of the building is clearly of less importance.

ARCHITECTURAL ELEMENTS OF THE INTERIOR is concerned with those rudiments of any interior so easily forgotten: a floor, some walls and – most important – light. 'The walls are in full brilliant light, or in half-shade or in full shade, giving an effect of gaiety, serenity or sadness.'

Only with ARRANGEMENT are we informed exactly how the various constituent qualities of a plan take effect: 'they are seen from the ground, the beholder standing up and looking in front of him' – a banal but equally radical statement. But the beholder also moves, inevitably along an axis. 'That axis is the regulator of architecture. ... Arrangement is the grading of axes, and so it is the grading of aims, the classification of intentions.' He then describes in some detail the effects of the implied axes on the Acropolis, Athens, and in the Forum and the House of the Tragic Poet at Pompeii.

THE EXTERIOR IS ALWAYS AN INTERIOR provides a complementary argument to A Plan Proceeds from Within to Without; just as the exterior is of relative unimportance' compared with the potential qualities of the interior, so it is similarly unimportant when compared with the impact of its setting – which for Le Corbusier would ideally be an undisturbed Virgilian landscape: 'your building may cube 100,000 cubic yards, but what lies around it may cube millions of cubic yards, and that is what tells'. Thus he seems to suggest that the actual enclosure of a building has no more importance than to serve as a membrane between the internal and external effects of a building. The only difference between these two kinds of experience is their scale, otherwise they should be treated as elements of the same composition and subjected to the same considerations i.e. related to various axes. Again he refers to the Acropolis, the Forum at Pompeii and Hadrian's Villa.

The last chapter of Architecture, PURE CREATION OF THE MIND, is at once the most stimulating in the whole book and the most difficult to reduce to a structured argument. In fact, it does not really have an argument; it is a celebration, with various afterthoughts thrown in, of the greatest thing that ever happened to Le Corbusier: six weeks studying the Acropolis and the Parthenon. 'Here everything was a shout of inspiration, a dance in the sunlight ... and a final supreme warning: do not believe until you have seen and measured ... and touched with your fingers.'[22] Clearly, the Parthenon represents for him the highest level of creation ever achieved and the only one still worth aspiring to. But to explain exactly why or how this should be so seems virtually impossible – either for Le Corbusier or anyone else.

His explanation is that certain sensations are pleasing and induce us into a state of harmony with our immediate surroundings, and beyond with nature and the universe. This is because of 'an axis of organization ... on which all phenomena and all objects of nature are based'. His evidence: 'If, through calculation, the airplane takes on the aspect of a fish or some object of nature, it is because it has recovered the axis. If the canoe, the musical instrument, the turbine, all results of experiment and calculation, appear to us to be "organised" phenomena, that is to say as having in themselves a certain life, it is because they are based upon that axis.' He then lists the characteristics of these 'organized' phenomena: they should be 'animated by a unity of the intention which is responsible for them'; and they should have their 'own special character'. The attainment of all these qualities at once is only possible through 'pure creation of the mind'.

But, whereas such high intentions are commonplace in other arts, in architecture they are rare: 'architecture is lowered to the level of its utilitarian purposes'. Such purposes ought to be well served but architecture is capable of much more: 'Architecture only exists when there is poetic emotion.' Presumably this refers back to the beginning of the argument so that such an emotion would be one that induced in us a particular state of harmony. Whether or not an architect is capable in this sense depends upon his ability to handle contours: 'contours are the touchstone of the architect; in dealing with them he is forced to decide whether he will be a plastic artist or not ... Greece, and in Greece the Parthenon, have marked the apogee of this pure creation of the mind: the development of profile and contour.' The text is illustrated by a series of excellent close-up photographs of the Parthenon, with captions which often suggest parallels between the quality of the mouldings and modern engineering techniques.

The last two chapters of *Vers une Architecture*, Mass-Produced Housing and Architecture or Revolution, are markedly different from any of the previous ones; thus Pure Creation of the Mind may be taken as concluding Le Corbusier's general proposals on the nature of architecture. So why was Banham so wrong in saying that 'the reader who goes straight through the book gets the impression that he is being conducted through an orderly argument in which machine-design stands as a necessary intermediate stage between certain Abstract fundamentals of design and the glories of the Parthenon'? On the whole, my presentation of Le Corbusier's writings would seem to support this as a fair, if somewhat flippant, summary of their contents and purpose. In fact, it has been my purpose so far only to make explicit and illusive impression which *Vers une Architecture* is likely to make on even the most attentive reader. But now we have a second problem of an equally illusive nature. How is it that the last two chapters seem so different from the previous ones?

The most obvious difference is their basic concern with social issues; there is no mention of any 'poetic emotion', only of the urgent need to establish better living conditions. 'The primordial instinct of every human being is to assure himself of a shelter. The various classes of workers in society to-day no longer have dwellings adapted to their needs; neither the artisan nor the intellectual. It is a question of building which is at the root of the social unrest of today.'[23] Now, it is my contention that this concern with general social conditions is present as a discontinuous sub-theme throughout the rest of *Vers une Architecture*, and that in the last two chapters it simply becomes explicit and of dominating importance. Thus, though the basis of their argument is different, the last two chapters do not represent a serious break with what has gone previously. And if there is an element of serious social concern running through the whole book, surely to ignore it, as Banham does, is to seriously misrepresent Le Corbusier's arguments.[24]

The reason why his remarks on social issues tend to go unnoticed throughout most of *Vers une Architecture* is probably that they are usually self-contained and inserted within a more obvious and continuous line of argument. Their characteristic form is to contrast a pessimistic view of the present – often employing similies with the human body – with an optimistic view of the near future. Thus at the very beginning of the Engineers' Aesthetic and Architecture: 'Our houses disgust us; we fly from them and frequent restaurants and night-clubs; or we gather together in our houses gloomily and secretly like wretched animals; we are becoming demoralized. Engineers fabricate the tools of their time. Everything that is to say, except houses and moth-eaten boudoirs.' Pure excitement at the potential of the latest engineering and production techniques is the usual reason for his optimism; and the most obvious purposes to which these techniques might be put in architecture is to produce houses. He concludes the first chapter: 'Our external world has been enormously transformed in its outward appearance and in the use made of it, by reason of the machine. We have gained a new perspective and a new social life, but we have not yet adopted the house thereto.'

But the implications of this statement clearly extend beyond the production of single houses to questions concerning their lay-out and town planning generally. These are taken up in PLAN where having concluded his remarks on the importance of the plan in individual buildings Le Corbusier moves straight on to town planning and a discussion of Tony Garnier's *Cité Industrielle*. (Fig. 45.3) But far more indicative than his comments in the main text, is an extended caption under an illustration showing some housing: 'In his important studies on the Manufacturing Town, Tony Garnier has taken for granted certain possibilities of social development, not yet brought to pass, which would permit of methods of normal expansion of towns. The public would have complete control of all building sites. A house for each family: only one half of the area would be occupied by buildings, the other half being for public use and planted with trees: hedges and fences would not be allowed. In this way the town could be traversed in every direction, quite independently of the streets, which there would be no need for a pedestrian to use. The town would really be like a great park.'

These observations on the *Cité Industrielle* contain in outline many of the ideas which Le Corbusier was to develop in his own planning studies which eventually resulted in the formulation of his ideal city, *La Ville Radieuse*. Another inspiration – the next thing he mentions – was Auguste Perret's apparently casual reference to the possibility of building a 'City of Towers' – 'A glittering epithet which aroused the poet in us. A word which struck the note of the moment because the fact itself is imminent.' Evidently Perrot never

45.3
Design for a housing district in an industrial city

From Tony Garnier, *Une Cité industrielle* (1917)

bothered to demonstrate his idea with a design; but Le Corbusier seems to have set to work immediately. In a drawing dated 1920 he shows six towers each in squares of parkland separated by arterial roads. They were to be 60 storeys high and from 250 to 300 yards apart – 'in spite of the great area devoted to the surrounding parks, the density of a normal town of today is multiplied many times over'. As business offices they would be located in city centres where their lay-out would relieve traffic congestion. He then describes the housing which would complement his office towers: 'No more courtyards, but flats opening on every side to air and light, and looking, not on the puny trees of our boulevards of today, but upon green sward, sports grounds and abundant plantations of trees.' Their continuity of lay-out – 'Streets with Set-backs' – he ascribes to the 'revolution in the aesthetics of construction' brought about by reinforced concrete, which in turn has led to, 'a new aesthetic of the plan'. So in this 'period of reconstruction and adaption to new social and economic conditions', he considered technical and aesthetic advances to be mutually self-supporting.

The 'City of Towers' and 'Streets with Set-backs' are Le Corbusier's most detailed town planning proposals in *Vers une Architecture*; his only reason for raising the topic again is to stress the urgent need for action: 'The time is ripe for construction, not for foolery.' This is in Liners where already he has committed himself to a topic of more immediate and direct importance. The 'build-up' is typical; first he states his disgust with the status quo: 'The roofs, these wretched roofs, still persist, an inexcusable paradox. The basements are still damp and cluttered up, and the service mains of our towns are invariably buried under stonework like atrophied organs.' Then one paragraph later, without the slightest warning, CRASH: 'A house is a machine for living in. Baths, sun, hot water, cold water, warmth at will, conservation of food, hygiene, beauty in the sense of good proportion.' It should be useful in the manner of a fountain pen, a typewriter, a telephone, office furniture, a safety razor, a briar pipe, a bowler hat or a limousine. Airplanes may be an example of the 'problem well stated'; but Le Corbusier is more interested in houses: 'But you will say, the Peace has set the problem in the reconstruction of the North of France. But then, we are totally disarmed, we do not know how to build in a modern way – materials, systems of construction, THE CONCEPTION OF THE DWELLING, all are lacking.' Then by contrasting the generally acceptable with the technically feasible, he attempts to define the problem of the house and summarizes his conclusions in the MANUAL OF THE DWELLING, a manifesto of personal expectation which he would have had 'printed and distributed to mothers of families'. To see how he envisaged his demands in terms of building it is necessary to turn back to Mass-Production Houses.

The greater part of MASS-PRODUCTION HOUSES is devoted to a survey of Le Corbusier's own projects, (Fig. 45.4) in the form of drawings with captions giving detailed technical information. The text too deals with technical matters though at a more general level. He

45.4
Housing at Pessac (1924)

From Le Corbusier, *Vers une Architecture* 2nd ed. (1924)

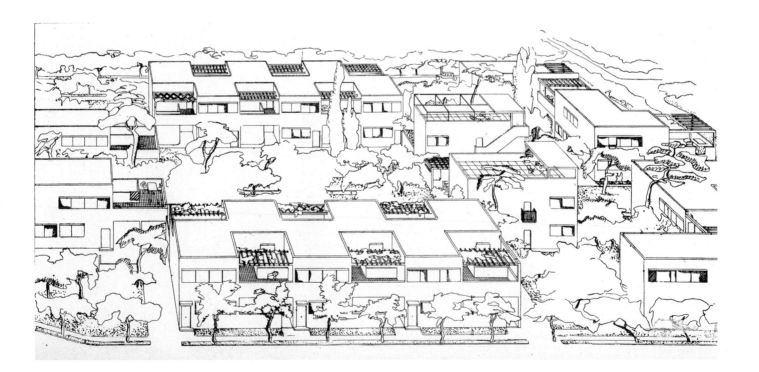

begins by referring to the *Loi Loucheur* which was supposed to authorise 'the construction of 500,000 dwellings to be built well and cheaply' as part of the post-war reconstruction programme – 'an exceptional event in the annals of construction' requiring 'exceptional means and methods'. But 'the right state of mind does not exist – the state of mind for mass-production houses, the state of mind for living in mass-production houses, the state of mind for conceiving mass-production houses'. Then, presumably to induce the 'mass-production spirit', he embarks on an instant survey of the latest developments in the building industry; he describes how an ever increasing number of building materials and components are manufactured 'off-site' and simply incorporated into the building during construction, and how engineers, besides rationalising the service systems necessary to a building, have also invented more efficient alternatives to traditional methods of construction. His conclusions, in their context, are optimistic; these developments, if pursued, must inevitably result in a totally rationalized building industry only capable of mass-production and socially responsible projects.

In the face of such radical changes to come, Le Corbusier can only have considered his own design proposals as provisional solutions on the way to full industrialization. But the technical characteristics of each of his three basic dwelling types are still startling today: in the Domino house standardised woodwork units (doors, cupboards and windows) are used to locate block walls between in-situ cast slabs at fixed heights; in the Monol (Fig. 45.5) house asbestos sheeting is used as permanent shutting for both walls and roofs permitting what would otherwise be sub-standard concrete work; and the Citrohan house has a structure of in-situ cast side walls of concrete reinforced with expanded metal.

There are perspectives showing interiors and possible collective lay-outs for each dwelling type, but probably the most important illustrations are of the *Immeubles-Villas*. These consist of Citrohan-type units, each with its own 'hanging garden', assembled into blocks five units high and ten units long, facing inwards onto garden courts and serviced by roads running between the backs of neighbouring pairs of blocks. All services – heating, hot water, food, domestic help – are organised centrally, car-parking is underground – beneath the central court – and on the roof of each block are a communal hall, a gymnasium and a running track. 'No actual rent is paid; the tenants take shares in the enterprise; these are payable over a period of 20 years, and the interest represent a very low rent.'

This project provides the most direct connection between Le Corbusier's design solutions for individual dwellings and his earlier town planning proposals, and demonstrates both the relevance and the feasibility of each. He knew he was 'dealing with an urgent problem of our epoch, or rather, with *the* problem of our epoch' – it only remained to convince society that he was right. To this end he wrote: ARCHITECTURE OR REVOLUTION.

This title is itself misleading due to the slightly unexpected meanings Le Corbusier attaches to both 'architecture' and 'revolution'. Throughout most of the chapter 'revolution' does not refer to the possibility of violent social reform but to various technical and organizational innovations whose effects, though widespread, have not been generally recognised: 'Industry has created new tools: the illustrations in this book provide a telling proof of this. Such tools are capable of adding to human welfare and of lightening human toil. If these new conditions are set against the past, you have Revolution.'

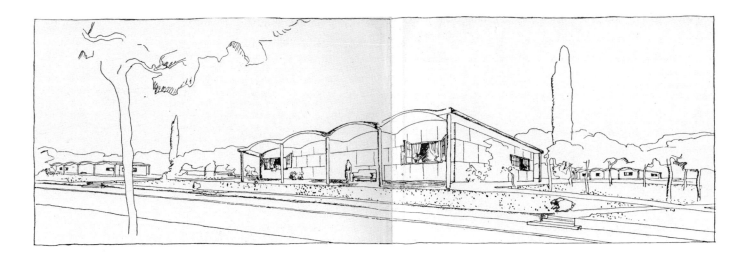

45.5
A 'Monol' house (1919)

From Le Corbusier, *Vers une Architecture*
2nd ed. (1924)

But despite these achievements, the physical condition of the general environment remains unchanged, much to the detriment of family life. 'Disturbed by the reactions which play upon him from every quarter, the man of today is conscious, on the one hand, of a new world which is forming itself regularly, logically and clearly, which produces in a straight forward way things which are useful and usable, and on the other hand he finds himself, to his surprise, living in an old and hostile environment. This framework is his lodging; his town, his street, his house or his flat rise up against him useless, hinder him from following the same path in his leisure that he pursues in his work, hinder him from following in his leisure the organic development of his existence, which is to create a family and to live, like every animal on this earth and like all men of all ages, an organised family life. In this way society is helping forward the destruction of the family, while she sees with terror that this will be her ruin.'

Thus Le Corbusier foresees a decline in family life leading to a general disintegration of existing social patterns – a second, and more conventional, concept of revolution. But clearly this kind of revolution would not be averted by 'the masterly, correct and magnificent play of masses brought together in light', although it might be by a large-scale reconstruction programme – so this must be architecture too. The book ends: 'Society is filled with a violent desire for something which it may obtain or not. Everything lies in that: everything depends on the effort made and the attention paid to these alarming symptoms. Architecture or Revolution. Revolution can be avoided.'

Conclusion

Vers une Architecture is an intoxicating book, an uninhibited combination of experience and learning, logic and emotion; thus it is both easy to read and equally easy to misunderstand. But conversely, any attempted interpretation must inevitably detract from its full scope and impact – and from its desperate seriousness. *Vers une Architecture* was not intended as a gesture for the titillation of an architectural élite; it was written in the confused years immediately after the 1914–18 war.

Probably the only way of more fully appreciating it is simply to continue reading Le Corbusier's later books, particularly *Urbanisme*[25] and *La Ville Radieuse*[26]. Although their form of presentation and manner of argument is essentially no different from *Vers une Architecture*, they are each more considered and deliberate in purpose. *Urbanisme* starts with a series of general propositions as to the nature of cities, again based mainly on historical evidence, then considers the condition and potential of existing cities, and ends with an exposition of 'A Contemporary City' and the *Plan Voisin* for Paris. In *La Ville Radieuse* reference to historical precedent is minimal; Le Corbusier's purpose is to define the collective goals of society and the rights of the individual within society, and to show how these may be achieved through a correct use of technology: 'We must build the places where mankind can be reborn. When the collective functions of the urban community have been organised, then there will be individual liberty for all.'[27]

Even his insistence on the importance of harmony is very much subdued: 'I confine myself to this negative observation: it is the lack of harmony, cacophony which has put the human biology and the heart out of order today.'[28] But when it comes to making proposals for some of the world's greatest cities there is no restraint; the old virtuosity at inventing and manipulating form bursts forth unabashed – how else could he have sketched the future of Rio de Janeiro from a plane and simply commented 'An idea is born'?[29] And when he formulates such ideas in more detail, his continuing preoccupation with axes, rhythm and harmony, though increasingly subtle in its manifestation, is equally apparent. So where is the connection between all that talk about society and technology, and these beautiful formal creations?

The answer is once more in his view of history, of the way in which civilisations advance and attain a state of culture. The idea is first outlined in brief in *Vers une Architecture*: 'Civilisations advance, they pass through the age of the peasant, the soldier and the priest and attain what is rightly called culture.'[30] In *Urbanisme* he is more explicit: 'Culture manifests itself in a full realisation of the equipment at our disposal, by choice, by classification, and by evolution.'[31] He then describes the stages by which this level of culture is attained: the first is the era of the savage who has an instinctive respect for 'universal laws' but makes no attempt to understand them; the second is the era of self-conscious nations who have lost their intuitive sensibility and are struggling to regain a state of equilibrium. The third and final stage is Le Corbusier's ideal: 'But the great moment is reached at length when every means has been proved, and where a complete equipment assures the perfect carrying out of rational schemes. A great calm is created by the power which had been acquired and which can be measured. The mind is able to create in a state of serenity. The period of struggle is over. The period of construction has arrived. And the spirit of construction has entered into our minds; we are able to appreciate and to measure; we can recognise what is best; we can bring proportion to bear.'[32]

The implication is clear. During such periods not only are practical building requirements dealt with as a matter of course, but great architecture is produced too. So construction for its own sake and architecture as 'pure creation of the spirit' are not mutually exclusive, but rather the existence of one ensures the possibility of the other. This is the clue to the apparent dichotomy which exists throughout Le Corbusier's writings, and is particularly obvious in *Vers une Architecture* at any time he is either invoking the 'spirit of architecture' or making a simple demand for a reconstruction programme. For him these aims were not contradictory, but complementary; if one could be achieved, the other would follow as a consequence. The alternative, if neither were achieved, would be an intolerable decline into general squalor and misery: 'There is a man who is not completely happy. On the verge of boredom almost. Then another man who is even less happy than the first. Then another, and another – millions of them.'[33] Architecture or Revolution. If only architecture were that important!

1   I have not used the translated title of *Vers une Architecture*, *Urbanisme* and *La Ville Radieuse* because in my opinion the original French titles are more explicit and exact.

2   Nikolaus Pevsner, *Pioneers of Modern Design*, Harmondsworth, 1960, p. 184.

3   See, for instance the introduction to the first volume (1910–29) of the *Oeuvre Complète* for remarks on Garnier, Perret and others – even Frank Lloyd Wright.

4   Letter to Charles L'Eplattenier translated and published in *L'Architecture d'Aujourd'hui*, no. 51, November 1965.

5   *Towards a New Architecture*, p. 69 (see footnote 11).

6   Op. cit., p. 128.

7   Le Corbusier and Ozenfant, 'Le Purisme' in *L'Esprit Nouveau*, no. 4, 1920. Translated by Robert L. Herbert and republished in *Modern Artists on Art*, New Jersey (Prentice-Hall) 1964, pp. 58–73.

8   Le Corbusier, *My Work*, London: Architectural Press, 1960, p. 217.

9   To avoid confusion, I have not distinguished between the orginal Charles-Edouard Jeanneret and Le Corbusier pseudonym he adoped in 1923 to separate his works as an architect and as a painter.

10   As footnote 4.

11   A revised and expanded edition was published in Paris in 1924 and translated by Frederick Etchells as *Towards a New Architecture* published by John Rodker, London 1927. The quotations I have used are taken from the 1946 edition of Etchells' translation, published by the Architectural Press.

12   Reyner Banham, *Theory and Design in the First Machine Age*, London: Architectural Press, 1960, p. 220.

13   Op. cit., p. 223.

14   Op. cit., p. 223.

15   See Ozenfant's *Art*, Paris, 1928 (translated by John Rodker as *Foundations of Modern Art* and published in London, 1931, and New York, 1952) and the extracts from his *Mémoires* published in *Architecture d'Aujourd'hui*, no. 51, November 1965 for an account of his collaboration with Le Corbusier on the original *L'Esprit Nouveau* articles.

16   *Theory and Design in the First Machine Age*, p. 248.

17   Quotations from *Towards a New Architecture* are only referenced when I have used them outside their original context.

18   In my treatment of Le Corbusier's arguments I have usually preferred to describe and edit rather than comment directly on their coherence.

19   *Towards a New Architecture*, p. 20.

20   Op. cit., p. 20.

21   Op. cit., p. 69.

22   *My Work*, p. 21.

23   *Towards a New Architecture*, p. 250.

24   In the last chapter of *Theory and Design in the First Machine Age* Banham finally dismisses the 'progressive architecture of the Twenties' as of only aesthetic interest. To this end it is clearly in his interests to restrict the previous discussion to a mainly aesthetic basis.

25   Le Corbusier, *Urbanisme,* Paris, 1925. *The City of To-morrow and its Planning*, translated by Frederick Etchells, published by Rodker, London, 1929, from which the quotations are taken.

26   Le Corbusier, *La Ville Radieuse,* Boulogne-sur-Seine 1935. *The Radiant City,* translated by Pamela Knight, Eleanor Levieux and Derek Coltman, New York: Orion Press, London: Faber & Faber, 1967, from which the quotations are taken.

27   *The Radiant City*, p. 152.

28   Op. cit., p. 36.

29   Op. cit., p. 223.

30   *Towards a New Architecture*, p. 128.

31   *The City of Tomorrow*, p. 34.

32   Op. cit., p. 35.

33   *The Radiant City*, p. 344.

Source: *AAQ*, vol 3, April/June 1971

Displacement of Concepts

By Alan Colquhoun

*The term is borrowed from Donald Schon.

What I mean by 'displacement of concepts'* is that a concept belonging to one field or associated with one set of functions becomes transferred to another. For instance, machine made objects of everyday use suffer a displacement when they become converted into an already existent architectural meaning system. This process can be observed in the whole of the early Modern Movement (for people in Constructivism), but nowhere is it so apparent as in the work of Le Corbusier. Le Corbusier never excluded on principle the classical architectural tradition, and this is fused with the newly displaced elements outside the architectural tradition, becoming modified or inverted by its application to new problems on the one hand, and its juxtaposition with these external concepts on the other. This results in a kind of tension and ambiguity in Le Corbusier's work which does not exist in the work of the early Modern Movement as a whole.

I have isolated a number of these complementary concepts. The list is provisional, not exhaustive, and in no particular order: (1) the classical tradition, (2) machines and engineering, (3) the folk tradition, (4) biological forms, (5) accidental and random elements.

These various derivations can be grouped basically into two opposites which Le Corbusier was constantly concerned with both stating and resolving. The first is the idea of values true for all time and in all places, and is associated with classical epistemology. The second is the idea of change and evolution, and is associated with post Hegelian historicism and Marxist materialism.

Two examples of the displacement of concepts can be seen in his projects for city super-blocks. The first is the almost literal up-turning of the garden city, so that houses are stacked one above the other, taking their gardens with them. This theme, making use of the two storey studio house established as an 'objet-type' (itself the result of displacement from an existing late 19th century prototype), runs through Le Corbusier's super-blocks from the Immeubles Villas of 1922 to the Unités of the 50's and 60's. The second is the *à redents* composition, which is derived from the Baroque Palace, of which we may take the Chateau Richelieu as a suitable example, by way, probably, of Fourier's *Phalanstères*. The alternative model of urban unités comes from such 'natural' acretions as Venice or the Arab quarter of Algiers, referring to which Le Corbusier says that the 'civilised' people are holed up like rats, while the 'barbarians' live in quietude and open space, and which he used both for his hill-side schemes of the 50s and the Venice hospital.

46.1
Old Vic Theatre Annex (now the National Theatre Studio), London (1958)

Architects: Lyons Israel & Ellis
Photographer unknown (1958)

Designed while the author was working for the architects Lyons Israel & Ellis and
showing a Corbusian aesthetic

46.2
Lecture diagram illustrating fenestration and the Cartesian skyscraper made by Le Corbusier to illustrate his lecture, 'The Golden Section', given at the Architectural Association, London (1947)

Some of the most striking examples of concept displacement can be seen in Le Corbusier's tower blocks. In the Cartesian sky-scraper (Fig. 46.2) a large 'window' is placed in the centre, and by this one magnified element, the unity of the block is established by a deliberate ambiguity of scale. In the Algiers tower, the articulation of the surface is less abrupt and more complex, but nonetheless creates the impression of two scales superimposed. In both cases the intention is to create a new *objet type* whose huge size and repetitive content is humanised by the introduction of transposed classical themes (the window, the portico, the *piano nobile*).

Le Corbusier's various urban models all involve the radical displacement of ideas that already existed in other historical or social contexts. If we look at individual buildings, we can observe the same process. The prototype of the liner is perhaps too well known to dwell on. The promenade decks of liners are transposed into such schemes as the villa at Garches and the shopping level in the Unité. What is perhaps more interesting is a comparison between the section through the liner and the section through the super-block. The section, rather than the plan, seems to express the idea of collectivity – of a unit that is more than the sum of its parts and which is structurally rigid. The concept of the ship as rigorously determined by outside constraints is carried over symbolically to the super-block, achieving its final practical apotheosis in the Unité d'Habitation. The similarity between the Unité and the ship is not intended as a purely visual analogy, but as an analogy of operation (function type).

257

In the 'generous' solution of Poissy, the ordering system is simplified to a theoretically regular grid of columns, and a square 'field'. It is here that the concept of the free plan is most lucidly presented, and it is here also that the plan, freed entirely from symmetry, achieves a knotted complexity that is surely related to those ingenious French hotel plans of the 17th century, where alternative service routes are hidden behind the orderly sequence of salons arranged *en suite*.

It is interesting to compare the factory at St Dié and one of the anonymous North American factories illustrated in *Vers une Architecture* (the comparison was first pointed out by Robert Maxwell).

At St Dié the horizontal stratification of the building is almost identical with that of the factory; a regular framework to which a number of chance and useful elements are attached. The sheds and ductwork on the roof of the original factory, are echoed by the penthouse and chimney at St Dié, and there is the same assymetrically placed office and entrance in each building.

Such elements modifying the neutral *Gestalt* of the frame building are a constant theme in Le Corbusier. Unlike Mies, Le Corbusier does not reduce the frame to a neo-classic symmetry, but presents elements of empirical convenience as markers by which transitory human needs are expressed and become part of the architectural message. These elements are, however, 'ordered' in accordance with compositional principles, and this distinguishes them from purely utilitarian structures where aesthetic content, where it occurs at all, is uncontrolled. But Le Corbusier transposes thematic material from the purely architectural tradition as frequently as he 'thematises' the world of empirical fact. Colin Rowe long ago drew attention to the similarities between the diagrammatic geometry of the Palladian Villa plan and that of the villa at Garches, that 'most difficult' of the four basic types of house plan illustrated in the *Oeuvre Complète*.

Source: *Architectural Design*, April 1972

A Philistine Attack

By Martin Pawley

This talk should have been called 'Le Corbusier: He's Sure Got a Lot to Answer For'. Part of what he has got to answer for is a tremendous naive vision of the City of the Future, which he conceived in various repetitive, slightly altering forms, like frames on a movie film, from the end of the First World War onwards. The most famous collection of these images is called *Ville Radieuse*, and that dates from 1930, and that image of *Ville Radieuse* is still current, 40 years later. It is still an idea which inspires urban development. The trouble with Le Corbusier's tremendous naive vision was that it was a vision from above; it was in itself, in all its thinking, in all its drawing, something which was seen from a distant standpoint; seen from an aeroplane, seen from a helicopter, seen from a bird's eye, seen from the top floor. There was never any real understanding of what was to go on at the smaller scale amongst those huge snaking blocks. The idea was clear enough, as we know, and as you have all probably heard; that you would get rid of all the scrubby little slums and all the confused piled-on-top-of-one-another-functions, simplify, straighten out the whole thing, and make it all very healthy. It cannot have passed your notice that Le Corbusier was a health nut; he was on to cycle racing. He was keen on large bathrooms, he was keen on physical fitness. And his *Ville Radieuse* reflects these small personal foibles, so that they become a social disease.

Le Corbusier's vision was inadequate, not because Corbusier was a stunted or minor thinker. It is evident, whether one agrees with him or not, that his vision of the city of the future has had a colossal impact and that impact continues; he cannot be dismissed as a minor figure. None the less, his grand design had no social details: it was like a kind of academic situation where one is called upon while working to produce one's answer, and one endlessly dissimulates and fails to do it. Le Corbusier for most of his life dissimulated and failed to produce the real social working of his visionary city. Let me explain what I mean; here is an example taken from his first post-war book *A Propos d'Urbanisme*. It consists of a number of answers to a questionnaire which was sent to France after the German occupation but before the end of the war, by an English architectural magazine. There were a number of questions concerning future development after the second World War. One of them, which strikes me as particularly important, was Question No. 12: How do you envisage the financing of the task of re-construction?

That is, presumably, the construction cost of *Ville Radieuse* and similar developments. His answer was this:

For the inventors, the realists, the strong, who toil at life with courage, money dies, and weakness is the love of money. All money becomes a single reservoir of wealth. What is for us clearly evident is the reality and urgency of the building programme. The equipment of our technical civilisation, a gigantic adventure, out of the horror of a world war there arose also some tremendous technical achievements, the fruits of mathematics and new techniques. Finance, to see that the house without walls, and without a roof, its foundations shattered, to take off one's jacket, roll up one's sleeves and get started. Let the farmer farm, the bricklayer lay bricks and the manufacturer manufacture. One eats to live; one does not live to eat ...

That was his answer to the highly specific question, 'How do you finance the construction?'

It was also another example of what is really the result of the lacunae and foibles in every man's thinking. It depends on the scale at which you think how serious these become. When you think on a global scale, on a city scale, as Le Corbusier did, these little foibles and weaknesses are magnified to colossal consequences.

Here is another example. He is dealing again with what he imagines is a kind of moaning half mumbled criticism of his grand design. In the United States it was suggested that instead of building high, height limits should be set at four or five storeys. In this way, it was claimed, lifts would not be necessary. His response?

Why this terror of lifts? One accepts without demur the electric tracks of trams and trolley buses, the petrol motor, the subterranean adventure of the electric railway, etc. I agree there may be occasions where the installation of automatic lifts may result in abuses by the irresponsible, but to this evil there is a simple remedy: the provision of lift attendants. This means three professional liftmen to cover the 24 hour day, to pay whom a large clientele is required. Another reason for the completion of dwelling units of adequate size, i.e. over 1,000, 1,500 or 2,700 inhabitants.

That is another superb answer to a highly specific question. If you have got trouble with the lifts have lift attendants! Who is going to pay for them? Well, we'll have more people, obviously.

Let us just consider the consequences of such responses applied to housing, as indeed they have been. A lot of low cost housing in this country, Europe and America has been inspired by *Ville Radieuse*. Le Corbusier's very hazy grasp of land values – for example I don't believe he ever understood them– his idea was that by turning a building up on end, by having what he called 'a vertical garden city', (Fig. 47.1) you would create 88% free park space, and only 12% built up area. Of course, if urban land values are of any importance – and urban land values are always important – this is a quite unrealisable possibility. In parts of the United States in the late 1930s densities of the kind he proposed, about 400 per acre, had been achieved several times over, but never with huge areas of parkland because the land itself was quite simply too valuable. The buildings have to be packed closer together in order to justify the fact of constructing them at all. If they are not packed closely together,

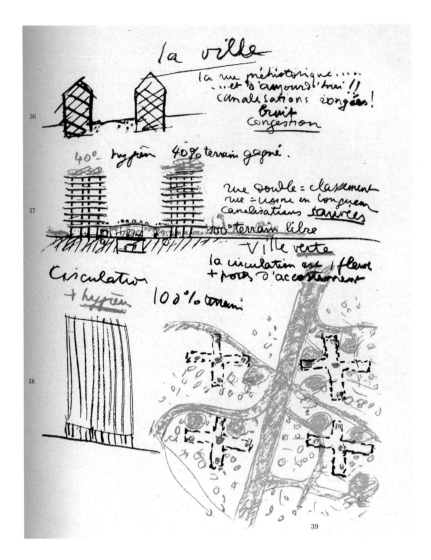

47.1

Sketch showing freeing up of space in the vertical garden city

From Le Corbusier, *Précisions sur un Etat Présent de l'Architecture et de l'Urbanisme* (1930)

then the cost of the land has to be greatly subsidised. Either these immense apartment blocks are intended for rich people who can afford to finance 88% free parkland in an urban area, or else they have to be subsidised. Those blocks have to be paid for by the public purse, and if those blocks and that free parkland are paid for by the public purse, then the consequence is that there is no money left for the schools, crèches, games areas, fives courts, swimming pools, all the fantastic gymnastic paraphernalia that Le Corbusier loved. All that stuff doesn't get built. And you can see anywhere around London (just tour around a local authority area where tower blocks have been built) the direct social consequences of the application of La Corbusier's images, and the failure of those concepts because his images lacked substance is revealed before your eyes. You will find immense tower blocks constructed more or less as his; people object and say the details are different, but it is only the details, the failure to provide the social support system that these tower blocks need proceeds from Corbusier's own myopic vision. That is, he did not understand how to do it or why it should be done; he only visualised. His ideas were taken and built, and the consequences have been disastrous. Disastrous because the social infrastructure for such developments is hardly ever built (it is not understood how to build it) in any case it is dubious if high rise is a feasible mode of living, compared to the one it replaces.

Just a couple more funny remarks by Le Corbusier. One of his attacks on the garden city interests me. He says: 'The gardens are illusory; they require unceasing unkeep; the roadways multiply; conflicts with neighbours have advantages.' A report from the *Daily Mail*, Saturday, July 3rd, 1971: 'A teenage mother alone in her new flat at the top of a 20 storey block delivered her own baby with scissors and string because she was too shy to knock up the neighbours.'

That story was illustrated by a photograph of a 26 storey tower block with an arrow pointing to one corner at the top, where the child was born. I think that story sums up what was wrong with this great man, and why he has got a lot to answer for.

If you are going to look at the city on such a scale, and if you are going to advise people to do things on that scale, if you are going to publish, perpetrate and advocate images on that scale, you have a responsibility to work out what happens inside.

Source: *Architectural Design*, April 1972

The Corb That Might Have Been

By Peter Cook

The English generation which I represent had Le Corbusier rammed down its throat. What interests me is the difference between the Le Corbusier that was rammed down our throats and the range of ideas that *can* be pulled out from the great range of his work. The critics have got between us and the Le Corbusier *that might have been*. They have looked at a great inventor who was able, over a period of time, to repeat some of his inventions and have decided that there are certain formal and elemental aspects of his work which show such *consistency* of invention that they are observable and even repeatable rules for others. But this aspect of Le Corbusier leaves aside his particular usefulness as an *inventor*.

Look at his drawings, and especially the model, for the Palace of the Soviets. (Fig. 48.1) The enormous range of different requirements – in particular the theatrical and rallying requirements – forced him not to do another piece of simplistic architecture, instead he put together a ramshackle array of gimmicks. What I like about this building is that it is extremely *unpleasant*. It is fascinating to see Le Corbusier on shaky territory – trying a few look-no-hands engineering ploys; stringing together a series of unrelatable building parts and drawing them out by way of a series of ramps and open roofs and bits of curved geometry. This is a *pot pourri* project.

48.1
Model for the Palace of the Soviets (1931)

263

48.2
**Philips Pavilion, 1958 World's Fair,
Brussels**

Photographer: John Donat (1958)

Another design I find interesting is the Pavillon de l'Espirit Nouveau. Again a look-no-hands structure, but not to the same extent as the previous project. It looks forward to the inevitable well-serviced shed, with its meaningful graphics. This is another Le Corbusier that *might have been*. You could argue that because it was a temporary exhibition he tried something outside the mainstream of his work, but I suspect that had the opportunities been more frequent this approach might have taken him into a territory totally different from that of heavyweight, elemental architecture.

My third choice – the Philips Pavilion at Brussels (Fig. 48.2) – is like the first, instantly distasteful, a corny, over-sculptural object. It was the first light show (if one can call it that) I experienced. It could just as easily have been a rectangular box. It's arguable that it might have been more effective for the kind of programme being presented in it, if it had been a circular box, which is much easier to deal with, but it wasn't.

He could have concentrated on the single mechanistic problem of an enclosure dealing with software or made a scaled-up twisted sculpture – Gabo-like. Had he been slightly less arrogant, perhaps, he wouldn't have tried the two things at once, but he did. It is slightly tatty and slightly incongruous, but again I think it illustrates an odd corner of his creativity. There are little corners in the broad stream of Le Corbusier's work in which he hinted at other talents and the ability to react inventively to *non-elemental* ways of making an environment.

Source: *Architectural Design,* April 1972

Towards a New Look at Le Corbusier

By Louis Hellman

Using the metaphor of the flower and the cube to represent the opposing tones in the polarity of western cultural conflict – the individual, romantic, organic as against the impersonal, intellectual, synthetic – the cube had by the end of the 1920s all but obliterated the flower in avant garde architectural circles.

The triumph of the mechanistic, 'functional' style was institutionalised by the foundation of CIAM in 1928.

The precepts governing the development of this 'functionalist' style of modern architecture had been formulated in Germany before the First World War, and can be summarised as follows:

Total reliance on machine production, the application of science and technological growth, and an aesthetic derived from the mass production of synthetic materials, or 'the marriage of art and technology'.

A new academicism deriving abstract laws from a synthesis of neo-classical discipline and the mechanical repetition of parts.

The belief in the power of design to change the world, to bring about a new society and to create a machine age utopia.

The first two principles had taken a firm foothold in Germany and Holland after the First World War through the activities of the constructivism and the teaching methods of the Bauhaus. The third doctrine, the idea of utopia through planning and architecture, was subsequently propagated by the work and writings of the leading figure in CIAM, Charles Edouard Jeanneret, who assumed the *nom de plume* Le Corbusier.

The buildings and pronouncements of Le Corbusier have had a greater influence on modern architects than those of any other leader of the Modern Movement, gripping the imagination of at least three post-war generations of designers.

Biographies from the old functionalist school of critics such as Blake or Furneaux Jordan tend to assume Michelangelo-comparity tunes of sycophantic adulation, and even the more perceptive historians of the school of Banham or Jencks finally submerge any criticisms on grounds of environment or political failings under blanket approval of the definition of 'genius'.

But while recognising Corb as a great formal innovator (leaving aside the question of the validity of mere forms) and rightly absolving him from responsibility for the mindless and artless apeing of his stylistic vocabulary perpetrated by his followers, it is as a propagandist for

49.1
Archi-têtes: late Corb

Artist (1984): Louis Hellman
A caricature by the author

utopia, both in words and buildings, that his great influence can be felt and his work assessed: 'The worst has prevailed for lack of organisation. With it we can have utopia tomorrow.'

For in a series of repetitive books, written in tones of strident and portentious rhetoric (a literary style parroted by the equally pretentious declamations of Modernists from Etchells to the Smithsons) Corb set out his universal remedies, mainly related to the problems of housing and town planning.

Le Corbusier was born in 1887 in the small watch-making town of la Chaux-de-Fonds in the Swiss Jura. He started out, naturally, as a watchmaker himself, but went on to study art and design and practice architecture, designing a few houses around his home town. But, like many artists born in that relatively cultureless land, he was soon off to seek out roots in German and French culture, first in Vienna in 1908 then to Paris, where he came under the influence of Auguste Perrot.

Perret had taken the new material, reinforced concrete, stripped it of its inherent qualities of plasticity and fluidity and straight jacketed it into a mean post and lintol system with which he built stripped classical structures whose depressing mediocrity was surpassed only by those of Tony Garnier. However it was more important to be seen as an innovator, and Garnier had also laid claims to this with his futurist project for an all-concrete industrial city which proposed a separation of functions into zones – a notion which was to have a great impact on Le Corbusier.

Le Corbusier soon returned to Germany to work for Behrens. In Germany in 1909 he met Gropius and Mies and was introduced to the new classicist/functionalist doctrines of the Werkbund whose above mentioned precepts he absorbed:

a great epoch has begun. There is a new spirit: it is the German spirit of construction and of synthesis guided by a clear conception.

However, like many Swiss, having succumbed to the power of teutonic culture, he entered feigned repudiation of it in one of the few perceptive statements made about one time nature of the factory aesthetic:

The Germans wished to make of their architecture one of the most active armaments of pure Germanism ... conceived to impose, to crush, to cry out absolute power.

Having turned down an offer to work with Hoffmann, Le Corbusier set off in 1910 on a Grand Tour of Europe – The Balkans, Asia Minor, Italy and Greece – a subconscious desire to redress the balance of the German influence by seeking out the Mediterranean origins of his ancestors. This aspect of conflict in his personality, Northern Alpine against Southern Mediterranean, is reflected in his work which represents a constant attempt to reconcile a clean Swiss mechanical precision with a classical monumentalism, and it accounts for the change in style from the Purism of the 20s and 30s to the Brutalism of the 50s and 60s.

Returning to the metaphor, this conflict has little in common with the reconciliation or transcending of the cube and the flower to be found in the work of Wright or Mackintosh, described by Corb himself as:

the two poles of architecture ... to construct buildings (realm of technique); and to embellish them and make them glorious, delightful etc (realm of sentiment) ... technicité et sentiment, synchronisme insécable

but rather a concentration on the plastic possibilities of the cube – a spatial manipulation, hollowing out and exploration of the form to its limits so that some parts of the obliterated flower might be revealed:

The technical consideration comes first before everything and is its condition, that it carries within it unavoidable plastic consequences, and that it lends sometimes to radical aesthetic transformations.

By the time Le Corbusier finally settled in Paris in 1913 his architectural philosophy had been established. Above all, he believed that the problems that modern architects should grapple with were the social problems of the present day, particularly the problem of living and housing. While this idea had been put forward by Morris 50 years before, in France it was unheard of – the architect's concern was felt to be monumental architecture with a capital A. However in Le Corbusier the notion that a new social order required new formal and aesthetic solutions was confused with the Teutonic idea that the physical form could come first and determine the political and social form of that society: 'the new built volumes which transform the condition of man'.

In addition Corbusier was in touch with the exhilarating post-cubist world of ideas of the Paris of the 20s, and in 1920 he collaborated with the painter Ozenfant to publish the avant garde journal, *L'Esprit Nouveau*, setting out to revolutionise the field of design.

What he could also not escape from was the all-persuading influence of the Beaux Arts classicist tradition (however much he railed against it), a tradition of Baroque axial megalomania reaching back through Ledoux to Haussmann and Le Nôtre, and which later emerged strongly in his own planning schemes.

In order to develop the new built form, Le Corbusier had first to invent a new form of living – a life style for the 20th century which would only be based on his own.

Do you know how to live soundly, strongly, gaily, free of the hundred stupidities established by human custom, and urban disorganisation?

Of all the austere, hardline, machine-age pioneers Le Corbusier was perhaps the most daunting. He hated children and despised and patronised women and had an uncompromising attitude to people generally. He epitomised the 20s intellectual and the Nietzschean cult of 'terrible isolation', the prophet of a new order 'intelligent, cold and calm.' He was a man of prolific ideas but of little real humanity, a builder of monuments to those ideas but not of places to feel at home in.

Le Corbusier's conception of the new life was therefore related to his own personality – a concept of individual, near monastic isolation in a commercial context – though he himself saw it in Krishnamurti's terms as 'a sign of nobility to be able to detach oneself from

49.2
Maisons La Roche-Jeanneret, Paris (1925)

Photographer: Lance Knobel (ca. 1984)

things'. This isolation is symbolised by the separation and expression of functions which are a hallmark of *le style Corbu* and which presupposes that only those forms which are 'clearly appreciated' are beautiful.

Thus the building is separated from the ground, the garden is separated from the earth and put on the roof, the roof is separated from the floor by continuous strip windows, the walls are separated from the structure as are the elements of the facade. The whole is a monument to an idea of how people ought to live, a form imposed from without rather than an 'organic appendage' of its inhabitants as Haering defined it.

In the book *Towards a (New) Architecture*, published in 1923, Le Corbusier brought together all his own writings from *L'Esprit Nouveau*. It was a book which became the most read and influential of any other from the modern movement. In the section entitled The Manual of the Dwelling, Corbusier check, lists the ideal house.

Most of this is concerned with his own obsession with physical fitness (there had been a series of articles in *L'Esprit* by a Dr Winter, an avowed fascist, and believer in spiritual health through physical fitness) and personal neatness – 'demand a bathroom looking South ... one wall to be entirely glazed, opening if possible on to a balcony for sun

49.3
Maisons La Roche-Jeanneret, Paris (1925)

From *Architecture Vivante*, Autumn 1927

baths; the most up-to-date fittings with a shower bath and gymnastic appliances ... *never undress in your bedroom. It is not a clean thing and makes the room horribly untidy* ... built-in fittings to take the place of much of the furniture, which ... takes up too much room and needs looking after ... keep your odds and ends in drawers or cabinets ... bear in mind economy in your actions, your household management and in your thoughts.'

There is relatively little guidance on environmental matters – a large living room, ventilation, diffused lighting and a kitchen on the top floor 'to avoid smells.'

Post-1918 France, unlike Germany, gave little scope or official support to progressive thinkers and machine-age visionaries in matters architectural.

Although the loss of her northern mining and industrial areas during the war had resulted in the rapid growth of the chemical and electrical industries so that by 1925 the recaptured old and the developed new had merged to double both her output and rail transport, official commissions for buildings were controlled by the conservative Beaux Arts establishment. The work of Perret was an exception.

Le Corbusier's first completed buildings therefore were private houses for middle-class artists and art patrons built in the leafy Parisian suburbs. They drew on the white cubist style of the time as well as the Paris studio vernacular with its large north facing windows, which also had to cope with tight sites, and combined these with the programme for new living.

Where the sites are restricted or particularly abundant in greenery as for the La Roche/Ozenfant pair of houses, (Fig. 49.2 and 49.3) the Villa or 'Les Terrasses' at Garches, Le Corbusier's mastery of the hollowed out cube is superb – the sharp white forms present a perfect foil to the surrounding natural environment; a human-scaled, domestic application of the principles of classical space that Le Corbusier had recognised with such perception during his visit to the Acropolis.

> The temples are turned towards one another, making an enclosure, as it were, which the eye readily embraces; and the sea which composes with the architraves.

The precise man made forms framing, and framed by, the natural environment.

Linked to the grasping of the essentials of classical form in Corbusier's mind was the platonic ideal of equating art and beauty with truth and good; of relating the laws of geometry with laws of nature, conduct and universal order.

'Culture is an orthogonal state of mind.' 'Calm, order, neatness and inevitability imposes discipline on the inhabitants.' 'You do me good, I am happy and I say "This is beautiful. This is architecture".'

In other words clean, chaste, geometrical forms dictate clean, chaste, orderly lives.

The extension of this imposed and abstracted building form and life style was the idea of the house as a 'machine for living in', a dwelling could be as impersonal and functional as a piece of machinery, and also be mass produced like a car or a plane, an idea that from then on gave the myth of the machine aesthetic new meaning for modern architects. The German 'functionalists' had made their buildings machine-like in the sense of repetition of standard units made of modern synthetic materials, but Corbusier made his buildings look like machines themselves, the smooth rounded casings, the articulation of parts or the appearance of bulk resting on slender supports.

The error lay in the confusion of process with result, a misconception that has been at the root of much that is wrong with modern architecture since. The products of machines are not themselves machine-like (unless they are themselves machines). The aesthetic evolved was one which attempted to ape the superficial appearance of machines, not allow itself to evolve from the principles of mass production.

Mass production techniques had of course been applied to building as early as the 17th Century when Coade stone mouldings had been produced in the forms of classical ornament. The components of the Crystal Palace were in a vaguely Gothic style. Neither was it any less a product of the machine for that. Today it is still the mass-produced building component that looks like a machine part (a bus window for example) that receives the approval of architects and buildings are still compared to 'aircraft carriers on hill tops' or 'ocean liners anchored in a Georgian square.' However, in buildings it is the human-serving function that is important, the machine-serving is minimal. In the home, for example, machines are required to be discreet, hidden or disguised – cookers and fridges have styled casings to make them 'domestic' and the ultimate solution is when the machine is entirely invisible. A house is a building for living in!

Apologists for Corb have protested that the famous phrase was completely misunderstood by architects. He meant 'machine' in the original Greek sense of 'contrivance' as when he called the Parthenon a 'terrible machine' akin to 'naked polished steel'.

But by this definition a thatched cottage could equally well be a 'machine for living in' and Corbusier's own houses of the time such as the well known Villa Savoye at Poissy-sur-Seine (1928) which has been likened to a 'helicopter poised to take off in a Virgilian landscape', belie the machine pastiche result, if not intention.

In *Towards a (New) Architecture*, Le Corbusier compares modern machines – cars, ships, planes – to classical buildings of Rome or Greece, ostensibly to point out the lessons that can be learned in terms of economy and function, but in reality the comparisons served to draw an analogy between the ephemeral products of technology and the enduring qualities of ancient monuments to reassure architects that they could be modern *and* build for posterity. Le Corbusier also saw the Parthenon as an example of 'selection applied to a standard' just as a machine or household object can reach its ideal form through refinements and modifications over time, and which in Le Corbusier's view always resulted in a Gestalt reversion to basic geometrical forms.

Anything of universal value is worth more than anything of merely individual value.' 'In place of individualism we prefer the commonplace, the everyday, the rule to the exception ...' 'Our eyes are made to see forms in light: cubes, cones, spheres, cylinders, or pyramids are the great primary forms.

The result of a simplistic view of architecture after Choisy in terms of structure and proportion divorced from its social or political context.

Since the Domino House project of 1917 and the later Citrohan House Le Corbusier had been constantly putting forward the idea of mass productions – 'we must create the mass production spirit' and of standardised houses, thus perpetuating the myth that if only houses could be run off the assembly lines like cars our problems would be solved at a stroke. Le Corbusier himself of course never employed such techniques in his pre-war houses, which were knocked up in accordance with the Parisian spec builder's well-tried method of frame-and-crude-rubble infill rendered over to give a smooth finish, but minus the traditional sills and copings which prevented the sudden deterioration of the surfaces.

However, if the middle-class patrons could afford the constant maintenance required to maintain the cubist image as well as convincing themselves that they were indulging in new ways of living in their cold, stark, overlit *machines à habiter*, when the same principles were applied to a mass housing problem as at Pessac in 1925, the results were quite different.

The Pessac housing was built by a factory owner near Bordeaux for his workers, and using a combination of standard two-storey and three-storey house types related to one another by a domino-like pattern to avoid monotony, Le Corbusier achieved a highly imaginative low-rise/high-density layout employing a sensible use of standardisation.

However, in detail the dwellings themselves with their soulless austerity, their shoddy and cheap finishes and their dogmatic application of the new living principles – unusable roof terraces, glare-producing strip windows and wasteful ground floor loggias – serve today as a warning of the dangers of trying to legislate for human behaviour through built form.

Those occupants who have been able to buy their dwellings have made pathetic attempts to provide them with some humanity, more often then not out of practical considerations – pitched roofs added on leaking flat ones, large windows reduced in width, sills and copings added to openings and loggias filled with room extensions.

Le Corbusier's later reaction to the Pessac scheme adaptations was the bitterly ironical: 'It's life that's always right and the architect who is wrong.'

Though his earlier statements were probably nearer to his real feelings – 'The right state of mind does not exist. There is no point of contact between the two sides involved: 'my plan (which is a way of life) and those for whom the law is made (the potential clients who have not been educated)' – and an excuse served up by architects to justify their failures ever since, the people do not understand the new way of life. They must be educated to appreciate it.

Originally the scheme was dubbed 'experimental' and the intention was to 'select suitable groups to live in the experimental buildings' and to 'teach them the know-how of dwelling'.

Thus paving the way again for all the ivory-tower fantasies with other people's lives which could be argued away under the label 'experimental'. It is about time we recognised that the experiment has been a failure – the hypothesis disproved time and again.

But in fact there is hardly a 'new' idea around today concerning architectural solutions for hypothetical new ways of living which cannot be traced back to one of Corbusier's projects or sketches. These include system-built terrace houses (Monol 1919), deck access maisonettes (Immeubles Cité Universitaire 1925), standardised low-rise/high-density (Pessac 1925), support system megastructures (Algiers 1931), staggered section terraces (Algiers 1931), co-operative villages (*Ferme Radieuse* 1934), self-build systems (*Murondins* 1941) and slab blocks (St Dié 1944). It is notable that the only type missing is the tower block which Corbusier condemned since 'family life would hardly be at home with them, with their prodigious mechanism of lifts'.

But Le Corbusier was basically a monumental architect. His correlation of classical architecture, machines and 'pure' forms (the Phileban solids) all conform to the idea of a building as an easily comprehensible object-to-be-viewed.

His definition of architecture as 'the masterly, correct and magnificent play of masses brought together in light' belies his essentially sculptor's approach to building as pure form.

And though he never subscribed to the doctrines of functionalism ('Architecture goes beyond utilitarian needs') his insistence on the spiritual refers to a superhuman, platonic plane.

When dealing with traditional monumental structures (church, monastery, museum, civic building) or when restricted in scale, Corb's facility in handling space and investing forms could produce superb results – Ronchamp is unquestionably the finest modern church in the world.

The problems of the modern world, however, do not generally demand monumental statements. Mass housing, hospitals, schools, old people's homes, urban design – the buildings for ordinary people – demand more flexible and practical solutions. No-one wants to live in an overblown monument to the housing problem or a 'temple to family life,' to use Corbusier's phrase.

So by 1922 Le Corbusier was turning his attention to the possibilities of stacking dwellings in the air, justifying it not only along the lines of Gropius' simplistic diagram which gave the illusion of proving that land could be saved by building high, but also in terms of saving in pipe runs, travelling time and building costs. His solutions first took the form of 'deck' access maisonettes – the Immeubles Villas of 1922 which also stacked attached gardens one above the other!

A prototype of one of their units was built as the Pavilion de l'Esprit Nouveau for the Exposition des Art Decoratifs in Paris, 1925. This building was also furnished with articles chosen by Le Corbusier to conform to his ideal of the *objets types*.

In 1930 Le Corbusier was able to put together a microcosm of these ideas with the design of the Swiss Pavilion in the University City, and at the same time undergo a change of attitude with regard to technology and materials. In the Swiss Pavilion the separation or articulation of parts is applied to a building larger than the domestic scale. The single bedroom cells are stacked in a block raised off the ground with a stair tower behind converting to a single storey communal building. But though the south facing elevation is fully glazed (a highly unfunctional but typical 'modern' error) the rest of the building has taken on a much coarser appearance.

The free standing columns are gathered together in curved *piloti* of smooth unpainted concrete, the back and ends of the bedroom block clad in stone and the north wall of the low block built of random rubble.

Le Corbusier had learnt from the by-now cracked, peeling and misty appearance of the houses of the 20s – there is no attempt at the previous smooth, homogenous envelope and the whole building has taken on a heavier, more permanent, aspect. Here too was a whole new set of formal references for European architects to copy blindly – blank end walls irrespective of orientation, 'built-in bomb damage' instead of roofs, *piloti* even when sited in a high street, random rubble walling in the midst of the city, articulated staircases where they could not be seen, etc etc.

But Le Corbusier's subsequent solutions for mass housing cannot be considered out of the context of his wider proposals for town planning, or more strictly speaking, urban design. In 1922 he published his first ideal town plan, the *Ville Contemporaine* or city for three million people, laid out axially on a strict regular grid of communication networks. The centre of the city was to be occupied by several ranks of glass office towers, the 'city's brains ... all the careful working out and organisation on which the general activity is based.'

These temples to bureaucracy and capitalism took the place of the cathedral or civic centre as the city's focal point. Around these were grouped two classes of linear superblocks planned in the form of vast landscaped squares, one for the middle class with accommodation for their 'maids, servants, governesses and nursemaids', and those on the periphery for the workers.

Parks and industry were zoned tidily away in between the grid of roads. Just as the functions of the house had been separated and articulated, so the function of the city –

housing, offices, industry, recreation, transport – were separated, articulated and mummified in zones.

For ironically, Le Corbusier's planning was really anti-city. Just as he hated messy houses, romanticism, the suburbs ('a leprosy, a scandal'), Gothic buildings ('not very beautiful ... a sensation of a sentimental nature ... not plastic') so he despised the tight, unplanned network of streets in the older parts of towns and cities as 'obsolete, antique, rotten', 'the detritus of dead epochs', admiring rather the grand boulevards of Haussmann in Paris, or Roman axial planning.

The city of today is a dying thing because it is not geometrical. To build in the open, would be to replace our present haphazard arrangements ... by a uniform layout.

Le Corbusier's great open areas of 'abundant foliage' (in summer at least) and sweeping vistas would do away with the 'untidy' sky lines of the past and impost order on the lives of the citizens. Their function was 'to dominate and control the mob'.

The *Voisin* plan for Paris exhibited at the same time as the *Ville Contemporaine*, applied this formula as a comprehensive redevelopment area to a vast section of Paris north of the Louvre stretching from Notre Dame almost to L'Etoile. This area included Les Halles, the market, and its working class residential surroundings (an area similar to Covent Garden in London) typifying that part of Paris that Corbusier hated most.

In the *Voisin* plan its 'cafes and places for recreation would no longer be that fungus which eats up the pavements of Paris; they would be transferred to flat roofs'.

If Le Corbusier had no time for old buildings, he had even less time for old communities, refusing to accept any of 'those principles which have animated former societies'.

This incredibly simplistic view of cities as objects not organisms has of course had a disastrous effect on town planning to this day. The present London Plan, for example, is based on the earlier Abercrombie Plan which derived from the MARS group plan of 1942 which itself was a watered down version of the *Ville Contemporaine*. As far as Paris is concerned the terrible legacy of this type of ministry can be seen today around Porte Maillot and beyond to the north.

It is not difficult to see why this simplistic and totalitarian view endured. Apart from the practical nature of some of the technical and economic solutions (motorways and private investment) such an image of utopia presupposes an oligarchy of technocrats and enlightened industrialists to direct operations ... 'The law givers, men with logical minds ... of initiative, of action, of thought ... the L E A D E R ...'

Little wonder that this role appealed to architects and politicians alike – detached from common problems and common people, dispensing inspired blueprints for the future from the safety of their converted ivory towers.

Though Le Corbusier always denied any political allegiances ('I have been very careful not to depart from the technical side of my problem. I am an architect: no-one is going to make a politician out of me') seeing himself as the apolitical technocrat, the environmental physician curing society's ills, few people, especially architects, can maintain such a position.

Le Corbusier's political stance as manifested in his housing and planning proposals, was clearly that of benevolent fascism. In fact he collaborated closely with fascists of various lands from the notorious Dr Winter of *l'Esprit Nouveau*, Stalinist Russia, the Vichy Government and Mussolini during the war.

His images of the calm, ordered, healthy, technological state with everything in its place demand a totalitarian system of one kind or another, and are very much in line with the realities of political polarisation in the 1930s and the idea of mass social reform going hand in hand with the new technology.

For Le Corbusier it was the captains of industry who were the ultimate prophets and dictators of the technological millennium – and he addresses these words to them in *Towards a (New) Architecture*.

> All your energies are directed towards this magnificent end which is the forging of the tools of an epoch, and which is creating throughout the whole world this accumulation of very beautiful things in which economic law reigns supreme, and mathematical exactitude is joined to daring and imagination. That is what you do; that to be exact is beauty.

The planners and architects would take their orders from these benevolent despots modelled on Louis XIV, the builder of The Louvre, 'a great town planner ... who conceived immense projects and realised them ... saying "we wish it" or "such is our pleasure".'

By the publication of *Ville Radieuse* in 1935, however, Le Corbusier's town planning proposals had become at the same time more flexible and more dispersed. The book contains proposals for a linear town strung along a communication route of motorways – 'a city made for speed is made for success' – off which are clusters of staggered superblocks – the Unités d'Habitation.

This idea of the superblock set in parkland derives from the 18th century philosopher Charles Fourier, who conceived a utopian social system based on cooperative socialism. This unit consisted of 400 families housed in a 'phalanstery', a vast structure for communal living in the middle of a 'square league' of cultivated land which the inmates worked combining their labour but controlled by one man.

Le Corbusier proposed to build these *villes radieuses* in several towns in France and all over the world, but in the economic crisis-ridden France of the 1930s with its continual collapse of governments, massive unemployment and inflation, the realisation of such grandiose schemes was out of the question, even if anybody had wanted to carry them out.

It was not until after the Second World War in 1946 when the French welfare state, built on a tradition of strong bureaucratic, paternalist natural government, was launched by the MRP party, that Le Corbusier was given the opportunity to put his theories of the Unité d'Habitation into practice in Marseilles.

Here the earlier ideals of living as expressed in the houses of the 1920s was augmented and translated into a communal solution – a 16-storey slab block housing almost 400 families in maisonettes of various sizes raised above the ground on massive *pilotis*, with balconies framing the distant landscape and the whole roof given over to recreational and sporting activities, was constructed in standardised precast concrete units with the service elements – escape stairs, flue, lift motor room articulated into sculptural motifs.

What had altered completely, a change signalled by the Swiss Pavilion and the earlier Weekend House, was the extreme finishes and the attitude to concrete – rough, crude exposed aggregate for the precast elements and for the in situ parts – mainly the *pilotis* – the pattern of unwrought timber framework left exposed – the whole conceived on a massive superhuman scale.

The *pilotis*, dwarfing the human being at ground level, have been compared to primeval ruins like Stonehenge and their 'anthropomorphic' qualities have been noted as relating to the sculptures of Henry Moore, both only confirming Le Corbusier's concern for monumental abstract sculpture at the expense of human scale and function – 'the business of architecture is to establish emotional relationships by means of brutal materials', and his desire to make of housing 'immense constructions on a noble scale.'

The Marseilles Unité was received by the architectural world with almost total adulation and immediately adopted in one form or another as the ultimate solution to workers' housing from Roehampton to Rio de Janeiro – those 'multi-fold' mistakes 'abjectly imitating a monumental failure' to use a phrase of Mumford, the only critic who dared to question the validity of the concept as a final solution to the housing question.

With hindsight, however, we can delineate the failures inherent in the basic approach – leaving aside the stylistic influences.

Firstly, the cost of the complex, compared to other possible solutions was enormous. It was for this reason that any plans for further blocks were abandoned and not because of reactionary opposition to the new way of living, as Le Corbusier would have had us believe. The technology and resources needed to provide the multi-storey solution with a fraction of the basic facilities which come cheaply and easily at ground-level shopping areas, recreation, terraces, circulation, parking, etc. are prohibitively high.

The Unité was originally intended for the Marseilles fishermen, but as costs soared it was turned over to rented accommodation for the professional and administrative classes.

Secondly, the building was intended to free the surrounding landscape for use by the occupants; 'a pact is sealed with nature. Nature is entered in the lease'.

But, as Mumford said, it was 'visual open space not functional open space which is the space human beings need for living in'.

In other words landscape to look at as one might gaze at the sea from the Acropolis. In a way the advantages of the open site are nullified by building high, cutting the tenants off from the ground without any good reason.

Thirdly, the long narrow form of the maisonettes themselves, a product of the need to cut costs by saving external wall, make for depressing environments. In spite of Le Corbusier's insistence on 'sun, light and air', over a half of each flat is deprived of those very things. There is no privacy between the various parts of the dwelling for in order to provide a view from each part they are open plan. Thus there is no escape from noise sources even in the bedrooms which are on open galleries over the living room and there is nothing to contain cooking smells from the internal kitchen.

The stated intention to provide 'vast spaces before every window of each dwelling' has certainly been achieved. The height of the balcony balustrades (necessary for safety) precludes any view of grass and trees from the upper levels or when sitting down.

The children's rooms, too, are long narrow corridors, bearing witness to Le Corbusier's ignorance of family life in general.

Fourthly, the communal areas, roof, shopping precinct, restaurants, are all now used, but how much more successful might they have been at ground level. In fact in the later Unités at Nantes and Briey-en-Forêt these modifications were made. As for the euphemism *rue intérieure*, for 'corridor', the less said the better.

The overall impression given by the Unités is one of power, a rather terrifying totalitarian image of a self contained, technological, workers' ghetto – a roaring rhetorical monument to one man's inflexible and dogmatic vision of how people ought to live. Presumably it is now full of architects and trend setters who have forced themselves to believe in and confirm to, that vision.

As if aware, after the failures of Pessac, that ordinary people would not fit into his idealised plans for new ways of living, Le Corbusier's initial reaction was to put his faith in the future and the dwellings that 'a future generation will know how to live in', proposing that primary schools start teaching children 'the efficient basis of domestic training' and lamenting that 'one could build beautifully designed houses, always provided the tenant was prepared to change his outlook'.

But eventually Le Corbusier was obliged to design an ideal human being to fit his ideal environment – the modular man. In the 20s following Choisy's narrow view of buildings in terms only of structure and proportion, he had devised some crude proportional rules of thumb based on the golden section.

The notion of rules of proportion and rules of machine production fitted together neatly with the concept of mathematics governing the universe. By the 50s Le Corbusier had rediscovered the Fibonari series of proportion and applied it to an idealised, standard 6ft high man. This world shattering discovery was inspired by the typical Bulldog Drummond-like hero of English detective novels with his 'eye level fixed at 5ft 6in'.

Of course, despite Le Corbusier's pronouncements about human scale and the relationship of built form to the human being, abstracted proportional games are quite irrelevant in matters of scale, and Le Corbusier's designs tried to distort the human anatomy to fit his theories, seeking 'with violence to accommodate human beings into the inflexible dimensions of his monumental edifice' (Mumford) and learning from Mumford the adjective 'procrustean' after the ancient mythical Greek robber who stretched or cut his captive's legs to make them fit a bed.

The image of modular man, staring out of the murky concrete at Nantes, is one of a plastic Frankenstein with arm upraised in a gesture of dumb protest possibly at the claustrophobic ceiling height in his modular pad.

At the foundation of CIAM there was only one voice to oppose the dominance of Le Corbusier and his proposals for the future direction of architecture, that of the German, Hugo Häring. Le Corbusier demanded a 'modern architecture', and a return to 'pure geometry', Häring 'a new way of building' and an 'organic architecture' following his desire to 'examine things and allow them to discover their own images. It goes against the grain with us to bestow a form on them from the outside, or to impose some abstract modular upon them ...'

It was inevitable that Le Corbusier's vision of a geometric/technological utopia should triumph for the following three decades, and if we are at last shaking free from his all-pervading influence and megalomania in the field of planning it will take a long time for the effect of his aesthetic prejudices to be confined to the history books.

These are still with us, not only in the disastrous theories of brutalism and exposed concrete – a material which does not weather, only deteriorates – but also in the obsession with the articulation of elements without reason, witness the sculptural boiler flues, lift rooms and staircases which still abound, not to mention ducting and fans painted in primary colours to emphasise the 'sculpture technology'.

In the final analysis, history's judgement on Corbusier will probably fall between Salvador Dali's sick-joke epitaph ('Le Corbusier simply went down for the third time because of his reinforced concrete and his architecture, the ugliest and most unacceptable building in the world') and the ecstatic eulogies of the 'functionalist' historians ('the greatest genius since Leonardo. His buildings will no doubt be preserved as museums [as is already happening]').

Le Corbusier's description of a teacher, one of his rare moments of human perception perhaps, sum up best his own position in the history of modern architecture.

A man who uproots you from that magnificent school of doubt provided by life itself, who is obliged by his profession to develop a hard core of certainties inside himself so that he can then pass them on to his listeners … Teaching the future? (he) will automatically become a pontiff, whether he likes it or not; his students will make him into one simply by believing him … they are all round him revering him … the future comes … and life gives him the lie.

Source: *Building Design*, 6 September 1974; 13 September 1974; 20 September 1974

With Corb in Chandigarh

By Max Fry

Following the death in a plane crash in 1950 of Matthew Nowicki, the extremely able young Polish architect associated with Albert Mayer in drawing up the original planning proposals for Chandigarh, the Punjab government deputed two senior officials to visit Europe with the object of finding two architects to return with them to India to implement the early stages of the plan.

They came to London and most probably advised by the RIBA (which knew of their African planning experience) met Max Fry and Jane Drew and offered them three-year contracts to work on Chandigarh. (Figs 50.1 and 50.2) Max Fry recalls that unfortunately, "Jane was engaged on our part of the Festival of Britain. I'd been asked to be director of that but I did not see it as my line and said to Gerald Barry, 'give us a nice big chunk of it and that'll do'. Jane therefore felt she could not leave immediately and this posed a great problem for the two Indians. They said they could create a place for Jane later, but now they needed to take back two people. 'If you can come', they said to me, 'then we must find another'.

It was then that Le Corbusier's name came up. They asked me what did I think about working with Corb? I replied, 'glorious for you all right, but bitter for me because I'm no disciple and I do not know what it would be like to work with him'. So we rang up Corb and went over to Paris to see him, and he swore on the book that he would work to Albert Mayer's master plan. When he came out of course the first thing that he did was to tear it up, at the bungalow in the old village at Chandigarh. I did stop him from trampling all over the plan though – he wanted a lot of skyscrapers there.

I was critical at times and Corb used to make fun of me; when Jane came out he and I were hardly speaking because I said I had detected a certain theatrical note about the High Court designs. Jane took him in hand at once however and he absolutely adored her. Until he died there was constant correspondence between them; books, pictures, drawings, everything.

I was having a rough time and having to work and work to get the housing and other buildings and the team going, as well as keeping Nehru happy. I have never worked so hard in my life, ever. We had no administrative machinery and we had these Indian public works engineers who were against us, most of them. The chief engineer in particular was a subtle and spiritual kind of man who had this gift of not telling you what was on his mind – one of the worst things of all to deal with.

50.1
Type 9F house, Chandigarh (1954)

Architect: Max Fry
Photographer unknown (1954)

About the time when Jane came, I handed in my resignation. I said, 'I've been here weeks and weeks and although I have given up a great deal to come here, nobody's been to see me. This chief engineer is so subtle-minded that I do not know how to deal with him: I'm going'. Thapar, the chief administrator, who was a great man in his way, practically put his arms around me and said, 'this man is my enemy as much as yours: Max, if you go I don't know what I shall do'. I said, 'all right', and I stayed out my three-year contract as senior architect.

We developed Sector 22, Jane and I, working as none of the others did, directly with the shopkeepers, the cinema owner and all the others concerned. The contractors were very good; I distrusted the public works engineers and trusted the contractors – they did what was wanted. We designed for the shopkeepers their shops and said: now look, what about the covered ways that lead to the market places, will you build them for us? And they said yes …

We went back to Chandigarh a little over a year ago and were driven round. It had grown up a great deal of course in the fifteen or twenty years. Trees were growing, public buildings and the university were getting on splendidly: my feeling is that this is a noble city and I believe that's also the feeling in India, they love it. With all its deficiencies, low standard of building, poor maintenance and so on.

We found Sector 22 to be full of life, still, whereas Corb's city centre is a gloomy affair, forbidding, without a tree. He did not really intend that, though, because I took quite a part in its early design with Corb and we both wanted to get a bazaar feeling at the centre of it – like our Sector 22 which he admired; give it to Corb that when he saw something he admired, he said so. We made a centre of life there which he intended to do also for the city centre, but he was too heavy-handed – that's to say that his setting was too heavy. The

50.2
Flats and shops in Sector 22, Chandigarh (1950s)

Architect: Jane Drew
Photographer unknown (1950s)

bazaar element would have been too lightweight on its own, what was needed was a combination of the two with strong integrating structure as the background to the life.

They have done several major buildings since Corb, under his influence, working through Indian architects which are such blank and hopeless buildings and very forbidding. The museum and the art gallery on the other hand are lovely buildings.

And then of course the lake: this was the chief engineer's thing. He had it up his sleeve all the time ... although this man was very difficult for me to deal with, we had a kind of admiration for him afterwards. For years after I left I got letters beseeching me to come: he wanted to commune with me, he was very spiritual you see and for a lot of them I was a sort of guru ...

Source: *Building,* 31 October 1975

The Price of Le Corbusier

By Christopher Booker

Last Sunday BBC2 showed Fritz Lang's parable about a city of the future, *Metropolis*. With its nightmare vision of vast, humming machines, tower blocks, elevated motorways and the 'Prisoners' Chorus' of workers being fed to the Moloch of technology, Lang's view of the future was at best ambivalent, at worst hostile. Nevertheless the film, made in 1926, was a fine expression of that astonishing decade when the machine as 'dream symbol' achieved a power over the Western imagination greater than any time before or since. The 1920s were the decade of Mayakovsky's hymn to Chicago ('City built upon a screw! Electro-dynamical-mechanical city ... five thousand skyscrapers, Granite suns ... mile high they gallop to heaven, crawling with millions of men'); of Lenin's hypnotic Dada invocation 'Electrification plus the Soviets equals Bolshevism'; of those myriad 'dithyrambs in praise of machinery' which Huxley called 'The New Romanticism.' This passage is as explicit as any:

> On that 1st day of October (1923) on the Champs Elysées, I was assisting at the titanic re-awakening of a comparatively new phenomenon ... traffic. Motors going in all directions, going at all speeds. I was overwhelmed, an enthusiastic rapture filled me ... the rapture of power ... we are part of that race whose dawn is just awakening. We have confidence in this new society which will in the end arrive at a magnificent expression of its power'.

This record of a 'mystical' experience, by a man who was as much moved by the image of the power implicit in machines as Marx had been by the potential of the great new army of the proletariat fifty years before, was set down by one of the most influential ideologists of our century. He was a revolutionary, a genius, a megalomaniac, unmistakably a totalitarian, whose ideas have profoundly touched all our lives in profound ways (and condemned tens of millions to the most intense misery). And yet, although we all know his name, because he is not normally thought of as 'political,' let alone as a totalitarian ideologist of the first rank, almost no one (perhaps one per cent of those reading this copy of *The Spectator*) will actually have read any of his works at all, let alone the two which can be claimed (alongside *Das Kapital* and *Mein Kampf*) to have been among the most far-reaching revolutionary texts of the twentieth century.

It is in fact exactly fifty years since the first of these two books, *Vers une Architecture*, was first published in English. Its author, from the homelands of Rousseau and Calvin, was a younger painter-architect in his late thirties, who had first sprung into prominence in Paris in 1920 with a manifesto in support of the pure geometry of post-Cubist painting. And like Stalin, 'the man of steel,' and all the best twentieth-century revolutionaries, Edouard Jeanneret chose to fantasise his historic role by adopting a *nom de guerre*, Le Corbusier ('crow-like').

In re-assessing Le Corbusier's importance to our century today (a task which has so far been confused by the fact that almost the only people who have bothered to read him are architects, who notoriously lack any sense of the world outside their own little narrow concerns), one must show two things. The first is the way that his writings did constitute a revolutionary ideology of the most explicitly political kind; the second is how that ideology has in fact been even more influential on our civilisation in the past fifty years than most of us supposed.

Written in short, declamatory paragraphs of great power (and with a mass of photographs and drawings), *Vers une Architecture* takes us at once into the beguiling world of the prophet of imminent revolution. 'A great epoch has begun. There exists a new spirit.' The age-old archetype is at work – the present age is infinitely corrupt, stifling and decayed: it must be swept away with insuperable violence: then paradise will emerge. Le Corbusier is in no doubt about how corrupt the present age (1923) is. Men are dying, suffocating under something much more fundamental than mere outmoded political systems: 'it is a question of building which is at the root of the social unrest of today.' Society is literally dying, because 'unworthy houses ... ruin our health and morale ... our houses disgust us; we fly from them and frequent restaurants and night-clubs ... we are becoming demoralised' (at this early stage it is all slightly comic).

But have no fear! A 'great epoch' is bursting into life all around us, the age of the machine, of the steamship, of the airplane, of the motor car – the age of mass-production (endless illustrations of all these wonderful things). We must throw off the past, or at least the European detritus of the past 2,000 years (a cathedral, for instance, is 'not very beautiful ... it interests us as the solution of a difficult problem'). But if we look at the clean lines of the latest Bugatti or American grain-elevators ('the magnificent FIRST FRUITS of the new age') we shall learn to claim 'in the name of the steamship, the airplane and the motor car, the right to health, logic, daring, harmony and perfection.' We must begin with the house, and recognise that it is (in the only phrase of Le Corbusier that most of us know) 'a machine for living in.' The challenge is to 'create the mass-production spirit. The spirit of constructing mass-production houses.' And above all 'the spirit of living in mass-production houses.'

Here speaks the totalitarian *pur et simple*, the architect who would create not just new buildings but new men – or rather the New Man. One of the most remarkable passages in *Vers une Architecture* is called 'The Manual of the Dwelling,' what the 'New Man' must learn to demand from his house (or rather how Corbusier insists he should live). 'Demand a new bathroom looking south, one of the largest rooms in the house or flat, the old drawing room for instance' (this must have 'the most up-to-date fittings' and 'gymnastic appliances'). 'Never undress in your bedroom' orders Le Corbusier, 'it is not a clean thing to do, and makes the room horribly untidy.' 'Put the kitchen at the top of the house.' 'Demand a vacuum cleaner' (who from, one might ask?). Corbusier was deeply offended by the idea of walls being cluttered up with pictures and books. You must have special fittings in which to hide these messy objects away, and 'bring out your pictures one at a time, when you want them.' Scarcely a detail of life escapes the all-supervising *diktat* (not even Stalin would have gone so far as to insist that 'the gramophone, the pianola or the wireless will give you exact interpretations of first-rate music, and you will avoid catching cold in the concert hall, and the frenzy of the virtuoso').

And so at last we arrive at the vision of the paradise that is within our grasp: 'One day Auguste Perret created the phrase 'A City of Towers.' A glittering epithet which aroused the poet in us. A word which struck the note of the moment because the fact itself is imminent! Almost unknown to us, 'the great city' engendering its plan' (we are on a great tide, part of something vast, mysterious and insuperable).

Just as no revolutionary can be without the mystical support of history's irresistible force (however much he condemns most of what it has to offer otherwise), so Corbusier then pauses to claim spiritual kinship with the spirit that built the Parthenon ('Phidias would have loved to live in this standardised age ... his vision would have seen in our epoch the conclusive result of his labours'). We finally get a long series of sketches of the ideal housing of the future (in which E V E R Y O N E will live)– vast blocks of flats, with communal open space, communal kitchens, communal sports facilities – built by a mighty industrial process that is an object of veneration in itself ('the building yards will be on a huge scale, run and exploited like government offices. Dwellings ... will be enormous and square-built, and no longer a dismal congeries ... an inevitable social evolution will have transformed the relationship between tenant and landlord ... our towns will be ordered instead of chaotic').

With his second book, *Urbanisme* (*The City of To-morrow*), published in 1924, the social revolutionary finally emerges in its most devastating form, as Le Corbusier turns his attention from the individual dwelling to whole cities. 'A town is a tool,' he begins, 'towns no longer fulfil this function. They are ineffectual; they use up our bodies, they thwart our souls.' 'The city is crumbling, it cannot last much longer.'

At last the enemy is in full view, the age-old city that grew up 'the Pack-Donkey's Way,' organically, over centuries, full of crooked streets, crooked houses and crooked people. So worked up by now is Le Corbusier at the appalling social catastrophe that is the existing city that he solemnly assures us that for the shorthand typist 'sleep is not sufficient to restore the nervous energy used up in office routine, she slowly wears herself out,' while 'it is admitted that the third generation to live in our great cities is generally sterile.' What is the answer to this crooked world? 'The right angle is the essential and sufficient implement of action,' and then (a solemn moment this, for our poor old twentieth century) 'therefore my settled opinion which is quite a dispassionate one is that the centres of our great cities must be pulled down and rebuilt.' The cataclysm is at hand! All must be destroyed! (Did Lenin ever go so far?) Some fools had suggested that there might be a ring of skyscrapers round the edge of Paris. 'Nonsense,' cries Le Corbusier, 'we must concentrate on the centre of the city ... which is the simplest solution, and more simply still the only solution.'

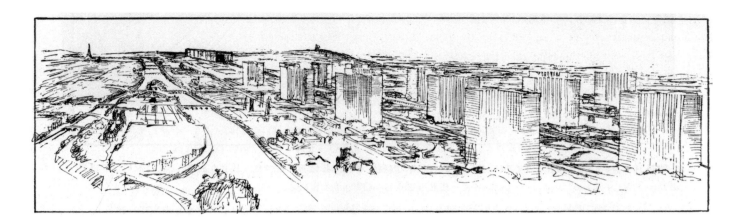

51.1
Sketch for the centre of Paris (1925)

From Le Corbusier, *The City of To-morrow and Its Planning* (1929)

We must, in short, tear down EVERYTHING, to erect *The City of To-morrow*. At its centre (oh beautiful symbolism) will be a gigantic station, the hub for railways, buses, cars and aircraft (from the mediaeval, cathedral-centred city, with ultimate stillness at its heart, we come full pendulum-swing to the image of a gigantic mandala-city centred on ultimate restlessness). Around the station, the focus of a rectangular grid of great motorways, criss-crossing the city, are grouped a cluster of gigantic skyscraper office-blocks, 700 feet high, with room for up to 50,000 people in each. Beyond them, set in a sea of parkland (communal open space) huge slab blocks of municipal housing, up to 160-feet high. The 'corridor street' (ultimate offence) will have been abolished, and the city will have been transformed into nothing but a network of vast housing estates, with motorways running between, and giant multi-storey car parks for commuters. On the edge of the city, tucked away, is sited 'the industrial zone.' Beyond that will be a 'green belt' of municipally-reserved woods and fields (containing the main airport); and finally a ring of satellite 'garden cities.'

So completely and perfectly is this a paradigm of the model which has dominated the minds of the planners who have sought to reshape our own towns and cities in the past thirty years (and which has landed us quite directly in our present appalling crisis), that it is absolutely vital at this time that we should go back to Le Corbusier and see precisely where it all came from. Of course Le Corbusier was completely mad. In 1924, he exhibited his so-called *Voisin* plan for a large chunk of Paris (which would have involved the demolition of the entire Marais District, the Place des Vosges and many others), which he saw as an entirely practical first step towards his ultimate dream of rebuilding all the cities of the Western world. (Fig. 51.1) Nothing made him more livid with rage than to be asked the question 'But where is the money coming from?' And he finally condescends (as, after all, an artist, a painter and a visionary) to take a few moments off to instruct us mere mortals as to how it could be done. His argument is that, if Haussmann's improvements of the nineteenth century had increased the value of land by five times, and if he was rebuilding to a density four times that of Haussmann, then the proceeds from a multiplication of the development value of land by twenty times would be enough to pay for his scheme many times over. QED. The triumph of Gallic logic! But unfortunately he forgets that, only a few pages earlier, one of the great arguments in favour of his new city was that the new buildings would only cover 5 per cent, or a twentieth, of the total land area (the rest would be taken up with agreeable trees and communal sports areas). In other words, even on his own batty arithmetic, the development value of the land would be precisely what it was before! I fear Le Corbusier would not have made a Harry Hyams or a Joe Levy.* No, he was a very different kind of visionary (he ends his book with a picture of Louis XIV, 'in homage to a great town-planner. This despot conceived immense projects and realised them').

We may laugh at all this now. But the fact is that, for thirty years now, we have all been paying a far greater price for the visions of Le Corbusier than the wretched inhabitants of Paris paid for those of Louis XIV. This of course will be denied by those absurd architects and planners who are now half-ashamed of Le Corbusier, and claim that his influence has been 'over-rated' and that he was 'just a great architect,' or why say defiantly that we laymen are not qualified to recognise what a great genius he was, and therefore should not talk about him. But I want to show just how those megalomaniac visions, of *Metropolis*, in fact, step by step, became the hypnotic orthodoxy which has all but killed off our cities.

Source: *The Spectator*, 26 March 1977

*Harry Hyams (b. 1928) and Joe Levy were the best-known of the speculative property developers in London in 1960s, Hyams is most associated with Centrepoint, and Levy the Euston Centre. (Eds)

How Wrong was Corbusier?

By Phil Windsor

A great epoch has begun.
There exists a new spirit

Those words first appeared, in Frederick Etchell's translation of *Vers une Architecture.* exactly half a century ago this year. It is now a truism to remark that the great epoch has been and gone, and the new spirit lies in tatters.

Since Corbusier first spoke his idea, that design should be based on geometrical simplicity derived from his admiration for the modern school of painting, has patently been enormously influential. A new movement appeared, flourished, and is now under siege. It seems not unnatural that some of the blame for what are held to be the failures of modern architecture should be aimed at Corbusier, for he indeed was, and had little hesitation in assuming the public mantle of, one of its progenitors.

But many other factors are to blame. How many architects actually studied Corbusier? How many took him to heart? How many misread him? How many, assuming they wanted to put his ideas directly into practice, were hamstrung by cost contingencies or explicit client requirements which prevented the degree of experimentation they desired? How many others taught a modified version of the same doctrine? In short, how much Corbusier was actually put into practice?

These considerations need study in depth and length, ideally with the benefit of greater historical hindsight than can yet be gained. But, it seems pertinent to enquire fifty years after their first appearance in English, how much of the blame for the failure of the modern movement can fairly be laid with Corbusier's doctrines themselves.

From a cursory re-examination of *Towards a New Architecture* it can be seen that many charges popularly levelled against Corbusier are quite groundless. For those who would confer on him the dubious distinction of suggesting high-rise housing we find his explicit warning, when discussing Perret's suggestion of a city of towers that 'family life would hardly be at home in them with their prodigious mechanism of lifts.'

Indeed Corbusier's suggestion that high land values in city centres, which discourage parks, should be compensated by tower blocks spaced among parkland looks as imaginative – and untried – as ever. He must therefore be specifically excluded from any indictment of the way in which town centre development has actually occurred: his tower block offices but without his parkland between them.

Some of the shortcomings of modern architecture, then, can only be laid at Corbusier's door if one is prepared to misread him almost wilfully, to disregard the words in black and white on the page. Which is foolish, when for those who would wish to trip him there are a multiplicity of contentious assertions.

For instance, Corbusier states:

The engineer, inspired by the law of Economy and governed by mathematical calculation, puts us in accord with the universal law. He achieves harmony.

Thus Corbusier moves towards a philosophy for an aesthetic of simplicity, so the above statement deserves close analysis.

Corbusier assumes that the engineer's approach is totally rational. He is faced with a problem, says Corbusier; he answers it with logic and mathematics.

It is highly debatable whether engineers work in any such way. Plainly the engineer's solution is dependent upon the technology which is open to him to solve that problem, and technology becomes progressively more sophisticated. This is to say that the solution of an engineer now can involve less waste, and more 'Economy' than it could in Corbusier's time. Logically bridges must therefore be more beautiful now.

Are they? If beauty is to be equated with the progress of ruthless efficiency, then plainly beauty should be increasingly prevalent with the progress of time.

To return to the same quotation, we see that Corbusier assumes that the engineer's solution is based exclusively on mathematical efficiency must certainly form a large part of the engineer's proposal so too will subjective experience – training, experience with one form of construction rather than another, and personal aesthetic preferences.

Otherwise it is difficult to explain why the two Forth bridges, for example, side by side, should be so different. What seemed the most rational and efficient proposal to one group of engineers in the eighteenth century no longer seemed so to another in the nineteen sixties. There is no universal law in this instance which can be eliminated from considerations of history and personality.

So Corbusier's rationale of the doctrine of efficiency is based on very subjective assertions; and his speaking of 'universal law' and 'harmony' begins to sound like rhetoric. Because the proposition does not hold water Corbusier seems to prop it up with intangible abstractions to conceal its weakness. The engineer does not work solely to the dictates of Economy (notice the capital E) and mathematical calculation; if he did its connection with the universal law is unexplained; and what is universal law anyway?

What Corbusier is plainly trying to express is a preference for an aesthetic based on simple forms. There is no reason why he should not do so, and certainly at the historical moment he chose to do so it was introducing a new and bold range of aesthetic possibilities to architecture.

But he is mistaken to imply that beauty can only be found in Cézanne's formula of 'cylinders, cones and spheres.' Elsewhere in *Towards a New Architecture* we see him going to quite unremarkable lengths to try and prove that the Cathedral of Notre Dame, for example, was designed according to strictly mathematical rules of proportion. (Fig. 52.1)

52.1
**Regulating lines applied to
Notre Dame, Paris**

From Le Corbusier, *Towards a New
Architecture* (1927)

That may be true, but to the observer much of the richness of Notre Dame is attributable to the flying buttresses, the glass, and the details of the west façade – exactly those elements of ornament that Corbusier claims are superfluous to true, mathematically simple beauty. Or again he shows the mathematical congruousness of the Parthenon, apparently forgetting – or not knowing – that in its original form the building was richly frescoed, painted, festooned with statues.

So much for the connection between proportion and beauty. Corbusier prefers the ruin.

But by taking the doctrine to, on occasion, extreme lengths, it can be more sinister. To cite one of the most celebrated passages of the book:

If houses were constructed by industrial mass-production, like chassis, unexpected but sane and defensible forms would soon appear, and a new aesthetic would be formulated with astonishing precision.

Corbusier's comparison with a chassis is immediately a bad one: he would have done better to compare with a whole car. Then he would not be able to ignore the all-important problem of user requirements, which effectively dictate what a car is to look like and how it will perform. Having discovered these a car is indeed designed to a largely mathematical formula, but its advantage over a house is that it is expected to be replaced as user requirements change.

Corbusier inverts the formula: the house is designed according to the rationalising principles of industrialism and the user is expected to conform to the product.

Nor does Corbusier stop here. It is plain that the earlier quotation that simple, clean, economical design is associated in his mind with moral superiority and 'natural law', and sure enough we find explicit moral guidance in the section of *Towards a New Architecture* on *The Manual of Dwelling*.

'Never undress in your bedroom' he exhorts us. 'It is not a clean thing to do.'

What is morally acceptable, however, is to 'bear in mind economy in your actions, and household management and in your thoughts.'

It matters little whether these sentiments are laudable or not. They demonstrate how very near the surface is Corbusier's obsession with cleanliness and economy, an obsession which has plainly strayed out of the field of moral and into his aesthetic philosophy.

Economy is morally laudable, he says; therefore so is design based upon what he believes to be economical principles. Whilst it is apparent that all fields of thought must be connected, it is questionable whether architects have any business enshrining their views on moral guidance in their designs on behalf of clients.

This brings us to one of Corbusier's most unacceptable tenets: architects as a means of social control, or in his terms 'architecture or revolution'. He suggests:

the man of today is conscious, on the one hand, of a new world which is forming itself regularly, logically and clearly, which produces in a straightforward way things which are useful and usable, and on the other hand he finds himself, to his surprise, living in an old and hostile environment. This framework is his lodging; his town, his street, his house or his flat rise up against him useless, hinder him from following the same path he pursues in his work …

Conformity with the rationalising principles of industrialism in the creation of a physical environment will, he believes, create a far more congruous human environment. This presupposes that man is, or has been made, a rational creature, disregarding evidence from a multiplicity of observers that man actually reacts against the constant rationalisation of his life that conformity with industrialism implies.

Why did Corbusier's equation of simple design forms and moral and social purity seem so persuasive when they are based on such intuitive rather than logical connections? The answer, if Brent Brolin's devastating hatchet job on the Modern Movement *The Failure of Modern Architecture* is to be believed, is in the nature of intuition as an involuntary, socially-induced perception rather than a rational one.

Brolin points to the social currency of the ideas of efficiency and rationalism brought about by the ruthless advance of efficiency in capitalist enterprise and technology. Modern architects, he suggests, 'using poetic associations devoid of any rational basis, relied on the moral weight of culturally accepted premises to enforce essentially unpopular aesthetic choices.'

Needless to say this perception, if correct, has very serious implications for any architect practising in the modern vernacular.

But Corbusier has shown that buildings based on simple geometrical forms can indeed be beautiful and for this, and for his own unsurpassed demonstration of the theory in practice at Ronchamp, we should be eternally grateful. But he has not shown that they will necessarily be beautiful, as the abominations of a school of less able followers proves, and in some cases attempting to rationalise the built environment with loose reference to his precepts has created the industrialised rabbit-hutches which are already demonstrating that what men need is less uniformity, not more. These findings are evident in *Towards a New Architecture* and could have been foreseen.

For aesthetically he does not free us from the conception of talent; that given a language of forms they will only combine to produce beauty in exceptional hands. Corbusier's aesthetic, like any other, may produce beauty; but there is no rationalising formula for beauty despite his insistence. Ultimately the forms themselves from which one works are irrelevant beside the application to which they are put.

Source: *The Architect*, April 1977

Corbusier: Architect of Disaster for the Millions who are Condemned to Live in a Concrete Jungle

By Christopher Booker

In recent weeks the nation has again been shocked by the details of one of the most horrific crimes of our time– the hacking to death of PC Blakelock.*

The murder trial at the Old Bailey has revived images of the terrible events in 1985 when Broadwater Farm in North London (Fig. 53.1) became like a scene out of hell – a crazed mob and the exploding petrol bombs amid the grim concrete towers, pedestrian decks and graffiti of an all-too-typical modern housing estate.

It all might seem to belong to a different world from the rarified atmosphere of an exhibition being staged in an art gallery a mile away across the Thames from the Old Bailey in homage to a Swiss architect born 100 years ago.

Here, admiring groups of architectural students, wander past brightly lit images of neat little houses, flats, even a monastery and a convent chapel, designed by the man proclaimed outside the Hayward Gallery as 'the architect of the century'– Charles Edouard Jeanneret, alias Le Corbusier.

One would never guess from this reverential exhibition, sponsored by some of the country's leading architects and property companies, that there was any connection between the ideas of Le Corbusier and the unspeakable inhumanity of the event at Broadwater Farm.

But there is in fact a very direct link indeed. And it is an appalling comment on the schizophrenia of our age that this connection is almost totally ignored by the wide-eyed organisers of the exhibition.

Just after the First World War, as an unknown experimental painter and architect living in Paris, the young man who called himself Le Corbusier became gripped by an extraordinary vision.

What was needed in the world, more than anything else, was a revolution in the way we looked at the architecture of our cities.

It was time we recognised we were living in an entirely new age, the age of the machine and mass-production. We should tear down our messy, stifling cities, built over the centuries in brick and stone, and rebuild them on a colossal scale, planned down to the tiniest detail, with gigantic towers and vast housing estates made of concrete.

Le Corbusier was in fact a revolutionary dreamer on the grandest scale. He saw architecture and town planning as the way to a new world, as a gigantic social blueprint, as the way to 'create a new type of human being.'

*PC Keith Blakelock was murdered during a riot at the Broadwater Farm, Tottenham, North London, housing estate, on 6 October 1985. (Eds)

53.1
**Broadwater Farm Estate, London
(1973)**

Architects: London Borough of Haringey
Architects Department
Photographer: Harry Metcalfe (ca. 1985)

53.2
Aylesbury Estate, London (1970)

Architects: Southwark Department of
Architecture & Planning
Photographer: Tony Ray-Jones (1970)

There was not even anything particularly new about his individual ideas – the sky-scraper, for instance, was already towering over American cities.

But what was new was the way he put all these ideas together in his vision of 'the city of the future', a vision of immense power – and by the Thirties Le Corbusier's ideas were beginning to exercise a strange fascination on a whole generation of younger architects, above all in Britain.

During the war, as Hitler's bombs laid waste large parts of Britain's major cities, a number of planners and architects were recruited to plan and rebuilding of those cities.

Some of the most influential of them, like Arthur Ling, the mastermind of the Abercrombie Plan for London, had been the most fanatical of Le Corbusier's pre-war disciples.

It was largely thanks to their influence that, in 1947, the Labour Government's Town and Country Planning Act gave local authorities unprecedented powers to plan and to organise redevelopment in Britain.

Ten years later, the first fruits of this silent revolution began to appear, as Britain saw the first monster buildings appear above the skyline.

In London, Liverpool, Glasgow, Birmingham, down came the old back-to-back neighbourly houses in their millions. Up went the gigantic new tower blocks and housing estates, like the Aylesbury in South London, (Fig. 53.2) the colossal Hulme Estate in Manchester, the towers of Everton and the Gorbals, Ronan Point, Broadwater Farm (completed in 1970) and thousands more.

Many were designed or inspired by those admirers of Le Corbusier in the Thirties, such as Basil Spence or Denys Lasdun, men who saw that their time to make history had come.

Then suddenly, in the early Seventies, came the horrified realisation of what had happened – that we had created an astonishing architectural and social catastrophe.

Almost overnight, tower blocks, comprehensive redevelopment, system building, concrete buildings on stilts and all the other Corbusian ideas were rejected.

But the damage had been done, and in the Eighties we have been beginning to count the cost. The huge, windswept housing estates into which millions, had been kennelled were not just soul-destroying to look at.

They were literally the most inhuman form of architecture ever conceived by the mind of man, creating frustration and loneliness, as well as their by-products, vandalism and crime, on an almost unimaginable scale.

Look back today at those original visions of Le Corbusier in the Twenties, and we know only too well what they would have meant in practice. Le Corbusier had the dream of using architecture and planning to 'create a new kind of human being'– and that is what we saw at Broadwater Farm.

Yet today, in the discreet hush of the Hayward Gallery, the architects, the academics and the property developers are staging their act of homage to Le Corbusier, the 'architect of the century' as if they had learned nothing of what his ideas really stood for in human terms at all.

In the name of the millions of hapless victims of that philosophy this exhibition is a vile offence.

But then the real tribute to the power of Le Corbusier's ideas in London at the moment is not that being staged in the Hayward Gallery. It is the one unfolding in that courtroom at the Old Bailey.

Source: *Daily Mail*, 16 March 1987

Architect of Our Sky-high Life

By Brian Appleyard

He was either the most comprehensively gifted visual artist since Michelangelo – or a monster of egotism and inhumanity whose works have contributed directly to the post-war desecration of our towns and cities. When it comes to Le Corbusier, it is difficult to find a fence on which to sit.

Britain does not have a single one of his buildings. Yet probably no town in the country has escaped his influence. His legacy is visible in every building raised on stilts, every exterior staircase turned into a geometric, concrete spiral, every strip of horizontal 'ribbon' windows and every huge, rectangular block of council flats. (Fig. 54.1)

The reputation of aggressively modern architecture has been poor in this country for 20 years. Above all others, Le Corbusier has been blamed. So an exhibition to mark the centenary of his birth, entitled *Le Corbusier: Architect of the Century*, might be said to be asking for trouble.

'His dream was fundamentally wrong,' says Rod Hackney, president of the Royal Institute of British Architects. 'His housing projects are the reason for the collapse of the whole Modern Movement in architecture and the cause of the housing problem in this country. All those designers who followed his ideas about streets in the sky and machines for living failed completely to realize that people cannot live like machines.'

For Hackney the disaster of Le Corbusier's legacy arises from his radical ideas on housing and urban planning. In the 1920s he produced schemes for vast cities with widely-spaced 60-storey blocks of flats. The argument was that, by building high, huge areas of greenery would be freed for the inhabitants.

It was from those schemes that the tower-block, so beloved of British councils during the 1960s, was born. But it was another Le Corbusier building – the Unité d'Habitation in Marseilles – that was to have the most profound influence. This vast concrete slab, set in open parkland, houses 1,600 people and was the model for thousands of disastrously poor imitations across the world. In the London suburb of Roehampton similar blocks did work, but southeast London is littered with soulless mimicry of the master's idea.

Hackney does not argue about the quality of some of Le Corbusier's other work. 'He was a schizophrenic artist,' he says. 'On the one hand there was the housing and on the other he showed himself to be a genius with individual buildings. With the chapel at Ronchamp and the monastery at La Tourette he demonstrated that he could produce buildings that did

54.1
Loughborough Road Estate, London (1957)

Architects: London County Council Architects Department
Photographer: John Pantlin (1956)

what architecture should do – lift the spirit.' In fact, most of Le Corbusier's finished buildings were meant to be one-offs rather than models for mass production.

He was born Charles Edouard Jeanneret in Switzerland and took Le Corbusier as a signature for his architecture in the 1920s. From the practice that he shared at the time with his cousin, Pierre Jeanneret, there emerged not only the visionary cities but also some of the most influential buildings of the age. These included one-off houses like the villa at Garches, near Paris, and the Villa Savoye at Poissy, cool, complex buildings which are still being analysed.

But Le Corbusier's inventiveness meant he could not stand still. He moved away quickly from the clinical look – planting a tree to grow through the roof of the Pavillon de l'Esprit Nouveau in 1925, building a wall of random rubble for the Swiss Students' Hostel in Paris in 1932.

'People often say that Corb and the other great figures of that generation threw away the past,' says Sir Denys Lasdun, architect of the National Theatre. (Fig. 54.2) 'But they

54.2
National Theatre, London (1976)

Architects: Denys Lasdun & Partners
Photographer unknown (1970s)

were really steeped in the past. Every word he wrote shows him attempting to come to terms with it.'

Many of the problems of the Le Corbusier legacy arise from the man himself. He was obsessed and arrogant, 'full of contradictions', explains Colin St John Wilson, Professor of Architecture at Cambridge and designer of the new British Library. 'Many of the things he wrote were contradicted by the things he built. But in the early 1920s he did establish the first new and complete canon of architecture since the 13th century. It was complete technically and complete stylistically.'

In his later years Le Corbusier was taken on by the British architect Maxwell Fry to build the administrative centre of the Indian city of Chandigarh. Along with Fry's wife Jane Drew, they worked together for three years.

'He was without doubt one of the great architects of the age,' Fry says. 'His influence is all around us. He was a difficult man to get on with because he was always so wrapped up in his work. He didn't suffer fools gladly, but he was a great friend.'

On one aspect of Le Corbusier's legacy everybody is agreed – it is too huge and too varied to be fully understood just yet.

Source: *The Times*, 4 June 1987

The Consequences of Le Corbusier

By Gavin Stamp

When Sam Webb, the tireless campaigner for the demolition of the notorious Ronan Point tower block, (Fig. 55.1) finally achieved his goal, he remarked that, 'blaming Le Corbusier for this is like blaming Mozart for Muzak.' In recent years, the Swiss-born Modernist, who died in 1965, has been blamed for most of the failings of modern British architecture – above all, for the socially disastrous policies of urban renewal and the construction of high-rise housing blocks. In Britain, the name of Le Corbusier is virtually synonymous with modern architecture.

It is for this reason that the Arts Council of Great Britain is justified in mounting a major exhibition about Le Corbusier at the Hayward Gallery even though the only work of his ever constructed in this country was a temporary exhibition stand at Olympia in 1930. It is rather sad that Erich Mendelsohn, whose centenary also falls this year and who did work here, is being ignored by the Arts Council but he had nothing like the influence Le Corbusier did over British architects.

For many, brought up on Modern Movement principles in the Thirties and Forties, 'Corb' was almost God. He still is for many unreconstructed modernists and this exhibition is clearly intended to be a reaffirmation of faith in these dark days of 'Post-Modernism'. Hence, also, the fact that Le Corbusier is virtually the Devil for many of modernism's critics.

Is this fair? What is curious is how much of Le Corbusier's influence was based on books he published back in the Twenties. Above all, there was *Towards a New Architecture* published in English in 1927 by John Rodker, who normally specialised in pornography. In this seductive volume, images of racing cars, ocean liners and aeroplanes were placed with photographs of the Parthenon, to help justify the famous cliché 'The house is a machine for living in'. Le Corbusier was a polemicist and a self-publicist who delighted in hyperbole. It may not be his fault that naive English admirers took many of his brilliant flights of imagination at face value, just as it may not be fair to blame him for the fact that English versions of his Unité d'Habitation were so crude and insensitive.

However, the same book also contains sketches of Le Corbusier's vision of 'A City of Towers' (the phrase was actually coined by Perret): serried ranks of giant skyscrapers arranged on a ruthless grid. This was developed as the *Ville Contemporaine* of 1922 with a great central avenue terminated by giant arches – not unrelated in spirit to Hitler's Berlin. In 1925 came the *Plan Voisin* which proposed replacing much of Paris by a rectilinear

55.1
Ronan Point, London, seen in the aftermath of the explosion (1968)

Architects: Newham Department of Planning & Architecture
Photographer unknown (1968)

pattern of tall blocks and in 1930 he suggested reconstructing Moscow as a grid, commenting that 'It is not possible to reconcile the past city with the present or future one'. The consequences of these megalomaniac fantasies have been catastrophic, as can be seen all over the world. Le Corbusier's apologists maintain that he never intended to house people in these blocks, but this is not true. *Vers une Architecture* contains a project of 1920 for 'Apartments or Flats, built as towers of 60 storeys ... pitiless but magnificent'. However, the tragedy is that British architects remained stuck with this terrible vision, for Le Corbusier himself moved on and what really matters is not all this theory but the buildings.

The exhibition, which is a stylish and imaginative arrangement of photographs, drawings and models, is not likely to change anyone's view of Le Corbusier, or make many converts.

The architect liked to have his buildings photographed with smart cars in the foreground, so as to emphasis the machine-like modernity of his designs. Today, of course, such images are compelling because the cars have period charm in contrast to the buildings which, when in good condition, are pure architectural statements of great refinement and control. Le Corbusier should be remembered not as a social engineer but as an artist.

He certainly thought of himself as an artist and made paintings and sculpture as well as buildings. His designs, particularly in plan, are often related to contemporary artistic developments, although there are rather too many of his paintings in the exhibition – mostly repetitive derivatives of Picasso and Fernand Léger. However, the important thing – and this contradicts the conventional view of the Modern Movement – is that Le Corbusier did not eschew ornament and decoration and in his late work he designed decorative enamelled doors and abstract relief sculpture in cast concrete on blank walls. *Béton brut* need not always be brutal.

The exhibition does have surprises. One is Le Corbusier's first building, a villa of 1906 in his birthplace, La Chaux-de-Fonds, which, along with his early decorative watercolours, shows the influence of Mackintosh, Wright and contemporary *Jugendstil*. But the most interesting section is devoted to the late, post-Second World War work. This confounded his English acolytes at the time, for it became sculptural, raw and very personal, often using natural materials. The masterpiece is the church at Ronchamp which, with its organic, almost formless plan, curving walls and rough finishes, baffled narrow British Modernists who thought architecture should be rectilinear, neat and smooth. With Ronchamp Le Corbusier rejected the machine aesthetic and, yet again, demonstrated his wayward individuality by ignoring the technological approach to architecture which came to dominate the West. Then there is the remarkable series of sculptural buildings at Firminy, a sort of French Aberfan. (Fig. 55.2) Recently, in defiance of the view that sees Modernism as Left-wing, a Communist council has tried to demolish some of them while the tenants of the local Unité d'Habitation actually protested that they liked living in 'Corbu'. That could surely never happen here.

Le Corbusier: Architect of the Century is the title of the exhibition and certainly no other architect so well represents our time. All the destructive forces of the 20th century are manifest in his life and work: machine-worship, utopianism and megalomania. Like other 'seminal figures' he was a man of colossal vanity and egotism. There are countless photographs of his cold, smug face embellished with his famous owl-like spectacles and he

55.2
Youth centre, Firminy, with relief by Le Corbusier (1965)

Photographer: Walter Rawlings (1967)

was often a pseud and a poseur, who spoke of himself in the third person. It is hard for an Englishman wholly to take seriously such a self-appointed genius, one who could adopt a pompous stage name: Le Corbusier (*corbeau* means raven in French). He was annoyed when his RIBA Gold Medal was engraved with his real name: Charles-Edouard Jeanneret. Perhaps such affectations seem less pretentious in France.

Yet he cannot be dismissed. Le Corbusier was an immensely resourceful and inventive architect who was always one jump ahead and is not easily categorized. He developed and enriched the language of the Modern Movement and was ultimately concerned with the emotional effect of three-dimensional forms. He was interested in the power of symbols, of shapes, of historical resonances and, in his late buildings, could rise triumphantly to the challenge of sacred architecture. He deserves to be remembered as a real architect rather than as a mischievous planner, whose work must remain a potent influence.

Just as the Lutyens exhibition ended with the triumph of New Delhi, so this homage to Le Corbusier ends with Chandigarh, the new capital of the Punjab commissioned by Nehru. (Fig. 55.3) Both cities were essentially alien, Western concepts imposed arrogantly on India (the former by order, of course, and the latter by choice). But whereas New Delhi is an

55.3
Secretariat, Chandigarh (1959)

Photographer: Valerie Winter (1959)

undoubted success, Chandigarh remains unfinished and political changes make it rather a failure, although at the end of its vast, dreary grid plan stand Le Corbusier's finest public buildings powerful and inventive masses of rough concrete strangely resonant of the monuments of the Ancient world. The irony is that, in this centenary year of its creator, Chandigarh is closed to foreign visitors because of the troubles of the Punjab. But in this case, for once, communal unhappiness cannot be blamed on the architecture of Le Corbusier.

Source: *Daily Telegraph*, 9 June 1987

The Relevance of Le Corbusier

By James Palmes

There is a moment in *Poet's Pub* when Professor Benbow, Eric Linklater's fictional academic, admits to being 'sick of scholarship and the graveyard way.' We delve into the motivations of the illustrious dead, when these so often, he implies, are perfectly simple. I do not think that the Professor would have had to dig very deep to find the influences which made C.E. Jeanneret into Le Corbusier.

The immigrant francophone community in Switzerland into which he was born drew its rugged strength of purpose from ancestral victims of religious and political persecution (in his family's case supposedly the Albigensian heretics of Languedoc) and in the 1880s or thereabouts from the skilled workers who flocked into the expanding clock and watch trade centred at La Chaux-de-Fonds, his birthplace. From these two sources welled, on the one side, his relentless didacticism and uncompromising antiestablishment attitude of mind and, on the other, his abiding interest in machine products and in the then new phenomenon of the mass-produced *objet-standard*, already evident at the turn of the century in cheap and accurate watches.

Often in later years Le Corbusier would claim that he was self-trained rather than school-trained, and no doubt this was largely true. But, in L'Eplattenier, who presided over his class in the School of Art at La Chaux-de-Fonds, he found an exceptionally gifted, sympathetic and informed adviser. It was this 'emancipated pedagogue', as he described him, who introduced the young Jeanneret not only to the *Grammar of Ornament* of Owen Jones, which incidentally he much admired, but to the work of Behrens, Berlage, and the Werkbund, and encouraged the student in a parallel commitment to painting and sculpture, guiding him towards that synthesis of the arts in architecture which developed more noticeably at the end of his career, and to a deep respect for the complementary function of the engineer. In 1908 Jeanneret went for a time to work as a draughtsman for Perret (then in some trouble for acting as his own contractor), and began to make his mark in the intellectual world of Paris, shunning of course the salons where the arts' establishment might be loitering. He was attracted to Cubism, to the study of forms reduced to their fundamental geometric shapes, and this led to association with Ozenfant, lifelong friendship with Léger, the sculptor Laurens, Picasso and other Cubists, which was first to blossom in *L'Esprit Nouveau*. It was in this magazine that Jeanneret presented his purist architecture, derived in part from Cubism, and assumed the pseudonym Le Corbusier, to which he clung henceforward.

56.1
**Mill Owners' Association building,
Ahmedabad (1954)**

Photographer: Valerie Winter (1959)

56.2
Villa Shodhan, Ahmedabad (1956)

Photographer: Valerie Winter (1959)

The pseudonym seems to have been given to him by Ozenfant and is a more dramatic version of Lecorbesier, the name of a family with which the Jeanneret was connected. His friends probably admired his raven-like features (*corbeau* = raven), but since the symbolic traits of the great carrion-crow in France as elsewhere are generally negative, it is unlikely that they would have wanted the resemblance over emphasised! The first significant architectural product of this period was the Pavilion de l'Esprit Nouveau built for the 1925 Exhibition of Decorative Arts in Paris, which was successful in bringing him to the notice of an international public. This was followed soon afterwards by the now familiar *maisons blanches*, at Garches and Poissy for example, and the Swiss Hostel for the Cité Universitaire de Paris.

This is the point when a few critics, incorruptible partisans of the Modern Movement, began to hesitate over the significance of what he built subsequently, at least in the Western World, and they have been lately joined by a larger contingent who detect a falling from excellence since the 1940s. There was of course little for him to build for more than a decade after 1931. The only major project that went ahead was the Ministry of Education building, Rio de Janeiro, completed during the Second World War under the supervision of Costa and Niemeyer. It was a period of anxiety and frustration, of ambitious plans obstructed or reduced to inconsequential dimensions, of early studies for *brise-soleils* – he was shocked by the effect of sunlight on the glass wall, even in temperate zones – and for his later *grille climatique* applicable to the tropics. On the credit side also there was the growing influence of his books and CIAM on architects.

In 1940 came the Murondin *pisé* housing proposals, designed for war refugees, which were immediately rejected by the authorities, and then various abortive plans for the Vichy government, which probably did little good for his postwar reputation, though there is no reason to think of him as a collaborator. The tide began to turn in his favour with the appointment of Raoul Dautry as Minister of Reconstruction. But not surprisingly, during the long pause of reluctant inactivity, Le Corbusier's ideas had evolved.

The basic principles had not changed. The *pilotis*, the free plan, the roof garden and open-air living space were still there, and usually the horizontal strip windows. But the monochrome cubist purity, characteristic of the 'white houses' of the interwar years, was now enlivened, some say, debauched by colour, and the simple basic geometric forms were no longer so simple, but mannered and seemingly distorted. Le Corbusier claimed that the complex polychrome treatment of the Unité d'Habitation at Marseilles required four thousand instructions to the painters, and one recalls that his sculpture is predominantly polychromatic, and that the young Jeanneret had been considered an outstanding cubist painter, at least during the colour and collage phases of the movement. What seems to have happened in the later years of this single-minded man was a gradual shift in philosophy, to a deeper understanding of that synthesis of the visual arts which L'Eplattenier had encouraged his students to seek at La Chaux-de-Fonds, and which he himself exemplified so brilliantly in India. (Figs 56.1 and 56.2) After World War II Corbu the painter and sculptor, not forgetting the tapestry weaver and ceramicist, played essential parts in the architect's designs. Perhaps, at Ronchamp and La Tourette, the visual impact of a building in a particular setting was becoming more important than the purpose for which the building was intended? And whether the result was sculpture or architecture is far from certain. I think it was poetry. It was certainly a long way from the button-bright prose of *La Ville* practical reality [...].

Source: *RIBA Journal*, March 1987

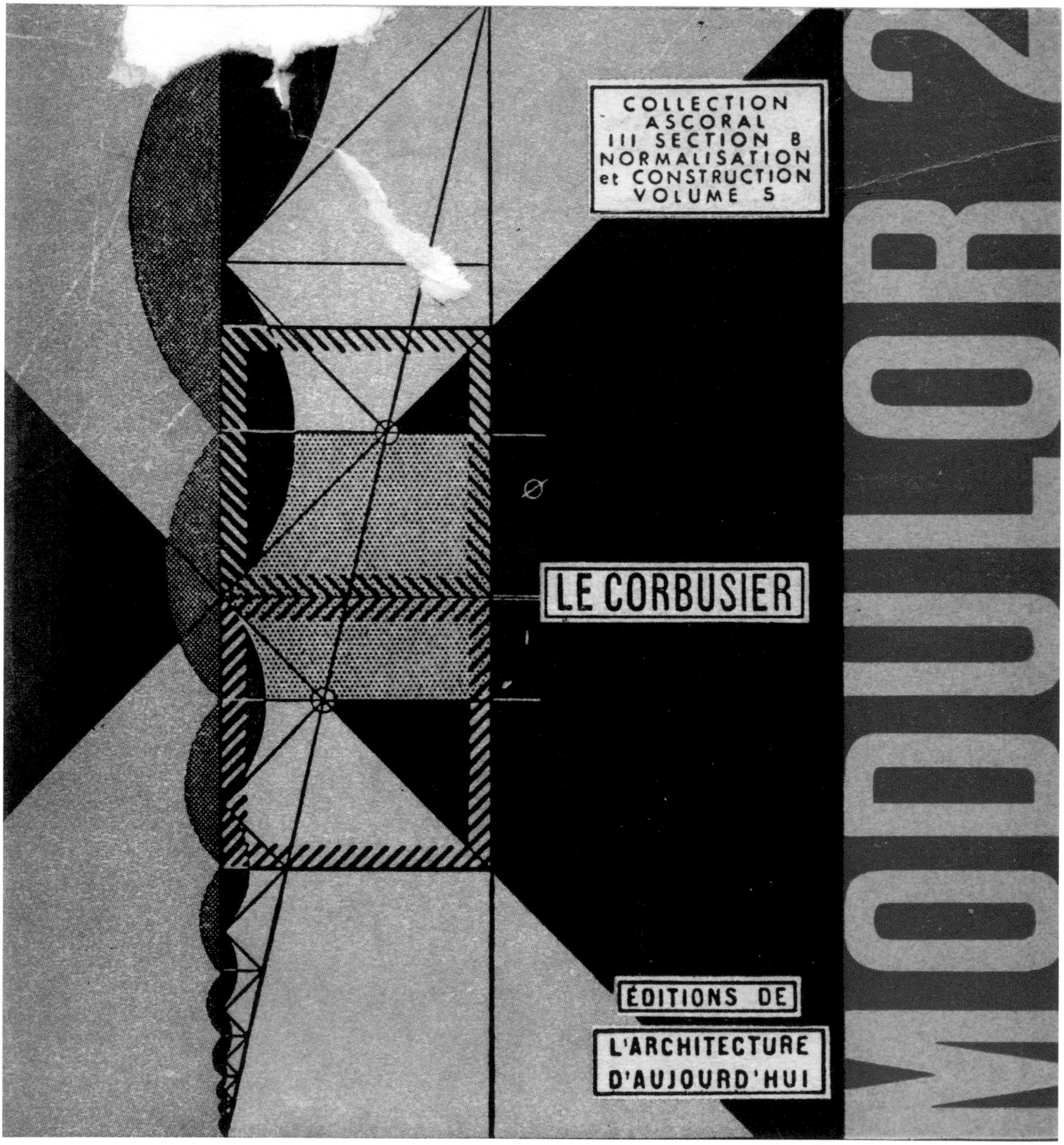
COLLECTION
ASCORAL
III SECTION B
NORMALISATION
et CONSTRUCTION
VOLUME 5
LE CORBUSIER
ÉDITIONS DE
L'ARCHITECTURE
D'AUJOURD'HUI
MODULOR 2

Bibliography

Julian Osley

Introduction

The purpose of the bibliography of over 650 references is to support the anthology and to demonstrate the sustained level of interest (both lay and professional) in Le Corbusier in Great Britain during his lifetime and beyond.

For the most part, the bibliography follows the chronological arrangement of the anthology, and, apart from one or two important exceptions (where British scholars' work has been published outside the United Kingdom), the bibliography is restricted to books and periodical publications published in Great Britain.

It has not, of course, been possible to compile a totally exhaustive bibliography, given the fact there are no indexes to many of the daily and weekly newspapers, although advances in digital technology have encouraged the development of online archival products, such as those provided by *The Daily Mirror, The Economist, The Guardian, The Observer, The Scotsman* and *The Times*: these have been invaluable.

Omitted are references to reviews of books *about* Le Corbusier, and to reviews of Le Corbusier exhibitions not held in Great Britain.

References to the texts in the anthology are marked with an asterisk.

Bibliography

1 Monographs by Le Corbusier

(1927) *Towards a New Architecture*, London: John Rodker [Trans. Frederick Etchells of *Vers une Architecture*].

(1929) *The City of To-morrow and Its Planning*, London: John Rodker [Trans. Frederick Etchells of *Urbanisme*, 8th edn].

(1935) *Aircraft*, London: The Studio.

(1946) *Towards a New Architecture*, New edn, London: Architectural Press.

(1947) *The City of To-morrow and Its Planning*, 2nd edn, London: Architectural Press.

(1947) *Concerning Town Planning*, London: Architectural Press [Trans. Clive Entwistle of *Propos d'Urbanisme*].

(1947) *The Four Routes*, London: Dennis Dobson [Trans. Dorothy Todd of *Sur les 4 Routes*].

(1948) *When the Cathedrals Were White: a Journey to the Country of Timid People*, London: Routledge [Trans. E. Hyslop of *Quand les Cathédrales étaient Blanches*].

(1953) *The Marseilles Block*, London: Harvill [Trans. Geoffrey Sainsbury of *L'Unité d'Habitation de Marseille*].

(1954) *The Modulor: a Harmonious Measure to the Human Scale Universally Applicable to Architecture and Mechanics*, London: Faber [Trans. Peter de Francia and Anna Bostock of *Le Modulor*, 2nd edn, 1951].

(1957) *The Chapel at Ronchamp*, London: Architectural Press [Trans. Jacqueline Cullen of *Ronchamp*].

(1958) *The Modulor 2, 1955: Let the User Speak Next: Continuation of The Modulor 1948*, London: Faber [Trans. Peter de Francia and Anna Bostock of *Modulor 2*, 1955].

(1960) *My Work*, London: Architectural Press [Trans. James Palmes of *L'Atelier de la Recherche Patiente*].

(1967) *The Radiant City: Elements of a Doctrine of Urbanism to Be Used as the Basis of Our Machine-age Civilisation*, London: Faber [Trans. P. Knight, E. Levieux and D. Coltman of *La Ville Radieuse*].

(1971) *The City of To-morrow and Its Planning*, 3rd edn, London: Architectural Press.

(1998) *The Decorative Art of Today*, Oxford: Architectural Press [Trans. James Dunnett of *L'Art Décoratif d'Aujourd'hui*]. Published as part of *Essential Le Corbusier*.

(2007) *Toward an Architecture*, London: Frances Lincoln [Trans. John Goodman of *Vers une Architecture*].

— and Pierrefeu, François de (1948) *The Home of Man*, London: Architectural Press [Trans. Clive Entwistle and Gordon Holt of *La Maison des Hommes*].

2 Reviews of monographs by Le Corbusier

Aircraft (1935)

*J.N.S. [John Summerson] (1936), 'The Voice of the Prophet', *Architect & Building News*, 145 (10 Jan.): 56–57.

Scholberg, Philip (1936) 'Sentimental Calvin', *Architects' Journal*, 83 (23 Apr.): 633–34.

Pascoe, Paul (1936) 'The New Age', *Architectural Review*, 80 (Sept.): 122.

Spens, Michael (1987) 'Le Corbusier and *Aircraft*', *Studio International*, 200 (Aug.): 18–19.

L'Art Décoratif d'Aujourd'hui (1959)

P.R.B. [Reyner Banham] (1960) 'Decorative Reprint', *Architectural Review*, 127 (Apr.): 227.

The Athens Charter (1973)

Smithson, Peter (1974) 'The Athens Charter', *Architecture Plus*, Mar./Apr.: 6.

The Chapel at Ronchamp (1957)

Rowntree, Diana (1958) 'Chapel in Concrete', *Manchester Guardian*, 18 Mar.

Maguire, Robert (1958) 'The Chapel at Ronchamp', *Architectural Association Journal*, 73 (May): 251.

(1958) 'The Chapel at Ronchamp', *Architectural Design*, 28 (Jun.): 255.

C.S. (1958) 'The Chapel at Ronchamp', *Architect & Building News*, 214 (13 Aug.): 243.

Des Canons, des Munitions? Merci! Des Logis, s.v.p (1938)

Bennett, Tim (1938) 'Oeuvre Plastique; and, Des Canons, des Munitions? Merci! Des Logis, s.v.p.', *Focus*, 2: 80–85.

The City of To-morrow and Its Planning (1929)

(1929) 'Speed Cities of the Future', *Daily Mail*, 1 Jul.

(1929) 'A Very Important Book', *Architect & Building News*, 122 (5 Jul.): 3–4.

*N.S.H. [Nora Shackleton Heald] (1929) 'The City of To-morrow: the Real Revolution Lies in the Solution of Existing Problems', *The Queen*, 24 Jul.: 8–9.

*Waugh, Evelyn (1929) 'Cities of the Future', *The Observer*, 11 Aug.

C.H.R. [Charles Reilly] (1929) 'The City of To-morrow', *Manchester Guardian*, 14 Aug.

*Bernard, Oliver P. (1929) 'The City of To-morrow', *The Studio*, 98 (Sept.): 612–24.

Edwards, A. Trystan (1929) 'The Dead City', *Architectural Review*, 66 (Sept.): 135–38.

*Pick, Frank (1929) 'The Way of To-morrow and the Traffic Problem', *The Studio*, 98 (Sept.): 624–28.

(1929) 'The Problem of the Great City', *The Studio*, 98 (Sept.): 611.

T.E.S. (1929) 'The City of To-morrow', *Building*, 4 Sept.: 428.

*Shand, P. Morton and Edwards, A. Trystan (1929) 'The City of To-morrow', *Concrete Way*, 2 (Sept.): 79–87.

(1929) 'The City of To-morrow', *Times Literary Supplement*, 10 Oct.: 785.

Chester, H.W. (1930) 'The City of To-morrow', *Journal of the Royal Institute of British Architects*, 37 (7 Jun.): 559.

The City of To-morrow and Its Planning, 2nd edn (1947)

G.J.H. [G. J. Howling] (1948) 'Corbusier Revisited', *The Builder*, 174 (23 Jan.): 104.

Tayler, Herbert (1948) 'The City of To-morrow', *Architect & Building News*, 193 (13 Feb.): 144.

(1948) 'The City of To-morrow', *Architectural Design*, 18 (Apr.) 1948: 91.

De Maré, Eric (1948) 'What Kind of Tomorrow?', *Architectural Review*, 103 (Jun.): 273.

Concerning Town Planning (1947)

Cox, A. (1947) 'Concerning Town Planning', *Journal of the Royal Institute of British Architects*, 55 (Dec.): 81.

Fedden, Robin (1948) 'Le Corbusier and the Passage of Taste', *Nineteenth Century and After*, Mar.: 172–77.

The Four Routes (1947)

(1948) 'Corbusier Again', *The Builder*, 174 (26 Mar.): 355–56.

Jones, A. Douglas (1948) 'The Four Routes', *Architect & Building News*, 194 (2 Jul.): 16.

The Home of Man (1948)

M.L. (1948) 'The Home of Man', *Architectural Design*, 18, (Dec.): 277.

Une Maison – un Palais (1929)

Tomlinson, Harold (1929) 'Une Maison – un Palais', *Architects' Journal*, 70 (18 Sept.): 433–34.

Poole, C.A. (1998) 'Theoretical and Poetical Ideas in Le Corbusier's *Une Maison – Un Palais*', *Journal of Architecture*, 3 (Spring): 1–30.

The Marseilles Block (1953)

Hoar, Frank (1953) 'Corbusiania: Two New Books', *The Builder*, 185 (24 Jul.): 132.

Abercrombie, Patrick (1953) 'The Marseilles Block', *Building*, 28 (Aug.): 284–86.

(1953) 'Innovation in Housing: the Marseilles Block', *The Times*, 1 Aug.

(1953) 'Vertical or Horizontal Living', *The Economist*, 12 Sept.: 682–83.

Horsburgh, Patrick (1953) 'The Marseilles Block', *Architect & Building News*, 204 (19 Nov.): 625.

M.L. (1953) 'Le Corbusier: the Marseilles Block', *Architectural Design*, 23 (Dec.): 356.

Le Modulor (1951)

Summerson, John (1952) 'Corbusier's Modulor', *New Statesman & Nation*, 23 Feb.: 213–14.

The Modulor (1954)

(1954) 'The Modulor', *Architectural Design*, 24 (Apr.): 118.

Banham, Reyner (1955) 'The Modulor', *Burlington Magazine*, 97 (Jul.): 231.

Pottage, A. (1996) 'Architectural Authorship: the Normative Ambitions of Le Corbusier's Modulor', *AA Files*, 31 (Summer): 64–70.

The Modulor 2, 1955 (Let the User Speak Next) (1958)

Voelcker, John (1958) 'Modulor 2', *Architects' Journal*, 128 (18 Sept.): 403.

H.R. (1959) 'Modulor 2: 1955 (Let the User Speak Next)', *Burlington Magazine*, 101 (Mar.): 113.

My Work (1960)

Keyte, Michael (1961) 'My Work', *Architects' Journal*, 33 (16 Feb.): 245–46.

Rowntree, Diana (1961) 'Across the Mind's Divisions ...', *The Guardian*, 16 Feb.

Howling, G.J. (1961) 'Corbusier's *My Work*', *The Builder*, 200 (31 Mar.): 619.

Read, Herbert (1961) 'The Poetry of Le Corbusier', *Architectural Review*, 129 (Jun.): 371.

Oeuvre Complète

Jarrett, E.R. (1931) '*Le Corbusier & Pierre Jeanneret: ihr Gesamtes Werk 1910–1929*', *Journal of the Royal Institute of British Architects*, 38 (2 May): 464.

Townsend, Robert (1935) 'The Preacher in Practice', *Architects' Journal*, 81 (25 Apr.): 638–39.

J.N.S. [John Summerson] (1937) 'Le Corbusier: the First Phase', *Architect & Building News*, 149 (5 Mar.): 308.

Osborn, F.J. (1937) 'Fantasies of Planning: the Tower and the Street', *Town & Country Planning*, 5 (Sept.): 119–21.

Bennett, Tim (1939) 'Le Corbusier and Pierre Jeanneret: Complete Work. 3: 1934–1938', *Focus*, 3 (Spring): 67–72.

*[Summerson, John] (1939) 'Le Corbusier', *Architect & Building News*, 159 (14 Jul.): 36.

Stephen, Nicholas (1939) 'The Artist, Philosopher, Architect', *Building*, 14 (Sept.): 399.

Wilton, John (1947) 'Le Corbusier: Oeuvre Complète 1938–1946', *Architect & Building News*, 191 (22 Aug.): 157–58.

J.M.R. [James Richards] (1951) 'Le Corbusier 1938–46', *Architectural Review*, 110 (Sept.): 204.

Hoar, Frank (1953) 'Corbusiania: Two New Books', *Builder*, 185 (24 Jul.): 132.

M.L. (1953) 'Le Corbusier 1946–52', *Architectural Design*, 23 (Dec.): 356.

McCallum, Ian (1953) 'Five – and Victory: Le Corbusier: Oeuvre Complète 1946–52', *Architectural Review*, 118 (Jul.): 50.

Banham, Reyner (1957) 'Le Corbusier, 65 to 70', *Architects' Journal*, 126 (26 Sept.): 456–61.

Q.S.C. (1958) 'Le Corbusier: Oeuvre Complète (vol. VI) 1952–57', *Architectural Review*, 124 (Sept.): 194.

Banham, Reyner (1966) 'Let the Avalanche Go ...', *RIBA Journal*, 73 (Jul.): 325.

Segal, Walter (1968) 'Oeuvre Incomplete', *Architects' Journal*, 147 (28 Feb.): 477.

Frampton, Kenneth (1969) 'Le Corbusier 1910–1965', *Architectural Design*, 39 (Nov.): 591.

Summerson, John (1970) 'Le Corbusier: Last Works', *Encounter*, 35 (Sept.): 65–68.

Oeuvre Plastique: Peintures et Dessins, Architecture (1938)
Bennett, Tim (1938) 'Oeuvre Plastique; and, Des Canons, des Munitions? Merci! Des Logis, s.v.p.', *Focus*, 2 (Winter): 80–85.

Précisions sur un Etat Présent de l'Architecture et de l'Urbanisme (1930)
*Read, Herbert (1931) 'The City of To-morrow', *The Listener*, 18 Feb.: 272–73.
*Read, Herbert (1931) 'The House of To-morrow', *The Listener*, 25 Feb.: 324.

Quand les Cathédrales étaient Blanches: Voyage au Pays des Timides (1937)
(1937) 'Corbusier Goes West ...', *Architect & Building News*, 151 (20 Aug.): 215–16.

The Radiant City (1967)
(1967) 'Right ... Wrong ... Right', *Architects' Journal*, 145 (12 Apr.): 874.
Osborn, F.J. (1967) 'Le Corbusier in Perspective', *Town & Country Planning*, 35 (Aug./Sept.): 405.

Towards a New Architecture (1927)
*Tomlinson, Harold (1927) 'Towards a New Architecture', *Architects' Journal*, 127 (21 Sept.): 378–79.
[Clutton-Brock, Alan] (1927) 'Modern Architecture', *Times Literary Supplement* (30 Oct.): 734.
*N.S.H. [Nora Shackleton Heald] (1927) 'Towards a New Architecture: When Architect and Engineer Work Together', *The Queen*, 23 Nov.: 17–20.
S.C.R. (1927) 'Towards a New Architecture' , *Architect & Building News*, 118 (23 Dec.): 850.
J.D.B. (1928) 'Towards a New Architecture', *Building*, 3 (Jan.): 36–37.
*Lutyens, Edwin (1928) 'The Robotism of Architecture', *The Observer*, 29 Jan.
Butler, A.S.G. (1928) 'M. Le Corbusier's Book', *Journal of the Royal Institute of British Architects*, 35 (Feb.): 269.
(1929) 'Towards a New Architecture', *Garden Cities & Town-Planning*, 19 (Feb.): 46.
Verlarde, F.X. (1929) 'Towards a New Architecture', *Town Planning Review*, 13 (May): 201–02.
*Allison, P. (1971) 'Le Corbusier: Architect or Revolutionary', *AAQ*, 3 (Apr./Jul.): 10–20.

Towards a New Architecture (1946)
(1947) 'Towards a New Architecture', *Architect & Building News*, 190 (11 Apr.): 37–38.
(1947) 'Towards a New Architecture', *Architectural Design*, 17 (May): 146.
Brett, Lionel (1947) 'First Principles', *Architectural Review*, 102 (Sept.): 103.

Vers une Architecture (1924)
Holt, Gordon (1924) 'Vers une Architecture', *Garden Cities & Town-Planning*, 14 (Jul.): 158.

*Rees, V. O. (1924) 'Vers une Architecture', *Architectural Association Journal*, 40 (Sept.): 64–67.

La Ville Radieuse / The Radiant City
J.N.S. [John Summerson] (1936) 'The Voice of the Prophet', *Architect & Building News*, 145 (10 Jan.): 56–57.
*Samuel, Godfrey (1936) 'Radiant City and Garden Suburb: Corbusier's Ville Radieuse', *Journal of the Royal Institute of British Architects*, 43 (4 Apr.): 595–99.
Gutkind, Erwin (1936) 'The Indivisible Problem', *Architectural Review*, 80 (Oct.): 171–73.

When the Cathedrals Were White (1947)
Scorer, Hugh (1948) 'When the Cathedrals Were White', *Journal of the Royal Institute of British Architects*, 55 (Aug.): 419–20.
(1948) 'When the Cathedrals Were White', *Architectural Design*, 18 (Dec.): 277.

3   Monographs about Le Corbusier

Architectural Association (2003) *Le Corbusier and the Architecture of Reinvention*, London: Architectural Association.
Baker, Geoffrey H. (1996) *Le Corbusier: an Analysis of Form,* 3rd edn, London: Spon.
Baker, Geoffrey H. (1996) *Le Corbusier: the Creative Search: the Formative Years of Charles-Edouard Jeanneret*, London: Spon.
Baltanas, Jose (2005) *Walking Through Le Corbusier: a Tour of His Masterworks*, London: Thames & Hudson.
Besset, Maurice (1987) *Le Corbusier,* 2nd edn, London: Architectural Press. First edn published as *Who was Le Corbusier?*, 1968.
Blake, Peter (1963) *Le Corbusier: Architecture and Form*, Harmondsworth: Penguin Books.
Brooks, H. Allen (ed.) (1987) *Le Corbusier: the Garland Essays*. New York, London: Garland.
Cohen, Jean-Louis and Benton, Tim (2008) *Le Corbusier le Grand*, London: Phaidon.
Curtis, William J.R. (1986) *Le Corbusier: Ideas and Forms*, Oxford: Phaidon.
Darling, Elizabeth (2000) *Le Corbusier*, London: Carlton.
Etlin, Richard A. (1994) *Frank Lloyd Wright and Le Corbusier: the Romantic Legacy*, Manchester: Manchester University Press.
Frampton, Kenneth (2001) *Le Corbusier*, London: Thames & Hudson.
Gardiner, Stephen (1974) *Le Corbusier*, London: Fontana.
Graves, Michael (intro.) (1981) *Le Corbusier: Selected Drawings*, London: Academy Editions.
Jencks, Charles (1987) *Le Corbusier and the Tragic View of Architecture*, Rev. edn, Harmondsworth: Penguin Books.
Jenger, Jean (1996) *Le Corbusier: Architect of a New Age,* London: Thames & Hudson.
Jordan, Robert Furneaux (1972) *Le Corbusier*, London: Dent.
Menin, Sarah and Samuel, Flora (2003) *Nature and Space: Aalto and Le Corbusier*, London: Routledge.

Padovan, Richard (2002) *Towards Universality: Le Corbusier, Mies and De Stijl*, London: Routledge.

Pawley, Martin (1970) *Le Corbusier*, London: Thames & Hudson.

Richards, Simon (2003) *Le Corbusier and the Concept of Self*, New Haven, CT; London: Yale University Press.

Samuel, Flora (2004) *Le Corbusier: Architect and Feminist*, Chichester: Wiley-Academy.

Samuel, Flora (2007) *Le Corbusier in Detail*, Oxford: Architectural Press.

Tzonis, Alexander (2001) *Le Corbusier: the Poetics of Machine and Metaphor*, London: Thames & Hudson.

Walden, Russell (ed.) (1977) *The Open Hand: Essays on Le Corbusier*, Cambridge, MA; London: MIT Press.

4 Articles by Le Corbusier

(1928) 'The Town and the House', *Architectural Review*, 64 (Dec.): 223–30.

(1929) 'Corbusierthology', *Architectural Review*, 66 (Aug.): 67–70. Part of the chapter entitled 'The Great City' from *The City of To-morrow*.

(1930) 'Twentieth-Century Living and Twentieth Century Building', *Decorative Art: the Studio Year Book*: 9–20.

*(1936) 'The Vertical Garden City', *Architectural Review*, 79 (Jan.): 9–10.

*(1937) 'The Crystal Palace: a Tribute', *Architectural Review*, 81 (Feb.): 72.

(1937) 'The Quarrel with Realism: the Destiny of Painting', in J.L. Martin, Ben Nicholson and N. Gabo (eds) *Circle: International Survey of Constructive Art*, London: Faber: 67–74.

(1938) 'If I Had to Teach You Architecture', *Focus*, 1 (Summer): 3–12.

*(1938) 'The MARS Group Exhibition of the Elements of Modern Architecture: Introduction', *Architectural Review*, 83 (Mar.): 109–10.

(1947) 'Crystal Palace Competition', *Architects' Year Book*, 2: 146–48.

*(1947) 'The Future of the Architectural Profession', *Plan: Architectural Students Association Journal*, 2: 4–6.

(1947) 'Housing Equipment for a Machinist Society', *Architects' Year Book*, 2: 76–78.

*(1947) 'Intervention during Discussion on Architectural Expression by CIAM, Bridgwater on Sept. 13, 1947', *Architects' Journal*, 106 (25 Sept.): 279.

(1947) 'M Le Corbusier, December 18, 1947 at the Architectural Association', *Architects' Journal*, 107 (8 Jan.): 35–36.

*(1948) 'M Le Corbusier Addresses the Students of the AA School', *Architect & Building News*, 193 (2 Jan.): 17–18.

(1948) 'New World of Space', *Horizon*, 18 (Oct.): 279–84.

(1949) 'Hélène de Mandrot', *Architectural Review*, 105 (Apr.): 194.

(1950) 'The UN Building', *Architectural Review*, 108 (Jul.): 69–71.

(1952) 'Description of the CIAM Grid, Bergamo, 1949', in J. Tyrwhitt, J.L. Sert and E.N. Rogers (eds), *The Heart of the City: Towards the Humanisation of Urban Life*, London: Lund Humphries: 41–52.

(1952) 'A Meeting Place for the Arts', in J. Tyrwhitt, J.L. Sert and E.N. Rogers (eds), *The Heart of the City: Towards the Humanisation of Urban Life*, London: Lund Humphries: 171–76.

*(1953) 'A New City for India', *The Observer*, 10 May.

(1961) 'The International Council of Museums Congress, Italy (May) 1961', *Architectural Design*, 31 (Aug.): 338–39.

(1983) 'Auguste Perret', *Architectural Education*, 1: 7–21.

(1989) 'Corb on Spontaneous Theatre', *Architectural Review*, 185 (Jun.): 80–82.

(2001) 'Le Corbusier Parle ... 1951', *Twentieth Century Architecture*, 5: 7–10.

(2003) 'Dessins', *Architectural Design*, 73 (May): 6–8.

5 Articles about Le Corbusier

Benoit Levy, Georges (1918) 'A French Garden Hamlet', *Town Planning Review*, 7 (Mar./Apr.): 251–52.

*Holt, Gordon (1924) 'Some French Views on Architectural Education: Interviews with Leading Parisian Architects', *Architects' Journal*, 60 (23 Jul.): 117–19.

Robertson, Howard (1927) 'Some Recent French Developments in Domestic Architecture', *Architectural Review*, 61 (Jan.): 2–7.

Robertson, Howard (1927) 'Modern French Architecture', *Journal of the Royal Institute of British Architects*, 34 (19 Mar.): 323–37.

Robertson, Howard and Yerbury, F.R. (1927) 'Architecture of the Modernist School: Some French Examples', *Architect & Building News*, 117 (29 Apr.): 745–50.

*Wornum, Miriam (1928) 'Houses Ancient & Modern: a Home to Live in, not a Mansion for "Occasions"', *Architect & Building News*, 120 (20 Jul.): 72–74, 78.

*Etchells, Frederick (1928) 'Le Corbusier: a Pioneer of Modern European Architecture', *The Studio*, 96 (Sept.): 156–63.

*(1928) 'Europe Discusses the House', *Architectural Review*, 64 (Dec.): 221–22.

Adshead, Stanley (1930) 'Camillo Sitte and Le Corbusier', *Town Planning Review*, 14 (Nov.): 85–92.

(1932) 'M. Le Corbusier Plans a New Flat', *Garden Cities & Town-Planning*, 22 (Apr./May): 87–88.

(1938) 'London of the Future: a Towering City of Glass, Steel and Concrete: French Architect's Vision', *The Observer*, 23 Jan.

(1938) 'The MARS Party', *Architects' Journal*, 87 (27 Jan.): 156.

(1938) 'Le Corbusier and the Week-end Cottage', *The Builder*, 155 (28 Oct.): 820–21.

*Summerson, John (1940) 'The "Poetry" of Le Corbusier: Part of a Lecture Delivered Recently at the Warburg Institute', *Architect & Building News*, 162 (5 Apr.): 4–6.

Donner, Peter F.R. (1941) 'Criticism', *Architectural Review*, 90 (Oct.): 124–26.

*Holt, Gordon (1945) 'Corbusier', *Building*, 10 (Oct.): 256–61.

(1947) 'Ascoral: a French Reconstruction Group', *Architects' Year Book*, 2: 74–75.

*Brett, Lionel (1947) 'The Space Machine: an Evaluation of the Recent Work of Le Corbusier', *Architectural Review*, 102 (Nov.): 147–50.

Ghyka, M. (1948) 'Le Corbusier's Modulor and the Concept of the Golden Mean', *Architectural Review*, 103 (Feb.): 39–42.

Entwistle, Clive (1951) 'How to Use the Modulor', *Plan: Architectural Students Association Journal*, 9: 2–6.

(1951) 'Derivation of a Module', *Plan: Architectural Students Association Journal*, 9: 7–11.

(1951) 'Corbusier on the South Bank', *Manchester Guardian*, 11 Jul.

Moore, Olive (1951) 'Man of the Month. 112: Le Corbusier', *Scope,* Sept.: 60–73.

(1953) 'Le Corbusier', *Concrete Quarterly*, 17 (Jan./Mar.): 13–20.

(1953) 'Profile: Le Corbusier', *The Observer*, 1 Feb.

(1953) 'Dinner in Honour of M. Le Corbusier', *AA Journal*, 68 (May): 195–97.

(1954) 'Le Corbusier: the Justification of a Rebel', *Consulting Engineer*, 10 (Jan.): 14–18.

Collins, Peter (1954) 'Modulor', *Architectural Review*, 116 (Jul.): 5–8.

Fry, Maxwell (1955) 'A Discursive Commentary', *Architects' Year Book*, 6: 7–10.

Gasser, Hans-Ulrich (1955) 'The Painter Le Corbusier', *Architects' Year Book*, 6: 35–44.

Read, Herbert (1956) 'The Architect as Universal Man', *Architects' Year Book*, 7: 6–10.

Banham, Reyner (1956) 'Ateliers d'Artistes: Paris Studio Houses and the Modern Movement', *Architectural Review*, 120 (Aug.): 75–83.

Moffett, Noel (1956) 'Intuitive Flash and Reasoned Argument: a Critical Examination of Le Corbusier's Recent Work in France', *Architecture & Building*, 31 (Oct.): 368–72.

(1957) 'Le Corbusier Honoured at His Birthplace', *The Times*, 19 Nov.

(1959) 'Portrait Gallery: Le Corbusier', *Sunday Times*, 1 Feb.

Pevsner, Nikolaus (1959) 'Time and Le Corbusier', *Architectural Review*, 125 (Mar.): 158–65.

*(1959) 'Le Corbusier: a Symposium', *AA Journal*, 74 (May): 254–62.

(1959) 'Cambridge: Corbusier Honoured', *Architects' Journal*, 130 (20 Aug.): 44–45.

Girsberger, Hans (1959) 'Le Corbusier', *Adam International Review*, 275: 20–23.

Ellis, T. (1960) 'The Discipline of the Route', *Architectural Design*, 30 (Nov.): 481–82.

Banham, Reyner (1961) 'The Return Curve', *Motif*, 6 (Spring): 82–88.

Ardagh, John (1962) 'Le Corbusier: an Anti-interview', *Twentieth Century*, 1014 (Summer): 128–30.

Thomas, Harford (1962) 'Dust to Dust: Ronchamp', *The Guardian*, 17 Dec.

Morris, A.E.J. (1963) 'Le Corbusier and Precast Concrete in France', *Industrial Architecture*, 6 (Feb.): 87–91.

Atkinson, Fello (1963) 'Le Corbusier in America', *The Listener*, 16 May: 822–24.

Gardiner, Stephen (1966) 'Le Corbusier: the Second Twenty Years', *London Magazine*, 5 (Jan.): 63–66.

Wells-Thorpe, John (1966) 'Harvard's Tribute to Le Corbusier', *Architectural Review*, 139 (Jan.): 5.

(1966) 'Le Corbusier and Charlotte Perriand', *Architectural Design*, 36 (Jul.): 361.

Jencks, Charles (1967) 'Charles Jeanneret-Le Corbusier', *Arena: Architectural Association Journal*, 82 (May): 299–306.

(1967) 'Posthumous Corb', *Architectural Review*, 142 (Oct.): 247–48.

Vidler, Anthony (1968) 'The Idea of Unity and Le Corbusier's Urban Form', *Architects' Year Book*, 12: 225–37.

Crosby, Theo (1968) 'To Le Corbusier Despite Enchantment: Review Article', *Studio International*, 175 (Jan.): 52–53.

Rosie, George (1969) 'Did Le Corbusier Fall Down?', *Twentieth Century*, 1042: 16–19.

Lynton, Norbert (1969) 'Le Corbusier Sale', *The Guardian*, 1 Jul.

(1969) 'Le Corbusier Sale Brings £170,690', *The Times*, 2 Jul.

Ahluwalia, J.S. (1970) 'Human Proportion in Buildings', *Build International*, 3 (Nov.): 339–44.

Herbert, Gilbert (1972) 'Le Corbusier and the Origins of Modern Architecture in South Africa', *AAQ*, 4 (Jan./Mar.): 16–30.

*Colquhoun, Alan (1972) 'Displacements of Concepts', *Architectural Design*, 42 (Apr.): 236.

Moos, Stanislaus von (1972) 'Cartesian Curves', *Architectural Design*, 42 (Apr.): 237–39.

*Pawley, Martin (1972) 'A Philistine Attack', *Architectural Design*, 42 (Apr.): 239–40.

*Cook, Peter (1972) 'The Corb that Might Have Been', *Architectural Design*, 42 (Apr.): 240.

(1974) 'Architects of the Glass Age. 4: Le Corbusier', *Glass Age*, 17 (May): 23–26.

*Hellman, Louis (1974) 'Towards a New Look at Corbusier', *Building Design*, 216 (6 Sept.): 13–15; 217 (13 Sept.): 19–21; 218 (20 Sept.): 17–19.

Gardiner, Stephen (1974) 'Four Keys to Le Corbusier', *The Observer Magazine*, 8 Dec.

Marsh, Paul (1975) 'Le Corbusier: Warts and All', *Concrete*, 9 (Mar.): 22–24.

Gardiner, Stephen (1975) 'Meeting with a Memory', *The Listener*, 10 Apr.: 469–70.

Lowman, Joyce (1976) 'Corb as Structural Rationalist: the Formative Influence of Engineer Max DuBois', *Architectural Review*, 160 (Oct.): 229–33.

Jencks, Charles (1977) 'Le Corbusier on the Tightrope of Functionalism', in Walden, Russell (ed.) *The Open Hand: Essays on Le Corbusier*, Cambridge, MA; London: MIT Press: 186–214.

Purdy, Martin (1977) 'The Spiritual and Technological Paradox of Le Corbusier', in Walden, Russell (ed.) *The Open Hand: Essays on Le Corbusier*, Cambridge, MA; London: MIT Press: 285–321.

Sutcliffe, Anthony (1977) 'A Vision of Utopia: Optimistic Foundations of Le Corbusier's *Doctrine d'Urbanisme*', in Walden, Russell (ed.) *The Open Hand: Essays on Le Corbusier*, Cambridge, MA; London: MIT Press: 216–43.

Winter, John (1977) 'Le Corbusier's Technological Dilemma', in Walden, Russell (ed.) *The Open Hand: Essays on Le Corbusier*, Cambridge, MA; London: MIT Press: 322–47.

Nairn, Ian (1977) 'Sacred Cows: the Blind Mechanic', *Sunday Times Magazine*, 20 Feb.

Booker, Christopher (1977) 'Death of an Image', *The Spectator*, 2 Apr.: 13–14.

Goldfinger, Ernö (1978) 'Le Corbusier's Works', *The Times*, 13 Mar.

Booker, Christopher (1978) 'Nothing to Gain by Chains', *Daily Telegraph*, 22 Apr.

LeCuyer, Annette (1979) 'Spotlight on Le Corbusier', *Building Design*, 436 (9 Mar.): 28–29.

Spencer, Rory (1980) 'Corbu's Early Years', *Building Design*, 498 (30 May): 22.

Benton, Charlotte (1981) '"L'Aventure du Mobilier": Le Corbusier's Furniture Designs of the 1920s', *Journal of the Decorative Arts Society 1890–1940*, 6: 7–22.

Buchanan, Peter (1981) 'Corbu's Carnets', *Architectural Review*, 169 (May): 297–99.

Manasseh, Leonard (1981) 'Le Corbusier Lives On', *RIBA Journal*, 88 (Jun.): 12–13.

Benton, Tim (1981) 'Clues: Le Corbusier and Corbusians: Review Article', *AAQ*, 13 (Oct.): 57–58.

Baker, Geoffrey (1982) 'Le Corbusier: Sketches and Drawings', *Architectural Design*, 52 (7/8): 64–69.

Rybczynski, Witold (1982) 'Myopic Master's Indian Experience', *Building Design*, 611 (24 Sept.): 20–21.

Boralevi, A. (1983) 'The Architectural Conception of the Museum in the Work of Le Corbusier', *International Journal of Museum Management and Curatorship*, 2: 177–89.

Soth, L. (1983) 'Le Corbusier's Clients and Their Parisian Houses in the 1920s', *Art History*, 2: 188–98.

Benton, Timothy (1983) 'Drawings and Clients: Le Corbusier's Atelier Methodology in the 1920s', *AA Files*, 3 (Jan.): 42–50.

Benton, Timothy (1984) 'Le Corbusier and the Loi Loucheur', *AA Files*, 7 (Sept.): 54–60.

Tzonis, Alexander (ed.) (1985) 'Drawings from the Le Corbusier Archive', *Architectural Design*, 55 (7/8): 1–88.

Swann, Dick (1985) 'Le Corbusier on Controlling the Environment: Utilising the Design of the Wall to Control the Internal Climate ("Mur Neutralisant")', *RIBA Journal*, 92 (Feb.): 42–43.

Dunnett, James (1985) 'The Architecture of Silence: Corbusier's Motivations in House and City Design', *Architectural Review*, 178 (Oct.): 69–75.

Dunnett, James (1986) 'Le Corbusier's Machine Rhetoric', *Crafts*, 79 (Mar./Apr.): 12–13.

Poole, Cynthia (1986) 'The Garden is Above: Roof Structures in the Corbusian House', *Issue*, 5 (Jul.): 14–20.

Jencks, Charles (1986) 'The Corb Industry', *Blueprint*, 33 (Dec./Jan.): 15–17.

Ellis, Charlotte (1986) 'Machines for Sitting in', *Blueprint*, 33 (Dec./Jan.): 18–20.

Meade, Martin (1986) 'Corb in India', *Blueprint*, 33 (Dec./Jan.): 22–23.

Baker, Geoffrey and Gubler, Jacques (1987) 'Le Corbusier: Early Works by Charles-Edouard Jeanneret-Gris', *Architectural Monographs*, 12.

(1987) 'Le Corbusier/Pierre Jeanneret: Five Points Towards a New Architecture', *A3 Times*, 9 (Winter): 13.

Buchanan, Peter (1987) 'Corb, Born 1887: Master of a Misunderstood Modernism', *Architectural Review*, 181 (Jan.): 19–20.

Etlin, Richard A. (1987) 'A Paradoxical Avant-garde: Le Corbusier's Villas of the 1920s', *Architectural Review*, 181 (Jan.): 21–32.

Farmer, John (1987) 'Battered Bunkers', *Architectural Review*, 181 (Jan.): 60–61.

Loach, Judi (1987) 'Studio as Laboratory', *Architectural Review*, 181 (Jan.): 73–77.

McLeod, Mary (1987) 'Furniture and Femininity', *Architectural Review*, 181 (Jan.): 43–46.

Schumacher, Thomas (1987) 'Deep Space, Shallow Space', *Architectural Review*, 181 (Jan.): 37–42.

Spring, Martin (1987) 'Le Corbusier: Master of the Modern Movement', *Building*, 252 (27 Feb.): 38–42.

(1987) 'Le Corbusier: Observer and Observed: AJ and AR 1924–65', *Architects' Journal*, 185 (11 Mar.): 35–69.

Blanc, Alan (1987) 'Private View: Charles et Pierre', *Architects' Journal*, 185 (25 Mar.): 89.

Strathern, Oona (1987) 'Le Corbusier: a Profile', *Arts Review*, 39 (27 Mar.): 205.

Dunnett, James (1987) 'Le Corbusier: the School of Paris and the Radiant City', *Art Monthly*, 105 (Apr.): 6–9.

Gardiner, Stephen (1987) 'Le Corbusier', *Studio International*, 200 (Aug.): 12–15.

Gold, John R. (1988) 'Le Corbusier as Town Planner: Notes on New Sources from the Centenary Year', *Planning History*, 10 (1): 4–7.

Buchanan, Peter (1988) 'Commemorating Le Corbusier', *Architectural Review*, 183 (Feb.): 4–6.

Adam, Peter (1989) 'Eileen Gray and Le Corbusier', *9H*, 8: 150–53.

Benton, Charlotte (1990) 'Le Corbusier: Furniture and the Interior', *Journal of Design History*, 3 (2/3): 103–24.

Gardiner, Stephen (1990) 'Palumbo's Palaces', *The Observer Magazine*, 1 Jul.

(1990) 'Wogenscky on Corbusier', *Architects' Journal*, 192 (19/26 Dec.): 45.

Stephenson, Gordon (1991) 'Chapters of Autobiography: I–III', *Town Planning Review*, 62 (Jan.): 7–36.

Glancey, Jonathan (1992) 'A Concrete Visionary', *Independent on Sunday Review*, 19 Apr.

Bearn, Gordon C.F. (1992) 'The Formal Syntax of Modernism: Carnap and Le Corbusier', *British Journal of Aesthetics*, 32 (Jul.): 227–41.

Vago, Pierre (1992) 'The Dog and the Skeleton: Memories of Le Corbusier and Auguste Perret', *World Architecture*, 20 (Nov.): 24–25.

Macfarlane, Stephen (1994) 'Le Corbusier: Architect and Artist', *Magazine of the Royal West of England Academy*, Jul.

Fawcett, Peter (1994) 'Back to the Future with Le Corbusier', *Building Design*, 1157 (28 Jan.): 20–24.

Coll, Jaime (1995) 'Le Corbusier: Taureaux: an Analysis of the Thinking Process in the Last Series of Le Corbusier's Plastic Work', *Art History*, 18 (Dec.): 537–67.

Coll, Jaime (1996) 'Structure and Play in Le Corbusier's Art Works', *AA Files*, 31 (Summer): 3–14.

Samuel, Flora (1998) 'Le Corbusier, Women and Nature', *Issues in Architecture, Art and Design*, 5 (2): 4–19.

Loach, Judi (1998) 'Le Corbusier and the Creative Use of Mathematics', *British Journal for the History of Science*, 31: 185–215.

Brittain-Catlin, Timothy (1998) 'Le Corbusier: the Soul of an Architect', *World of Interiors*, 18 (Apr.): 170–71.

Bibliography

Naegele, Daniel (1998) 'Le Corbusier and the Space of Photography: Photo-murals, Pavilions and Multi-media Spectacles', *History of Photography*, 22 (Summer): 127–38.

Gold, John (1998) 'Creating the Charter of Athens: CIAM and the Functional City, 1933–43', *Town Planning Review*, 69 (Jul.): 225–47.

Read, Alice Gray (1998) 'Le Corbusier's "Ubu" Sculpture: Remaking an Image', *Word & Image*, 14 (Sept.): 215–26.

Arrhenius, Thordis (1999) 'Restoration in the Machine Age: Themes of Conservation in Le Corbusier's *Plan Voisin*', *AA Files*, 38 (Spring): 10–22.

Samuel, Flora (1999) 'Le Corbusier, Teilhard de Chardin and "The Planetisation of Mankind"', *Journal of Architecture*, 4 (Summer): 149–65.

Epstein-Pliouchtch, Marina (2002) 'Le Corbusier and Alexander Vesnin', *Journal of Architecture*, 7 (Spring): 57–76.

Harrod, Tanya (2002) 'Le Corbusier', *Crafts*, 176 (May/Jun.): 26–27.

Maycroft, Neil (2002) 'Repetition and Difference: Lefebvre, Le Corbusier and Modernity's (Im)moral Landscape: a Commentary', *Ethics, Place and Environment*, 5 (Jun.): 135–44.

Smith, M. (2002) 'Ethical Difference(s): a Response to Maycroft on Le Corbusier and Lefebvre', *Ethics, Place and Environment*, 5 (Oct.): 260–69.

Benton, Tim (2003) 'From Jeanneret to Le Corbusier: Rusting Iron, Bricks and Coal and the Modern Utopia', *Massilia*: 28–39.

Bergdoll, Barry (2003) 'Le Corbusier', *Burlington Magazine*, 145 (Mar.): 252–53.

Gans, Deborah (2003) 'Still Life After All: the Paintings of Le Corbusier', *Architectural Design*, 73 (May/Jun.): 25–30.

Liang, Ming-Kang (2004) 'Cyclic and Progressive: Le Corbusier's Dualistic View of History', *E.A.R.: Edinburgh Architecture Research*, 29: 53–59.

Epstein-Pliouchtch, Marina (2004) 'Le Corbusier and Walter Gropius: Contacts Prior to the Second World War', *Journal of Architecture*, 9 (Spring): 5–22.

Pearson, Christopher E.M. (2005) 'Authority Figures: Sculpture in Le Corbusier's Projects for Public Buildings, 1928–1938', *Sculpture Journal*, 13: 48–71.

Spencer, Clare (2005) 'Designing the Person: Sociological Assumptions Embodied Within the Architecture of Charles Rennie Mackintosh and Le Corbusier', *Irish Journal of Sociology*, 14 (1): 141–62.

Willmert, Tod (2006) 'The "Ancient Fire, the Hearth of Tradition": Combustion and Creation in Le Corbusier's Studio Residences', *ARQ: Architectural Research Quarterly*, 10 (1): 57–78.

Birksted, Jan Kenneth (2006) 'Beyond the Clichés of the Hand-books: Le Corbusier's Architectural Promenade', *Journal of Architecture*, 11 (Feb.): 55–132.

Richards, Simon (2007) 'The Antisocial Urbanism of Le Corbusier', *Common Knowledge*, 13 (Winter): 50–66.

Birksted, Jan Kenneth (2007) 'The Politics of Copying: Le Corbusier's Immaculate Conceptions', *Oxford Art Journal*, 30 (2): 305–326.

Attlee, James (2007) 'Towards Anarchitecture: Gordon Matta-Clark and Le Corbusier', *Tate Papers*, 7 (Spring).

Bottoms, Edward (2007) 'Corb at the AA', *AArchitecture Newsletter*, 4 (Summer): 23–25.

Sheldrake, Philip (2007) 'Placing the Sacred: Transcendence and the City', *Literature and Theology*, 21: 243–58.

Dunnett, James (2008) 'L'Homme Vert: Le Corbusier and Sustainability', *Architectural Review*, 223 (Feb.): 66–69.

6 Articles about Le Corbusier's buildings and projects

The dates of buildings and projects follow those established by the Fondation Le Corbusier.

1905 Villa Fallet (La Chaux-de-Fonds, Switzerland)

Geoffrey Baker and Gubler, Jacques (1987) 'Le Corbusier: Early Works by Charles-Edouard Jeanneret-Gris', *Architectural Monographs*, 12: 26–29, 50–57.

1907 Villa Jacquemet (La Chaux-de-Fonds, Switzerland)

Baker, Geoffrey and Gubler, Jacques (1987) 'Le Corbusier: Early Works by Charles-Edouard Jeanneret-Gris', *Architectural Monographs*, 12: 34–35, 66–73.

1907 Villa Stotzer (La Chaux-de-Fonds, Switzerland)

Baker, Geoffrey and Gubler, Jacques (1987) 'Le Corbusier: Early Works by Charles-Edouard Jeanneret-Gris', *Architectural Monographs*, 12: 30–33, 58–65.

1912 Villa Favre-Jacot (Le Locle, Switzerland)

Baker, Geoffrey and Gubler, Jacques (1987) 'Le Corbusier: Early Works by Charles-Edouard Jeanneret-Gris', *Architectural Monographs*, 12: 40–43, 82–91.

1912 Villa Jeanneret (La Chaux-de-Fonds, Switzerland)

Baker, Geoffrey and Gubler, Jacques (1987) 'Le Corbusier: Early Works by Charles-Edouard Jeanneret-Gris', *Architectural Monographs*, 12: 36–39, 74–81.

1914 Maison Dom-Ino (project)

Atkinson, George (1987) 'Standard Solution', *Building*, 252 (27 Feb.): 43.

1916 Cinéma "La Scala" (La Chaux-de-Fonds, Switzerland)

Baker, Geoffrey and Gubler, Jacques (1987) 'Le Corbusier: Early Works by Charles-Edouard Jeanneret-Gris', *Architectural Monographs*, 12: 48, 102–10.

1916 Villa Schwob (La Chaux-de-Fonds, Switzerland)

Baker, Geoffrey and Gubler, Jacques (1987) 'Le Corbusier: Early Works by Charles-Edouard Jeanneret-Gris', *Architectural Monographs*, 12: 44–47, 92–101.

Mead, Andrew (1998) 'Letter from La Chaux-de-Fonds', *Architects' Journal*, 208 (17 Sept.): 10–13.

1921 Villa Berque (Paris)

Benton, Tim (2007) *The Villas of Le Corbusier and Pierre Jeanneret 1920–1930*, New edn, Basel: Birkhäuser: 20–25.

1922 Atelier Ozenfant (Paris)

Benton, Tim (2007) *The Villas of Le Corbusier and Pierre Jeanneret 1920–1930*, New edn, Basel: Birkhäuser: 34–43.

1922 Villa Besnus (Vaucresson)

Manley, R.H. (1951) 'Le Corbusier's Buildings Improved', *Architectural Design*, 21 (Dec.): 375.

Benton, Tim (2007) *The Villas of Le Corbusier and Pierre Jeanneret 1920–1930*, New edn, Basel: Birkhäuser: 27–33.

1923 Villa Le Lac (Corseaux, Switzerland)

Dunster, David (1985) *Key Buildings of the Twentieth Century. 1: Houses 1900–1944,* London: Architectural Press: 26.

1923 Villa Marcel (Paris) (project)

Benton, Tim (2007) *The Villas of Le Corbusier and Pierre Jeanneret 1920–1930*, New edn, Basel: Birkhäuser: 78–83.

1923 Villa Ternisien (Boulogne-sur-Seine)

Dunster, David (1985) *Key Buildings of the Twentieth Century. 1: Houses 1900–1944,* London: Architectural Press: 27.

Benton, Tim (2007) *The Villas of Le Corbusier and Pierre Jeanneret 1920–1930*, New edn, Basel: Birkhäuser: 96–105.

1923 Villas La Roche-Jeanneret (Paris)

Robertson, Howard and Yerbury, F.R. (eds) (1928) *Examples of Modern French Architecture*, London: Benn: plates 43–46.

Blanc, Alan (1972) 'Charles Edouard and Pierre', *Architects' Journal*, 156 (8 Nov.): 1053.

Benton, Tim (2007) *The Villas of Le Corbusier and Pierre Jeanneret 1920–1930*, New edn, Basel: Birkhäuser: 46–77.

1923 Villas Lipchitz-Miestchaninoff (Boulogne-sur-Seine)

Benton, Tim (2007) *The Villas of Le Corbusier and Pierre Jeanneret 1920–1930*, New edn, Basel: Birkhäuser: 86–95.

1924 Lotissement de Lège

Benton, Tim (2004) 'Pessac and Lège revisited: standards, dimensions and failures', *Massilia*: 64–99.

1924 Quartiers Modernes Fruges (Pessac, Bordeaux)

Robertson, Howard and Yerbury, F.R. (1927) 'A Modern Housing Scheme', *Architect & Building News*, 118 (2 Sept.): 390–94; 118 (9 Sept.): 425–28.

Robertson, Howard and Yerbury, F.R. (eds) (1928) *Examples of Modern French Architecture*, London: Benn: plates 43–46.

Foyle, Arthur (1951) 'Le Corbusier's (1925) Housing Experiment at Pessac', *Architectural Design*, 21 (May): 142–43.

Hicks, David T. (1967) 'Corb at Pessac', *Architectural Review*, 142 (Sept.): 230.

Goldfinger, Ernö (1969) 'Le Corbusier at Pessac', *RIBA Journal*, 76 (Sept.): 381–82.

Jameson, Conrad (1972) 'Le Corbusier's Pessac: a Sociological Evaluation: an Essay-review', *AAQ*, 4 (Jul./Sept.): 51–56.

Abel, Chris (1979) 'Rationality and Meaning in Design', *Design Studies*, 1 (Oct.): 69–76.

Miller, Mervyn (1992) 'The First Machines for Living in', *World Architecture*, 19 (Sept): 48–53.

Benton, Tim (2004) 'Pessac and Lège revisited: standards, dimensions and failures', *Massilia*: 64–99.

1924 Maison Casa Fuerte (Paris) (project)

Benton, Tim (2007) *The Villas of Le Corbusier and Pierre Jeanneret 1920–1930*, New edn, Basel: Birkhäuser: 78–83.

1924 Villa Planeix (Paris)

Benton, Tim (2007) *The Villas of Le Corbusier and Pierre Jeanneret 1920–1930*, New edn, Basel: Birkhäuser: 124–35.

1925 Villa Meyer (Paris) (project)

Benton, Tim (2007) *The Villas of Le Corbusier and Pierre Jeanneret 1920–1930*, New edn, Basel: Birkhäuser: 139–47.

1925 Villa Mongermon (Paris) (project)

Benton, Tim (2007) *The Villas of Le Corbusier and Pierre Jeanneret 1920–1930*, New edn, Basel: Birkhäuser: 78–83.

1926 Maison Guiette (Antwerp)

Benton, Charlotte (1987) 'Keeping Faith with Modern History', *Building Design*, 834 (1 May): 10.

1926 Villa Cook (Boulogne-sur-Seine)

Benton, Tim (2007) *The Villas of Le Corbusier and Pierre Jeanneret 1920–1930*, New edn, Basel: Birkhäuser: 148–59.

1926 Villa Stein-de Monzie (Garches)

Robertson, Howard and Yerbury, F.R. (1929) 'The Quest of the Ideal: the Villa at Garches', *Architect & Building News*, 121 (10 May): 621–25; 121 (17 May): 653–58.

*Robertson, Mrs Howard [Doris Lewis] (1929) 'A Vision Realised: in a Country Villa Le Corbusier Proves His Theories', *The Queen*, 7 Aug.: 8–9.

McGrath, Raymond (1934) *Twentieth-Century Houses*, London: Faber: example 65.

Yorke, F.R.S. (1934) *The Modern House*, London: Architectural Press: 76–77.

*Rowe, Colin (1947) 'The Mathematics of the Ideal Villa: Palladio and Le Corbusier Compared', *Architectural Review*, 101 (Mar.): 101–04.

*Stirling, James (1955) 'Garches to Jaoul: Le Corbusier as Domestic Architect in 1927 and 1953', *Architectural Review*, 118 (Sept.): 145–51.

Dunster, David (1985) *Key Buildings of the Twentieth Century. 1: Houses 1900–1944,* London: Architectural Press: 34–37.

Ward, James (1985) 'Les Terrasses', *Architectural Review,* 177 (Mar.): 64–69.

DuBois, Marc (1987) '2 into 1', *Architectural Review,* 181 (Jan.): 33–36.

Benton, Tim (2007) *The Villas of Le Corbusier and Pierre Jeanneret 1920–1930,* New edn, Basel: Birkhäuser: 160–81.

1927 Villa Church (Ville-d'Avray)

Benton, Tim (2007) *The Villas of Le Corbusier and Pierre Jeanneret 1920–1930,* New edn, Basel: Birkhäuser: 106–23.

1927 Villa Cook (Boulogne-sur-Seine)

Yorke, F.R.S. (1934) *The Modern House,* London: Architectural Press: 45.

Benton, Tim (2007) *The Villas of Le Corbusier and Pierre Jeanneret 1920–1930,* New edn, Basel: Birkhäuser: 148–59.

1927 League of Nations (Geneva) (project)

(1927) 'League Building Designs: Artistic Paris Enraged: Political Influences Enraged: Mussolini Insists', *Manchester Guardian,* 22 Dec.

Frampton, Kenneth (1968) 'The Humanist v. the Utilitarian Ideal', *Architectural Design,* 38 (Mar.): 134–36.

Frampton, Kenneth (1982) 'Le Corbusier's Design for the League of Nations, the Centrosoyus, and the Palace of the Soviets 1926–1931' in *Le Corbusier Archive,* 3, New York, London: Garland: ix–xxii. Reprinted in *Le Corbusier: the Garland Essays* (1987) New York, London: Garland.

1927 Villas Weissenhofsiedlung (Stuttgart)

Robertson, Howard and Yerbury, F.R. (1927) 'The Housing Exhibition at Stuttgart', *Architect & Building News,* 118 (11 Nov.): 763–67; 118 (18 Nov.): 799–803; 118 (25 Nov.): 829–32.

Robertson, Howard and Yerbury, F.R. (eds) (1928) *Examples of Modern French Architecture,* London: Benn: plates 41–42.

McDonald, John (1931) *Modern Housing: a Review of Present Housing Requirements in Gt. Britain, a Resumé of Post-War Housing at Home and Abroad, and Some Practical Suggestions for Future Housing,* London: Tiranti.

Yorke, F.R.S (1934) *The Modern House,* London: Architectural Press: 72–75.

Jones, Peter Blundell (2002) *Modern Architecture Through Case Studies,* Oxford: Architectural Press, 2002: 24–27.

Mead, Andrew (2006) 'Le Corbusier/Stuttgart: it Still Looks Like a Vision of the Future That Never Came to Pass', *Architects' Journal,* 223 (1 Jun.): 25–37.

1928 Centrosoyus (Moscow)

Frampton, Kenneth (1982) 'Le Corbusier's Design for the League of Nations, the Centrosoyus, and the Palace of the Soviets 1926–1931' in *Le Corbusier Archive,* 3, New York, London :Garland: ix–xxii. Reprinted in *Le Corbusier: the Garland Essays* (1987). New York, London: Garland.

1928 Villa Ocampo (Buenos Aires) (project)

Benton, Tim (2007) *The Villas of Le Corbusier and Pierre Jeanneret 1920–1930,* New edn, Basel: Birkhäuser: 138–47.

1928 Villa Savoye (Poissy)

McGrath, Raymond (1934) *Twentieth-Century Houses,* London: Faber: example 66.

Yorke, F.R.S. (1934) *The Modern House,* London: Architectural Press: 41, 78–82.

Shand, P. Morton (1935) 'Houses 1825–1930', *Architectural Review,* 77 (Mar.): 103–04.

Gardiner, Stephen (1969) 'The Villa Savoye', *The Listener,* 30 Jan.: 145–47.

Curtis, William J.R. (1975) *Le Corbusier: the Evolution of His Architectural Language and Its Crystallization in the Villa Savoye in Poissy* [...], Milton Keynes: Open University Press.

Cohen, Stuart (1981) 'The Twentieth Century House', *Architectural Review,* 170 (Sept.): 139–40.

Benton, Tim (1984) 'Villa Savoye and the Architects' Practice', in Le Corbusier Archive, 7, New York, London: Garland: ix–xxii. Reprinted in *Le Corbusier: the Garland Essays* (1987). New York, London: Garland.

Dunster, David (1985) *Key Buildings of the Twentieth Century. 1: Houses 1900–1944,* London: Architectural Press: 54–55.

Benton, Tim (1986) 'Historic Architecture: Le Corbusier: Villa Savoye, Monument of the Modern Movement at Poissy', *Architectural Digest,* 43 (May): 182–87, 232.

Krier, Leon (1992) 'SOS Villa Savoye', *Architectural Design,* 62 (May/ Jun.): xxxvi.

Powers, Alan (1994) 'Villa Savoye, Ile-de-France: the Property of the French Government', *Country Life,* 188 (7 Jul.): 74–77.

Slessor, Catherine (1999) 'Delight', *Architectural Review,* 205 (Jun.): 98.

Jones, Peter Blundell (2002) *Modern Architecture Through Case Studies,* Oxford: Architectural Press: 111–22.

Tinniswood, Adrian (2002) *The Art Deco House: Avant-garde Houses of the 1920s–1930s,* London: Mitchell Beazley.

Weston, Richard (2004) *Plans, Sections and Elevations: Key Buildings of the Twentieth Century,* London: Lawrence King: 62–63.

Botton, Alain de (2006) *The Architecture of Happiness,* London: Hamilton.

Benton, Tim (2007) *The Villas of Le Corbusier and Pierre Jeanneret 1920–1930,* New edn, Basel: Birkhäuser: 182–201.

1929 Appartement De Beistégui (Paris)

Watt, Alexander (1936) 'Fantasy on the Roofs of Paris: the Surprising Apartment of M. Carlos De Beistégui', *Architectural Review,* 79 (Apr.): 155–59.

Benton, Tim (2007) *The Villas of Le Corbusier and Pierre Jeanneret 1920–1930,* New edn, Basel: Birkhäuser: 202–12.

1929 Armée du Salut, Cité de Refuge (Paris)

Robertson, Howard (1934) 'The Salvation Army Cité-Refuge, Paris', *Architect & Building News,* 137 (2 Feb.): 165–69.

Manley, R.H. (1951) 'Le Corbusier's Buildings Improved', *Architectural Design,* 21 (Dec.): 375.

1929 Salon d'Automne: l'Équipement de l'Habitation: des Casiers, des Chaises, des Tables

Robertson, Howard and Yerbury, F.R. (1931) 'Problems of the Interior: Rooms and Furnishings by Le Corbusier and Jeanneret and Charlotte Perriand, I & II', *Architect & Building News*, 125 (2 Jan.): 18–20; 125 (16 Jan.): 117–19.

1930 Immeuble Clarté, Geneva

Yorke, F.R.S. and Gibberd, Frederick (1937) *The Modern Flat*, London: Architectural Press: 149–52.

(1969) 'Save Clarté', *Architectural Review*, 146 (Aug.): 153.

(1970) 'Clarté Safe', *Architectural Review*, 148 (Oct.): 263.

1930 Maison Errazuriz (Chile) (project)

Yorke, F.R.S. (1934) *The Modern House*, London: Architectural Press: 37.

1930 Palace of the Soviets, Moscow (project)

Frampton, Kenneth (1982) 'Le Corbusier's Design for the League of Nations, the Centrosoyus, and the Palace of the Soviets 1926–1931' in *Le Corbusier Archive*, 3, New York, London: Garland: ix–xxii. Reprinted in *Le Corbusier: the Garland Essays* (1987) New York, London: Garland.

1930 Pavillon Suisse, Cité Universitaire (Paris)

(1933) 'Pavillon Suisse, Cité Universitaire, Paris', *Architects' Journal*, 78 (12 Oct.): 451–53.

Yorke, F.R.S. and Gibberd, Frederick (1937) *The Modern Flat*, London: Architectural Press: 181–82.

(1957) 'Thoughts in Progress: The Pavillon Suisse as a Seminal Building', *Architectural Design*, 27 (Jul.): 223–24.

Smithson, Peter (1959) 'Progress Report: Maison de Brésil, Cité Universitaire, Paris', *Architectural Design*, 29 (Jul.): 283–84.

Cantacuzino, Sherban (1966) *Great Modern Architecture*, London: Studio Vista: 84–89.

Weston, Richard (2004) *Plans, Sections and Elevations: Key Buildings of the Twentieth Century*, London: Lawrence King: 70–71.

1930 Venesta Exhibition Stand (London)

(1930) 'The Stand of Venesta Ltd at the Building Trades Exhibition', *Architect & Building News*, 124 (29 Aug.): 265.

(1930) 'An Isometric Sketch of the Venesta Stand at the Building Trades Exhibition, Olympia, London', *Architectural Review*, 68 (Sept.): plate I.

(1930) 'A Modernistic Exhibition Stand', *Architects' Journal*, 72 (24 Sept.): 444.

Pritchard, Jack (1984) *View from a Long Chair: the Memoirs of Jack Pritchard*, London: Routledge & Kegan Paul: chapter 6.

Dean, David (1985) *The Architect as Stand Designer: Building Exhibitions 1895–1983*, London: Scolar Press: 2, 53–55.

Berdini, Paolo (1987) 'Le Corbusier in England: the Venesta Stand of 1929', *AA Files*, 15 (Summer): 14.

1930 Ville Radieuse (project)

Samuel, Godfrey (1936) 'Radiant City and Garden Suburb: Corbusier's *Ville Radieuse*', *Journal of the Royal Institute of British Architects*, 43 (4 Apr.): 595–99.

Yorke, F.R.S. and Gibberd, Frederick (1937) *The Modern Flat*, London: Architectural Press: 189–98.

Frampton, Kenneth (1969) 'The City of Dialectic', *Architectural Design*, 39 (Oct.): 541–46.

1931 Immeuble Nungesser et Coli – Appartement Le Corbusier (Paris)

Robertson, Howard (1935) 'An Apartment House in Paris', *Architect & Building News*, 141 (11 Jan.): 45–49.

Shand, P. Morton (1935) 'A First Instalment of the Immediate Future: Flat of the Parc de Princes, Paris by Le Corbusier and Jeanneret', *Architectural Review*, 77 (Feb.): 73–76 (Decoration supplement, 2)

Yorke, F.R.S. and Gibberd, Frederick (1937) *The Modern Flat*, London: Architectural Press: 64–65.

1934 Maison de Week-end (La Celle Saint Cloud)

(1935) 'Two Villas by Le Corbusier & Jeanneret', *Architect & Building News*, 144 (13 Dec.): 318–23.

Benton, Tim (2002) 'The Little "Maison-de-weekend" and the Parisian Suburbs', *Massilia*, 2002: 112–19.

1935 Villa Le Sextant (La Palmyre-Les Mathes)

(1935) 'Two Villas by Le Corbusier & Jeanneret', *Architect & Building News*, 144 (13 Dec.): 318–23.

1936 Ministry of Education and Health (Rio de Janeiro)

(1943) 'Office Building for the Ministry of Education and Health, Rio de Janeiro', *Architect & Building News*, 174 (16 (Apr.): 45.

(1944) 'Ministry at Rio de Janeiro, Brazil', *Architects' Journal*, 99 (25 May): 389–92.

Loweth, Sidney (1945) 'Ministry of Education & Health, Rio de Janeiro: a Description of the New Building', *Official Architect*, 8 (Jun.): 286–91.

1945 La Sainte Baume (Saint-Maximin-la-Sainte-Baume)

Samuel, Flora (1999) 'The Philosophical City of Rabelais and St Teresa: Le Corbusier and Edward Trouin's Scheme for St Baume', *Literature and Theology*, 13 (2): 111–25.

Samuel, Flora (2001) 'Le Corbusier, Rabelais and the Oracle of the Holy Bottle', *Word & Image*, 17 (Dec.): 325–38.

1945 Unité d'Habitation, Marseilles

See also reviews of: The Marseilles Block (1953)

Macfarlane, Stephen (1949) 'Unité d'Habitation', *Plan: Architectural Students Association Journal*, 4: 23–27.

Zegel, Sylvain (1949) 'A Vertical Community: Le Corbusier's Project at Marseilles', *Manchester Guardian*, 2 Feb.

(1949) 'Le Corbusier and the Minister', *Building*, 24 (Mar.): 75.

(1949) 'Unité d'Habitation, Marseilles', *Architectural Design*, 19 (Dec.): 295–96, 308–09.

(1949) 'Unité d'Habitation Le Corbusier', *Architect & Building News*, 196 (2 Dec.): 595–98.

(1949) 'His Skyscraper Is in the Air at Both Ends: it Begins 20ft up', *Daily Mirror*, 6 Dec.

(1950) 'Progress at Marseilles', *Architectural Design*, 20 (Feb.): 51.

Moutonnier, Denise (1950) 'Flats at Marseilles', *Architectural Review*, 107 (May): 347–48.

Spiwak, H.J. (1950) 'A Vertical Community', *Building*, 25 (Dec.): 451–60.

Moffett, Noel (1951) 'Le Corbusier's Unité d'Habitation at Marseilles: a Critical Analysis', *Architectural Design*, 21 (Jan.): 1, 3–7.

Hoar, Frank (1951) 'Corbusier at Marseilles: the Unité d'Habitation', *The Builder*, 180 (12 Jan.): 40–42.

*London County Council Architect's Department Housing Division (1951) 'Le Corbusier's Unité d'Habitation', *Architectural Review*, 109 (May): 292–300.

(1951) 'High Thinking at High Lea', *Town & Country Planning*, 19 (Sept.): 407.

Pilliet, G. (1951) 'The Marseilles Flats: a French View', *Town & Country Planning*, 19 (Nov.): 496–99.

Jordan, Robert Furneaux (1951) 'Le Corbusier's Experiment at Marseilles', *The Listener*, 13 Dec.: 1011–13.

Carey, Oliver and Charlotte (1952) 'Unité d'Habitation', *Architects' Year Book*, 4: 130–36.

(1952) 'Formez Voz Piloti!', *Town & Country Planning*, 20 (Feb.): 79–80.

(1952) 'Marseilles and Le Corbusier', *Town & Country Planning*, 20 (Apr.): 181.

(1952) 'Marseille Building Experiment: Symbol of L.C.C. Dispute', *Manchester Guardian*, 9 Apr.

*Osborn, F.J. (1952) 'Concerning Le Corbusier', *Town & Country Planning*, 20 (Jul.): 311–16; 20 (Aug.): 359–63.

Fairclough, Alan (1952) 'Design for Living (on Stilts) Meets a Snag', *Daily Mirror*, 14 Jul.

(1952) 'Radiant City Lawsuit: the Rules Defied at Marseilles', *The Times*, 15 Oct.

McNab, G.A. (1952) 'L'Unité d'Habitation at Marseille: Memoir of Studies', *Quarterly Journal of the Royal Incorporation of Architects in Scotland*, 80 (Nov.): 28–43.

Dunn, Robin and Maxwell, Robert (1952) 'Radiant City', *Manchester Guardian*, 8 Nov.

(1952) 'Radiant City Lawsuit: Complaint of Brutal Realism', *The Times*, 4 Dec.

Jones, H. Dennis (1953) 'Le Corbusier's Unité d'Habitation: a French Experiment in Vertical Housing', *The Builder*, 184 (27 Mar.): 480–81.

Pilliet, G. (1953) 'The Le Corbusier Lawsuit', *Town & Country Planning*, 21 (Apr.): 173–74.

Tomkinson, Donald (1953) 'The Marseilles Experiment', *Town Planning Review*, 24 (Oct.): 193–214.

Wright, Lance (1953) 'House or Home: a Commentary on Le Corbusier's Unité d'Habitation', *Blackfriars*, 34 (Oct.): 450–55.

(1953) 'Life Chez Le Corbusier: Community Existence in New Flats', *The Times*, 20 Oct.

Dunbar, Mary (1953) 'All This and ...', *Sunday Times*, 25 Oct.

(1953) 'The Corbusier at Marseilles', *Town & Country Planning*, 21 (Dec.): 659.

(1954) 'Unité d'Habitation, Marseilles', *Architectural Design*, 24 (Jul.): 203.

Ratcliff, John (1955) 'Impressions of L'Unité d'Habitation', *AA Journal*, 71 (Jul./Aug.): 61.

Yorke, F.R.S. and Gibberd, Frederick (1958) *Modern Flats*, London: Architectural Press: 101–06.

Banham, Reyner (1966) 'Unité d'Habitation, Marseilles', in his *The New Brutalism*, London: Architectural Press: 16, 21–27.

Cantacuzino, Sherban (1966) *Great Modern Architecture*, London: Studio Vista: 90–95.

Golzari, Nassar (1987) 'The Individual and Collectivity: l'Unité d'Habitation, Marseille 1947–1952: Le Corbusier', *A3 Times*, 9 (Winter): 10–13.

Aldersey-Williams, Hugh (1989) 'A Chip Off the Old Block', *Building Design*, 958 (20 Oct.): 40–41.

Jenkins, David (1993) *Unité d'Habitation, Marseilles: Le Corbusier*, London: Phaidon Press.

Mackenzie, Christopher (1993) 'Le Corbusier in the Sun', *Architectural Review*, 192 (Feb.): 71–74.

Hussell, Lesley and Raftery, Paul (1997) 'Le Corbu', *Architectural Review*, 201 (Jun.): 76–82.

Melhuish, Clare (1999) 'Le Corbusier's Beautiful Scapegoat', *Architects' Journal*, 210 (2 Sept.): 12.

Mulhearn, Deborah (2000) 'A Life in Architecture: Tom Bloxham', *Architects' Journal*, 212 (6 Jul.): 26.

Broughton, Philip Delves (2002) 'Architect's Failed Vision Celebrated 50 Years On', *Daily Telegraph*, 17 Oct.

Weston, Richard (2004) *Plans, Sections and Elevations: Key Buildings of the Twentieth Century*, London: Lawrence King: 98–99.

Arfin, Ferne (2005) 'Concrete Ambition', *Daily Telegraph*, 5 Jun.

1946 Usine Duval (Saint Dié)

(1963) 'Le Corbusier at St Die', *Industrial Architecture*, 6 (Mar.): 165–68.

1949 Curutchet House (La Plata)

(1956) 'House of Dr Curutchet at La Plata', *Architectural Design*, 26 (Mar.): 86–88.

Dunster, David (1990) *Key Buildings of the Twentieth Century. 2: Houses 1945–1989*, London: Butterworth Architecture: 20–21.

Corona Martinez, Alfonso (1998) 'Le Corbusier's Curutchet House in La Plata', *AA Files*, 37 (Autumn): 33–39.

1950–65 Chandigarh

Drew, Jane (undated) 'Le Corbusier: the Relevance of his Work in Chandigarh for India', unpublished manuscript, Frey & Drew Papers, RIBA British Architectural Library.

Drew, Jane (1953) 'Chandigarh: Capital City', *Architects' Year Book*, 5: 56–66.

(1953) 'New Capital of the Punjab: a Geometrical City', *The Times*, 9 Jan.

Fry, Maxwell (1953) 'Chandigarh: a New Town for India', *Town & Country Planning*, 21 (May): 217–20.

(1953) 'A New City for India', *The Observer*, 10 May.

(1953) 'The Capitol, Chandigarh', *Architectural Review*, 113 (Jun.): 348.

(1953) 'Punjab's New Capital: Most Modern City', *The Times*, 8 Oct.

Cliff, Norman (1953) 'Chandigarh', *Building*, 28 (Nov.): 404–06.

(1953) 'Chandigarh: the New Capital of the Punjab', *Architect & Building News*, 204 (26 Nov.): 669–71.

(1954) 'Pioneer City of the Punjab: New Capital With a Western Look', *The Times*, 8 Jan.

(1954) 'Houses at Chandigarh', *Architects' Journal*, 119 (4 Feb.): 159–68.

Fry, Maxwell (1955) 'Chandigarh: the Capital of the Punjab', *Journal of the Royal Institute of British Architects*, 62 (Jan.): 87–94.

Fry, Maxwell (1955) 'Chandigarh: the Capital of the Punjab', *The Builder*, 188 (7 Jan.): 7–9.

Blee, Michael (1958) 'Chandigarh and the Sense of Place', *Architectural Review*, 123 (Mar.): 201–03.

(1961) 'The Civic Centre, Chandigarh', *Architectural Design*, 31 (Feb.): 63.

Cockburn, Charles and Cynthia (1963) '[Housing at Chandigarh]', *Interbuild*, 10 (Jan.): 36–40.

Mathur, Bhanu (1965) 'Chandigarh Realised', *Architects' Year Book*, 11: 270–78.

Chowdhury, Eulie (1965) 'Le Corbusier in Chandigarh: Creator and Generator', *Architectural Design*, 35 (Oct.): 504–13.

Dunn, Cyril (1966) 'Le Corbusier's City May Wither', *The Observer*, 12 Jun.

Thapar, P.N. (1966) 'Indian City as Monument to the Genius of Le Corbusier', *The Times*, 21 Nov.

Perkin, George (1967) 'Far East Journey', *Concrete Quarterly*, 75 (Oct./Dec.): 15–20.

Anand, Mulk Raj (1971) 'Postscript', *Architectural Review*, 150 (Dec.): 389–92.

*Fry, Maxwell (1975) 'With Corb in Chandigarh', *Building*, 229 (31 Oct.): 57.

Morris, A.E.J. (1975) 'Chandigarh: the Plan Corb Tore Up?', *Built Environment Quarterly*, 1 (Dec.): 229–34.

Fry, Maxwell (1977) 'Le Corbusier at Chandigarh', in Walden, Russell (ed.) *The Open Hand: Essays on Le Corbusier*, Cambridge, MA; London: MIT Press: 350–63.

Glancey, Jonathan (1978) 'Chandigarh's Reality', *Architects' Journal*, 168 (8 Nov.): 876–87.

Davies, Rob (1985) 'Chandigarh Revisited', *Building Design*, 744 (21 Jun.): 9.

Brown, Derek (1987) 'The Master Plan That Took No Account of Indian Reality', *The Guardian*, 10 Mar.

Hellier, Chris (1989) 'Chandigarh: City Out of Context', *Geographical Magazine*, 61 (Jun.): 34–36.

Caputo, Silvio (1990) 'Corb's Dream Come True?', *Building Design*, 982 (20 Apr.): 40–41.

Rattenbury, Kester (1990) 'Constant Companion', *Building Design*, 984 (4 May): 2.

Moore, Rowan (1991) 'Chandigarh Now', *Blueprint*, 80 (Sept.): 22–25.

Mackenzie, Christopher (1993) 'Le Corbusier in the Sun', *Architectural Review*, 192 (Feb.): 71–74.

Singh, Patwant (1994) 'India's Oddest City Under Threat', *The Independent*, 13 Jul.

Popham, Peter (1999) 'Flying to the Defence', *RIBA Journal*, 106 (Jan.): 6–9.

P.D. [Peter Davey] (1999) 'Celebrating Chandigarh', *Architectural Review*, 205 (Feb.): 11.

Sharp, Dennis (1999) 'Fifty Years of Love and Hate in City of the Future', *Concrete Quarterly*, 190 (Spring): 15.

Orton, Jason (2001) 'Partition's New Town', *Blueprint*, 181 (Mar.): 54–59.

Antoniou, Jim (2003) 'Chandigarh: Once the Future City', *Architectural Review*, 213 (Mar.): 70–75.

Glancey, Jonathan (2008) 'The Pearl of the Punjab', *The Guardian*, 28 Jan.

1950 Chapelle Notre Dame du Haut, Ronchamp

(1955) 'Shape without Reason', *Architects' Journal*, 121 (23 Jun.): 839–40.

Gasser, M. and H.U. (1955) 'Chapel of Notre Dame de Ronchamp', *Architectural Design*, 25 (Jul.): 214–18.

(1955) 'Notre Dame du Haut, Ronchamp', *Architect & Building News*, 208 (11 Aug.): 174–75.

(1955) 'Notre Dame du Haut at Ronchamp', *Architectural Review*, 118 (Dec.): 354.

Stirling, James (1956) 'Ronchamp: Le Corbusier's Chapel and the Crisis of Rationalism', *Architectural Review*, 119 (Mar.): 155–61.

(1956) 'Further Views of Ronchamp', *Architectural Design*, 26 (Apr.): 139.

Spence, Basil (1956) 'The Modern Church', *Journal of the Royal Institute of British Architects*, 63 (Jul.): 372–74.

Moffett, Noel (1956) 'Intuitive Flash and Reasoned Argument: The Chapel at Ronchamp', *Architecture & Building*, 31 (Nov.): 425–29.

(1958) 'Milestone or Millstone', *Architects' Journal*, 128 (18 Dec.): 870.

Howell, W.G. (1959) 'Intention and Poetry', *Architects' Journal*, 129 (19 Mar.): 460.

Banerji, Anupam (1979) 'Ronchamp: the Home of Le Corbusier's Man', *AAQ*, 11 (3): 36–48.

Glancey, Jonathan (1994) 'And Then There was Light', *The Independent*, 8 Aug.

Evans, Robin (1995) *The Projective Cast: Architecture and its Three Geometries*, Cambridge, MA; London: MIT Press: chapter 7.

Giles, Richard and Carey, Graham (1997) 'Ronchamp Revisited', *Church Building*, 47 (Sept./Oct.): 26–27.

Samuel, Flora (1997) 'A Door of Experience: Le Corbusier's Chapel at Ronchamp', *Things*, 7 (Winter): 76–85.

Samuel, Flora (1999) 'The Representation of Mary in the Architecture of Le Corbusier's Chapel at Ronchamp', *Church History*, 68 (Jun.): 398–416.

Singmaster, Deborah (1999) 'A Life in Architecture: Anthony Caro', *Architects' Journal*, 210 (28 Oct.): 32.

Towers, Brian (2001) 'Le Corbusier's Chapel: Notre Dame du Haut at Ronchamp, France', *Access by Design*, 88: 25.

Liang, Ming-Kang (2002) 'Le Corbusier's Transformation of Travel Sketches into Architecture in his Chapel at Ronchamp', *E.A.R.: Edinburgh Architecture Research*, 28: 66–77.

Weston, Richard (2004) *Plans, Sections and Elevations: Key Buildings of the Twentieth Century*, London: Lawrence King: 104–05.

Chrisafis, Angelique (2006) 'Convent to Bring Spirit Back to Chapel', *The Guardian*, 4 Dec.

(2007) 'Great Modern Buildings: Notre Dame du Haut, Le Corbusier', *The Guardian*, 18 Oct.

1950 Governor's Palace and Garden (Chandigarh)

Constant, Caroline (1987) 'From the Virgilian Dream to Chandigarh', *Architectural Review*, 181 (Jan.): 66–72.

1950 Master Plan (Bogota)(project)

(1957) 'Master Plan for Bogota, Colombia', *Architectural Design*, 27 (Jun.): 192–203.

1951 Cabanon Le Corbusier (Roquebrune Cap Martin)

Brittain-Catlin, Timothy (2003) 'Corbusier Stripped Bare', *World of Interiors*, 23 (Apr.): 144–49.

Amadei, Gian Luca (2007) '[Cabanon]', *Blueprint*, 258 (Sept.): 29.

1951 City Museum (Ahmedabad)

Lannoy, Richard (1956) 'Two Buildings in India: Museum at Ahmedabad', *Architectural Design*, 26 (Jan.): 21–22.

1951 Delgado-Chalbaud Funerary Chapel (Caracas) (project)

Lapunzina, Alejandro (2001) 'The Pyramid and the Wall: an Unknown Project of Le Corbusier in Venezuela', *ARQ: Architectural Research Quarterly*, 5 (3): 255–70.

1951 Maisons Jaoul (Neuilly-sur-Seine)

*Stirling, James (1955) 'Garches to Jaoul: Le Corbusier as Domestic Architect in 1927 and 1953', *Architectural Review*, 118 (Sept.): 145–51.

(1956) 'Jaoul Completed', *Architectural Review*, 119 (Jan.): 1.

Lasdun, Denys (1956) 'Maison Jaoul, Paris', *Architectural Design*, 26 (Mar.): 75–77.

Moffett, Noel (1956) 'Intuitive Flash and Reasoned Argument: Nantes and the Maisons Jaoul', *Architecture & Building*, 31 (Dec.): 448–52.

Yorke, F.R.S. (1957) *The Modern House*, 8th edn, London: Architectural Press: 226–27.

Banham, Reyner (1966) 'Les Maisons Jaoul. Neuilly', in his *The New Brutalism*, London: Architectural Press: 85–86, 96–101.

(1971) 'A Flight of Fancy', *Architectural Design*, 41 (Jun.): 386.

Hanson, Michael (1988) 'Converted to Corbusier', *Country Life*, 182 (4 Feb.): 86.

Seulliet, Philippe (2002) 'Le Corbusier the Colourist', *World of Interiors*, 22 (Aug.): 76–85.

Weston, Richard (2004) *Plans, Sections and Elevations: Key Buildings of the Twentieth Century*, London: Lawrence King: 108–09.

1951 Mill Owners Association Building (Ahmedabad)

Lannoy, Richard (1956) 'Two Buildings in India: Mill Owners Association Building, Ahmedabad', *Architectural Design*, 26 (Jan.): 18–20.

1951 Villa Sarabhai (Ahmedabad)

Dunster, David (1990) *Key Buildings of the Twentieth Century. 2: Houses 1945–1989*, London: Butterworth Architecture: 32–33.

Falbe, Jody de (1998) 'Le Corbusier was Here', *Elle Decoration*, 72 (Jul./Aug.): 62–71.

1951 Villa Shodhan (Ahmedabad)

Lannoy, Richard (1956) 'House at Ahmedabad', *Architectural Design*, 26 (Mar.): 93–95.

1952 Art Gallery (Chandigarh)

Ellis, Charlotte (1986) 'Chandigarh's Newest Pavilion', *The Architect: Journal of the Royal Institute of British Architects*, 93 (Sept.): 42–43.

1952 High Court (Chandigarh)

(1954) '[High Court of Justice, Chandigarh]', *Architectural Review*, 116 (Sept.): 144.

(1956) 'Progress Report: Secretariat and High Court Buildings, Chandigarh', *Architectural Design*, 26 (May): 159–62.

1952 Museum of the City (Chandigarh)

(1968) 'Chandigarh Museum', *Architectural Design*, 38 (Apr.) 152.

Morley, Grace L. (1970) 'Museums of Chandigarh', *Museum*, 23 (4): 290–99.

1952 Unité d'Habitation de Rezé (Nantes)

(1954) 'Unité no. 2: First Photographs', *Architects' Journal*, 120 (15 Jul.): 69.

(1954) '[Unité d'Habitation, Nantes]', *Architectural Review*, 116 (Sept.): 144.

(1954) 'Construction: Complete Structures: Unité d'Habitation, Nantes', *Architects' Journal*, 120 (2 Dec.): 689–93; 120 (23 Dec.) 1954: 787–89.

(1955) 'New Flats at Nantes', *Manchester Guardian*, 9 Mar.

P.R.B. [Reyner Banham] (1955) 'Nantes-Rezé', *Architectural Review*, 118 (Nov.): 327–29.

Moffett, Noel (1956) 'Intuitive Flash and Reasoned Argument: Nantes and the Maisons Jaoul', *Architecture & Building*, 31 (Dec. 1956): 448–52.

(1956) 'Flats at Nantes-Rezé, France', *Architects' Journal*, 123 (12 Jan.): 53–58.

Yorke, F.R.S. and Gibberd, Frederick (1958) *Modern Flats*, London: Architectural Press: 109–15.

(1966) 'Homes Le Corbusier Designed', *The Times Supplement on France*, 30 Jun.

1953 Couvent Sainte Marie de La Tourette (Eveux-sur-Arbresle)

(1957) 'Corb's Friary', *Architectural Review*, 121 (Jun.): 401.

(1957) 'Corbusier's Monastery Near Lyons', *Architects' Journal*, 126 (28 Nov.): 801, 832.

Evans, Kit (1958) 'Convent de La Tourette, Eveux-sur-Arbresle', *Architectural Design*, 28 (Jan.): 25.

Q.S.C. (1958) 'La Tourette', *Architectural Review*, 124 (Nov.): 339–40.

Smithson, Alison (1958) 'Convent de La Tourette, Eveux-sur-Arbresle, Nr Lyon', *Architectural Design*, 28 (Nov.): 462.

Evans, Illtud (1959) 'Le Corbusier's Masterpiece', *The Listener*, 27 Aug.: 314–17.

(1959) '[Convent de La Tourette]', *Journal of the Royal Institute of British Architects*, 66 (Sept.): 374.

Baker, William B. (1960) 'Couvent de La Tourette, Eveux-sur-Arbresle, Near Lyons, France', *Architectural Design*, 30 (Aug.): 318–20.

(1960) 'La Tourette', *Architects' Journal*, 132 (20 Oct.): 567–76.

Evans, Illtud (1960) 'La Tourette', *Architect & Building News*, 218 (2 Nov.): 555–64.

(1961) 'Couvent de La Tourette, Eveux-sur-Arbresle, France', *Architectural Design*, 31 (Jan.): 23–25.

Rowe, Colin (1961) 'Dominican Monastery of La Tourette, Eveux-sur-Arbresle, Lyons', *Architectural Review*, 129 (Jun.): 400–10.

Perkin, George (1962) 'Le Corbusier's Monastery of La Tourette: a Simple, Austere and Powerful Building with Subtly Calculated Crudities', *Concrete Quarterly*, 53 (Apr./Jun.): 14–19.

Gardiner, Stephen (1964) 'The Monastery on a Hill', *The Listener*, 2 Apr.: 545–47.

Evans, Illtud (1964) 'Heard and Seen: Le Corbusier's Monastery at Work', *Blackfriars*, 45 (Jun.): 274–75.

Cantacuzino, Sherban (1966) *Great Modern Architecture*, London: Studio Vista: 96–101.

Henze, A. (1966) *La Tourette: the Le Corbusier Monastery*, London: Lund Humphries.

(1971) 'La Tourette', *Architectural Design*, 41 (Mar.): 194.

Buchanan, Peter (1987) 'La Tourette and Le Thoronet', *Architectural Review*, 181 (Jan.): 48–59.

Singmaster, Deborah (1999) 'A Life in Architecture: Amanda Levete', *Architects' Journal*, 209 (29 Apr.): 18.

Glancey, Jonathan (2000) 'Poverty and Chastity', *The Guardian*, 25 Sept.

Worsley, Kate (2000) 'Pure Inspiration: Forty Years After Its Construction This Extraordinary Concrete Seminary in the South of France Remains a Place of Pilgrimage for Followers of Le Corbusier', *The Independent*, 28 Oct.

Glancey, Jonathan (2002) 'Divine Inspiration: it Is Severe, Cold and Crumbling, but Le Corbusier's Monastery Must Be Saved', *The Guardian*, 14 Jan.

(2003) 'Corbusier Monastery Appeals for 26 Million Pounds to Assist in Repairs', *Architects' Journal*, 217 (16 Jan.): 5.

Weston, Richard (2004) *Plans, Sections and Elevations: Key Buildings of the Twentieth Century*, London: Lawrence King: 114–15.

Coleman, Nathaniel (2005) *Utopias and Architecture*, Abingdon: Routledge: chapter 6.

O'Connor, Helen and Repellin, Didier (2007) 'Le Corbusier/La Tourette', *Architects' Journal*, 226 (12 Jul.): 27–35.

1953 Maison du Brésil, Cité Universitaire (Paris)

Rykwert, Joseph (1959) 'The Brazilian Students' Hostel in Paris', *Architecture & Building*, 34 (Oct.): 394–95.

1953 Secretariat (Chandigarh)

(1951) 'Preliminary Sketches for the Administrative Centre at Chandigarh, India', *Architect & Building News*, 200 (6 Sept.): 253.

(1956) 'Progress Report: Secretariat and High Court Buildings, Chandigarh', *Architectural Design*, 26 (May): 159–62.

(1961) 'Chandigarh: the Secretariat', *Architectural Design*, 31 (Feb.): 60–61.

1954–1965 Firminy Vert

Loach, Judi (1982) 'Le Corbusier: Politics and Laisser-Faire at Firminy', *RIBA Journal*, 89 (Nov.): 46–47.

Gardiner, Stephen (1987), 'The Master Builder', *The Observer Magazine*, 1 Mar.

1955 Assembly Building (Chandigarh)

(1961) 'The Assembly Building, Chandigarh', *Architectural Design*, 31 (Feb.): 62.

Correa, Charles (1964) 'The Assembly, Chandigarh', *Architectural Review*, 135 (Jun.): 404–12.

Weston, Richard (2004) *Plans, Sections and Elevations: Key Buildings of the Twentieth Century*, London: Lawrence King: 110–11.

1955 Tombe Le Corbusier (Roquebrune-Cap-Martin)

(1973) '[Corb's Tomb]' *Architects' Journal*, 158 (14 Nov.): 1149.

1956 Gymnasium, Sports Centre (Baghdad)

Taj-Eldin, Suzanne (1987) 'Baghdad: Box of Miracles', *Architectural Review*, 181 (Jan.): 78–83.

1956 Unité d'Habitation (Briey-en-Forêt)

(1964) 'Cite Radieuse, Briey-en-Forêt, (M. et M.), France', *Architectural Design*, 34 (Jun.): 292–303.

(1990) 'Baby Bauhaus in the Making', *Architects' Journal*, 191 (6 Jun.): 9.

1957 Museum of Western Art (Tokyo)

(1962) 'Museum of Western Art, Tokyo', *Architectural Review*, 132 (Sept.): 165–66.

1957 Unité d'Habitation (Berlin)

(1957) 'Skyscraper Type Berlin', *Architectural Design*, 27 (Sept.): 320.

(1957) 'Progress Report: Unité d'Habitation, Berlin', *Architectural Design*, 27 (Nov.): 424–25.

Yorke, F.R.S. and Gibberd, Frederick (1958) *Modern Flats*, London: Architectural Press: 130–31.

1958 Philips Pavilion (Brussels)

(1958) 'Philips Pavilion', *The Builder*, 194 (2 May): 801.

(1958) 'Philips Pavilion', *Architects' Journal*, 127 (29 May): 799.

(1958) 'Philips Pavilion', *Architect & Building News*, 214 (16 Jul.): 99.

(1958) 'Phillips [*sic*] Pavilion', *Architectural Design*, 28 (Aug.): 322.

(1958) 'Philips Pavilion', *Architectural Review*, 124 (Aug.): 83.

Sykes, J.H.M. (1959) 'The Philips Pavilion at the Brussels Exhibition: Unique Pre-Stressed Concrete Construction Housing the *Poème Electronique*', *Discovery*, 20 (Mar.): 120–24.

1960 Eglise Saint Pierre (Firminy-Vert)

(1978) 'Le Corbusier's Last Battle', *The Times*, 4 Mar.

Loach, Judi (1983) 'Le Corbusier and the Battle of Firminy', *Building Design*, 660 (7 Oct.): 24–26.

Curtis, William J.R. (2006) 'Building Study: Le Corbusier/Firminy: Is it Possible to Keep the Soul of an Architectural Idea in Such Conditions?', *Architects' Journal*, 223 (13 Apr.): 27–39.

Booth, Robert (2006) 'Hymn to a Higher Power', *The Independent Supplement Extra*, 3 May.

West, Daniel (2006) 'Le Corbusier', *Icon*, 040 (Oct.): 50.

(2006) 'Better Late Than Never', *Building Design*, 1749 (1 Dec.): 3.

Dyckhoff, Tom (2006) 'Praise Be: the Corb Is Risen', *The Times Arts Section*, 19 Dec.

Lichfield, John (2006) 'The Legacy of Le Corbusier', *The Independent*, 19 Dec.

Woodman, Ellis (2007) 'Return of the Saint', *Building Design*, 1756 (2 Feb.): 10–11.

Webb, Michael (2007) 'Miraculous Rebirth', *Architectural Review*, 221 (Mar.): 62–67.

Mamet, Catherine (2007) 'Church Triumphant', *World of Interiors*, 27 (May): 210–17.

1961 Carpenter Center for the Visual Arts, Harvard University, (Cambridge, MA)

Ritter, Paul (1962) 'Harvard Visual Arts Centre', *Architects' Journal*, 136 (12 Dec.): 1311.

(1963) 'New Buildings U.S.A.: Corb in Bloom', *Interbuild*, 10 (Feb.): 12–13.

Collins, Peter (1963) 'A Primitive at Harvard', *The Guardian*, 28 Mar.

(1963) 'Carpenter Center for the Visual Arts, Harvard', *Architectural Design*, 33 (Apr.): 190–91.

Monk, A.J. (1963) 'Carpenter Centre for the Visual Arts, Harvard University, Cambridge, Massachusetts', *Journal of the Royal Institute of British Architects*, 70 (May): 183–87.

(1963) 'The Visual Arts Centre, Harvard University: Typically Le Corbusier, and the Master's First Building in the United States', *Concrete Quarterly*, 58 (Jul./Sept.): 35–37.

Ambler, Peter (1963) 'Visual Arts Centre, Harvard University', *Architectural Review*, 134 (Dec.): 400–07.

(1964) 'Carpenter Center, Harvard', *Architect & Building News*, 225 (1 Jan.): 13–16.

Morris, James Shepherd (1966) 'Corb at Harvard', *RIBA Journal*, 73 (Aug.): 360–65.

1963 Centre Le Corbusier (Zurich)

Segal, Walter (1967) 'Corb in Corb's Country', *Architects' Journal*, 146 (29 Nov.): 1331–33.

(1967) 'Centre Le Corbusier, Zurich', *Architectural Design*, 37 (Dec.): 574–77.

(1968) 'Centre Le Corbusier, Zurich', *Architectural Review*, 143 (Mar.): 213–17.

Winter, John (1968) 'Frame and Panel Systems', *Architectural Review*, 143 (Mar.): 217–18.

Sairally, Mahmood (1968) 'Centre Le Corbusier in Zurich', *Architect & Building News*, 233 (19 Jun.): 930–35.

Gardiner, Stephen (1972) 'Corbusier's Ideal Home', *The Observer Magazine*, 29 Oct.

Sutherland, Charlie and Hussey, Charlie (1998) 'Steel Design: Building Favourites', *Architects' Journal*, 208 (23 Jul.): 45.

1964 French Embassy, Brasilia (project)

Colquhoun, Alan (1966) 'Formal and Functional Interactions: a Study of Two Late Projects by Le Corbusier', *Architectural Design*, 36 (May): 221–34. Reprinted in his *Essays in Architectural Criticism: Modern Architecture and Historical Change* (1981), Cambridge, MA; London: MIT Press.

1964 Hospital, Venice (project)

(1965) 'Corb's Skylit Beds', *Architectural Review*, 137 (Jun.): 403.

(1965) 'Italy: Hospital by Le Corbusier', *Interbuild*, 11 (Jul.): 10–11.

(1965) 'Corb', *Architectural Review*, 138 (Oct.): 235.

Colquhoun, Alan (1966) 'Formal and Functional Interactions: a Study of Two Late Projects by Le Corbusier', *Architectural Design*, 36 (May): 221–34. Reprinted in his *Essays in Architectural Criticism: Modern Architecture and Historical Change* (1981), Cambridge, MA; London: MIT Press.

(1967) 'Le Corbusier Hospital Chapel, Venice', *Architectural Design*, 37 (Jun.): 270–74.

(1971) '[Venice Hospital]', *Architectural Review*, 149 (May): 318.

7   Catalogues and reviews of Le Corbusier exhibitions

1953 (Institute of Contemporary Arts, London): Le Corbusier: Painting, Drawings, Sculpture and Tapestry, 1918–1953

(1953) 'A Corbusier Show', *Manchester Guardian*, 23 Apr.

(1953) 'Corb Again', *Architects' Journal*, 117, (30 Apr.): 539, 541–42.

(1953) 'Le Corbusier as a Painter: London Exhibition', *The Times*, 30 Apr.

J.B. [John Berger] (1953) 'Le Corbusier at the ICA', *New Statesman & Nation*, 9 May: 548.

*Banham, Reyner (1953) 'Painting and Sculpture of Le Corbusier', *Architectural Review*, 113 (Jun.): 401–04.

(1953) 'A Neglected Painter', *Building*, 28 (Jun.): 237.

1954 (Hanover Gallery, London): Le Corbusier

Gasser, Hans Ulrich 'Le Corbusier's Paintings', *Architectural Design*, 24 (Dec.): 380.

1958 (Walker Art Gallery, Liverpool)/1959 (Building Centre, London): Le Corbusier: Architecture, Painting, Sculpture, Tapestries

Crosby, Theo (ed.) (1958) *Le Corbusier: Architecture, Painting, Sculpture, Tapestries*, Liverpool, Walker Art Gallery, 1958; London, Building Centre, 1959. Exhibition catalogue.

(1958) 'All-Round View of Le Corbusier: Birthday Exhibition Reaches England', *The Times*, 9 Dec.

Sewter, A.C. (1958) 'The Humanism of Le Corbusier: a Striking Exhibition', *Manchester Guardian,* 10 Dec.

Jordan, Robert Furneaux (1958) 'Le Corbusier on Show', *The Observer*, 14 Dec.

(1958) 'Le Corbusier in Liverpool', *Architect & Building News*, 214 (17 Dec.): 794.

Fry, Maxwell (1958) 'Opening of Le Corbusier's Exhibition', *Architect & Building News*, 214 (17 Dec.): 801–03.

O'Donahue, James and Wilson, Colin R. (1958) 'Corbusier Exhibition, Liverpool', *Architects' Journal*, 128 (18 Dec.): 873–75.

Thearle, Herbert (1958) 'Le Corbusier at Liverpool', *The Builder*, 195 (19 Dec.): 1031–32.

Drew, Jane (1959) 'An Exercise in One, Two & Three Dimensions', *Architecture & Building*, 34 (Feb.): 60–61.

(1959) 'Le Corbusier Exhibition at the Building Centre, 3 Feb.–6 Mar', *Architectural Design*, 29 (Feb.): 55.

(1959) 'Le Corbusier Exhibition', *Architectural Review,* 125 (Feb.): 84–85.

Mullaly, Terence (1959) 'Painting and Sculpture in Le Corbusier Exhibition', *Daily Telegraph*, 4 Feb.

Gowan, James (1959) 'Le Corbusier Exhibition, London, 1959', *Architect & Building News*, 215 (11 Feb.): 177–80.

Rowe, Colin (1959) 'Le Corbusier: Utopian Architect', *The Listener*, 12 Feb.: 287–89.

Marriott, Basil (1959) 'Le Corbusier Exhibition', *The Builder*, 196 (13 Feb.): 305.

(1959) 'The Corb Exhibition', *Architect & Building News*, 215 (18 Feb.): 208–09.

Mudie, Robin (1959) 'Lay Eyes on Corb', *Architects' Journal*, 129 (19 Mar.): 427, 429.

Grenfell Baines, George (1959) 'A Cat Looks ...', *Town & Country Planning*, 27 (Apr.): 147–48.

1987 (Hayward Gallery, London): Le Corbusier: Architect of the Century

Pearman, Hugh (1986) 'Building Corb on London's South Bank', *Blueprint*, 33 (Dec./Jan.): 6.

Raeburn, Michael and Wilson, Victoria (eds) (1987) *Le Corbusier: Architect of the Century*, London: Arts Council of Great Britain. Exhibition catalogue.

Sudjic, Deyan (1987) 'The Architect as Outsider', *Arena* (Spring): 12–13.

Baker, Tom (1987) 'Le Corbusier', *The Face*, 38 (Mar.): 96–97.

Moore, Rowan (1987) 'Le Corbusier at the Hayward', *Vogue* (Mar.): 22–24.

Seymour, Helen (1987) 'Le Corbusier: Expose', *Design Week*, 2 (10): 14.

Sudjic, Deyan (1987) 'Genius or Vandal', *London Daily News*, 2 Mar.

Barker, Paul (1987) 'Making the Point', *Evening Standard*, 3 Mar.

*Appleyard, Brian (1987) 'Architect of Our Sky-High Life', *The Times*, 4 Mar.

Amery, Colin (1987) 'A Dangerous Genius', *Financial Times*, 5 Mar.

Latham, Ian (1987) 'Homage to Modernism', *Building Design*, 826 (6 Mar.): 2.

(1987) 'The Master Concrete Pourer', *The Economist*, 7 Mar.: 98.

Pawley, Martin (1987) 'Changer of the Garde', *The Guardian*, 7 Mar.

Taylor, John Russell (1987) 'A Mystical Realist', *The Times*, 7 Mar.

Vaizey, Marina (1987) 'Le Corbusier: the Prince of Space', *Sunday Times*, 8 Mar.

Gardiner, Stephen (1987) 'The Right Man Using the Right Means', *The Observer*, 8 Mar.

Shepherd, Michael (1987) 'A Genius Frustrated', *Sunday Telegraph*, 8 Mar.

*Stamp, Gavin (1987) 'The Consequences of Le Corbusier', *Daily Telegraph*, 9 Mar.

Buchanan, Peter (1987) 'Complex Corb', *Architects' Journal*, 185 (11 Mar.): 30–31.

Gradidge, Roderick (1987) 'Father of the Concrete Jungle? Le Corbusier at the Hayward', *Country Life*, 181 (12 Mar.): 102–03.

Nuttgens, Patrick (1987) 'Man of Concrete', *The Listener*, 12 Mar.: 32–33.

(1987) 'Pilgrim's Guide to Saint Corb', *Building*, 252 (13 Mar.): 20.

Games, Stephen (1987) 'Coping with Architect's Block', *The Independent*, 13 Mar.

Stamp, Gavin (1987) 'Misunderstood Modernism?', *The Spectator*, 14 Mar.: 38–39.

(1987) 'All That Glisters', *Architects' Journal*, 185 (18 Mar.): 6–7.

(1987) 'Old Pre-Stressed Corbusier: the Man Who Started the Nightmare', *Punch*, 18 Mar.: 59.

Blanc, Alan (1987) 'Behind the Façade', *Building Design*, 828 (20 Mar.): 16–17.

Harbison, Robert (1987) 'Architectural Alchemy', *Building Design*, 828 (20 Mar.): 14–15.

Hatton, Brian and Benton, Tim (1987) 'Rhetoric and Reality', *Building Design*, 828 (20 Mar.): 18–21.

Hatts, Leigh (1987) 'Genius of the Odd and Bizarre', *Catholic Herald*, 20 Mar.

Bayley, Stephen (1987) 'Fantasy and Reality', *Evening Standard*, 26 Mar.

Berryman, Larry (1987) 'Le Corbusier: Architect of the Century', *Arts Review*, 39 (Mar.): 204–05.

Clarke, Michael (1987) 'Master of Space', *Times Educational Supplement*, 27 Mar.: 32.

Perkin, George (1987) 'From Corb to Classicism', *Concrete Quarterly*, 153 (Apr./Jun.): 36–39.

(1987) 'Corb out of Context', *Designers' Journal,* 25 (Apr.): 6.

Homes, Bill (1987) 'Vers un Corb', *Art Monthly*, Apr.: 9–12.

Pawley, Martin (1987) 'No Information at the Hayward's Corbusier Exhibition', *The Architect: Journal of the Royal Institute of British Architects*, 94 (Apr.): 83.

Sawtell, Jeff (1987) 'Le Corbusier: Legend in His Own Lifetime', *Morning Star*, 1 Apr.

Sewell, Brian (1987) 'Over the Credit Limit', *Evening Standard*, 2 Apr.

Bibliography

Ambrose, Eric (1987) 'Understanding Corbusier', *Building Design*, 830 (3 Apr.): 13.

(1987) 'A Critical Century', *Building Design*, 831 (10 Apr.): 16–17.

(1987) 'Corbusier Considered', *Building Design*, 833 (24 Apr.): 14–15.

Nugent, Kenneth (1987) 'Le Corbusier: Concrete Abstractions', *The Month*, 20 (May): 191–95.

Broadbent, Geoffrey (1987) 'Confusion at the Hayward', *Building Design*, 837 (22 May): 14.

(1987) 'Le Corbusier Reviewed', *Building Design*, 838 (29 May): 18–19.

Buchanan, Peter (1987) 'Exhibiting Architecture', *Architectural Review*, 181 (Jun.): 4–6.

Spurrier, Raymond (1987) 'Corbu: the Paradoxical Utopian', *The Artist*, 102 (Jun.): 38–39.

1988 (ASB Gallery, London): Le Corbusier Paintings

Buchanan, Peter (1988) 'Concrete Vision', *Architects' Journal*, 187 (9 Mar.): 24–25.

Bowness, Sophie (1988) 'Le Corbusier Was a Painter', *Studio International*, 201 (Apr.): 44–47.

2001 (City Art Gallery, Leeds): Le Corbusier: the Sculptural Collaboration with Savina

(2001) 'Nationwide Choice: Le Corbusier Exhibition at Leeds City Hall, Feb. 3–Apr. 29, 2001', *The Times*, 3 Feb.

Mead, Andrew (2001) 'Different Dimension', *Architects' Journal*, 213 (1 Mar.): 68.

8   Le Corbusier and the RIBA Royal Gold Medal

(1953) 'Foreword', *Architects' Year Book*, 5: 7–8.

(1953) 'Architectural Honour for Le Corbusier: Royal Gold Medal Award', *The Times*, 27 Jan.

(1953) 'A Great Architect', *The Times*, 27 Jan.

(1953) 'Royal Gold Medal for Architecture, 1953', *Architectural Design*, 23 (Feb.): 55–56.

(1953) 'Royal Gold Medal', *Building*, 28 (Feb.): 41.

(1953) 'Royal Gold Medal 1953', *Journal of the Royal Institute of British Architects*, 60 (Feb.) 1953: 126.

(1953) 'R.I.B.A. Gold Medal', *Architectural Review*, 113 (Apr.): 271.

*(1953) 'Presentation of the Royal Gold Medal to Le Corbusier (Charles Edouard Jeanneret)', *Journal of the Royal Institute of British Architects*, 60 (Apr.): 215–18.

(1953) 'Architects Honour Le Corbusier', *The Times*, 1 Apr.

(1953) 'Morality and Architecture', *Manchester Guardian*, 1 Apr.

(1953) 'Le Corbusier Accepts Royal Gold Medal', *Architects' Journal*, 117 (9 Apr.): 451.

(1953) 'The Royal Gold Medallist, 1953: Presentation to M Le Corbusier at the RIBA', *The Builder*, 184 (10 Apr.): 556–57.

(1987) '[Sketches Made by Le Corbusier in 1953 When in London to Accept the RIBA Royal Gold Medal]', *Building Design*, 834 (1 May): 1.

(1987) 'Corb's Revenge', *Architects' Journal*, 185 (6 May): 9.

9   Obituaries and appreciations

(1965) 'Architect Dies on Swim', *Daily Sketch*, 28 Aug.

(1965) 'Architect of Fantasy World', *Northern Echo*, 28 Aug.

(1965) 'Architects' Picasso is Dead', *Daily Mirror*, 28 Aug.

(1965) 'Corbusier Dies in Holiday Swim', *Daily Worker*, 28 Aug.

(1965) 'Corbusier Dies While Swimming', *Sheffield Telegraph*, 28 Aug.

(1965) 'Death of a Giant', *Daily Telegraph*, 28 Aug.

Ellison, John (1965) 'The City Maker', *Daily Express*, 28 Aug.

(1965) 'Famous French Architect Drowned', *Birmingham Post*, 28 Aug.

Gillie, Darsie (1965) 'Corbusier Drowned After Heart Attack', *The Guardian*, 28 Aug.

Hopkirk, Peter (1965) 'The Man Who Built Tomorrow', *The Sun*, 28 Aug.

(1965) 'Le Corbusier: a Chapter Ends', *Financial Times*, 28 Aug.

(1965) 'Le Corbusier, Architect of the Century, Dies', *Yorkshire Post*, 28 Aug.

(1965) 'Le Corbusier, Architect: Controversial High Priest', *Daily Telegraph*, 28 Aug.

(1965) 'Le Corbusier Dies While Swimming', *Glasgow Herald*, 28 Aug.

(1965) 'Le Corbusier, the Free-Style Architect, Dies', *Liverpool Post*, 28 Aug.

(1965) 'Le Corbusier: the Outstanding Architectural Figure of His Time', *The Times*, 28 Aug.

(1965) 'Leading World Architect Dies While Bathing', *Nottingham Guardian Journal*, 28 Aug.

(1965) 'Noted Architect Dies While Swimming', *East Anglian Times*, 28 Aug.

(1965) 'Pioneer Architect Drowned', *Western Mail*, 28 Aug.

Rowntree, Diana (1965) 'Le Corbusier', *The Guardian*, 28 Aug.

Smyth, Robin (1965) 'Corbu: Genius Who Made Homes Reach for the Sky', *Daily Mail*, 28 Aug.

(1965) 'World-famous Architect is Drowned', *Aberdeen Press & Journal*, 28 Aug.

Harling, Robert (1965) 'Urban Visionary', *Sunday Times*, 29 Aug.

Jordan, Robert Furneaux (1965) 'Corbusier: Greatest of the Lot', *The Observer*, 29 Aug.

Clifton-Taylor, Alec (1965) 'Le Corbusier', *The Observer*, 12 Sept.

Smyth, Geoffrey (1965) 'Le Corbusier', *Arena: Architectural Association Journal*, 81 (Sept./Oct.): 5–9.

*Yates, Peter (1965) 'Le Corbusier: a Personal Appreciation', *Northern Architect: Journal of the Northern Architectural Association*, Sept.: 566. Reprinted in *The Builder* (1965), 209 (22 Oct.): 865.

Hollingworth, Clare (1965) 'Paris Pays Homage to Le Corbusier', *The Guardian*, 2 Sept.

(1965) 'Le Corbusier', *The Builder*, 209 (3 Sept.): 491.

G.J.H. [G.J. Howling] (1965) 'A Personal Appreciation', *The Builder*, 209 (3 Sept.): 491.

Causey, Andrew (1965) 'Le Corbusier', *Illustrated London News*, 4 Sept.: 7–9.

(1965) 'Corb', *Architects' Journal*, 142 (8 Sept.): 523–26.

*Segal, Walter (1965) 'The Unknown Giant', *Architects' Journal*, vol. 142 (8 Sept.): 526–30.

Zinkin, Taya (1965) 'No Compromise with Corbusier', *The Guardian*, 11 Sept.

Goulden, Gontran (1965) 'Le Corbusier', *Architect & Building News*, 227 (15 Sept.): 486.

*Powell, Philip and Drew, Jane (1965) 'Le Corbusier: Appreciations', *Architects' Journal*, 142 (15 Sept.): 1592–93.

Tallet, Margaret (1965) 'Le Corbusier', *The Guardian*, 16 Sept.

(1965) 'Corb', *RIBA Journal*, 72 (Oct.): 483.

Goldfinger, Ernö (1965) 'Vers une Architecture', *Architectural Design*, 35 (Oct.): 474–75.

(1965) 'Le Corbusier (1887–1965)', *Town & Country Planning*, 33 (Oct.): 365.

Drew, Jane (1965) 'A Personal Note', *Journal of the Town Planning Institute*, 51 (Nov.): 380–81.

Tetlow, John (1965) 'Le Corbusier', *Journal of the Town Planning Institute*, 51 (Nov.): 380.

Ambrose, Eric (1965) 'The End – and the Beginning of a Chapter', *Ideal Home*, 92 (Dec.): 113–14, 116.

Drew, Jane (1977) 'Le Corbusier as I Knew Him', in Walden, Russell (ed.) *The Open Hand: Essays on Le Corbusier*, Cambridge, MA; London: MIT Press: 364–73.

10 Influence, reaction and reputation

Jenkins, Gilbert H. (1927) 'Modernism in Architecture', *Architectural Association Journal*, 53 (Nov.): 151–71.

Robertson, Howard (1927) 'The English House by Modern Methods', *The Queen*, 14 Dec.: 16–18.

Shackleton, Edith (1927) 'Let's Make Ourselves More Comfortable: Why Go on Living in Houses a Century Behind Our Needs?', *Evening Standard*, 17 Nov.

Shackleton, Edith (1927) 'A Machine for Living in: Quaint Old Worldery as "Sham-Sentimental Bosh"', *Evening Standard*, 24 Nov.

Robertson, Howard and Yerbury, F.R. (1928) 'England, France and the Ultra Moderns', *Architect & Building News*, 119 (27 Jan.): 153–56.

H.H.D. (1928) 'Modernist Movement in Architecture: Exhibition in Liverpool', *Manchester Guardian*, 25 Apr.

(1928) 'Modernism in Architecture', *Architect & Building News*, 119 (25 May): 766–69.

Stratton, P.M. (1928) 'The Line from France', *Architectural Review*, 64 (Jul.): 1–2.

Todd, Dorothy (1929) 'The Modern Interior', *Decorative Art: 'The Studio' Year Book*: 59–84.

(1929) 'Modernism in Architecture: Some British Examples: the Rise of a New Style', *The Observer*, 10 Feb.

Summerson, John (1930) 'Modernity in Architecture: an Appeal for the New Style', *The Scotsman*, 21 Feb.

Maufe, Mrs Edward (1931) 'The Home Beautiful and Quiet: a Woman's View on Decoration', *Manchester Guardian*, 10 Dec.

(1933) 'Is Modern Architecture on the Right Track?', *The Listener*, 26 Jul.: 123–28.

Blomfield, Reginald and Connell, Amyas (1934) 'For and Against Modern Architecture', *The Listener*, 28 Nov.: 885–88.

Reilly, C.H. (1935) 'The Modern Dwelling-House', *Manchester Guardian*, 16 Aug.

(1936) 'Dulce Domum', *The Times English Home Number*, 3 Mar.

MARS Group (1938) *New Architecture: an Exhibition of the Elements of Modern Architecture*, London: MARS Group.

Fry, Maxwell (1941) 'The New Britain Must Be Planned', *Picture Post*, 4 Jan.: 16–20.

Reilly, C.H. (1941) 'Mechanised City of Towers: an Architect's Dream', *Manchester Guardian*, 18 Mar.

*Wilson, Colin St John (1952) 'The Vertical City', *The Observer*, 17 Feb.

Smithson, Alison and Peter (1953) 'An Urban Project', *Architects' Year Book*, 5: 48–55.

Smithson, Alison and Peter (1955) 'The Built World: Urban Reidentification', *Architectural Design*, 25 (Jun.): 185–88.

(1956) 'Experiment and Inspiration in L.C.C. Building: New Schools and Housing Estates', *Manchester Guardian*, 25 May.

(1957) 'The Continuous Street', *Town & Country Planning*, 25 (Apr.): 167–78.

Smithson, Alison (ed.) (1962) 'Team 10 Primer', *Architectural Design*, 32 (Dec.): 559–602.

(1965) 'Builder of Genius', *Glasgow Herald*, 28 Aug.

*Spence, Basil (1965) 'Our Debt to Le Corbusier', *Sunday Telegraph*, 29 Aug.

Wilson, Colin St John (1965) 'The Committed Architect', *Society of Architectural Historians Journal*, 24 (Mar.): 65.

Hinton, Denys (1965) 'Corb', *Architects' Journal*, 142 (29 Sept.): 721.

Berger, John (1965) 'The Only Machine for Living in', *New Statesman*, 8 Oct.: 533.

(1965) 'Le Corbusier: His Impact on Four Generations', *RIBA Journal*, 72 (Oct.): 497–500.

Banham, Reyner (1965) 'Corbolatry at County Hall', *New Society*, 4 Nov.: 26–27.

*Banham, Reyner (1966) 'Le Corbusier: the Last Formgiver', *Architectural Review*, 140 (Aug.): 97–108.

Giedion, Sigfried (1967) 'Le Corbusier and the Coming Generation', in *Planning and Architecture: Essays Presented to Arthur Korn by the Architectural Association*, London: Barrie & Rockliff: 87–90.

Martin, Leslie (1967) 'Architects' Approach to Architecture', *RIBA Journal*, 74 (May): 191–200.

Banham, Reyner (1967) 'Gurus of Our Time. 1: Le Corbusier', *New Society*, 14 Sept.: 353–55.

Lambert, Richard (1968) 'Not So Skyscraping Now', *The Times Building Supplement*, 12 Nov.

Fawcett, Austen P. (1974) 'New Assessments of Le Corbusier', *Yorkshire Architect*, 35 (Mar./Apr.) 1974: 21–23.

Rowe, Colin and Koetter, Fred (1975) 'Collage City', *Architectural Review*, 158 (Aug.): 66–91.

Jameson, Conrad (1977) 'British Architecture: Thirty Wasted Years', *Sunday Times Magazine*, 6 Feb.

*Booker, Christopher (1977) 'The Price of Le Corbusier', *The Spectator*, 26 Mar.: 11–12.

*Windsor, Phil (1977) 'How Wrong Was Le Corbusier?: How Much of the Text of Le Corbusier's *Towards a New Architecture* Is Still Relevant Today?', *The Architect*, Apr.: 36–37.

Bibliography

Booker, Christopher (1978) 'Nothing to Gain but Chains', *Daily Telegraph*, 22 Apr.

Marmot, Alexi (1981) 'The Legacy of Le Corbusier and High-rise Housing', *Built Environment*, 7 (2): 82–95.

Lipstadt, Hélène (1983) 'Polemic and Parody in the Battle for British Modernism', *AA Files*, 3 (Jan.): 68–76.

Scruton, Roger (1984) 'Keep this Monster in Its Grave', *The Times*, 1 May.

Ezard, John (1986) 'Dissection of Ronan Point Begins', *The Guardian*, 17 May.

Forty, Adrian (1987) 'Le Corbusier's British Reputation,' in Raeburn, Michael and Wilson, Victoria (eds) *Le Corbusier: Architect of the Century*, London: Arts Council of Great Britain: 35–41.

Lyall, Sutherland (1987) 'Guru or Anti-Christ?', *Building*, 252 (27 Feb.) 44–45.

*Palmes, James (1987) 'The Relevance of Le Corbusier', *The Architect: Journal of the Royal Institute of British Architects*, 94 (Mar.): 48–52.

Latham, Ian (1987) 'Missed Opportunity', *Building Design*, 827 (13 Mar.): 2.

*Booker, Christopher (1987) 'Corbusier: Architect of Disaster for the Millions Condemned to Live in a Concrete Jungle', *Daily Mail*, 16 Mar.

Atwell, David (1987) 'Après Le Corbusier', *Building Design*, 829 (27 Mar.): 9.

Dunnett, James (1987) 'Words of Wisdom', *Building Design*, 838 (29 May): 20–21. On John Rodker, Le Corbusier's first English publisher, and Frederick Etchells, his translator.

Coleman, Alice (1987) 'Planners' Crimes: Dreams That Went Sour', *Geographical Magazine*, 59 (Nov.): 560–65.

Dunnett, James (1989) 'Heirs to Modernism', *World Architecture*, 1 (Apr.): 66–71.

Dunnett, James (1989) 'Object-lesson', *Architects' Journal*, 189 (14 Jun.): 26–33.

Maxwell, Robert (1994) 'Truth Without Rhetoric: the New Softly Smiling Face of Our Discipline', *AA Files*, 28 (Autumn): 3–11.

Neumann, Eve-Marie (1996) 'Architectural Proportion in Britain 1945–1957', *Architectural History*, 36: 197–221.

Weston, Richard (2000) 'Influence Without Anxiety: Jørn Utzon, Silkeborg Museum and Le Corbusier', *ARQ: Architectural Research Quarterly*, 4 (2): 106–21.

Gregory, Robert (2000) 'Heroism Versus Empiricism', *Architectural Review*, 207 (Jan.): 68–73.

Dunnett, James (2000) 'Future Cities: Contemplative or Delirious?', *Architects' Journal*, 212 (6 Jul.): 20–21.

Fawcett, A. Peter (2001) 'Learning from Le Corbusier and Lubetkin: the Work of Ryder and Yates', *Journal of Architecture*, 6 (Autumn): 225–48.

Dunnett, James (2001) 'Tower Power', *Building Design*, 1513 (7 Dec.): 8.

Hartoonian, Gevork (2001) 'The Limelight of the House-machine', *Journal of Architecture*, 6 (Spring): 53–79.

Calder, Barnabas (2007) 'The Education of a Modern Architect: Denys Lasdun in the 1930s', *Twentieth Century Architecture*, 8: 117–27.

Knevitt, Charles (2007) 'Life is Right: Le Corbusier's British Legacy', in *Le Corbusier: the Art of Architecture*, Weil am Rhein: Vitra Design Museum: 359–69.

Pevsner, Nikolaus (2007) 'The Modern Movement in Britain', *Twentieth Century Architecture*, 8: 11–38.

11 General and related titles

Allan, John (2002) *Berthold Lubetkin*, London: Merrell.

Banham, Reyner (1976) *Megastructure: Urban Futures of the Recent Past*, London: Thames & Hudson.

Banham, Reyner (1960) *Theory and Design in the First Machine Age*, London: Architectural Press.

Banham, Reyner (1966) *The New Brutalism: Ethic or Aesthetic*, London: Architectural Press.

Benton, Tim (2006) *The Modernist Home*, London: V&A Publications.

Benton, Tim, Benton, C. and Sharp, D. (1975) *Form and Function: a Source Book for the History of Architecture and Design 1890–1939*, London: Crosby Lockwood Staples.

Bertram, Anthony (1935) *The House: a Machine for Living in: a Summary of the Art and Science of Homemaking Considered Functionally*, London: Black.

Blomfield, Reginald (1934) *Modernismus*, London: Macmillan.

Bullock, Nicholas (2002) *Building the Post-war World: Modern Architecture and Reconstruction in Britain*, London: Routledge.

Coleman, Alice (1990) *Utopia on Trial: Vision and Reality in Planned Housing*, Rev. edn, London: Shipman.

Colquhoun, Alan (1989) *Modernity and the Classical Tradition: Architectural Essays 1980–1987*, Cambridge, MA; London: MIT Press.

Colquhoun, Alan (2002) *Modern Architecture*, Oxford: Oxford University Press.

Dannatt, Trevor (1959) *Modern Architecture in Britain: Selected Examples of Recent Building*, London: Batsford.

Darling, Elizabeth (2007) *Re-forming Britain: Narratives of Modernity Before Reconstruction*, Abingdon: Routledge.

Dean, David (1983) *The Thirties: Recalling the English Architectural Scene*, London: Trefoil.

Doordan, Dennis P. (2001) *Twentieth-century Architecture*, London: Lawrence King.

Elwall, Robert (2000) *Building a Better Tomorrow: Architecture in Britain in the 1950s*, Chichester: Wiley-Academy.

Esher, Lord [Lionel Brett] (1981) *A Broken Wave: the Rebuilding of England 1940–1980*, London: Allen Lane.

Frampton, Kenneth (2007) *Modern Architecture: a Critical History*, 4th edn, London: Thames & Hudson.

Glendinning, Miles and Muthesius, Stefan (1994) *Tower Block: Modern Public Housing in England, Scotland, Wales and Northern Ireland*, New Haven, CT: Yale University Press.

Gloag, John (1931) *Men and Buildings*, London: Country Life.

Gold, John R. (1997) *The Experience of Modernism: Modern Architects and the Future City 1928–53*, London: Spon.

Gold, John R. (2007) *The Practice of Modernism: Modern Architects and Urban Transformation 1954-1972*, Abingdon: Routledge.

Higgott, Andrew (2007) *Mediating Modernism: Architectural Cultures in Britain*, Abingdon: Routledge.

Hill, Oliver (1950) *Fair Horizon: Buildings of Today*, London: Collins.

Jackson, Anthony (1970) *The Politics of Architecture: a History of Modern Architecture in Britain*, London: Architectural Press.

Jencks, Charles (1985) *Modern Movements in Architecture*, 2nd edn, Harmondsworth: Penguin Books.

Lyall, Sutherland (1980) *The State of British Architecture*, London: Architectural Press.

Maxwell, Robert (1972) *New British Architecture*, London: Thames & Hudson.

Pawley, Martin (2000) *20th Century Architecture: a Reader's Guide*, Oxford: Architectural Press.

Pevsner, Nikolaus (1960) *Pioneers of Modern Design*, Rev edn, Harmondsworth: Penguin Books.

Powers, Alan (2005) *Modern: the Modern Movement in Britain*, London: Merrell.

Powers, Alan (2007) *Britain*, London: Reaktion.

Richards, J.M. (1940) *An Introduction to Modern Architecture*, Harmondsworth: Penguin Books.

Robertson, Howard and Yerbury, F.R. (1989) *Travels in Modern Architecture 1925–1930*, London: Architectural Association.

Sharp, Dennis (2002) *Twentieth Century Architecture: a Visual History*, Rev. edn, Mulgrave: Images.

Smithson, Alison (1982) *The Emergence of Team 10 out of C.I.A.M.*, London: Architectural Association.

Smithson, Alison and Peter (1981) *The Heroic Period of Modern Architecture*, London: Thames & Hudson.

Summerson, John (1949) *Heavenly Mansions and Other Essays on Architecture*, London: Cresset Press.

Taut, Bruno (1929) *Modern Architecture*, London: Studio.

Todd, Dorothy and Mortimer, Raymond (1929) *The New Interior Decoration: an Introduction to Its Principles, and International Survey of Its Methods*, London: Batsford.

Tubbs, Ralph (1943) *Living in Cities*, Harmondsworth: Penguin Books.

Weston, Richard (1996) *Modernism*, London: Phaidon.

Weston, Richard (2002) *The House in the Twentieth Century*, London: Lawrence King.

Wilks, Christopher (ed.) (2006) *Modernism 1914–1939: Designing a New World*, London: V&A Publications.

Notes on the Contributors

PETER ALLISON

Architectural critic and teacher at South Bank University, London

BRIAN APPLEYARD

Journalist and broadcaster, author of *Richard Rogers: a Biography* (1986)

PETER REYNER BANHAM (1922–88)

Influential architectural writer, critic, and professor, author of *Theory and Design in the First Machine Age* (1960)

OLIVER PERCY BERNARD (1881–1939)

Architect of the Art Deco foyer of the Strand Palace Hotel, and designer of interiors of the Lyons Corner Houses in London

CHRISTOPHER BOOKER (B. 1937)

Journalist who campaigned vigorously against tower blocks in the 1970s; author with Candida Lycett Green of *Goodbye London: an illustrated Guide to Threatened Buildings* (1973)

LIONEL BRETT (4ᵀᴴ VISCOUNT ESHER) (1913–2004)

Architect and planner of post-war new towns in England, author of *A Broken Wave: the Rebuilding of England 1940–1980*

ALAN COLQUHOUN (B. 1921)

Architect, teacher and critic, author of *Essays in Architectural Criticism: Modern Architecture and Historical Change* (1981)

PETER COOK (B. 1936)

Architect, teacher and writer, founder member of Archigram

Contributors

JANE DREW (1911–96)
Architect, partner of Max Fry, worked with Le Corbusier at Chandigarh, mainly on housing

ARTHUR TRYSTAN EDWARDS (1885–1973)
Town planner, author and architectural critic, passionate advocate of the new towns movement

FREDERICK ETCHELLS (1886–1973)
Artist and architect, translator of *Vers une Architecture* (1927) and *Urbanisme* (1929)

EDWIN MAXWELL FRY (1899–1987)
Architect, partner of Jane Drew, worked with Le Corbusier at Chandigarh, mainly on housing

HUBERT DE CRONIN HASTINGS (1902–86)
Influential editor and later editorial director of the *Architectural Review* and the *Architects' Journal* from 1927 to 1973, and ardent proponent of Modernism

NORA SHACKLETON HEALD (D. 1961)
Journalist, worked on various national newspapers, before becoming editor of *The Queen*, and, until 1954, editor of *The Tatler*; elder sister of Edith Shackleton Heald (d. 1976), sometime leader writer on the *Evening Standard*

LOUIS HELLMAN (B. 1936)
Architect, best known for his work as a cartoonist for the *Architects' Journal* and *Building Design* magazines

GORDON HOLT
Former Captain in the Royal Air Force, developed an interest in Le Corbusier after studying the benefits of aerial photography and architecture

EDWIN LUTYENS (1869–1944)
The leading architect of his generation, instrumental in the design and building of New Delhi

FREDERIC JAMES OSBORN (1885–1978)
Town planner, leading member of the garden city movement, chairman of the Town & Country Association

JAMES PALMES (1908–2001)
Librarian of the Royal Institute of British Architects, 1948–69; translator of *L'Atelier de la Recherche Patiente* (1960)

MARTIN PAWLEY (1938–2008)
Architectural critic, and writer and editor, author of *Theory and Design of the Second Machine Age* (1990)

FRANK PICK (1878–1941)
Managing Director of the London Underground Group, and later Chief Executive of the London Passenger Transport Board, 1933–40

HERBERT READ (1893–1968)
Poet and literary critic, advocate and interpreter of the Modern Movement in art and architecture

VERNER OWEN REES (1886–1966)
Architect and planner specialising in public and university buildings in a stripped Neo-classical manner

MRS HOWARD ROBERTSON [DORIS ADENEY LEWIS] (1899–1981)
Born in Australia, one of the first women to attend the Architectural Association, ceased to practise after her marriage to Howard Robertson in 1927, specialising instead in interior design

COLIN ROWE (1920–99)
Architectural historian and critic, his most influential writings published in *The Mathematics of the Ideal Villa and Other Essays* (1976)

GODFREY SAMUEL (1904–82)
Partner in Berthold Lubetkin's Tecton Group, architects of Highpoint, Highgate, London, member of the Modern Architectural Research Group (MARS) Group, and later Secretary of the Royal Fine Art Commission

WALTER SEGAL (1907–85)
Architect, pioneer of the self-build housing movement in Great Britain, author of *Home and Environment* (1948)

PHILIP MORTON SHAND (1888–1960)
Architectural critic and writer, founder member of the Modern Architectural Research Group (MARS), and joint founder of Finmar, a company dedicated to importing and selling Alvar Aalto-designed furniture in England

PETER SMITHSON (1923–2003)
Architect and theorist, with his wife Alison (1928–93), designer of Hunstanton School, the Economist Building and Robin Hood Hardens housing complex, East London

Contributors

BASIL SPENCE (1907–76)
Scottish architect, most well-known for his rebuilding of Coventry Cathedral, the British Embassy at Rome, Sussex University and the now-demolished Hutcheson Block C in the Gorbals district of Glasgow

GAVIN STAMP (B. 1948)
Architectural historian, journalist and broadcaster, former Chairman of the Twentieth Century Society

JAMES STIRLING (1926–92)
Architect of Ham Common flats (based on his study of the Maisons Jaoul) Leicester University Engineering Building, the Clore Gallery extension to the Tate Gallery and the Staatsgalerie, Stuttgart

HAROLD TOMLINSON (1899–1951)
Architect of buildings in the Cambridge area and occasional contributor to architectural journals

EVELYN WAUGH (1903–66)
Celebrated author of *Decline and Fall* (1928), *A Handful of Dust* (1934) and *Brideshead Revisited* (1945)

COLIN ST. JOHN WILSON (1922–2007)
Architect, worked at the London County Council Architects Department, 1950–55; best known for his British Library building

PHIL WINDSOR
Assistant editor of *The Architect* magazine

MIRIAM WORNUM (1898–1989)
Artist and designer, wife of George Grey Wornum (1888–1957), architect of the London headquarters of the Royal Institute of British Architects

PETER YATES (1920–82)
Worked with partner Gordon Ryder (1919–2000) on buildings in the North of England in a Modernist style influenced by Le Corbusier and Berthold Lubetkin

Index

IMAGE CREDITS

© Architectural Association Archives
  31.1, 31.2

© FLC/ADAGP, Paris and DACS, London 2008
  8.3, 13.3, 32.3, 34.3, 37.1, 37.2, 37.3, 37.4

Architectural Press Archive / RIBA British Architectural Library Photographs Collection 2.3, 32.2, 35.1,
  40.3, 40.4, 43.1, 46.1, 49.1, 53.1, 54.1

Architectural Press Archive / RIBA British Architectural Library Photographs Collection /
  © FLC/ADAGP, Paris and DACS, London 2008
  9.1, 25.1, 32.4, 32.5, 34.2, 39.5, 41.5, 49.2, 55.2, 55.3, 56.1, 56.2

RIBA British Architectural Library Books & Periodicals Collection
  2.2, 45.3

RIBA British Architectural Library Books & Periodicals Collection /
  © FLC/ADAGP, Paris and DACS, London 2008
  1.1, 2.1, 3.1, 4.3, 5.1, 6.1, 6.2, 7.1, 7.2, 8.1, 8.2, 11.1, 11.2, 12.1, 12.2, 13.1, 13.2, 14.1, 16.1, 17.1, 18.1,
  18.2, 20.1, 20.2, 20.3, 21.1, 21.2, 24.1, 25.2, 26.2, 26.4, 27.1, 27.2, 28.2, 30.1, 30.2, 30.3, 30.4, 34.1,
  35.2, 35.3, 42.2, 45.2, 45.4, 45.5, 47.1, 49.3, 51.1, 52.1

RIBA British Architectural Library Drawings Collection /
  © FLC/ADAGP, Paris and DACS, London 2008
  31.3, 31.4, 46.2

RIBA British Architectural Library Photographs Collection
  2.4, 4.1, 4.2, 16.2, 19.1, 19.2, 19.3, 22.1, 22.2, 23.1, 23.2, 28.1, 29.1, 38.2, 38.3, 39.1, 39.3, 40.2, 40.5,
  41.2, 41.3, 41.4, 41.6, 44.1, 44.2, 45.1, 50.1, 50.2, 53.2, 54.2, 55.1

RIBA British Architectural Library Photographs Collection /
  © FLC/ADAGP, Paris and DACS, London 2008
  1.2, 2.5, 6.3, 9.2, 9.3, 9.4, 9.5, 10.1, 15.1, 26.1, 26.3, 26.5, 32.1, 33.1, 36.1, 36.2, 38.1, 39.2, 39.4, 40.1,
  41.1, 42.1, 48.1, 48.2

TEXT CREDITS

The editors and publishers gratefully acknowledge the above for permission to reproduce material
in the book. Every effort has been made to contact copyright holders for the permission to reprint
material in this book. The publishers would be grateful to hear from any copyright holder who is not
acknowledged here and will undertake to rectify any errors or omissions in future editions of the
book.

Text sources

The following texts are published with the kind permission of the authors (or the authors'
descendents) and the publishers.

P. Allison, 'Le Corbusier: Architect or Revolutionary: a Re-appraisal of Le Corbusier's First Book on
    Architecture', *Architectural Association Quarterly*, vol. 3, April/July 1971, pp. 10–20.
Brian Appleyard, 'Architect of Our Sky-High Life', *The Times*, 4 March 1987.
Reyner Banham, 'Painting and Sculpture of Le Corbusier', *Architectural Review*, vol. 113, June 1953,
    pp. 401–04. Copyright © by Reyner Banham 1953. Reproduced by kind permission of Mrs Mary
    Banham and Shelley Power Literacy Agency.

Reyner Banham, 'Le Corbusier: the Last Formgiver', *Architectural Review*, vol. 140, August 1966, pp. 97–108. Copyright © by Reyner Banham 1953. Reproduced by kind permission of Mrs Mary Banham and Shelley Power Literacy Agency.

Oliver P. Bernard, 'The City of To-morrow', *The Studio*, vol. 98, September 1929, pp. 612–24. Courtesy The Studio Trust. www.studiointernational.com

Christopher Booker, 'The Price of Le Corbusier', *The Spectator*, 26 March 1977, pp. 11–12.

Christopher Booker, 'Corbusier: Architect of Disaster for the Millions Condemned to Live in a Concrete Jungle', *Daily Mail*, 16 March 1987.

Lionel Brett, 'The Space Machine: an Evaluation of the Recent Work of Le Corbusier', *Architectural Review*, vol. 102, November 1947, pp. 147–50.

Alan Colquhoun, 'Displacements of Concepts', *Architectural Design*, vol. 42, April 1972, p. 236.

Peter Cook, 'The Corb that Might Have Been', *Architectural Design*, vol. 42, April 1972, p. 240.

Frederick Etchells, 'Le Corbusier: a Pioneer of Modern European Architecture', *The Studio*, vol. 96, September 1928, pp. 156–63. Courtesy The Studio Trust. www.studiointernational.com

Maxwell Fry, 'With Corb in Chandigarh', *Building,* vol. 229, 31 October 1975, p. 57.

N.S.H. (Nora Shackleton Heald), 'Towards a New architecture: When Architect and Engineer Work Together', *The Queen*, 23 November 1927, pp. 17–20.

N.S.H. (Nora Shackleton Heald), 'The City of To-morrow: the Real Revolution Lies in the Solution of Existing Problems', *The Queen*, 24 July 1929, pp. 8–9.

Louis Hellman, 'Towards a New Look at Corbusier', *Building Design*, no. 216, 6 September 1974, pp. 13–15; no. 217, 13 September 1974, pp. 19–21; no. 218, 20 September 1974. pp. 17–19.

Gordon Holt, 'Some French Views on Architectural Education: Interviews with Leading Parisian Architects', *Architects' Journal*, vol. 60, 23 July 1924, pp. 117–19.

Le Corbusier, The Future of the Architectural Profession', *Plan: Architectural Students Association Journal*, no. 2, 1947, pp. 4–6.

Le Corbusier, 'Intervention during Discussion on Architectural Expression by CIAM, Bridgwater on September 13, 1947', *Architects' Journal*, vol. 106, 25 September 1947, p. 279.

'Le Corbusier: a Symposium', *Architectural Association Journal*, vol. 74, May 1959, pp. 254–62.

Le Corbusier, 'A New City for India', *The Observer*, 10 May 1953.

Edwin Lutyens, 'The Robotism of Architecture', *The Observer*, 29 January 1928.

F.J. Osborn, 'Concerning Le Corbusier', *Town & Country Planning*, vol. 20, July.

James Palmes, 'The Relevance of Le Corbusier', *The Architect: Journal of the Royal Institute of British Architects*, vol. 94, March 1987, pp. 48–52.

Martin Pawley, 'A Philistine Attack', *Architectural Design*, vol. 42, April 1972, pp. 239–40.

Frank Pick, 'The Way of To-morrow and the Traffic Problem', *The Studio*, vol. 98, September 1929, pp. 624–28. Courtesy The Studio Trust. www.studiointernational.com

Philip Powell and Jane Drew, 'Le Corbusier: Appreciations', *Architects' Journal*, vol. 142, 15 September 1965, pp. 1592–93.

'Presentation of the Royal Gold Medal to Le Corbusier (Charles Edouard Jeanneret)', *Journal of the Royal Institute of British Architects*, vol. 60, April 1953, pp. 215–18.

Herbert Read, 'The City of To-morrow', *The Listener*, 18 February 1931, p. 272–73.

Herbert Read, 'The House of To-morrow', *The Listener*, 25 February 1931, p. 324.

V. O. Rees, 'Vers une Architecture', *Architectural Association Journal*, vol. 40, September 1924, pp. 64–67.

Mrs Howard Robertson (Doris Lewis), 'A Vision Realised: in a Country Villa Le Corbusier Proves his Theories', *The Queen*, 7 August 1929, pp. 8–9.

Colin Rowe, 'The Mathematics of the Ideal Villa: Palladio and Le Corbusier Compared', *Architectural Review*, vol. 101, March 1947, pp. 101–04.

Godfrey Samuel, 'Radiant City and Garden Suburb: Corbusier's Ville Radieuse', *Journal of the Royal Institute of British Architects*, vol. 43, 4 April 1936, pp. 595–99.

Walter Segal, 'The Unknown Giant', *Architects' Journal*, vol.142, 8 September 1965, pp. 526–30.

P. Morton Shand and A. Trystan Edwards, 'The City of To-morrow', *Concrete Way*, vol. 2, September 1929, pp. 79–87.

Credits

Basil Spence, 'Our Debt to Le Corbusier', *Sunday Telegraph*, 29 August 1965.

Gavin Stamp, 'The Consequences of Le Corbusier', *The Daily Telegraph*, 9 March 1987.

James Stirling, 'Garches to Jaoul Le Corbusier as Domestic Architect in 1927 and 1953', *Architectural Review*, vol 118, September 1955, pp. 145–51.

Harold Tomlinson, 'Towards a New Architecture', *Architects' Journal*, vol. 127, 21 September 1927, pp. 378–79.

Evelyn Waugh, 'Cities of the Future', *The Observer*, 11 August 1929.

Colin St. John Wilson, 'The Vertical City', *The Observer*, 17 February 1952.

Phil Windsor, 'How Wrong was Le Corbusier?: How Much of the Text of Le Corbusier's Towards a New Architecture is Still Relevant Today?', *The Architect*, April 1977, pp. 36–37.

Peter Yates, 'Le Corbusier: a Personal Appreciation', *The Builder*, vol. 209, 22 October 1965, p. 865.